REFOCUSING CRIME PREVENTION:
COLLECTIVE ACTION AND THE QUEST FOR COMMUNITY

D0555241

Despite widespread concern over urban crime, public participation in local crime prevention programs is generally low and limited to a small, homogeneous group of middle-class, home-owning residents. Conspicuously absent from these programs are the very people who are the most vulnerable to crime: the poor, immigrants, and visible minorities.

In *Refocusing Crime Prevention* Stephen Schneider explores the capacity of disadvantaged neighbourhoods to organize around issues related to local crime and disorder. He identifies obstacles to community mobilization, many of which are strongly related to demographic and socio-psychological factors, including low socio-economic status and a lack of local social integration. Other obstacles stem from weaknesses in program implementation, such as inappropriate or ineffectual community outreach and communications, a lack of resources, and leadership voids. Many of these barriers flow from broader structural forces, including political and economic conditions that contribute to the concentration of poverty, crime, and apathy in certain areas; a culture of pervasive individualism; and a reliance on the welfare state for solving social problems. Based on extensive ethnographic research, *Refocusing Crime Prevention* identifies and critically examines the many factors that obstruct public participation in community crime prevention programs, while formulating strategies and theories that attempt to empower disadvantaged and marginalized communities.

STEPHEN SCHNEIDER is an assistant professor in the Department of Sociology and Criminology at Saint Mary's University.

STEPHEN SCHNEIDER

Refocusing Crime Prevention

Collective Action and the Quest for Community

UNIVERSITY OF TORONTO PRESS
Toronto Buffalo London

© University of Toronto Press Incorporated 2007
Toronto Buffalo London
Printed in Canada

ISBN-13: 978-0-8020-3550-9 (cloth)
ISBN-10: 0-8020-3550-7 (cloth)

ISBN-13: 978-0-8020-8420-0 (paper)
ISBN-10: 0-8020-8420-6 (paper)

Printed on acid-free paper

Library and Archives Canada Cataloguing in Publication

Schneider, Stephen, 1963–
   Refocusing crime prevention : collective action and the quest for
community / Stephen Schneider.

   Includes bibliographical references and index.
   ISBN-13: 978-0-8020-3550-9 (bound)
   ISBN-13: 978-0-8020-8420-0 (pbk.)
   ISBN-10: 0-8020-3550-7 (bound)
   ISBN-10: 0-8020-8420-6 (pbk.)

   1. Crime prevention – British Columbia – Vancouver – Citizen
participation.   2. Crime prevention – Social aspects –
British Columbia – Vancouver.   3. Mount Pleasant (Vancouver, B.C.) –
Social conditions.   I. Title.

   HV7431.S36 2006   364.4'30971133   C2006-904168-7

University of Toronto Press acknowledges the financial assistance to
its publishing program of the Canada Council for the Arts and the
Ontario Arts Council.

University of Toronto Press acknowledges the financial support for
its publishing activities of the Government of Canada through the
Book Publishing Industry Development Program (BPIDP).

To my mother and father, who, no doubt,
kept me from a life of crime

'But where are the people? ... Mount Pleasant residents have plenty to get aroused about. Why aren't you? Why are there, usually, only a handful of people, if that, at any of the Area Council meetings, although they're talked up and announced in the neighbourhood newspapers?'

Louisa Rogers, *Mount Pleasant Resource Catalogue*

Contents

Preface

When first I moved to East Vancouver's Mount Pleasant neighbour-hood to conduct participant observation research into crime and com-munity safety for my doctoral dissertation, I had little idea how much "participation" this research would actually entail. In the space of eight months, a bicycle was stolen from the balcony of my third-floor flat, the door of my apartment was jimmied open as part of an attempted break and enter, and there were two separate thefts from my car (both occurring in the "secure" underground parking lot of the apartment complex). The final act was the torching of my building by a young arsonist who deliberately started a bonfire on the patio of his ground-floor apartment that quickly spread throughout the wood-framed building, sending me scurrying into the night in my slippers with a draft of my dissertation protectively clutched to my chest. After a few minutes of standing outside and nervously watching the flames inch closer and closer to my apartment, my feeling of helplessness finally forced me to leave. My temporary home for the next few days was the Patricia Hotel, located in the heart of Vancouver's Downtown East-side, considered Canada's poorest, most crime-ridden neighbourhood. Thinking that my luck could not possibly get any worse that night, I went in search of food, oblivious to my attire of sweatpants, a worn hockey jersey, and green corduroy slippers – the clothes I was wearing when I fled my burning building. My dishevelled appearance did not go unnoticed by the legion of drug dealers who hounded me on every block, offering a smorgasbord of illicit pharmaceuticals.

In hindsight, what interested me the most about these street-level entrepreneurs was the businesslike and organized approach to their trade. One drug dealer recited a list of narcotics he had for sale, like a pharmacist taking inventory, and assured me that if he did not have what I wanted he could quickly have it delivered by a colleague within a few minutes. I eventually found out that Frank (not his real name) was part of a trio; he would solicit orders, his girlfriend would hang on to the money, and his brother would run and get the drugs. I wasn't entirely surprised by the level of organization I encountered, having spent the last year in Mount Pleasant observing local drug dealers, prostitutes, pimps, thieves, addicts, and fences, some of whom were connected through an intricate network. These observations prompted me to think, If only the legitimate, law-abiding residents could become so well organized, perhaps poor neighbourhoods like the Downtown Eastside or Mount Pleasant could reverse the downward spiral of crime, disorder, and poverty that engulfs them. This rumination reflected important questions that had already confronted my research in Mount Pleasant, such as: What are the obstacles to a broad-based mobilization of poor neighbourhoods around crime? Why don't more people come to the defence of their neighbourhood by participating in local crime prevention programs? and What can be done to increase the level of participation in community crime prevention activities or other forms of local collective problem solving, especially within disadvantaged neighbourhoods? This book represents the culmination of my efforts to answer these questions.

I would like to express my most sincere appreciation to everyone who took part in the research for this book. Most importantly, I would like to thank all the residents of Mount Pleasant who participated in this study. A special thanks is extended to the board of directors of the Mount Pleasant Safer Community Society, as well as two former coordinators of the Mount Pleasant Community Crime Prevention Office – Megan Stubbs and Deborah Dolly Entwhistle – who greatly facilitated my data collection. This research also benefited from the assistance of other community leaders, in particular Martha Welsh of the Mount Pleasant Business Improvement Association and Sharon Babu of the Mount Pleasant Neighbourhood House. I also received tremendous input from the coordinators of other Vancouver crime prevention offices, in particular Chris Taulu, Peter Symons, Adrian Balazs, Clair MacGougan, and Patrick Kwok. Thank you to those Vancouver Police Department members – especially Brian McGuiness, Gord Pirrie, Pat Hudson, Steve Callander, and Joanne McCormack – for helping me access police data and for allowing me to take up their valuable time with questions, observations, and unsolicited advice. Finally, I would like to thank my doctoral dissertation committee at the University of British Columbia: Robert Ratner, Henry Hightower, and especially Peter Boothroyd, who provided invaluable guidance and encouragement throughout this study.

REFOCUSING CRIME PREVENTION:
COLLECTIVE ACTION AND THE QUEST FOR COMMUNITY

Introduction

This book explores the capacity of disadvantaged neighbourhoods to organize around significant local problems. In particular, through field research conducted in Vancouver, Canada, this study identifies and examines the factors that obstruct poor, high-crime neighbourhoods from effectively mobilizing around local crime and disorder problems. Based upon these findings, a subsequent objective is to develop crime prevention organizing theories and strategies that are commensurate with the unique environments of these neighbourhoods. While this study focuses on community crime prevention (CCP), it speaks to broader issues such as the impact of the political economy at the local level and the spatial concentration of poverty, crime, and community "immobilization," as well as to topics central to the governance of civil society, including citizen participation in public affairs, local social problem solving, and neighbourhood organizing. Community crime prevention provides an illuminating exploration of these issues due to the apparent connections between political economic forces, poverty, crime, and community immobilization; the prominence that crime has assumed as a focal point for community organizing; the heightened status that proactive and preventative approaches have been accorded in government crime control agendas; and the accompanying proliferation of crime prevention theories, strategies, and programs in recent years. The ascension in the popularity and currency of CCP in the past thirty or so years can be attributed to the real and perceived limitations of the criminal justice system, and because, to some, community-based preventative approaches represent a more effective salvo in the battle against crime and disorder. While the theory and practice of crime prevention is grounded in a seemingly common sense approach that is built upon such instrumental actions as rational planning, proactive interventions, citizen involvement, and multi-institutional partnerships, its attractiveness is also based upon its association with the highly idealized notion of "community." Indeed, a normative basis for crime prevention theory and practice is the quest for community. Within the praxis of CCP, the sociological concept of community is regarded as the essential resource to be mobilized in the battle against crime; it is the vortex around which the winds of collective action, local social problem solving, and community safety swirl. At the service of this quest is a body of research confirming the critical role played by the constituent elements of community – social interaction and cohesion, a shared identity, local attachment and belonging, collective efficacy, and informal social control – in fostering successful crime prevention programs and practices.

What is an unlikely source for the popularity of CCP are the many empirical studies that have evaluated the effectiveness of applied crime prevention programs implemented at the local level. For a majority of these assessments have concluded that many CCP strategies fail to meet their stated objectives, which is due, in part, to the low levels of participation in local crime prevention programs. This problem is especially apparent in those neighbourhoods that need crime prevention programs the most. In fact, perhaps the most persistent and exigent dilemma facing the field of crime prevention today is *the inability of CCP programs to initiate and sustain a broad-based mobilization of poor, high-crime neighbourhoods*. The well-documented difficulties faced by CCP groups in their attempts to organize the often diverse spectrum of residents that populate disadvantaged neighbourhoods[1] constitute a significant quandary for the field of crime prevention for at least two reasons. First, CCP theory and practice is fundamentally reliant on the mobilization of neighbourhood residents to meet its objectives. Second, disadvantaged neighbourhoods are in the most need of crime prevention programs, yet it is these neighbourhoods that most often have the greatest aversion to organization. As Freidman (1998: 1462) succinctly states, when one considers the increased likelihood of victimization among "those who live in low-income neighborhoods, it is clear that there is significant under-participation by these groups in relation to the need."

In an attempt to better understand the failings of CCP theory and practice in poor, high-crime neighbourhoods, this research addresses such largely unanswered questions as: Why do CCP programs fail to effect a broad-based mobilization of disadvantaged neighbourhoods? Is this lack of success the result of theory failure or program implementation failure (or both)? What accounts for the widely varying participation levels in CCP programs among different demographic groups? What can be done to maximize participation in crime prevention programs, especially among those groups and individuals who traditionally do not become involved? By answering these questions, this book addresses the scarcity of research that explores impediments to a broad-based mobilization of disadvantaged neighbourhoods around crime and community safety. Despite the empirical evidence substantiating the failures of CCP to rally local populations, especially within poor, high-crime neighbourhoods (Podolefsky and Dubow, 1981; Lavrakas and Herz, 1982; Rosenbaum, Lewis, and Grant, 1985; Fowler and Mangione, 1986; Hope, 1988; Rosenbaum, 1988b; Dowds and Mayhew, 1994; Sherman, 1997b; Hancock, 2001; Skogan, 2004) there have been no empirically informed analyses that systematically and comprehensively identify and deconstruct the many impediments to local collective action around crime and disorder problems. Most studies have focused on identifying and examining factors related to participation in CCP groups and activities and have paid only tangential attention to those that may impede participation. These gaps in knowledge are symptomatic of a larger void in crime prevention scholarship: a lack of attention to the essential collective action underpinnings of community crime prevention. What's more, despite the abundant literature that has critiqued and questioned the theoretical tenets of CCP and its application to disadvantaged neighbourhoods (Lewis and Salem, 1981; Boostrom and Henderson, 1983, 1988; Lewis, Grant, and Rosenbaum, 1988; Rosenbaum, 1988a; Skogan, 1990; Buerger, 1994; Hope, 1995; Crawford, 1997; Garland, 2001; Young, 2001), there have been few, if any, attempts to develop alternatives to traditional CCP models that may be more appropriate for these unique and challenging environs. In short, existing crime prevention scholarship has failed to directly identify, comprehensively detail, and critically examine the many factors that obstruct participation in CCP programs; it has ignored decades of relevant research into local collective action, social movements, and public participation; and it has neglected to develop alternative theories and strategies that can potentially overcome obstacles to the mobilization of disadvantaged neighbourhoods.

This book strives to make a modest contribution to the crime prevention literature by addressing these voids. This is accomplished through ethnographic research that sets out to identify and dissect the obstacles that impede the broad-based mobilization of residents of Mount Pleasant, a poor, high-crime, inner-city neighbourhood in Vancouver, British Columbia. Mount Pleasant is a cogent example of those disadvantaged neighbourhoods that previous studies have identified as in great need of crime prevention programs, but where widespread participation has been lacking. As detailed in chapter 2, the research undertaken in Mount Pleasant reveals that CCP programs have generally been unable to spawn a broad-based mobilization of residents, despite widespread concern over local crime problems. Participation in CCP groups and activities is largely confined to a narrow, demographically homogeneous group of residents who are distinguishable as white, educated, middle-class homeowners with a strong attachment to their neighbourhood.

While the Mount Pleasant case study shows that barriers to successful crime prevention organizing are numerous and complex, the results of this research has been to classify all obstacles into the following four categories: personal, community, organizational, and structural. After providing a theoretical and empirical overview of community crime prevention and the Mount Pleasant case study in chapters 1 and 2, respectively, the subsequent three chapters explore these four categories of obstacles to crime prevention organizing. Chapter 3 examines those demographic and socio-psychological factors related to participation and non-participation at the level of the individual resident. These factors are then extrapolated to the local population as a whole in order to discern aggregate demographic and socio-psychological barriers to collective action at the neighbourhood level. Because most Mount Pleasant residents do not participate in local CCP programs, a strong correlation between demographic characteristics and non-participation cannot be established through this study. However, what became abundantly clear in Mount Pleasant was that those who make up the majority of the local population – the poor, recent immigrants, members of visible minority groups, the undereducated, non-professionals, and renters – were disproportionately absent from CCP groups and activities. Significant socio-psychological variables that appear to correlate with non-participation include a lack of attachment and commitment to the neighbourhood and minimal social interaction with other local residents. At the neighbourhood level, these demographic and socio-psychological factors came together to form formidable obstacles to a broad-based mobilization; Mount Pleasant is characterized by widespread poverty, demographic heterogeneity, a high population turnover, and a lack of social cohesion, all of which undermine the capacity of the local population to effectively mobilize around crime and disorder problems. Chapter 4 analyses obstacles to an inclusive mobilization that stem from local crime prevention organizations and program implementation; that is, how CCP programs and organizers can unintentionally encumber participation. The organizational obstacles identified in this research include inappropriate or ineffectual outreach and communications, leadership weaknesses, a lack of resources, and the nurturing of a narrow and exclusionary identity of crime prevention participants. Chapter 5 analyses structural obstacles to local collective action that are rooted in the dominant institutions and forces of advanced Western societies, such as a political economy that spatially concentrates poverty, crime, and community immobilization; a culture of pervasive individualism; and a post-war reliance on the welfare state for local problem solving.

The sheer variety of, and interconnections between, the aforementioned obstacles guarantee that no single variable can be held unilaterally responsible for the problems disadvantaged neighbourhoods encounter when attempting to organize around crime. The determinants of participation and non-participation are not simple, unilateral, or mutually exclusive; they are the product of a complex interaction of many factors manifested at the individual, community, organizational, and structural levels. The documented lack of success that CCP programs have realized in attempting to effect a broad-based mobilization of poor, inner-city neighbourhoods, combined with the apparent inability of CCP theories to anticipate, recognize, and directly address obstacles to participation, raises fundamental questions about the assumptions, theories, and epistemologies underlying traditional CCP paradigms, especially when applied to disadvantaged neighbourhoods. Given the persistent failure of CCP programs to take root in poor, high-crime neighbourhoods, a principal focus of this book is a critical analysis of the application and applicability of the dominant theories of community crime prevention in these locales.

As detailed in chapter 5, traditional crime prevention theory, research, and practice have been guided overwhelmingly by a technical instrumentality – a preoccupation with tweaking the tactical and logistical aspects of program delivery – to maximize success. Yet, this fixation with the technical fine-tuning of CCP theory and programs ignores the broader structural environment, and politico-economic forces in particular, which greatly influence the causes, scope, and spatial distribution of crime, as well as the ability of collective crime prevention programs to take root in particular neighbourhoods. As Adam Crawford (1997: 260) states, "Questions about the direction and methods of crime control and prevention are inherently political and not purely technical or administrative." As such, like the causes, nature, scope, and impact of crime itself, any discussion of normative crime prevention theory at the local level must incorporate a politico-economic perspective. The relatively high crime rate in disadvantaged neighbourhoods like Mount Pleasant can ultimately be traced to external economic and political forces that create and perpetuate impoverished neighbourhoods by spatially concentrating the prerequisites of crime and criminality, including poverty, unemployment, family breakdown, overcrowding, social disorganization, instability, weak local institutions, the negative socialization of children and youth, drug trafficking and substance abuse, social exclusion, and a lack of local social cohesion and informal social control. Moreover, as the extensive body of literature on local collective action and social movements demonstrates, a perennial catch-22 is in effect: these spatially concentrated social problems are instrumental in undermining and constricting a level of local mobilization that is necessary to address such problems (Milbrath, 1965; Piven, 1966; Hyman and Wright, 1971; Huckfeldt, 1979; Gittell, 1980; Perkins et al., 1990; Prokopy, 1998; Marsh, 1999; Greenberg, 2001; Hall et al., 1997; Hall, McKeown, and Roberts, 2001). As this study and other research suggests, there is a strong positive correlation between socio-economic status and participation in local collective action. This means that crime prevention organizing capacities and initiatives are most prevalent in middle-class and affluent neighbourhoods. Conversely, it is those neighbourhoods where poverty is concentrated that organizing around community safety and other social problems is least likely to bear fruit. In short, the impediments to a broad-based mobilization of disadvantaged neighbourhoods at the individual, community, and organizational levels can be linked ultimately to the broader political economy of advanced Western societies, which bifurcates society along the lines of socio-economic status and which constitutes a significant dynamic in determining where local (crime prevention) organizing will meet with success.

The correlation between socio-economic status and participation in local collective action also has profound implications for organizing populations that are demographically heterogeneous, a defining characteristic of Canada's poor, inner-city neighbourhoods. When viewed through the prism of the Mount Pleasant case study, it can be argued that an inclusive mobilization of residents is frustrated in "mixed status" neighbourhoods, in part because local crime prevention programs, organizers, and participants cultivate community safety programs that can exclude residents based on demographic characteristics. As detailed in chapter 7, the "opportunity reduction" crime prevention programs that predominate in Mount Pleasant – in particular, Neighbourhood Watch – have become a means by which a small, homogeneous group of middle-class, home-owning residents nurture a collective identity based on shared demographic characteristics, values, and goals. In turn, this self-nurtured collective identity may serve to exclude, both intentionally and unintentionally, those who do not share similar demographic characteristics and who are perceived as the source of local crime and disorder problems. These identity-based, opportunity reduction programs coalesce with and stem from a broader ideological approach to the governance of crime that emphasizes punitive sanctions, zero tolerance, and situational measures, all of which not only ignore the politico-economic and social environmental root causes of crime and criminality, but also promote a demographically based labelling of and delineation between the "normal" law-abiding citizen and the "pathological" criminal (Crawford, 1997: 200–1). As one anonymous reviewer of the original manuscript for this book wrote, "crime (and hence crime prevention) are not natural categories of behaviour, but are socially and politically constructed labels that are applied by those in positions of power and which form the basis for politically motivated social responses (including crime prevention)." As socio-political constructs, the scope and spatial concentration of crime, as well as the dominant opportunity reduction approach to local crime prevention, parallel and reinforce the socio-economic cleavages that are forged by the prevailing political economy and fortified by a governance of crime that revolves around promulgating stereotypical and oppositional identities of law-abiding citizens (white, middle-aged, middle-class homeowners) and pathological offenders (poor young renters, visible minorities, drug addicts). For David Garland (1996: 460), traditional theories of situational crime prevention, along with zero tolerance policing and "three strikes" laws, are part of a new "criminology of the alien" that is built upon "essentialized differences" whereby the "alien other" represents criminals as dangerous members of distinct racial and social groups which bear little resemblance to the law-abiding "us" (a delineation that has been bolstered by the unique racial and religious profiling inherent in the suspicion-laden post-9/11 era). This tendency to bifurcate the law-abiding citizen from the criminal along demographic lines has serious repercussions for inclusive, broad-based, collective action crime prevention within heterogeneous neighbourhoods, such as Mount Pleasant.

Refocusing and Reconceptualizing Community Crime Prevention

The inadequacies of traditional crime prevention theories and strategies, especially when applied to poor, high-crime neighbourhoods, expose the need for the development of alternative theoretical models for these environments. The final two chapters of this book attempt to refocus and reconceptualize community crime prevention for disadvantaged neighbourhoods in order to promote a more inclusive, broad-based mobilization of residents, with particular emphasis on soliciting the participation of those who traditionally do not become involved in local collective action. In doing so, the main exhortations of these chapters are twofold. First, there is a need to shift the focus of crime prevention theory and practice to its collective action underpinnings, which involves nurturing a better understanding of crime prevention as local collective behaviour and an appreciation of those factors that obstruct and promote participation in collective action and local problem solving. Second, there is a need to reformulate CCP theory specifically for disadvantaged neighbourhoods. This involves moving away from a technical preoccupation that characterizes traditional theories and approaches to a more critically oriented outlook that addresses the common causes underlying the spatial concentration of poverty, crime, and civic disengagement. Central to these attempts to refocus and reconceptualize CCP theory and practice are action-oriented prescriptions intended to promote a more inclusive, broad-based mobilization of disadvantaged neighbourhoods through local social development and community building.

Chapter 6 begins this reconceptualization process by examining community crime prevention through the theoretical and empirical rubric of collective action, social movements, and public participation. The goal of this chapter is to examine CCP as collective action, and ultimately to examine the factors that impede the capacity of disadvantaged neighbourhoods to mobilize around local issues. Like the results of CCP research, empirical studies into local collective action and social movements acknowledge that active volunteering for local groups and causes in developed societies is restricted to a small number of people who often share similar demographic and socio-psychological characteristics (Olson, 1965; Lipsky, 1969; Salisbury, 1969; Garnson, 1975; Henig, 1982; Muller, 1990; Stoecker, 1990; Clapper, 1995; Williams, 1995; Marsh, 1999; Munk, 2002). In the vernacular of those studying neighbourhood movements, the popular use of the acronym "NIMBY" (Not In My Back Yard) may increasingly be overshadowed by a more prevalent one: "DIM" (Don't Involve Me). The latter should be viewed as a more alarming development because it stems from, and contributes to, the breakdown of socially cohesive and empowered communities and their ability to address local problems, a cornerstone of civil society.

A reconceptualization of CCP theory for disadvantaged neighbourhoods culminates in chapter 7 with the formulation of a critically oriented, development-based, integrated approach to crime prevention organizing and community building – what I simply call Crime Prevention through Community Development. This alternative model replaces the technical and instrumental preoccupation characteristic of traditional CCP theory and practice with a critically oriented philosophy that views the causes of crime and the obstacles to crime prevention as social, political, and economic in nature. A critically oriented approach to CCP organizing is concerned with the long-term goal of addressing the underlying politico- and socio-economic structural factors that concentrate poverty, crime, disempowerment, and civic disengagement in certain neighbourhoods. This development-based, politically charged strategy strives towards the empowerment of disadvantaged neighbourhoods to address not just crime, but other local social programs and their shared causes. This is achieved by working towards such civic ideals as local socio-economic prosperity; an engaged and activist population; greater neighbourhood control over decision-making and the allocation of public resources; strong, inclusive, and democratic community institutions; and expanded social interaction and cohesion. Ultimately, the goal is to transform poor neighbourhoods into prosperous, cohesive, caring, healthy, non-alienating, civically engaged, democratic, and politically empowered communities. While the intent of this prescriptive framework is to address the interrelated problems of disadvantaged neighbourhoods through a long-term developmental approach, the immediacy of promoting inclusive collective action alongside or even in the absence of such development is also paramount. As such, a community development approach to crime prevention incorporates complementary short-term, pragmatic, and innovative community organizing and outreach strategies that are directly concerned with engaging neighbourhood members and maximizing participation in local collective action. Despite the idealistic nature of its goals, this alternative CCP model recognizes that many will continue to decline to become involved in neighbourhood groups and activities. Thus, the goal is not necessarily to fully mobilize disadvantaged neighbourhoods, but to promote a broad-based, inclusive collective effort that is truly representative of the community as a whole. Particular emphasis is placed on creating opportunities for the empowerment and civic engagement of those who are marginalized from mainstream society and who traditionally refrain from participating in local collective action.

Research Design

Primary research for this book entailed a case study approach that employed ethnographic research methods in the East Vancouver neighbourhood of Mount Pleasant. The period covered by the secondary and primary research stretches from 1995 to 2003. During this time, field research was conducted at two separate times. The original primary research was undertaken between September 1995 and May 1997. Follow-up field research was carried out between May and August 2003. The research design for the overall study was qualitative in nature and the principal method used for the field research was participant observation. Supplementing the participant observation research were other methods, including a media and literature review, personal interviews, focus groups, document analysis, and quasi-experiments.

Participant observation research involves the collection of information in a natural setting through direct observation facilitated by the researcher's participation in both the community and the specific phenomena under examination. In general, this method was used in Mount Pleasant to identify the factors, patterns, and processes contributing to and obstructing the mobilization of residents around local crime prevention groups and projects. Specifically, the main objectives of the participant observation research were to observe, record, and analyse: (1) indicators of collective and individualistic crime prevention behaviours among neighbourhood residents, (2) the demographic and socio-psychological characteristics of crime prevention participants and non-participants, (3) the demographic and socio-psychological factors at the neighbourhood level that may promote or obstruct collective action, (4) data that assesses the activities undertaken by local CCP groups and the ability of such groups to promote participation in collective crime prevention programs, and (5) factors that may reveal structural obstacles to collective action. To maximize the utility of this research method, I immersed myself in the neighbourhood, living in Mount Pleasant (during the original research phase only) and becoming involved in crime prevention and community policing projects, first as a volunteer with the Mount Pleasant Community Crime Prevention Office (September 1995 to February 1996) and then in a paid capacity as the coordinator for this office (February to September 1996). From September 1996 to May 1997, much of my research consisted of interviews and focus groups, although I also continued a more limited form of participant observation by volunteering with other local crime prevention groups and activities. This included observing community policing projects carried out by Vancouver Police Department members in Mount Pleasant. In 2003, I returned to Mount Pleasant to conduct a second phase of primary research (from May to September), which consisted of observational research, interviews, focus groups, and document analysis.

In both my volunteer and paid capacities at the Mount Pleasant Community Crime Prevention Office (CPO), I had the opportunity to observe the vehicle that would be central to crime prevention efforts in the neighbourhood during the eight-year period covered by this study. My participant observation research with this CPO, and other local crime prevention programs, allowed me to directly measure and examine the dependent variables of participation and non-participation, while identifying and analysing those independent variables that influenced them. I observed and interviewed residents who volunteered for or used the services of the CPO, attended numerous crime prevention functions and group meetings, and participated in ridealongs with police officers responsible for community policing and crime prevention projects in Mount Pleasant. I also became involved in numerous community outreach initiatives spearheaded by the CPO, which allowed me the opportunity to contact and interview both participants and non-participants. Through my volunteer and paid work at the CPO, I was also able to collect data through quasi-experimental research that involved the implementation of certain crime prevention, community outreach, and communication strategies, which were meant to test hypotheses regarding the scope and nature of local participation, and to profile participants and non-participants. During my tenure as paid coordinator, I was also responsible for organizing and training Neighbourhood Watch (NW) members. This meant coordinating and participating in a number of meetings with NW captains, members, and prospective members, which were used for research purposes.

Numerous interviews were conducted as part of the research, including those with Mount Pleasant residents (CCP participants and non-participants), crime prevention practitioners (civilian and police), and community leaders (including representatives of various community organizations and ethnic groups). Interviews were also held with crime prevention organizers and activists in other Vancouver neighbourhoods. In total, forty-three interviews were conducted during the original phase of the research. In the summer of 2003, twenty-three interviews were undertaken, mostly with crime prevention organizers and participants in Mount Pleasant and other Vancouver communities but also with Vancouver Police Department officials. The purpose of the interviews with Mount Pleasant residents in both periods was to elicit information on the demographic and socio-psychological characteristics of collective crime prevention participants and non-participants, to identify reasons for participation and non-participation, and to identify (perceptions of) the strengths and weaknesses of local crime prevention initiatives and outreach strategies in relation to their efficacy in promoting local participation. Interviews with crime prevention organizers and community leaders solicited information concerning who participates and who does not, why they do or do not participate, their views on the obstacles to participation, and the strengths and weaknesses of local crime prevention programs in relation to inviting and sustaining local participation.

Focus groups were also held with Mount Pleasant residents and were divided between those who participated in collective crime prevention programs and those who did not. The objectives of the focus groups with CCP participants were to elicit data concerning their level of concern over crime and previous victimization (if any); their demographic and socio-psychological characteristics; the reasons underlying their participation in collective efforts; their individualistic crime prevention behaviours; their awareness, perceptions, and assessment of local crime prevention initiatives; and their perceptions of the strengths and weaknesses of these initiatives. The objectives of the focus groups involving non-participants were to elicit data on their concern over crime and previous victimization (if any); their demographic and socio-psychological characteristics; their reasons for not participating; their individualistic crime prevention behaviours; the extent of their awareness of local crime prevention initiatives; and their perceptions and assessments of these initiatives. During the original research period, twenty-two focus groups were held with approximately 148 Mount Pleasant residents. Of these focus groups, fourteen were held with CCP program participants, most of them taking place after scheduled meetings of residents involved in local crime prevention groups or activities. Eight focus groups were held with Mount Pleasant residents who did not participate in collective crime prevention groups and activities. Those who took part in these focus groups were individuals who had declined to become involved in CCP programs when asked as part of the community outreach effort of the CPO. In the follow-up research undertaken in the summer of 2003, six focus groups were conducted, with fifty-two participants in total. Four of these focus groups were held with forty-two Mount Pleasant East residents who participated in the local Neighbourhood Watch program, while two focus groups were held with a total of ten residents who lived on streets that had a NW program in effect, but did not participate. Personal interviews were also held with eight residents who did not participate in the NW program on their street.

Finally, this study analysed documents and communications related to the efforts of neighbourhood crime prevention groups and the Vancouver Police to mobilize the local population. These papers included planning and strategy documents, minutes of meetings, promotional literature, and correspondence. The documents examined were made available through the crime prevention groups, the City of Vancouver, and the Vancouver Police Department. Numerous other government and police documents were available through the Internet.

The research design incorporated a number of measures to maximize the validity and reliability of the findings. These included triangulation (the use of multiple sources of data and research methods to corroborate the emerging findings), data confirmation (confirming the data collected and my interpretation with research participants), peer and colleague review (examining the plausibility of findings with other researchers studying crime prevention and/or Mount Pleasant), and detailed notes. (All salient observations were systematically recorded in a journal, recordings were made of all structured interviews and focus groups, and then were transcribed; all notes were stored in a binder in the chronological order of the research.) Before the research was undertaken, it was subject to an ethical review prior to its implementation, which was carried out by Office of Research Services and Administration at the University of British Columbia. While this ethical review applied only to the period covered by my doctoral research (September 1995 to August 1996), I employed the same ethical standards and methods throughout the research. This included having participants sign an informed consent form, which alerted them to the objectives and methods of the research, the confidentiality of their participation, and how the security of the data was to be protected. I also made every effort to ensure that anyone I encountered as part of my capacity as volunteer and paid coordinator of the CPO was alerted to the fact that I was also conducting research. However, this was not always possible, such as in crisis situations or encounters that were only momentary in nature. In general, informed consent forms were distributed and signed only in those occasions where I was conducting interviews and focus groups as a research adjunct to my CPO volunteer and coordinator responsibilities.

PART ONE

Theoretical and Empirical Background

1 Community Crime Prevention: A Theoretical and Empirical Overview

The field of crime prevention is exceptionally broad, ranging from approaches that address the root causes of criminal behaviour to those that attempt to deter the opportunity for criminal acts to occur in a particular time and place. Crime prevention theory and practice also encompasses society's most significant institutions, including the family, the school, the neighbourhood, the community, the labour market, the police, and other state agencies. This book concentrates on community crime prevention, and, more specifically, on the "community mobilization" model, which Lawrence Sherman (1997b: 65) contends is "the most visible community-based crime prevention strategy in the latter Twentieth Century." Under the community mobilization model, neighbourhood residents agree to act collectively to reduce the opportunity for crime by assuming a more vigilant and proprietary concern over their neighbourhood. Simply put, the community mobilization approach presumes that "what seems most clearly needed to prevent most instances of crime and other antisocial incidents in neighbourhoods is a caring and vigilant citizenry" (Lavrakas, 1985: 88). The theory underlying this crime prevention strategy is that once educated about the processes and benefits of a collective effort to address crime, concerned residents will participate in local crime prevention programs, or at the very least keep a watchful eye out for suspicious people or activities during their daily routines. Given these objectives, inherent within the community mobilization model of community crime prevention (CCP) is a situational approach to crime prevention that is primarily concerned with reducing criminal opportunities from occurring in a particular time and place. The crime prevention program that has become universally associated with this situational, community mobilization model is Neighbourhood Watch.

The purpose of this chapter is to provide a theoretical and empirical overview of community crime prevention, and the community mobilization model in particular. Close attention will be paid to collective action underpinnings and issues of central concern to this study: citizen participation, factors related to participation and non-participation, and the obstacles to the mobilization of (disadvantaged) neighbourhoods around crime.

Community Crime Prevention and Its Component Parts: A Theoretical Overview

Central to the community mobilization model of crime prevention are four fundamental constituent parts: a community-based orientation, collective action, informal social control, and opportunity reduction.

The Community

A community-based approach to crime prevention is predicated on the assumption that private citizens play a major role in maintaining order in a free society, and therefore should be encouraged to accept more responsibility for interventions aimed at reducing or precluding criminal acts from occurring in their neighbourhoods (Lurigio and Rosenbaum, 1986: 19). In this respect, the philosophy of CCP espouses a partial transfer in responsibility for proactive, preventative efforts from the state to the citizenry. Shonholtz (1987: 46) emphasizes that, despite modern perceptions of crime control as the exclusive purview of the state, in fact the (re-)emergence of crime prevention in the United States beginning in the late 1960s represented the type of responsibilities that for centuries had been carried out by local communities: "Historically Americans turned to community and religious institutions for the early settlement of conflict and promotion of community social values. In fact, swearing a police oath was considered in many communities to be a violation of individual moral responsibility and a sign that the community was lax in enforcing social norms. The Judaeo-Christian base of American democratic thought stressed the responsibilities of individuals and the obligation of society in maintaining cooperative associations and support systems. Historically, civic justice has been understood to be a community undertaking, outside and separate from the more narrow and formal responsibility of the state's exercise of formal control."

In the United States, the groundwork was laid for the future development of CCP scholarship and practice by the 1967 Presidential Crime Commission, which stressed the need for an active and involved citizenry in preventing crime. A key assumption of this report, and subsequent federal crime control policies, was that "the formal criminal justice system by itself cannot control crime without the help from neighbourhood residents." As such, the "community should play the central role in defining community crime prevention and that organized groups of residents are perhaps the best vehicle for responding to local crime" (U.S. Department of Justice, 1978: 3). In 1977, Congress authorized the creation of the Law Enforcement Assistance Administration's Community Anti-Crime Program, which dispensed millions of dollars in grants to "assist community organizations and neighbourhood groups to become involved in activities designed to prevent crime, reduce fear of crime, and contribute to neighbourhood revitalization" (1). For American federal policy makers, the prevention and control of crime would now be shared between the state and the citizenry through an implicit division of labour, which was reflected in the preamble to the Juvenile Delinquency Prevention Act of 1974: "The responsibility for control, primary punishment, and rehabilitation of identified juvenile criminals remains with the court, but the responsibility for prevention has been given back to the community." The centrality of the community to crime prevention has been reflected in government crime control agendas in other countries, including Canada. In their 1993 report on crime prevention, the Canadian Standing Committee on Justice and the Solicitor General recommended that future federal crime control policies be premised on the belief that "crime occurs in communities and priorities concerning crime prevention are best determined at the local level" (Standing Committee on Justice and the Solicitor General, 1993: 33). One of the results of this report was the creation of the National Crime Prevention Centre, which includes a "community mobilization" funding component that aims to help communities develop localized initiatives to deal with crime and victimization (Léonard et al., 2005: 237).

The intellectual genesis of CCP can be found in the first half of this century with the pioneering work of sociologists at the University of Chicago (Merton, 1938; Shaw and McKay, 1942) who examined the influence of social conditions and neighbourhood characteristics in an attempt to explain deviant and delinquent behaviour. The Chicago School of Sociology's enduring legacy for crime prevention was its emphasis on community organization and development in addressing local crime and disorder problems. More than fifty years later, in one of the most comprehensive reports written on the theory and practice of crime prevention in the United States, a principal author evoked the essential role that the institution of community plays in crime prevention: "Communities are the central institution for crime prevention, the stage on which all other institutions perform. Families, schools, labor markets, retail establishments, police, and corrections must all confront the consequences of community life. Much of the success or failure of these other institutions is affected by the community context in which they operate. Our nation's ability to prevent serious violent crime may depend heavily on our ability to help reshape community life, at least in our most troubled communities" (Sherman, 1997b: 57).

In the lexicon of crime prevention theorists and practitioners, the concept of community has traditionally been defined in physical and spatial terms – the residential neighbourhood. Within the crime prevention field, community is also conceptualized in sociological terms, as an organic collective of people who are bound together by enduring personal ties and networks, a high level of social interaction and cohesion, a shared identity and goals, and a sense of wholeness (Crank, 1994: 336–7; Leighton, 1988: 359). A dominant etiological theory of crime upon which CCP is premised is that the loss of the socially cohesive community has contributed to crime and disorder within Western societies. For those who subscribe to this "community lost" perspective, the scale and complexity of mass society has robbed individuals in urban areas of "solidary bonds," which is theorized as an essential form of interpersonal attachments that prevent people from victimizing one another. When community is lost, "Urbanites become uprooted, isolated, and interpersonally disorganized resulting in intrapersonal outcomes of anomie, alienation, and internal disorganization that propel them toward crime and deviance" (Leighton, 1988: 353). Given these arguments, an underlying assumption of CCP is that the efficacy of crime prevention programs at the neighbourhood level is contingent on the existence of solidary bonds at the local level. These localized bonds are commonly referred to as local social cohesion or "a sense of community." Bursik and Grasmick (1993a) believe that for local neighbourhoods to combat crime successfully, programs must provide for the development of strong networks of association among local residents and between residents and local institutions. Greenberg, Rohe, and Williams (1985: 17) recommend that communities "develop programs that familiarize local residents with each other and with the neighbourhood to help encourage intervention and reduce fear." For Mukherjee and Wilson (1987: 2), increasing social interaction, integration, and cohesion directly contributes to greater community safety: "The most important element of community crime prevention appears to be to bring about social interaction, whereby residents of the community maintain a degree of familiarity with each other. Such interaction and familiarity should, in theory at least, make it possible to detect strangers in the community. And finally, crime prevention theory suggests that such interactions may lead to a cohesive neighbourhood. The basic philosophy of community crime prevention is that social interaction and citizen familiarity can play an important role in preventing, detecting, and reporting criminal behaviour." In short, CCP theory is premised on the belief that both the problem of and the solutions to crime are strongly influenced by the sociological concept of community. While some may view the neighbourhood as simply the spatial locale in which crime prevention programs are implemented, a socially cohesive community in and of itself forms the heart of a distinct crime prevention philosophy. Like the family, the school, or the labour market, the community is viewed as an "institution" through which crime is controlled and prevented.

Informal Social Control

One implication of the shift in crime prevention responsibilities from the state to local communities is the increased importance of informal social control, which is said to prevent crime locally when exerted by private citizens acting collectively. Within the realm of crime prevention, informal social control is central to, and an enduring part of, the spatial community. CCP is concerned with reinforcing or modifying individual and collective behaviours of community residents to produce or strengthen a local social environment that can informally regulate itself, which includes preventing the opportunity for criminal and disorderly acts to occur. While formal social control is derived from state-imposed sanctions codified in written laws and regulations that are enforced by the police and the courts, informal social control is based on, and is said to restrict, crime and incivilities through a proprietary enforcement by community members of local custom, common agreement, social norms, and unwritten rules that guide what they consider to be appropriate and accepted behaviour for their neighbourhood. James Wilson (1975: 24) defines informal social control as "the observance of standards of right conducted in the public places in which one lives and moves, those standards to be consistent with, and supportive of, the values and life style of the particular neighbourhood." Theoretically, neighbourhoods with a strong sense of informal social control will not tolerate behaviour that is contrary to established or conventional norms. As a response to undesirable behaviour, instruments of informal social control include the spontaneous and subtle (e.g., raised eyebrows, gossip, or ridicule), direct confrontation by individual community members (e.g., verbal reprimands, warnings, physical intervention), and the structured activities of local groups, such as Neighbourhood Watch or citizen patrols (Greenberg et al., 1985: 1; Rosenbaum, 1988a: 327). Thus, informal social control is premised upon and incorporates "the threat of peer-imposed stigma if individuals violate norms endorsed by peers and the threat of self-imposed guilt feelings if actors violate norms they themselves have internalized" (Grasmick, Jacobs, and McCallum, 1983: 361).

The intellectual history of CCP is replete with references to the role of informal social control. Explicit in the social disorganization theory of crime and deviance originated by the Chicago School of Sociology (Merton, 1938; Shaw and McKay, 1942) is the perceived inability of local institutions to regulate the activities of residents and the need for the promotion of harmonious human relationships in "less socially integrated" neighbourhoods by creating or strengthening these local institutions. The concept of informal social control is also implicit in the influential writings of urban theorist Jane Jacobs (1961: 31–2) who insists, "The first thing to understand is that the public peace ... is not kept primarily by the police, as necessary as police are. It is kept primarily by an intricate, almost unconscious, network of voluntary controls and standards among the people themselves." In their "broken windows" metaphor, Wilson and Kelling (1982) further this theoretical doctrine by articulating the sequence of events that erodes the capacity of a community to invoke informal control mechanisms and which consequently contributes to a spiral of decline that invites crime. Just like an unrepaired broken window may spur damage against other intact windows, it is hypothesized that untended deviant behaviour can lead to the perception of social disorder and the concomitant breakdown of local informal control mechanisms. While this theory has most commonly been used as a basis for zero tolerance policing, it also advocates that efforts to address crime and disorder problems, as well as community decline in general, can only be truly successful when community residents collectively reassert a sufficient level of informal social control (Kelling and Coles, 1996). For Wesley Skogan (1990: 12), local stability is contingent upon the capacity of a neighbourhood to continually reproduce itself as a social system. Unstable social systems lack steering mechanisms capable of making mid-course corrections, and the result is that neighbourhoods slip into a perpetual cycle of decline. Informal social control represents one such steering mechanism. According to Barker and Linden (1985: 29), the leverage for responding to threats to the "moral order" is found in increasing the social control capacity of local institutions. Simply stated, when informal social control is present at the local level, residents only feel and act as though they are a part of the neighbourhood, but feel and act as if they are in control of their neighbourhood (Lavrakas, 1985: 99).

As intimated above, a fundamental prerequisite for informal social control (and hence successful crime prevention programs) is social cohesion. The essential elements of informal social control – residents' proprietary concern over their environment, increased vigilance, a willingness to intervene in suspicious circumstances or disorderly conduct – are forged through a commitment and attachment to the neighbourhood by individual residents and a strong sense of social cohesion at the collective level. For Findlay and Zvekic (1988), the local crime control objective is advanced through a cohesiveness, which in turn is established through the integration and socialization of community members that involves the inculcation of norms and values and the creation of a collective consciousness. Numerous studies have postulated a causal relationship between social cohesion and informal social control, on the one hand, and lower rates of crime and disorder on the other. For example, research has indicated that crime and related problems are lower in areas where residents have a strong attachment to, and greater responsibility and control over, what happens in their neighbourhood (Greenberg et al., 1982; Skogan and Maxfield, 1981; Taylor, Gotfredson, and Bower, 1984; Taub, Taylor, and Dunham, 1984; Gatti and Tremblay, 2000); where the perception exists that one's neighbours will provide assistance when needed (Newman and Franck, 1982; Fowler and Mangione, 1982); and where there is a willingness of residents to intervene in observed criminal activity (Maccoby, Church, and Church, 1958; Clotfelter, 1980). Greenberg et al. (1984: 6) note that cohesive groups are better able to respond to threats by outsiders and are more likely to adopt protective actions compared to groups that are less cohesive. Research conducted by Gillis and Hagen (1983) suggests that bystanders are more likely to intervene in an appropriate way when the victim is a friend or an acquaintance and when the incidence occurs in their own neighbourhood.

A particularly important variable in community crime prevention, according to Sampson, Raudenbush, and Earls (1997), is "collective efficacy," a concept that combines social cohesion with informal social control and which has variously been defined as "the linkage of mutual trust and the willingness to intervene for the common good" (919) or the realization of "common values and the ability of groups to regulate their members according to desired principles" (Crawford, 1999: 518). In a study of Chicago residents, Sampson and colleagues (1997) found that rates of violence were lower in neighbourhoods characterized by collective efficacy, which led to the conclusion that the willingness of local residents to intervene for the common good depends in large part on conditions of mutual trust and solidarity. The best predictors of crime reporting among members of immigrant and ethnic minority groups, according to Davis and Henderson (2003: 577) "were the measures of community empowerment: persons who said that their ethnic community was likely to work together to solve local problems and those who believed that their community wielded political power were more likely than those whose communities were disenfranchised to say that they would report crimes." Another study found that residents who trusted their neighbours were also more likely to have confidence in the police. This is because attitudes towards police are "part of global attitude system" of individuals and communities so that "mutual trust between neighbors brought down the mutual suspicion and promoted mutual understanding. Consequently, informal collective security bred confidence in the broader system, police being one of the larger systems, and reduced community disorder and restored public trust in the police" (Rena et al., 2005: 62). In contrast to all of the above, William Rohe (1985) writes that there is little strong evidence that the level of informal social control is related to crime rates. This position is also supported by a study carried out in English council estates by Hope and Foster (1992) who found that some high-crime areas also had high levels of informal social control.

Informal social control is said to develop locally in one of two ways.

It can develop *naturally* within a neighbourhood, where there is a low rate of population turnover, where patterns of local association and interaction are well established, and where social cohesion is strong. Some have argued that informal social control – and by extension greater community safety – can be *induced* in a neighbourhood where it does not currently exist through the implementation of community development programs. Some have gone so far as to tout CCP as a means to nurture the social cohesion preconditions necessary for informal social control through its emphasis on collective action, which in turn promotes common goals and stimulates resident interaction and mutual helpfulness (Durkheim, 1933; Dubow and Emmons, 1981; Lewis and Salem, 1981: 415; Greenberg et al., 1985; Rosenbaum, 1986; Lewis et al., 1988; Enns and Wilson, 1999). This "implant" or "transplant" hypothesis raises important questions about the ability of disadvantaged neighbourhoods to mobilize around crime through social engineering and behavioural modification strategies. Such questions include the following: Can social cohesion be nurtured in low-income, heterogeneous, high-crime neighbourhoods? Can informal social control exist or be induced in neighbourhoods that are characterized by a low level of social cohesion? Can the introduction of collective crime prevention programs help foster social cohesion and informal social control? and Can the introduction of crime prevention programs promote a collective, active, and vigilant stand against crime and disorder by neighbourhood residents?

Collective Action

One way to classify the many strategies that fall within the field of crime prevention is to make a distinction between those that are individualistic or "private-minded" in nature (e.g., target hardening, self-defence classes, carrying weapons, avoiding certain parts of a city) and those that are collective or "public-minded" in nature, such as Neighbourhood Watch, citizen patrols, and community safety groups (Schneider and Schneider, 1978). While both are necessary to address crime at the local level, when relied upon exclusively the former is viewed by some as potentially negative behaviour because it may serve to undermine the collective action, social cohesion, and informal social control underpinnings of CCP. As the U.S. National Advisory Council on Criminal Justice Standards and Goals (1973: 46) warned, while the retreat behind locks, bars, alarms, and guards may "be steps in self-protection, they can lead to a lessening of the bonds of mutual assistance and neighbourliness" so crucial to CCP. Put more tersely, Oscar Newman (1972: 3) believes, "When people begin to protect themselves as individuals and not as a community, the battle against crime is effectively lost."

Central to a community-based crime prevention effort is a collective response in which individuals act jointly to undertake activities that they generally could not accomplish on their own (Barker and Linden, 1985: 15). The "community mobilization" moniker itself indicates the importance of collective action in CCP, and this model has become so associated with community crime prevention that the two terms are often used interchangeably (a convention adopted by this book). The importance of collective action in promoting community safety has not been lost on policy makers. One of the first federal crime prevention agencies in the United States – the Law Enforcement Assistance Administration, created by Congress in 1977 – was to prioritize "programs and activities that are public minded in the sense that they are designed to promote a social or collective response to crime and fear of crime at the neighbourhood level in contrast to private minded efforts that deal only with the actions of citizens as individuals or those that result from the provision of services that in themselves do not contribute to the organization of the neighbourhood" (U.S. Department of Justice, 1977: 58). The argument that crime can only be prevented through efforts that transcend the capacity of the individual is reinforced by the considerable role played by social cohesion and informal social control in community crime prevention. Successful CCP programs are not only dependent upon the existence of social cohesion, but, as discussed earlier, it has been proposed that collective crime prevention programs can contribute to the cohesiveness of a block or neighbourhood. Lewis (1979) contends that when a neighbourhood can respond collectively, crime prevention can integrate residents by affirming common values and goals. For Conklin (1975: 99), promoting collective responses is the best way to counter "the disorganized community that is unable to exercise informal social control over deviant behaviour." According to Lewis and colleagues (1988: 136), CCP theory posits a set of reform strategies that sees welfare improved through initiatives that engage citizens with their fellow residents: "Solidarity will, in turn, lead to less crime and more political power for the community. If we build and fund community, we prevent crime. But it is done together, not individually."

Opportunity Reduction

Since the early 1970s, the opportunity reduction or "situational" model has dominated crime prevention scholarship, public policy, and practice. This broad crime prevention approach is concerned with removing or reducing the opportunity for a criminal act to occur in a particular time and place, rather than addressing the root causes of criminal and deviant behaviour. Reducing the opportunity for a criminal act to occur is the single greatest crime prevention goal of CCP and its most popular vehicles: Neighbourhood Watch and citizen patrols. In general, the opportunity for crime can be reduced in one of two ways: through the management and/or design of the physical environment (e.g., target hardening, entry control, crime prevention through environmental design, etc.) or by influencing the individual and collective behaviours of residents to minimize their vulnerability to crime through both personal and collective measures (e.g., Neighbourhood Watch, citizen patrols, etc.) (Lavrakas, 1981). Either way, preventing the opportunity for a criminal event to transpire involves increasing the risk of detecting criminal opportunities and events and apprehending offenders. Within the context of CCP, increasing the risk of detection and apprehension as a means to reduce crime opportunities is contingent upon collective action and informal social control conditions, including the formation of community safety groups, and the willingness of residents to look out for one another, to watch over public as well as private spaces, and to intervene in criminal acts (primarily by alerting police).

**Summary: The Theorized Processes of
Community Crime Prevention**

A theoretical premise of the community mobilization model is that the implementation of crime prevention initiatives will marshal the concern of residents into a collective effort that promotes vigilance, encourages social interaction and cohesion, and fosters an atmosphere of informal social control within their neighbourhood. The collective and sustained effort of a cohesive and vigilant neighbourhood – in partnership with the police – is then expected to lead to the preclusion or decline of local crime and disorder problems. For disadvantaged neighbourhoods, the community mobilization model is said to help reverse the self-feeding, downward cycle that diminishes a neighbour-

Figure 1.1 A conceptual model of the community crime prevention cycle

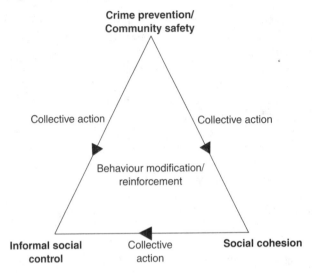

hood's informal control mechanisms, not to mention the local quality of life. The theoretical framework for CCP is built upon the interconnections among five essential concepts: collective action, informal social control, crime prevention, behaviour modification, and social cohesion. Figure 1.1 illustrates how the theorized potential of CCP entails a positive and symbiotic interaction between crime prevention/community safety, social cohesion, and informal social control. Social cohesion is essential to the success of CCP due to its role as the foundation for informal social control and collective action. Once a social environment conducive to producing informal control has been created, the capacity to prevent crime and disorder is greatly enhanced. In turn, control over negative local forces increases the likelihood that local social cohesion (and hence informal social control) can be established. The engine that drives the interaction between these three variables, and which steers a neighbourhood toward greater social cohesion and informal social control, is collective action. At the core of this tripartite relationship is the promotion or reinforcement of positive social behaviour among community members that includes a commitment to working with one's neighbours to protect the area.

Thus, mobilizing neighbourhoods around crime and disorder

involves initiating or furthering a positive cycle by modifying the social behaviour of neighbourhood residents to achieve the interrelated objectives of social interaction, local integration, cohesion, informal control, and the prevention of crime. In this respect, CCP is premised upon the conceptual constructs of systems theory: communities are self-guiding, goal-oriented, adaptive systems that continuously function through feedback loops that can intensify either a downward spiral of disorder, decay, and crime, or an upward cycle of informal social control, crime prevention, and community development. In their "community hypothesis" Dubow and Emmons (1981) articulate the theoretical tenets of CCP as such: (1) neighbourhood residents can be mobilized by community organizations to participate in collective crime prevention projects; (2) involvement in these activities creates a stronger community because people will take greater responsibility for their collective protection and interactions among neighbours will increase; (3) an increase in social interaction and a stronger sense of community leads to more effective informal social control; and thus, (4) apart from the direct effects of community crime prevention activities in reducing crime or fear of crime, these activities may also reduce crime or fear by rebuilding local social control in the neighbourhood. Notwithstanding this logic, the catch-22 discussed earlier in relation to the mobilization of poor communities to address local social problems is relevant to CCP theory and practice, and the implant hypothesis specifically: the implementation of collective crime prevention programs are meant to help invoke social interaction, cohesion, and informal control; however, these same variables constitute the foundation which must be present for CCP programs to take root in a locality in the first place.

Empirical Overview: CCP Research and Program Evaluations

Much of the research in the field of CCP has involved evaluating the application of crime prevention theories and programs. While different assessments of comparable crime prevention theories, strategies, and programs often contradict one another, much of the empirical research has shown that applied CCP programs have generally fallen short of the expectations set by their normative theoretical prescriptions. A host of individual studies and meta-analyses of these studies have demonstrated that various CCP strategies and applied programs have had only a modest or no impact on crime and fear of crime at the local level (Rosenbaum et al., 1985; Taylor and Gottfredson, 1986; Lewis et al., 1988; Rosenbaum, 1988a; Pennell et al., 1989; Bennett and Lavrakas, 1989; Garofalo and McLeod, 1989; Norris and Kaniasty, 1992; Hope, 1995; Sherman 1997b; Savolainen, 2005). A number of studies also conclude that CCP programs have generally been unable to engineer the social and behavioural preconditions (e.g., collective action, social interaction and cohesion, informal social control, etc.) necessary for applied CCP programs to reach their ultimate crime-control objectives (Merry, 1981; Greenberg et al., 1984; Taylor et al., 1984; Rosenbaum et al., 1985; Rosenbaum, 1987; Sherman 1997b; Lewis et al., 1988, Miller, 2001; Thacher, 2001; DeKeseredy et al., 2003).

Three leading crime prevention scholars have conducted separate reviews of the literature on CCP research and program evaluations (Rosenbaum, 1988a; Hope, 1995; Sherman, 1997b). Each arrived at the same conclusion: there is scant evidence that collective crime prevention programs have achieved their desired impact at the local level. Rosenbaum (1988a) concludes that there is little hard proof to assert that CCP is effective in reducing community crime rates, encouraging collective action, or building community cohesion, a result he blames on a combination of theory failure, program implementation failure, and the lack of reliable research findings. He writes, "Perhaps the most important set of findings to emerge from these evaluations is that community organizing was unable to activate the intervening social behaviors that are hypothesized as necessary (according to informal social control and opportunity reduction models) to produce the desired changes in crime, fear and social integration." His summary of past research suggests that crime prevention programs produce "very few changes in social interaction, surveillance, stranger recognition, crime reporting, home protection behaviors, feelings of control, efficacy and responsibility, satisfaction with the neighborhood and attitudes towards the police" (Rosenbaum, 1988a: 362). Hope (1995: 23) concurs: "Much of the effort to alter the structure of communities in order to reduce crime has not been noticeably successful or sustainable." As part of a meta-analysis of research findings on CCP programs, Sherman (1997b: 89) contends that "there are no community-based programs of proven effectiveness by scientific standards to show with reasonable certainty that they work in certain kinds of settings." For Sherman (1997b: 59), the results of evaluations of community-based programs are "generally discouraging" although, like Rosenbaum, he acknowledges that the research and evaluation designs used for examining and assessing CCP programs "have generally been quite weak."

Participation in Community Crime Prevention:
Theoretical and Empirical Scholarship

Research that has focused specifically on participation in CCP programs has produced mixed findings regarding the ability of crime prevention groups and activities to successfully mobilize neighbourhood residents. On the positive side, some program evaluations have documented encouraging findings about participation levels. Fowler and Mangione (1986) report on a neighbourhood group in Hartford, Connecticut, that fruitfully organized residents around street closures and short-term intensive law enforcement initiatives. In the two years after local police activity was reduced, resident mobilization rose to its highest levels. As part of their research into crime prevention programs sponsored by non-profit community groups in ten low-income neighbourhoods in the United States, Bennett and Lavrakas (1989) report that eight of the sites successfully implemented programs chosen during the planning process. Skogan (1996) provides evidence that in Chicago crime prevention and community policing meetings held in high-crime neighbourhoods have enjoyed good attendance. Donnelly and Majka (1998) describe a highly successful drive by community organizers to mobilize residents of a disadvantaged neighbourhood in Dayton, Ohio, around crime, which included community meetings where attendance topped more than 300 people. An evaluation of a Neighbourhood Watch program in Coquitlam, British Columbia, concluded, "the program appears to have met its basic objectives – to get local residents involved and interested in looking out both for themselves and their neighbours" (Consultation Centre, 1987: 2). In addition to these studies, the fact that Neighborhood Watch has been one of the fastest growing community-based programs in North America since the early 1980s cannot be ignored. Based on his review of the U.S. Bureau of Justice Statistics national crime survey data on crime prevention behaviours, Freidman (1998) estimates that from 1992 to 1997, between 39 million and 47 million Americans knew about a Neighbourhood Watch or other anti-crime activity in their neighborhood, while participation in such activities ranged between 18 million and 19 million volunteers. "Roughly one in twelve Americans, twelve years of age and over, participated in neighborhood efforts aimed at improving public safety and the general well-being of their neighbours" (1460).

Despite these findings, the majority of studies examining participation in CCP and community policing programs reveal that they had minimal success in initiating and sustaining a broad-based mobilization of neighbourhood residents (Podolefsky and Dubow, 1981; Lavrakas and Herz, 1982; Taub et al., 1984; Roehl, 1984; Rosenbaum et al., 1985; Whitaker, 1986; Forst and Bazemore, 1986; Lindsay and McGillis, 1986; Fowler and Mangione, 1986; Fagen, 1987; Schneider, 1987; Hope, 1988; Dowds and Mayhew, 1994; Gillham and Barnett, 1994; Grine, 1994; Sherman, 1997b; Miller, 2001; Thacher, 2001; DeKeseredy et al., 2003). Research findings have consistently shown that only between 10 and 30 per cent of the targeted population participate in neighbourhood crime prevention (Podolefsky and Dubow, 1981; Skogan and Maxfield, 1981; Lavrakas and Herz, 1982; Rosenbaum, 1988b; Dowds and Mayhew, 1994; Yarwood and Edwards, 1995; Chicago Community Policing Consortium, 1999). Based upon their observations of three test sites, McConville and Shepherd (1992) argue that NW cannot be described as a success because there is a general lack of participation, projects quickly become dormant, and they have little impact on crime. Even on blocks where NW exists, according to Gillham and Barnett (1994: 25), an appreciable proportion of residents decline to become involved. Findings from the 1988 British Crime Survey found that the 14 per cent of households were members of a NW program. For those households located on a block with an active NW program, the participation level was slightly higher at 18 per cent. The 1992 British Crime Survey found that 20 per cent of survey respondents stated that they participated in Neighbourhood Watch while 28 per cent of those who lived on a block with a program participated (Dowds and Mayhew, 1994: 1). While a review of NW studies led Garofalo and McLeod (1989) to conclude that this community safety program has had some modest success in reducing certain kinds of crimes, particularly residential burglaries, the authors expressed scepticism about the potential for NW to have a sustained impact on crime because of the difficulty in maintaining citizen involvement. "The hope that Neighbourhood Watch will play a role in the development of a sense of community and shared purpose in U.S. neighborhoods – and that this will be accompanied by a strengthening of informal social control – also faces some difficult realities" (Garofalo and McLeod, 1989: 336). In their research, Lewis et al. (1988: 114) found that increases in neighbourhood surveillance, social interaction, bystander intervention, and specific crime prevention behaviours as a result of situational crime prevention interventions are rare.

The neighbourhoods that appear to be the most averse to CCP organizing, and where levels of participation are the lowest, are those that are in the greatest need of crime prevention programs: low-income, high-crime, inner-city neighbourhoods (Merry, 1981; Skogan and Maxfield, 1981; Greenberg et al., 1982; Taub et al., 1984; Haeberle, 1987; Dowds and Mayhew, 1994; Chicago Community Policing Consortium, 2000; Miller, 2001; DeKeseredy et al., 2003). In his review of U.S. Bureau of Justice statistics on participation in crime prevention programs, Freidman (1998: 1462) notes, "when one considers the great likelihood of victimization among Blacks and Hispanics, the less-educated, and those who live in low-income neighborhoods, it is clear that there is significant under-participation by these groups in relation to the need." In highlighting the limitations of CCP, Hope and Lab (2001: 7) establish what they view as two main "facts" that have emerged in "discussions of crime prevention programming." The first is that official agents of social control, particularly the police, cannot prevent crime and disorder without the significant participation of the public. The second is that engendering citizen participation is, at best, difficult. These facts suggest that successful crime prevention may be an elusive goal.

Factors Related to Participation and Non-participation in CCP

Researchers have identified a myriad of factors that are related to participation (and to a lesser extent, non-participation) in CCP programs, although a consensus appears to be emerging as to those that are the most powerful predictors of a successful neighbourhood crime prevention mobilization effort. Naturally, one of the predominant hypotheses is that the issue of crime represents the most salient factor in prompting citizen involvement in collective anti-crime measures. In other words, participation is assumed to grow directly from an individual's concern over crime, including past or possible future victimization as well as perceptions of the scope and nature of local crime problems. Some social theorists, as far back as Emile Durkheim (1933), believe that crime unites people and strengthens community ties through a collective response. As part of his research into community policing in Chicago, Wesley Skogan (1990; 1996) found that the best-attended meetings around crime were in the police districts with the highest crime rates. Similarly, Perry (1989) observed that public support for and participation in the Guardian Angels was greatest in those areas experiencing high rates of victimization. In their study of Neighbourhood Watch participants in rural parts of England, Yarwood and

Edwards (1995: 454) observed that prior to initiating a NW scheme on their block, 26 per cent of the block captains had personally been victims of crime, 55 per cent knew friends who had been victimized, and 59 per cent also knew neighbours who had experienced some form of crime. In a poll undertaken in Melbourne, Australia, NW captains also expressed personal motivations for their involvement that included concerns about rising crime rates (Davids, 1995). A telephone survey of more than 2,500 residents in the Philadelphia metropolitan region that assessed engagement in civic affairs found that those involved in community policing and crime prevention were "very cognizant" of crime and disorder problems in their area (Greenberg, 2001).

In direct contradiction to the above studies, numerous other empirical inquiries appear to reject a strong correlation between the personal and contextual salience of crime and participation in collective crime prevention groups and activities (Dubow and Podolefsky, 1979; Lewis and Salem, 1981; Skogan and Maxfield, 1981; Lavrakas, 1981; Podolefsky and Dubow, 1981; Lavrakas and Herz, 1982; Troyer and Wright, 1985; Lab and Stanich, 1993; Dowds and Mayhew, 1994; Perkins, Brown, and Taylor, 1996; Savolainen, 2005). Lewis and Salem (1981) conclude there is no systematic evidence that an individual's attitude towards crime is associated with participation in collective responses; communities with higher concerns about robbery or burglary, for example, do not exhibit a greater number of burglary prevention programs. Lavrakas and Lewis (1980) found that no relationship existed between perceptions of crime in a neighbourhood and participation in collective crime prevention activities. Based on their analysis of British Crime Survey data, Podolefsky and Dubow (1981) also could not establish a correlation between an individual's concern over crime and participation in local anti-crime initiatives. Troyer and Wright (1985) discovered that people's willingness to participate in local citizen patrols actually correlates with a lower-than-average fear of crime, while Dowds and Mayhew (1994) use 1992 British Crime Survey data to show that the level of participation in Neighbourhood Watch was highest in low-risk areas (25 per cent of residents participated) compared with medium-risk (14 per cent participated) and high-risk (14 per cent participated) areas. In their review of studies examining factors associated with citizen participation in crime prevention activities, Hope and Lab (2001) acknowledge that the accumulated research has produced conflicting findings on the extent to which the victimization affects participation in crime prevention programs: "Where some studies report a relationship between victimization and prevention, others claim that victimization is not a predictor of participation." In the end, the authors conclude: "The expectation that prior victimization would increase the tendency to take preventive action is not borne out in the research" (9). Also relying on British Crime Survey data, Podolefsky and Dubow (1981: 104) not only "question the impact of fear of crime on involvement in community groups, but more importantly we question the salience of crime perceptions for an understanding of why people participate in collective responses to crime when a full range of anti-crime activities is examined."

Given the above, what is clear is that the relationship between one's personal and contextual perceptions of and experiences with crime, on the one hand, and participation in collective crime prevention activities, on the other, is complex, multifaceted, and highly individualized. The complicated nature of the relationship between victimization and participation in CCP programs is reflected in the results of a city-wide survey of residents of Cork, Ireland, in 1984, which assessed people's attitudes towards Neighbourhood Watch and their willingness to participate based on perceptions of local crime and actual victimization. An analysis of the data suggests that while serious crime deters involvement, victimization from certain types of minor offences results in a greater willingness to participate (Hourihan, 1987).

Other research indicates that participation in collective crime prevention programs may have less to do with crime concern and more to do with the influence of a number of other personal and environmental variables, including demographic characteristics (age, socio-economic status, education, tenure of residence, etc.), feelings of attachment and belonging to the neighbourhood in which one lives, one's feelings of personal efficacy, the extent to which one's friends and neighbours are involved in crime prevention activities, and the presence and perceived credibility of local crime prevention programs. Just as there are numerous explanations as to why some neighbourhoods have successfully mobilized around crime while others are stubbornly resistant to crime prevention organizing, there are multiple factors, often interacting with and influencing one another, that account for an individual's participation (or non-participation) in CCP groups and activities. Using data from the 1994 British Crime Survey, Hope and Lab (2001) identify three general categories of predictors affecting citizen participation in crime prevention groups and activities: demographic variables, community characteristics, and individual perceptions of safety in one's community. They also make the important point that predictors of participation will vary according to different crime prevention activities. They note the relative consistency of such demographic factors as age, gender, race, tenure of residence, education level, and income in predicting participation in Neighbourhood Watch. The typical participants in a NW program are "older individuals, women, whites, home owners, and those with higher incomes and higher levels of education" (Hope and Lab, 2001: 12). In a study conducted into a comprehensive anticrime initiative in Milwaukee, Wisconsin, Zevitz (2002: 133) suggests age, gender, and home ownership strongly correlate with involvement; participants tended to be older, females were disproportionately represented, and home owners somewhat outnumbered renters. Research into a Neighbourhood Watch program in New Haven, Connecticut, found that the typical block captain was an employed female homeowner who has lived in the community for over twenty years (Yanay, 1994). In a survey of crime prevention coordinators in Hereford and Worcester in England, Yarwood and Edwards (1995) found that most volunteers, especially those in leadership positions, tended to be middle-class, older, retired, male residents. Based on their literature review, Hope and Lab (2001: 9) also point to the relationship between certain demographic characteristics and participation in collective crime prevention, while also acknowledging the contradictions among the numerous studies: "In general, men, more educated people, and those with higher incomes all appear to participate more than their counterparts, although various analyses report that women and lower-income respondents participate more. Age and ethnicity do not show any consistent results across studies, with some analyses suggesting that older individuals participate more while others argue that younger citizens predominate. Similarly, in America, both whites and non-whites emerge as participants in different studies."

Socio-economic status is one demographic variable that research indicates is strongly related to participation in CCP programs. Although there are exceptions, most studies have found that a typical participant in collective crime prevention activities is a middle-class homeowner, while lower-income renters are the least likely to participate. Accordingly, middle-class neighbourhoods demonstrate the highest level of resident participation, while lower-income neighbourhoods demonstrate the lowest (Merry, 1981; Skogan and Maxfield, 1981; Greenberg et al., 1982; Taub et al., 1984; Whitaker, 1986; Haeberle, 1987; Dowds and Mayhew, 1994; Skogan, 2004). The 1992 British Crime Survey found that "affluent suburban areas" posted the highest rate of membership in Neighbourhood Watch: 33 per cent of households in neighbourhoods rated as "affluent" were members of a NW program. By contrast, low-income, multi-racial areas displayed the lowest rate with only 11 per cent participating in a NW program (Dowds and Mayhew, 1994: 2). In her research in Merseyside, Hancock (2001: 168) concludes that community crime prevention groups "are largely made up of middle-class people." Yarwood and Edwards (1995) found tenure to be a significant factor in determining where NW programs were located: 85 per cent of all programs surveyed included owner-occupied dwellings. Similarly, Skogan and Maxfield (1981) suggest that home ownership and long-term residence in a neighbourhood are closely related with organized responses to crime prevention. In his analysis of community policing in Chicago, Wesley Skogan (2004) found a strong middle-class bias among those who attended community meetings organized by police. In his survey of Philadelphia residents, Greenberg (2001) cited a relatively high socio-economic status, as well as home ownership, as significant determinants of participation in anti-crime activities.

According to Hope and Lab (2001: 17), the socio-economic status of an individual is likely to be an important factor in determining participation because those with more "disposable capital" have greater opportunities to engage in preventive measures, and greater personal and collective capacities to undertake them. In a statistical analysis of census data from Chicago, Sampson and colleagues (1997) conclude that higher socio-economic status and homeownership promote collective efforts to maintain local social control because these variables are prerequisites for elevated levels of "collective efficacy." In his review of the U.S. Bureau of Justice Statistics national crime survey findings, Freidman (1998: 1461) found that middle- and upper-middle-class households were disproportionately represented in Neighbourhood Watch programs: "Half of the volunteers came from households earning more than $50,000 a year, while only 39 per cent of the population lived in such households." His review of the data also indicates that participation strongly correlates with education levels. Conversely, as part of a study into factors related to participation in NW schemes in London, Trevor Bennett (1989: 217) notes, almost parenthetically, that income level, educational attainment, and employment status are not significant factors in determining participation. Bennett and Lavrakas (1989) found that socio-economic status influenced awareness of crime prevention programs but not actual participation.

The extent to which race and ethnicity influence crime prevention participation is also complex and largely unanswered. Some studies reveal a substantial participation of racial and ethnic minorities in CCP that is disproportionate to their population size (Lavrakas and Herz, 1982; Lab, 1990; Sasson and Nelson, 1996; Freidman, 1998). Based on the Bureau of Justice Statistics survey data, Freidman (1998: 1461) writes that 14 per cent of African Americans stated they participate in collective crime prevention activities, while making up only 12 per cent of the U.S. population. Whites accounted for 82 per cent of participants, which reflects the fact that they made up 84 per cent of the U.S. population during the years covered by the survey. Sasson and Nelson (1996) discovered that while both white and African American neighbourhoods in Boston formed NW programs, the latter were generally more resistant to organization. Grine (1994) lays much of the blame for this resistance on discriminatory attitudes and practices by police, including relatively less promotion of these programs by police in African American communities, the fact that this racial community most often bears the brunt of excessive law enforcement attention and abuses, and the resulting high levels of hostility and distrust that are expressed towards police by members of African American neighbourhoods, especially those that have a low socio-economic level and a high crime rate.

While race and ethnicity by themselves appear to be poor predictors of citizen participation in CCP, the racial and ethnic homogeneity of a neighbourhood has emerged as a significant factor that positively correlates with successful crime prevention organizing. Numerous studies demonstrate that participation rates are generally higher in neighbourhoods that are racially homogeneous, particularly those where the residents are predominately white (Merry, 1981; Rosenbaum, 1987, Skogan, 1990; Thacher, 2001). CCP programs are more likely to take root in middle-class, racially homogeneous neighbourhoods because they are often more socially cohesive with a stronger informal social control contrivance (Rosenbaum, 1987). In contrast, ethnically and racially heterogeneous neighbourhoods, especially those that also have a low socio-economic status, demonstrate lower levels of social cohesion, and hence are less fertile grounds for the organic development of informal social control and collective crime prevention programs. Several studies have found that shared norms for public behaviour are less likely to develop in low income, ethnically heterogeneous neighbourhoods compared with middle-class, racially homogeneous neighbourhoods (Merry, 1981; Skogan and Maxfield, 1981; Greenberg et al., 1982; Taub et al., 1984; Thacher, 2001). According to Skogan (1990: 132), in multiracial areas, there are often conflicting views of both the causes of local problems and what should be done about them. Where neighbourhoods are divided by race, concern about crime and disorder can be an expression of conflict between groups. Watching for suspicious people easily becomes defined as watching for people of a particular race. As Greenberg et al. (1984: 19) argue, "residents of low income, culturally heterogeneous neighbourhoods tend to be more suspicious of each other, to perceive less commonality with each other, and to feel less control over their neighbourhood than do residents of more homogeneous neighbourhoods." Racial and ethnic heterogeneity also disrupts local social networks, writes Paul Bellair (1997: 685–6), "because racial and ethnic groups often embrace different traditions, ways of life, and stereotypes about out-group members. Within a social context characterized by heterogeneity, communication among residents is thought to be tenuous and the ability of residents to recognize and solve common problems impeded."

The homogeneity of an area is also linked to another variable that research indicates is a strong neighbourhood-level predictor of collective action: social cohesion. Numerous studies have noted that a prerequisite for the effective mobilization of local communities around crime is a strong sense of social cohesion (Fowler and Mangione, 1982; Maccoby et al., 1958; Jacobs, 1961; Clotfelter, 1980; Newman and Franck, 1982; Skogan and Maxfield, 1981; Greenberg, et al., 1982; Taylor et al., 1984; Taub et al., 1984; Mukherjee and Wilson, 1987; Findlay and Zvekic, 1988; Bursik and Grasmick, 1993a; Sampson et al., 1997; Freidman, 1998; Hancock, 2001). Based on their ten-year study of Chicago neighbourhoods, researchers at the Harvard School of Public Health found that local social cohesion and informal social control is linked to reduced violence (Sampson et al., 1997). According to the authors, "these results suggested that dense personal ties, organizations, and local services by themselves are not sufficient; reductions in violence appear to be more directly attributable to informal social control and cohesion among residents" (1997: 923). This research proposes that lower rates of crime and violence are based on a strong sense of informal social control, which is cultivated from social cohesion, which in turn is due to the existence of a large proportion of long-time residents. This high level of neighbourhood stability means that neighbours get to know and trust each other and are willing to intervene to protect the well-being of fellow residents and the community as a whole (1997: 919). The hypothesis that residential stability is related to informal social control, social cohesion, and collective action is supported by U.S. Bureau of Justice Statistics survey findings, which found that homeowners and long-time residents are more likely to participate in community safety activities than were renters or newcomers (Freidman, 1998: 1464).

Social cohesion, informal social control, and collective efficacy are the products of an aggregated sense of local belonging and attachment among individual residents, which have also been cited as a direct determinant of participation in collective crime prevention (Skogan and Maxfield, 1981; Greenberg et al., 1982; Hunter and Baumer, 1982; Gillis and Hagen, 1983; Taylor et al., 1984; Taub et al., 1984; Hourihan, 1987; Perkins et al., 1996; Chicago Community Policing Consortium, 1999). In his study of sixty-six Baltimore neighbourhoods, Ralph Taylor (1996) found evidence that attachment to, involvement in, and the stability of neighbourhoods are important prerequisites for collective responses to disorder. Based on their research in Middle England, Girling, Loader, and Sparks (2000) infer that a resident's "connection to place" shapes their perception of and response to perceived problems with local youth. Neighbourhood residents who spoke most emphatically about groups of teenagers who "hang about" are those who have made the greatest material and emotional investment in their area; that is, they tend to be homeowners who have lived in the neighbourhood for many years. This suggests that a resident's sense of local attachment, belonging or "social integration" is often a product of his or her financial investment in a neighbourhood (i.e., home ownership). For Barker and Linden (1985: 27), involvement in CCP appears to be strongly related to one's financial investment in a community, and as such is strongly related to socio-economic status.

The research also indicates that participants in local collective crime prevention activities tend to be involved in two or more volunteer groups and activities, which itself stems from a high level of social integration, community attachment, and civic mindedness (Dubow and Podolefsky, 1979; Lewis and Salem, 1981; Lavrakas and Herz, 1982; Fowler and Mangione, 1986; Yarwood and Edwards, 1995; Hancock, 2001; Hope and Lab, 2001). In their evaluation of Chicago's community policing program, the Chicago Community Policing Consortium (1999) categorized participants who attended police-sponsored training sessions within three groups according to the extent of their affiliations within community organizations: those with no affiliations, those with one to three affiliations, and those with four or more affiliations. A questionnaire survey of a sample of these trainees indicated that the largest number fell into the middle category: 66 per cent had one to three affiliations; 19 per cent had no affiliations; and 15 per cent had four or more. The researchers also found that 80 per cent of survey respondents with four or more community organization affiliations stated they were involved in local crime prevention groups or activities, compared to 63 per cent of participants with one to three community organization affiliations and 48 per cent of participants with no such affiliation. In their analysis of local anti-crime groups in Salt Lake City, Baltimore, and New York City, Perkins et al. (1996) found that informal neighbouring, civic responsibility, community attachments, and participation in religious or other community organizations are the most consistent predictors of participation in local anti-crime groups across all three cities. In a study of Neighbourhood Watch participants in rural England, Yarwood and Edwards (1995) documented that nearly half of the coordinators (45 per cent) were also involved in running other local voluntary activities. According to Lavrakas and Herz (1982), "it appears that organized group anti-crime activities were better viewed as a manifestation or extension of a general tendency toward voluntary action rather than as a result of a fear of crime." Podolefksy and Dubow (1981: 104) agree: "Participation in collective responses to crime develops out of more general involvement in community groups." For Hope and Lab (2001: 9),

> one of the most consistent findings about participation is the propensity of those who are involved in crime prevention also to be involved in other group activity. Various studies note that people who join community crime-prevention groups are often members of a wide array of other community groups, such as residents' associations, fraternal organizations, school-based organizations, business alliances, and others. These individuals may feel a collective or even "civic" responsibility toward their community, regardless of the issue, and see crime prevention as another concern to be addressed. Additionally, these "joiners" may be able to draw upon the well of "social capital" within their groups and organizations, providing them with the trust they need in their fellow members both to initiate new crime-prevention ventures and to maintain the group solidarity and support to sustain them.

Podolefsky and Dubow (1981: 111) believe that in stable, socially integrated neighbourhoods, people are more likely to belong to a local group, which means it is easier to persuade them to become involved in other groups or community activities. The authors cite British Crime Survey statistics indicating that, while overall participation in CCP activities is 10 per cent, more than 50 per cent of those involved in a neighbourhood group participate in collective anti-crime activities.

The aforementioned research intimates a correlation between the presence of a community organization and participation in collective crime prevention activities by neighbourhood residents. Not only do community groups create opportunities for such involvement, but their very existence may be reflective (and often the natural outcome) of local social cohesion, collective efficacy, and a sense of belonging among the local population. Susan Bennett (1995: 74) believes that community organizations may be a more important influence on levels of participation in CCP than the issue of crime, especially if these groups are effective in recruiting members. Relatively few individuals begin participating because they are concerned about crime or other community problems. Instead, individuals are generally "recruited through face-to-face encounters with acquaintances or with community organizers." In their survey of NW programs in England, Yarwood and Edwards (1995: 454) indicate that 39 per cent of these programs emerged out of other local groups, such as village forums, parish councils, and residents' associations. This reflects a national government policy of using existing organizations to promote and initiate NW programs.

Finally, it has been hypothesized that one must look beyond the community and local organizations and acknowledge the role of broader structural factors – those rooted in the dominant ideologies and institutions of advanced western societies – in determining whether the essential preconditions exist for neighbourhoods to effectively mobilize around crime and other local issues. The many attributes of modernity, such as rising levels of welfare and education, high employment levels, and increased equality for women and racial minority groups have been cited as significant contributors to local collective action, civic engagement, and social movements in the post-war era (Inglehart, 1988). Conversely, it has been argued that the dominant ideologies and institutions of advanced western societies, such as individualism, positivism, a state-centred approach to local social problem solving, market forces, and the neo-liberal political economy undermine efforts to generate local collective action (McPherson and Silloway, 1981; Lavrakas, 1982; Boostrom and Henderson, 1988; Lewis et al., 1988; Garofalo and McLeod, 1989; Pepinsky, 1989; Skogan, 1990; O'Malley, 1992; Rutherford, 1993; Crawford, 1994, 1998, 1999; Garland, 2001; Young, 2001).

Conclusion

Community crime prevention theory, and the community mobilization hypothesis in particular, proposes that the implementation of crime prevention programs will harness the energies and shared concerns of neighbourhood residents, while promoting a collective mobilization and greater vigilance. However, numerous studies reveal that collective crime prevention programs have failed to reach both their substantive goals (i.e., reduction in crime) and process-oriented goals (e.g., widespread participation). This is especially true in disadvantaged neighbourhoods. The body of research examining factors related to participation and non-participation is often contradictory, but some semblance of a consensus appears to be emerging. The salient issue of crime itself – including victimization, fear of crime, perceptions of neighbourhood crime problems, and area crime rates – may not be powerful enough unilaterally to explain why an individual or an entire neighbourhood mobilizes around crime. Instead, one needs to consider personal demographic and socio-psychological characteristics of individuals, the "contextual and situational factors of the neighborhood," as well as the "contextual factors beyond the neighborhood's boundaries" (Henig, 1982: 203).

Demographic characteristics, such as socio-economic status, tenure of residence, and the amount of time spent in a neighbourhood, as well as socio-psychological characteristics, in particular concern over crime and attachment to one's neighbourhood, are predictors of participation in local collective crime prevention groups and activities. Past studies suggest that participants in CCP groups and activities tend to be middle-class, well-educated, middle-aged homeowners who are socially integrated in and committed to their neighbourhood, have a high level of social interaction with neighbours, and who are involved in more than one local community group or civic activity. Important neighbourhood contextual variables related to the proclivity of local populations to mobilize around crime include the aggregate socio-economic status of neighbourhood residents and their tenure of residence specifically, population turnover, demographic homogeneity, and the existence of local (crime prevention) groups or other relevant opportunity structures. Specifically, the research suggests that collective action crime prevention programs are more prone to take root in demographically homogeneous, middle-class, single-family homeowning neighbourhoods, with minimal population turnover and a strong sense of social cohesion.

Demographic and socio-psychological factors related to non-participation in CCP groups and activities include low socio-economic status, a high level of mobility, and a lack of attachment to one's neighbourhood. (Despite this typology, constructing a typical profile of a non-participant is next to impossible, because, as the research shows, regardless of the demographic and socio-psychological traits of individuals, as well as the situational and contextual characteristics of a neighbourhood, most people do not participate in collective crime prevention programs.) Poverty, demographic heterogeneity, high population turnover, a lack of social interaction and cohesion, and the absence of strong local leadership and organizations all represent neighbourhood-level obstacles to the collective mobilization of residents around crime. As a result, crime prevention programs are least likely in low-income, ethnically and socio-economically heterogeneous, transient, high-crime neighbourhoods. Given the increased likelihood of victimization among those who live in high-crime, low-income neighbourhoods, there is significant under-participation by such neighbourhoods in relation to the need for community crime prevention programs.

The inability of CCP programs to effect the broad-based mobilization of residents, especially in disadvantaged neighbourhoods, raises significant questions about the theoretical foundations of CCP, in particular the hypothesis that the implementation of CCP programs in poor, high-crime neighbourhoods will result in the mobilization of residents, the development of informal social control, and, ultimately, a decrease in crime and an increase in community safety. The objective of the second part of this book is to explore further the implant hypothesis and the broader community mobilization model, while trying to better understand the forces that influence collective action; differing participation levels among individuals, groups, and communities; and the obstacles to participation in collective crime prevention programs in disadvantaged neighbourhoods.

2 Mount Pleasant, Community Crime Prevention, and Participation in Local Collective Action

Located on the east side of Vancouver, Mount Pleasant is one of the city's oldest settled parts. An inner-city neighbourhood that is adjacent to the downtown core, Mount Pleasant is one of twenty-two officially designated communities in the City of Vancouver (see fig. 2.1). The boundaries of Mount Pleasant are Cambie Street on the west, Sixteenth Avenue and Kingsway on the south, Knight Street and Clark Drive on the east, and Great Northern Way and First Avenue on the north. As indicated in figure 2.2, for planning purposes the community is officially made up of five parts: Mount Pleasant Industrial, Mount Pleasant North, Mount Pleasant West, the Main Street Core, and the Mount Pleasant Triangle.

Census data for 2001 show that there were 12,655 private households in Mount Pleasant, with a total population of 24,535, a 3.5 per cent growth from 1996 census estimates (compared to a 6.2 per cent growth for Vancouver as a whole).[1] For much of the twentieth century, Mount Pleasant East was a working-class neighbourhood. Now it is one of Vancouver's most diverse areas, ethnically, socio-economically, and in terms of housing stock. Despite its designation as one community, and its official delineation into five parts, Mount Pleasant is in fact made up of two distinct neighbourhoods that are distinguished by differing socio-economic levels, racial and ethnic makeup and diversity, and tenure of residence. The dividing line between the more affluent west side of Mount Pleasant and its eastern half is (paradoxically) Main Street. Because of the significant differences between these two halves, this study focuses primarily on the east side of Mount Pleasant, which is one of Vancouver's most disadvantaged areas, characterized by low socio-economic status, a lack of locally available jobs, a high crime rate,

Figure 2.1 The City of Vancouver and its official communities

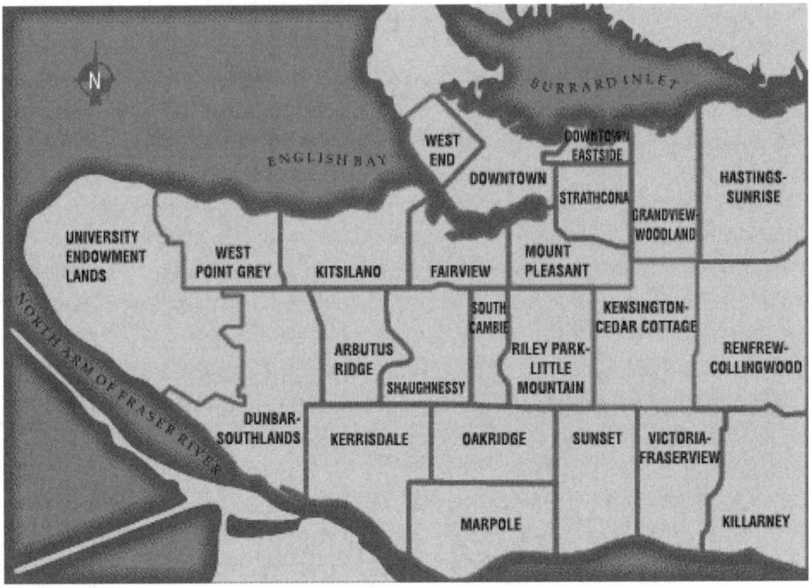

Source: City of Vancouver, http://www.city.vancouver.bc.ca/community_
profiles/CommunityList.htm.

demographic heterogeneity, rapid population turnover, and physical
deterioration.[2] These problems are particularly acute in the northeast
corner of Mount Pleasant, which reflects the heavy concentration of
poverty and crime in the northeast quadrant of Vancouver. In contrast,
the west side of Mount Pleasant (and Vancouver) is characterized by
a higher socio-economic status, relatively greater racial homogeneity,
a greater number of owner-occupied, single-family dwellings, and a
lower crime rate. Local journalist John Mackie (1999a) describes the
different solitudes of Mount Pleasant as such: "But it isn't one big
homogeneous neighbourhood. Mount Pleasant is made up of several
distinct areas. West Mount Pleasant (Main to Cambie, Broadway to
16th) is filled with beautiful heritage homes and quiet, tree-lined
streets. If you're thinking of walking around the area, there is a large
concentration of immaculate heritage homes between Ontario and
Columbia streets on West 10th and West 11th. East Mount Pleasant
(Main to Clark, Great Northern Way to 16th) is slowly becoming gen-

Figure 2.2 Mount Pleasant's official boundaries and five designated parts

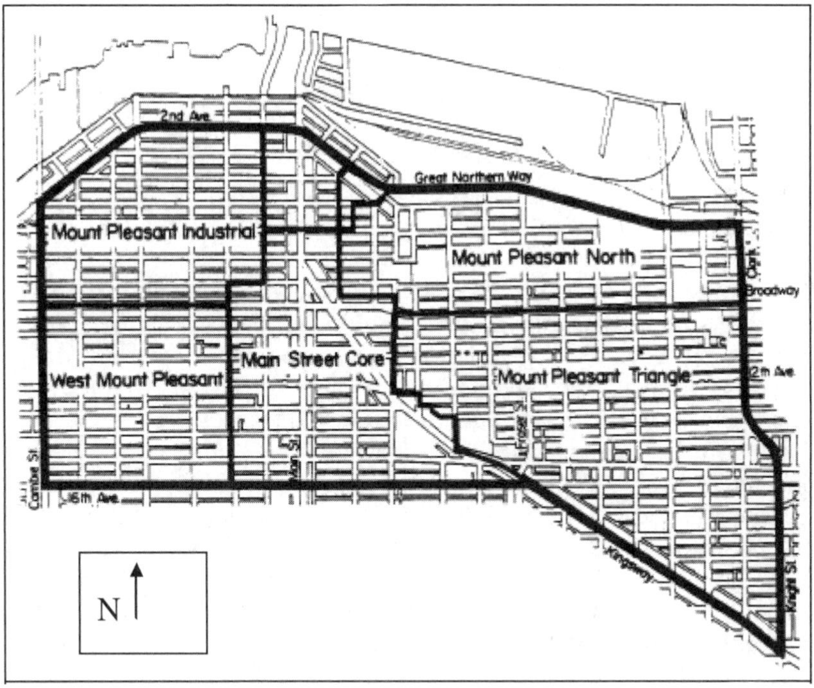

trified, but the area north of Broadway is one of the poorest, and roughest, in the city, with a big crack and prostitution problem."

Mount Pleasant can be viewed a spatial microcosm for the socio-economic disparities that divide the more affluent west side of Vancouver from its poorer eastern half. As Mackie (1999b) writes in another article, "Mount Pleasant is where Vancouver splits into east and west, literally (the dividing line is Ontario Street, two blocks west of Main). And nowhere else in the city is the division between the haves and have-nots so sudden, or so striking. West Mount Pleasant may be undergoing a renaissance, but in east Mount Pleasant near Fraser and Broadway, it's another world."

According to 1996 census data, individual income for adults over 15 years of age who live in Mount Pleasant as a whole was $18,031, compared to $26,295 for the population of the province of British Columbia (Government of British Columbia, 1996). The average family income for Mount Pleasant, according to 1996 census data, was $39,616 com-

Table 2.1 Personal income and unemployment rates: Mount Pleasant east and west

Census Year	Mount Pleasant	Mount Pleasant West	Mount Pleasant East	MP East as a % of MP West
Average personal income				
1996	$24,613	$30,348	$18,877	62.20%
2001	$26,143	$38,472	$22,933	59.19%
Average	$25,378	$34,410	$20,905	60.75%
Unemployment rates				
2001	7.71	5.3	9.53	179.81%

pared to $60,544 for Vancouver. The census data for 2001 estimates the average Mount Pleasant family income at $49,722, compared to $69,190 for Vancouver as a whole. The lower average income level for Mount Pleasant is mostly the product of its poorer eastern half, and a break-down by census tracts reveals the income disparity between its two halves. For the census tracts west of Main Street, the average personal income for residents over fifteen years of age was $30,348 for the 1996 census and $38,472 for the 2001 census. For census tracts east of Main Street, average personal income for residents over fifteen years of age was $18,877 for the 1996 census and $22,933 for the 2001 census.[3] Labour force statistics for the 2001 census (based on a 20 per cent sample of the total population) estimate an unemployment rate of 7.71 per cent for Mount Pleasant as a whole, and 13.5 per cent for males between the ages of fifteen and twenty-four. For Mount Pleasant East, the unemployment rate rises to 9.53 per cent, compared to 5.3 per cent for Mount Pleasant West. For males between the ages of fifteen and twenty-four, the unemployment rate for Mount Pleasant East was 15.6 per cent compared to 10.7 per cent for Mount Pleasant West. A compar-ison of the differences in average personal income and unemployment between Mount Pleasant East and West is summarized in table 2.1.

The 2001 census reported that 10.29 per cent of the Mount Pleasant population was dependent upon some type of government subsidy. For Mount Pleasant West, the proportion was 5.6 per cent. For Mount Pleasant East it was 13.82 per cent. Contributing to the high rate of poverty and government support is the large proportion of single-parent families; according to 2001 census data, of the 5,500 families liv-ing in Mount Pleasant, 24.5 per cent are single-parent households (compared to 17 per cent for Vancouver as a whole). Moreover, the per-centage of the Mount Pleasant population that lived in "low-income households" was 35.6 per cent, compared to 27 per cent for the city as a

Figure 2.3 Population in low-income households as a percentage of the total population of the community

Low-Income Households

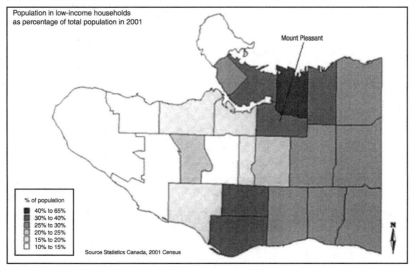

Source: City of Vancouver, Community Services. http://www.city.vancouver. bc.ca/commsvcs/Census2001/Maps/lowincome.htm.

whole. As indicated in figure 2.3, a spatial analysis of the distribution of low-income families shows that Mount Pleasant is one of six communities, all located on the eastern half of Vancouver, where the city's low-income households are predominately concentrated.

In a study investigating the relationship between the socio-economic status of Vancouver neighbourhoods and the preparedness of children to learn at school, Clyde Hertzman, a University of British Columbia epidemiologist specializing in population health, found children were most at developmental risk on the east side, due primarily to poorer socio-economic conditions. In a spatial mapping of this "development vulnerability," children living in Mount Pleasant East were consistently ranked at the bottom in terms of school readiness. His findings indicated that in all the kindergarten readiness tests – social competence, emotional maturity, physical health and well-being, communication skills and language and cognitive development – the students in the bottom tenth percentile all lived in the Mount Pleasant, Downtown

Eastside, and northeast sectors of the city: "In other words, there are large and consistent differences in developmental vulnerability across Vancouver's neighbourhoods, with the greatest vulnerability being in the Downtown Eastside, Lower Mount Pleasant, and the Grandview-Woodlands neighbourhoods" (Hertzman et al., 2002: 9). In a media interview, Dr Hertzman was quoted as saying, "If I was a single parent on welfare, I would want to live in a Kitsilano basement suite rather than a house in the Downtown Eastside or Mount Pleasant. My kids would do better because of the context they would be in" (Gram, 2001).

The socio-economic "context" that characterizes Mount Pleasant appears to have changed little during the post-war era. A 1962 economic study of the neighbourhood provides evidence that around this time, income levels in this neighbourhood were some of the lowest in the city. The report states that the population of Mount Pleasant is made up of "residents who lack the social and economic resources to move to a more 'desirable' location ... a large number of families and single persons in the area are dependent upon some form of social assistance" (Hicks, 1962: 60–1). A neighbourhood improvement report written in 1976 conceded that "the area is well below the city average in many socio-economic characteristics" (Mount Pleasant Triangle, 1976: 8). The 1989 Mount Pleasant Community Development Plan cites statistics compiled by the city's social planning department, which estimates that 36 per cent of the local population was dependent upon public income subsidies. Out of a population of approximately 21,000, around 4,300 residents (20.5 per cent) received government welfare cheques, 2,600 (12.4 per cent) were on unemployment insurance, and 400 (1.9 per cent) received senior and disabilities pensions (Mount Pleasant Citizens' Planning Committee, 1989: 17). To accommodate different special needs populations, the neighbourhood has several residential facilities that house seniors, refugees, abused women and youth, low-income families, and the mentally ill. According to 1994 figures, Mount Pleasant has 750 dwelling units in twenty-three government-assisted housing projects that provide housing for special needs groups (City of Vancouver, 1994: 4–5). A 2001 report, entitled *State of Social Housing in Vancouver*, indicated that Mount Pleasant had 783 non-market dwelling units. This constituted 6.6 per cent of the total housing stock of the community, which is less than 8.5 per cent for the city as a whole (City of Vancouver, 2001).

The population of Mount Pleasant is also one of the most transient in Vancouver. Census data for 2001 indicates that 64.2 per cent of Mount

Pleasant residents had moved in the last five years, compared to 51.7 per cent for Vancouver as a whole. The 1996 census documented that 70.6 per cent of Mount Pleasant residents had moved in the previous five years (compared to 57.7 per cent of Vancouver residents). One of the reasons accounting for Mount Pleasant's highly mobile population is that it is home to a large proportion of low-cost rental properties (which is particularly true on the east side). Many of the larger homes have been subdivided and converted into some of Vancouver's most inexpensive rental units, which for years have become home to poor, immigrant families. According to census data, 71.7 per cent of all dwellings in Mount Pleasant are rental, compared to 56.2 per cent for Vancouver generally. Only 5.6 per cent of all dwellings in Mount Pleasant are single-detached housing, compared to 27.7 per cent for Vancouver. For 2001, the average rent in Mount Pleasant was $692 compared to $796 for Vancouver as a whole.

Despite the generally low socio-economic status and transient nature of Mount Pleasant East residents, there remains a small cadre of middle-class, homeowning residents that contributes to the heterogeneity of the neighbourhood's population. In addition, since the early 1990s, some parts of Mount Pleasant East have slowly gentrified through the construction of medium-rise condominiums, and artist live-work lofts, which has attracted a small but growing population of young professionals and artisans. The portion of Main Street located in Mount Pleasant has also enjoyed what one media report described as a "minor" renaissance, with the location of a number of new Chinese, Vietnamese, Cambodian, Japanese, Russian, and Hungarian restaurants (Mackie, 1999c). A $2 million renovation of the Kingsgate Mall – to which some have applied the unfortunate nickname of "Hellsgate Mall" – was also undertaken in 1999 and 2000 to enhance its appearance (Warwick, 2001). The rebirth of Mount Pleasant's central business district, however, has been dwarfed by the commercial resurgence on the west side of Mount Pleasant that began in the early 1990s when a number of large retailers moved in along Broadway Avenue and "breathed new life into what was basically a thoroughfare to the suburbs" (Mackie, 1999c).

A final defining characteristic of the Mount Pleasant population is its diverse ethnic makeup and large proportion of new immigrants and visible minorities. According to 2001 census data, neighbourhood residents are predominately of non-European origin: less than one in four residents identify a single European heritage, 44.3 per cent claim a

Table 2.2 First languages spoken at Mount Pleasant East elementary schools

Mount Pleasant		Florence Nightingale		Queen Alexandria	
English	31%	English	23%	Vietnamese	29%
Cambodian	13	Vietnamese	23	English	24
Chinese	11	Cambodian	19	Chinese	19
Vietnamese	10	Chinese	16	Spanish	6
Polish	6	Spanish	5	Tagalog	4
Spanish	6	Tagalog	3	Cambodian	4
Hindi	4	(18 others)	10	Bengali	2
Tagalog	4			Hindi	2
Korean	2			Romanian	2
(26 others)	13			(13 others)	9
Total	100%		99%*		101%*

Source: Vancouver School Board, 1995.
*Total does not add up to 100 per cent due to rounding.

mother tongue other than English, and 44 per cent were born outside Canada. Of this immigrant population, over two-thirds emigrated from a developing country. Of those immigrants who have lived in Canada since at least 1981, 81.4 per cent are from Asia, primarily China, Hong Kong, Vietnam, the Philippines, and Sri Lanka. Residents from forty-two other ethnic groups were identified in Mount Pleasant, according to the 2001 census. This diversity is particularly extensive in Mount Pleasant East, which may very well be "the most ethnically diverse community in the province" (Mackie, 1999b). The variety of different ethnic groups is also illustrated by examining the mother tongue of students within the three Mount Pleasant East elementary schools. Vancouver School Board Statistics for the 1994/95 school year reveals that twenty-two languages were spoken at Queen Alexandria, twenty-four languages at Florence Nightingale, and thirty-five languages at Mount Pleasant Elementary School. As table 2.2 indicates, when an average is taken of the three elementary schools, only 26 per cent of the students spoke English as their first language.

Crime and Disorder in Mount Pleasant

As indicated in figure 2.4 below, Mount Pleasant has one of the higher crime rates in the city. It should be noted that the statistics in figure 2.4 do not adequately reflect the distribution of crime in Mount Pleasant – a disproportionate amount of property, personal, and consensual crime

Figure 2.4 2003 Crime rates by Vancouver communities

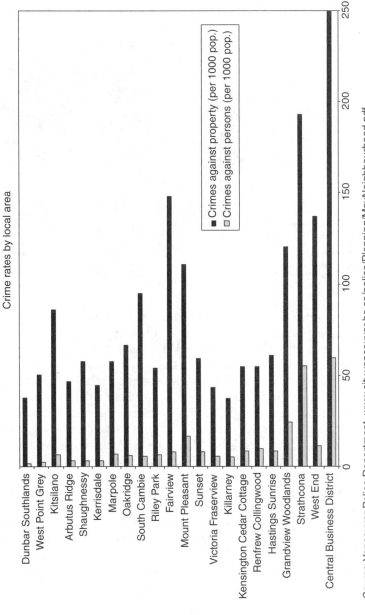

Crime rates by local area

- Crimes against property (per 1000 pop.)
- Crimes against persons (per 1000 pop.)

Dunbar Southlands
West Point Grey
Kitsilano
Arbutus Ridge
Shaughnessy
Kerrisdale
Marpole
Oakridge
South Cambie
Riley Park
Fairview
Mount Pleasant
Sunset
Victoria Fraserview
Killarney
Kensington Cedar Cottage
Renfrew Collingwood
Hastings Sunrise
Grandview Woodlands
Strathcona
West End
Central Business District

0   50   100   150   200   250

Source: Vancouver Police Department, www.city.vancouver.bc.ca/police/Planning/MayNeighbourhood.pdf.

Figure 2.5 Neighbourhood crime rate per capita, 2000 (all crimes) and proportion classified as violent, property, and other

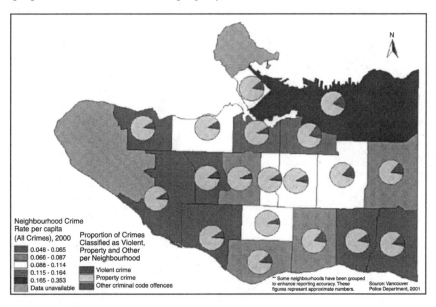

Neighbourhood Crime
Rate per capita
(All Crimes), 2000
  0.048 - 0.065
  0.066 - 0.087
  0.088 - 0.114
  0.115 - 0.164
  0.165 - 0.353
  Data unavailable

Proportion of Crimes
Classified as Violent,
Property and Other
per Neighbourhood
  Violent crime
  Property crime
  Other criminal code offences

** Some neighbourhoods have been grouped
to enhance reporting accuracy. These   Source: Vancouver
figures represent approximate numbers.   Police Department, 2001

is concentrated in its eastern half, which for years has had a reputation as a hub for prostitution and drug trafficking. Once again, the spatial distribution of crime within Mount Pleasant is a microcosm for Vancouver as a whole, which in turn roughly parallels the city's geographical distribution of socio-economic disparities: with some exceptions, the crime rate is much higher on the poorer, east side of Vancouver and is highest in the northeast corner, where poverty is most concentrated. Hertzman and colleagues (2002) mapped out crime rate statistics across the city and found that "there are not only four-fold differences in aggregate crime rates by neighbourhood, but also variation in terms of the proportion of crimes that may be classified as violent." East side neighbourhoods have higher rates for most offences, including violent offences. A spatial mapping of this data is presented in figure 2.5, which shows how the crime rate for Vancouver generally increases from west to east, with the highest crime rate located in the northeast corner of the city.

Straddling the eastern and western halves of Vancouver, Mount Pleasant internalizes these east-west crime rate disparities. As a *Van-*

couver Sun article described it: "West Mount Pleasant may be quiet, but east Mount Pleasant is overflowing with street life, and not all of it legal. Prostitutes linger on the corners, drug dealers sell their wares openly, and crackheads and junkies do their bizarre chicken walk up and down the street. 'There's a lot of crack, and it's related to prostitution,' says Constable Steve Callender of the Mount Pleasant Community Policing Centre. 'The prostitution here for the most part has been drug-driven. They're drug-addicted prostitutes. And we have a lot of street drug dealing'" (Mackie, 1999b). Prostitution and drug trafficking have been viewed as the most prevalent crime problems facing Mount Pleasant East since at least the early 1980s. Interviews and focus groups conducted for this research with police, municipal government officials, community activists, and local residents consistently ranked street prostitution and drug trafficking as the most pressing problems facing Mount Pleasant East. While street prostitution in Mount Pleasant can be traced as far back as the 1970s, it was during the mid-1980s that the problem began to intensify. As one community newspaper article stated in 1984, "Nothing better characterizes the problems facing Mount Pleasant and its residents than the recent influx of hookers into the district" (*East Ender*, 13 September 1984).

Two significant external events occurring in the mid-1980s helped trigger the escalation of the sex trade in Mount Pleasant. One was Expo 86, a successful international fair that attracted a large number of tourists to the city. The other was the migration of street prostitutes from the West End of Vancouver, due to the highly organized and effective protests of residents in that neighbourhood. Groups such as Concerned Residents of the West End and Shame the Johns were organized around the single purpose of ridding the West End of street prostitution, and, according to one media report, these campaigns developed into a "political force that was hard to ignore" (Cler-Cunningham, 2001). West End organizers made a series of submissions to the municipal, provincial, and federal governments demanding that street prostitution be removed from the area "regardless of where it might end up," according to criminologist and prostitution expert John Lowman (1992: 7). The political pressure eventually led to an unprecedented legal strategy by the provincial government: the issuing of civil nuisance injunctions against prostitutes, which provided police with the powers to remove them from the West End neighbourhood. It was a combination of these actions that pushed many street prostitutes into other Vancouver neighbourhoods, including Mount Pleasant. Between

Table 2.3 Counts of Vancouver street prostitutes, averages for the periods 1985–8 and 1988–93

Location	1985–8	1988–93
Richards-Seymour	44%	48%
Downtown Eastside	14%	28%
Mount Pleasant	26%	11%
Boystown	16%	12%

Source: Lowman and Fraser, 1995b.

the mid-1980s and early 1990s, street prostitution in Mount Pleasant increased dramatically. While prostitutes were most visible along main commercial thoroughfares such as East Broadway, Kingsway, and Fraser Street, they also plied their trade on residential streets and back alleys. In its 1989 development plan for the neighbourhood, the Mount Pleasant Citizens' Planning Committee (1989: 28) acknowledged that street prostitution was now "one of the foremost problems facing Mount Pleasant." Vancouver police statistics indicate that between January 1986 and April 1990, 1,517 prostitution-related charges under the Criminal Code were laid in Mount Pleasant, accounting for 30.8 per cent of all prostitution-related charges for the city during this period (Vancouver Police Department, 1990).

In their research, Lowman and Fraser (1995b) estimated that between 1982 and 1994 there were seventeen different prostitution "strolls" in Vancouver, with four or five more active than others at any one period of time. From 1982 through 1995, the researchers conducted "head counts" in the various strolls to monitor levels of street activity and to record displacement of street prostitution in response to various law enforcement and neighbourhood initiatives. The results of these head counts are summarized in the table 2.3. According to these estimates, between 1985 and 1993, the proportion of street prostitutes working in Mount Pleasant decreased from 26 to 11 per cent, although in a later article Lowman (2000: 993–4) identifies the emergence of another stroll, beginning in 1991, in a commercial area located in the northern most portion of Mount Pleasant, which increased the number of prostitutes working the neighbourhood. During the original research period covered by this study (1995 to 1997), street prostitutes continued to be visible in certain parts of Mount Pleasant East; along East Broadway Avenue, St George Street, Kingsway, the commercial area located in the north-eastern corner of the neighbourhood, and at the corner of Fraser Street and Tenth Avenue (one block south-east of the Mount Pleasant Community Crime Prevention Office). During a one-month period in 1996, some residents even reported sightings of a prostitute who intermittingly stood just outside the crime prevention office after it was closed for the day. These and other "prostitute sightings" were the most frequent types of reports made to the local crime prevention office during the original research period. Based on interviews conducted in 1996 with local crime prevention organizers and other community activists, as well as with Vancouver police patrol officers assigned to Mount Pleasant, the estimates of the average number of streetwalkers who plied the local streets on the east side of the neighbourhood were between fifteen and thirty. Observational research conducted for this study from 1995 to 1997 indicated, on average, a smaller number: between five and ten street prostitutes were seen working the streets of Mount Pleasant East on any given evening. (This total does not include prostitutes that worked out of apartments and houses in the neighbourhood.) In a 1996 interview, the Vancouver police inspector in charge of patrols for Mount Pleasant stated that the number of prostitutes "has increased in the past year. On any given night there are between six and ten in the area, and we have identified fifty who come and go." According to crime statistics for 1995 and 1996, Mount Pleasant accounted for 33.6 per cent of all solicitation arrests in the city in those two years. Due to intensive police crackdowns and ongoing citizen measures during the early to mid-1990s, the prostitution problem appeared to move east and north-east, primarily to the Strathcona community, which is located just north of Mount Pleasant. By 2003, according to Vancouver Police Department statistics for January to May, Mount Pleasant accounted for just 2 per cent of all prostitution-related offences for the city. Based on observations during the summer of 2003, I estimated that five prostitutes consistently worked the streets of Mount Pleasant East (most of whom were located along the major thoroughfare of Kingsway).

One of the most tragic repercussions of Vancouver's street-level sex trade has been the violence perpetrated against prostitutes, which reaches almost unimaginable proportions. Police believe that between 1982 and 1998, more than sixty women in the city's sex trade were murdered. Almost half of these are believed to be the victim of one accused serial killer, who became the target of the largest police investigation in the history of British Columbia (Saunders and Thompson, 2004; *Canadian Press*, 2006). According to Lowman and Fraser (1995c), the streetwalkers most vulnerable to violence are located in the strolls on the east side of Vancouver: "As with most of our other information about where women experience the highest rate of bad dates, by far the largest number of complainants appearing in these files had been working in one of the East Vancouver strolls. Of the 35 women for whom we have this information, 63% had met the attacker in one of the Downtown Eastside/Strathcona area strolls, and another 25% had been working in Mount Pleasant (i.e., in North Mount Pleasant/1st Avenue or Fraser/Broadway)." While conceding that "there is a lot of missing information in this regard," Lowman and Fraser (1995a) conclude the "murder victims come disproportionately from the east Vancouver strolls (Mount Pleasant and Strathcona)." While Mount Pleasant and the Downtown Eastside accounted for about 40 per cent of the nightly prostitute population from 1985 through 1993, nearly all the murder victims during this period came from these two areas (Lowman, 2000: 993–4).

The escalation of the drug trade in Mount Pleasant has also been linked to street prostitution, in part because many streetwalkers and pimps are chronic drug users. In a 1989 media interview, Inspector Don Keith, who at the time was the officer in charge of a joint Vancouver Police Department–RCMP drug enforcement task force, said cocaine trafficking in particular is on the increase in certain areas of Mount Pleasant. "We can expect to find some drug trafficking in all parts of the city, but we've had a lot more cases recently in Mount Pleasant" (Pemberton, 1989a). During the period that I worked in the crime prevention office, reports of street-level drug trafficking were the most persistent complaints made to the CPO and to police (outnumbering prostitution complaints). Cocaine and heroin was readily available in street-level quantities, from houses or apartments, corner stores, restaurants, nightclubs, cars, and even from bicycle couriers. During an interview conducted in 1996 for this study, one Vancouver police patrol officer noted, with no humour intended, that by simply placing a phone call, cocaine or heroin could be delivered to a Mount Pleasant address faster than a pizza. Drug use is conspicuous in many parts of the eastern half of the neighbourhood: needles for intravenous injections can be found on the street, in parks or bushes; addicts use public spaces to shoot up; and abandoned buildings have been converted into "shooting galleries." A local organization responsible for needle exchange makes daily stops in various locations throughout Mount Pleasant. While drug use and narcotics enforcement statistics are not available on a neighbourhood level for Vancouver, the city is a major port of entry for heroin from Southeast Asia (Royal Canadian Mounted Police, 2004) and has Canada's highest per capita population of heroin and crack cocaine addicts and drug overdoses, as well as one of the country's highest rates of illegal drug offences and drug-related crime (McLean, 2000).

Gang-related violence is also evident in Mount Pleasant and became of particular concern when, on 6 April 1996, three people were stabbed to death in a gang-related dispute at the Tulip Club, a karaoke bar located on the east side of the neighbourhood. According to one media article, "the weekend slayings brings to at least six the number of violent incidents at B.C. karaoke bars in the last seven months. Since 1991, 10 people have been killed and 13 wounded in nine separate incidents." The article goes on to list eight British Columbia addresses where the killings took place, four of which are in Mount Pleasant (Crawley, 1996). Another criminal spin-off of the concentration of the drug trade and addicts in Mount Pleasant is the high rate of local property crime. Vancouver Police Department crime statistics indicate that break and enters increased from 324 in 1994 to 1,233 in 1996 (a 280 per cent increase). During the same period, reported residential break and enters for Vancouver as a whole also increased, but only by 26 per cent. Crime rate statistics for the first six months of 2004 also indicate that Mount Pleasant has one of the highest property crime rates (including break and enters, robbery, theft, and motor vehicle theft), as well as one of the highest rates of assault (Vancouver Police Department, 2004a).

Helping to fuel the prostitution and drug problems in Mount Pleasant East is the high rate of absentee landlords, some of whom are accused of turning a blind eye, tolerating, and sometimes even welcoming tenants engaged in prostitution, pimping, and drug trafficking. Many of the persistent complaints about "problem premises" made to the police and the Mount Pleasant Community CPO during the initial research period concerned low-rent, subdivided houses. Most of the complaints revolved around drug trafficking and use, prostitution, late-night parties, constant vehicular and pedestrian traffic, untended garbage, unattended children and youth, and unsafe or unsanitary living conditions. Some of these problem premises were owned by the same people, and a small number of owners became notorious in Mount Pleasant as slum landlords (who in turn became the target of persistent community and city action). Drug trafficking appears to be most prevalent within rented dwellings. According to a former Vancouver police inspector in charge of drug enforcement: "For years there has been a lot of low-rental housing there and as a result drug-users have moved in ... Wherever they start hanging around the demand becomes such that they need a supplier" (Pemberton, 1989a). Another factor contributing to the instability of the neighbourhood is the presence of a liquor store in the Kingsgate Mall. A 1983 report by the city health department concluded that alcohol-related problems stemming from this liquor store escalated since the closing of the liquor store at Hastings and Main in the impoverished Downtown Eastside because "the clientele from that area are now appearing at the liquor store in Kingsgate Mall" (*East Ender*, 13 September 1984). Thus, as with street prostitution, the problems associated with the Mount Pleasant liquor store were exacerbated by external events.

In sum, Mount Pleasant suffers from one of the higher crime rates in the city, and, although statistics are not available for Mount Pleasant East, it is widely acknowledged that this section of Vancouver has one of the highest rates of crime in the city. Street prostitution has frequently been cited as the epicentre around which many other of Mount Pleasant East's problems – criminal and otherwise – revolve. Prostitution is seen as a powerfully negative force that undermines the community's delicate informal social control, directly and indirectly contributing to its social, economic, and physical decay. In this respect, Wilson and Kelling's (1982) broken windows theory – which argues that an unchecked incivility or illegality can initiate a chain reaction leading to more incivilities, disorder, criminality, and the deterioration of a neighbourhood – could potentially be applied to Mount Pleasant. There is sufficient historical evidence to suggest that the persistent presence of street prostitution in Mount Pleasant since the early 1980s has instigated, or at least contributed to, an intensification of crime, disorder, incivilities, and a downward spiral of this neighbourhood. Street prostitution in Mount Pleasant has brought with it increases in vehicular traffic, property crime, sexual assaults on women, the murder of street prostitutes, drug trafficking and abuse, gang-related activities, and other violence. The role of the sex trade in promoting the perception of social disorder, and, concomitantly, the chain of events suggested by Wilson and Kelling is articulated in the *Community Development Plan for Mount Pleasant* (Mount Pleasant Citizens' Planning Committee 1989: 28–9), an analysis that deserves to be quoted at length:

Street prostitution continues to be one of the foremost problems facing Mount Pleasant. The effects go beyond disruption of "normal" day-to-day life in areas such as traffic, noise and loss of personal safety, to include general deterioration of the social fabric of the community and, probably most destructive in the long run, a decline of the overall image of the community region-wide. The net effect is a community unable to bring about the changes necessary to improve liveability for residents and to improve economic viability for businesses ...

Traffic, stopping and going of vehicles and the many loud exchanges are the first intrusions. As the activity has increased, women not involved in the activity of prostitution are hassled by customers who cannot distinguish them from the prostitutes. Customers can be pressing and persistent. Gradually residents of the area are uneasy about living in Mount Pleasant. Prospective residents avoid the area. Personal safety is threatened by direct exchanges between aggravated residents and stubborn prostitutes, customers and agents (pimps and boyfriends).

As the area gains a reputation as a "safe place" for prostitution, prostitutes, a limited number of pimps and boy-friend managers and other individuals involved in related activities move into the community. Use of apartment suites for "business" brings the activity off the street into apartments. Increased coming and going, loud exchanges, confrontation, violence and poor attitudes are then brought right into the home environment.

Over time, the area gains a reputation as a "hooker haven," attracting more customers and more prostitutes. Activity levels increase throughout the night, often into the early morning. At this point residents who will not put up with the increased activity move. At a later stage, long-term residents contemplate moving. Ultimately the stable base of residents is gone and "skid row" has arrived.

The value of any positive change to improve liveability is negated, as residents tend to focus on the day-to-day problems of street prostitution and the image of the community. Property values decline, adding to the frustration of owners. Residents may lose the incentive to maintain or improve their properties, as they perceive this to be a poor investment. Current and potential stable, long term, or family-oriented residents leave or avoid the community.

Mount Pleasant has already experienced several of these impacts. Long-term residents are beginning to leave. One community leader recently sold a property at 8th and St. George at a price estimated to be

$10,000 to $15,000 less than its value might have been if the community's reputation had not deteriorated. Apartment buildings along Broadway and between Fraser and Glen Drive indicate a number of vacant apartments.

The report acknowledges that the many factors contributing to the decline of a community are not mutually exclusive, but critically interconnected. The progression of events that have contributed to the deterioration of Mount Pleasant is depicted in figure 2.6.

As in much of North America, the overall crime rate declined in Vancouver throughout the latter half of the 1990s, yet prostitution and drug problems stubbornly persisted in Mount Pleasant and neighbouring communities. A 27 October 2000 newspaper article summarized the continuing problems, as seen through the eyes of various area residents:

> It was his eight-year-old son who spotted a used condom in the parking lot behind the restaurant. "That kind of caught me by surprise." A week later, his son noticed another used condom at Kingsway and St. Catherine's. Last week, he found one on the street in front of his house. The yard at Charles Dickens elementary school on Glen Street was so littered with debris from the sex and drug trade that before the school could open this fall, maintenance staff had to hose down the property, he said ... Neighbours have told him they have seen prostitutes working in the alley behind the school. A vice-principal told [a meeting of residents] that administrators sometimes have to chase people stoned on drugs away from the school before it opens in the morning. (Zacharias, 2000)

Fears also surfaced that an intensive crackdown in the Downtown Eastside by Vancouver police that began in 2003 would result in the displacement of its drug and prostitution trade to Mount Pleasant (Bula and Fong, 2003). In a letter to the editor of a community newspaper, the minister of a United Church in Mount Pleasant East wrote:

> No doubt folks vested in the Hastings corridor are pleased by the continuing police cleanup of prostitutes, pimps, pushers and pernicious characters of all sorts. That sense of relief is not at all shared by those of us who have served as the dustpan for this effective sweep. I am minister of a small church in the northeast corner of the Kingsway Fraser junction. Over the past two weeks, I have been working night and day to manage

Figure 2.6 External factors and a chain of events contributing to deterioration of Mount Pleasant

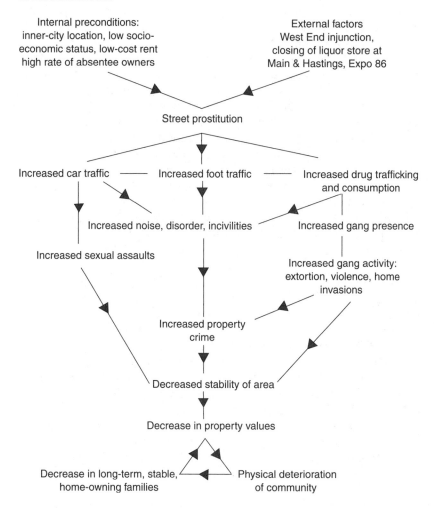

the increased presence of working girls, the pushers who supply their habits and the johns who pay the way. On any given day we have two to six people gathered on the back stairs of the church. This has caused a great deal of anxiety for the neighbourhood. (Feenstra, 2003)

Community Crime Prevention in Mount Pleasant

The ongoing crime problems have not gone unchallenged by Mount Pleasant residents. Since at least the mid-1980s, the community has been home to a number of organizations and activities that have focused exclusively or overwhelmingly on street-level crime (and prostitution in particular). Some of the more active groups include the Mount Pleasant Neighbourhood Association, Shame the Johns, the Carolina Street Neighbourhood Group, the Mount Pleasant Action Group, the Mount Pleasant Block Neighbours, the Mount Pleasant Safer Community Society, the Mount Pleasant Community Crime Prevention Office, Neighbourhood Watch, and the Dickens Community Group. The contemporary history of crime prevention groups in Mount Pleasant can be traced to September 1984 when the Mount Pleasant Neighbourhood Association (MPNA) sponsored a community meeting, the objective of which was to "formulate an anti-hooker battle plan." William Wood, the MPNA president at the time, noted that in order to address the problem of prostitution, "There has to be a cooperative effort, a joint approach. The meeting will be about what we, as a community, will do to respond to the street prostitution problem" (*East Ender*, 13 September 1984). The consensus of this meeting was that Mount Pleasant residents would place pressure on the Vancouver City Council and the Vancouver Police Department to remove the prostitutes from their area. This decision provided the impetus for what would become a string of increasingly confrontational tactics by local groups to combat prostitution and other crime problems in Mount Pleasant. One of the first acts of protest was a demonstration held on East Broadway during the summer of 1985 (Lowman, 1992: 9). In the same year, political pressure from neighbourhood groups prompted Vancouver City Council to approve a plan to move prostitutes into an informal red light district on the north western side of Mount Pleasant, which consisted primarily of industrial businesses. However, the result, according to John Lowman, was "they moved street prostitution to the front doorstep of a woman who was to become prominent in the Mount Pleasant Action Group, another one-issue lobby group organized to confront street prostitution." One of the tactics used by the Action Group was to stage a "sleep-in" at City Hall. Group members argued that since it was impossible to get any rest in their own neighbourhood they would sleep in the council chambers (10). Despite these efforts, prostitution continued to flourish in Mount

Pleasant in the mid- and late 1980s. Frustrated with the perceived inaction by City Council and police, local groups began to escalate their confrontational tactics. Through the Mount Pleasant Action Group and the Mount Pleasant Block Neighbours, some residents started citizen patrols that confronted the streetwalkers and their customers on the street. On one night, according to a news report, fifteen protestors gathered in the rain on a street corner where prostitutes often congregated. Some carried placards and signs while others recorded the licence plate numbers of cars carrying the prostitutes' prospective customers, and "within ten minutes of the groups' arrival about six hookers dispersed" (*Vancouver Sun*, 17 May 1986, as cited in Lowman, 1992: 9). The combined tactics of street-level confrontations and political pressure did realize some success when the Vancouver police convened a series of task forces in Mount Pleasant each summer from 1987 through 1992, which gradually displaced a number of prostitutes into nearby Strathcona (Lowman and Fraser, 1995a).

As the 1980s wore on, much of the local organizing continued to focus on crime and disorder problems. In 1989, members of the MPNA travelled to Ottawa to testify at parliamentary committee hearings into Bill C-49, a street solicitation law passed in 1985. During the early 1990s, residents of Carolina Street organized to protest a number of problem premises on their block, which evolved into a larger city-wide campaign to force absentee landlords to accept a greater responsibility for their properties. One notorious slum landlord who owned a number of properties in East Vancouver at the time was targeted by this informal collection of neighbours, which eventually became known as the Carolina Street Neighbourhood Group. (According to the lead organizer, who was interviewed for this research, at its peak the group totalled sixty people.) When no action was taken by the owner in response to the group's demands, they took their fight to City Council, and in March 1992 the council proposed a by-law authorizing the city to bill the landlord for visits to his houses by the police, the sanitation department, and the health department (Kines, 1992). Between 120 and 150 people attended the council meeting to support the appeals of the protest organizers, prompting veteran city councillor Don Bellamy to comment that in his experience, "this was the very first time that a whole neighbourhood had shown up to raise hell" (*Vancouver Echo*, 12 March 1992). The ongoing effort of the Carolina Street Neighbourhood Group ultimately resulted in the suspension of the owner's licence to rent his premises located on this street. In 1993, local residents who were active in the fight against prostitution, problem premises, and other community ills formed the Mount Pleasant Neighbourhood Association. According to one founding member interviewed for this research, this group was formed as an alternative to the MPNA, which was perceived as being too apolitical: "We weren't satisfied with the present organized groups; like they didn't seem to be really addressing the issues, like crime." One of their most successful campaigns was to block the opening of a proposed beer and wine store at a Mount Pleasant East hotel.

In July 1994, a crowd estimated at 350 people attended a community meeting to discuss the ongoing prostitution problem. (The crowd was so large organizers had to set up a sound system outside for people who could not fit into the auditorium at the Mount Pleasant campus of the Vancouver Community College.) The result of this meeting was the resurfacing of a local citizen's group that would confront prostitutes and their customers, this time under the Shame the Johns moniker first used by West End residents. During the height of its activism in the latter half of 1994, the leaders of the Mount Pleasant rendition of Shame the Johns claimed an active membership of fifty people. The group also actively lobbied city and provincial government officials, and even met with the provincial premier, demanding a five-year minimum sentence for pimps exploiting youths under eighteen years of age and seizure of the cars of johns caught buying sex (Gram, 1994). The same group also prepared community victim impact statements, which Crown attorneys agreed to present at the trials of accused johns. The group went so far as to develop advertisements to be placed in the city's largest daily newspaper, the *Vancouver Sun*, which would list the names of men convicted of prostitution-related offences. After the newspaper refused to accept the proposed ads, the group then considered projecting the names of johns at night on the blank walls of buildings (Bula, 1994), although that proposed tactic never came to fruition.

The leaders of this anti-prostitution campaign also began the process of establishing an organization dedicated to crime prevention in Mount Pleasant, which ultimately led to the founding of the Mount Pleasant Safer Community Society (MPSCS) in 1994. The formation of the MPSCS can be seen as an evolution in crime prevention organizing in the neighbourhood from single-issue, informal groups to more formal organizations mandated to address crime, community safety, and neighbourhood development in the broadest of terms. The immediate precursors of the MPSCS, such as Shame the Johns and the Carolina Street Neighbourhood Group, were largely informal, non-hierarchical, and ad hoc in nature. They materialized on the scene quickly to address specific crime and disorder problems in their neighbourhoods (prostitution and problem houses, respectively), resisted formalization (such as incorporating as a society), and disbanded soon after the worse part of their problems subsided. In contrast, the MPSCS was a legally incorporated society with a board of directors, members, and charitable status. According to its charter, the mandate of the society was to (1) reduce crime in Mount Pleasant, (2) make Mount Pleasant a safer place and promote the reality of Mount Pleasant as a safer place, (3) assist in the coordination and integration of government, non-profit, and community services in Mount Pleasant, and (4) improve the liveability of Mount Pleasant. Almost from the outset, those behind the MPSCS sought to establish a community crime prevention office. Their efforts were rewarded in February 1995 with the opening of the Mount Pleasant Community CPO at the corner of Fraser and Broadway, a location considered the epicentre for drug trafficking in the neighbourhood. Spurred in part by the Oppal Commission on Policing in British Columbia (Oppal, 1994), which emphasized the need for more community-based policing and crime prevention, especially in poor areas, the office received start-up grants of $45,000 from the provincial government and $6,000 from the city government. It was the second community crime prevention office to open in Vancouver. By 2000, there were twenty-one CPOs in Vancouver that delivered local crime prevention and community policing services (Lee, 2000).

Promotional literature distributed by the Mount Pleasant CPO describe its main objectives as follows: (1) reduce criminal activity and increase the safety and security of residents through the dissemination of crime prevention information and coordinating crime prevention activities, (2) create a bridge between the community and the police, and (3) build community by developing greater social interaction and cohesion, sponsoring beautification projects, reducing crime, encouraging community-based problem solving, and providing a visible presence for residents concerned with crime. The same promotional literature states that the Mount Pleasant CPO "emphasizes a partnership between the community and the police in developing ongoing, long-term solutions to community problems. Community members must be empowered to solve their problems, with critical support from the police and the CPO." According to information included in an application for provincial government funding, the programs and services offered by the Mount Pleasant CPO were described as follows:

Problem-Solving of General Crime and Disorder Issues and Concerns
- Community liaison through storefront access and counter service
- Police liaison on ongoing crime and disorder problems (e.g., prostitution task forces and drug suppression unit)

Opportunity Reduction Measures for Crimes against Property and Persons
- Crime Free Multi-Housing Program to deal with apartment security and landlord/tenant relations
- Neighbourhood Watch training and information distribution
- Distribution of crime prevention literature on property and personal safety precautions, access to property engraving equipment, crime statistics, as well as various community events throughout the year

Public Education and Social Development-Oriented Crime Prevention
- Community forums on prostitution, violent crime, and general safety issues
- Ethnic outreach
- Seminars for businesses
- Child safety programming
- Self defence seminars

Beautification Initiatives
- "Banners on Broadway" annual public art project sponsor
- Graffiti paint-out
- Anti-graffiti mural projects
- Garbage clean-up

Despite the use of terms such as "problem solving" and "social development-oriented crime prevention" in their literature, the crime prevention programs and strategies implemented by the Mount Pleasant CPO were predominately situational in nature. In fact, little emphasis was placed on social development strategies by the Mount Pleasant CCP groups studied as part of this research.[4]

Despite the initial enthusiasm that surrounded the opening of the CPO, from almost the beginning of its existence it teetered on the brink of extinction. By 2003, both the MPSCS and the CPO were no more. During those eight years of operation, the intertwined lives of the two organizations would be highly precarious and often tumultuous, marred by ongoing fiscal crises, the successive resignation or firing of six CPO coordinators, a civil suit against the MPSCS by one fired coordinator, acrimonious resignations of directors, accusations that funds were misspent and even misappropriated, the withdrawal of Vancouver police cooperation and city funding, the eviction of the CPO from its free office space, and the revocation of the legal society status of the MPSCS by the provincial government. The fate of the crime prevention office appeared to be foreshadowed long before its death, as it staggered along on unstable financial grounds and negligible community support. Barely six months after opening its doors, the CPO began to run out of money. As a result, the coordinator was forced to reduce her hours by half and had to spend much of her time fund-raising (Bula, 1995). Around the same time, the Mount Pleasant CPO joined with other crime prevention offices to lobby the provincial government for a $65,000 stipend for each office to pay for overhead and coordinators' salaries. Although the appeals for cash were initially rejected, the provincial Attorney-General eventually acquiesced by proposing a one-time cash injection of up to $20,000 per office, contingent upon these funds being matched by the City of Vancouver. On 16 October 1996 Vancouver City Council, with support from the Vancouver Police Department, approved a joint Community Safety Funding Program with an annual grant budget of $150,000 to be spread out over three years (1997 to 1999).

Despite the cash injection, the Mount Pleasant CPO continued to lack stability, which was epitomized by the hiring and resignation or firing of four different coordinators in the span of two years. In February 1996, the original coordinator resigned and was replaced by two part-time coordinators (including myself). In September of that year, I was fired by the board of directors. (The initial rationale for my firing was that I had failed to clean graffiti quickly enough off the front window of the office. However, a board member later confided that the real reason behind the firing was that, without informing the board, I had communicated with senior Vancouver Police Department officials, which included an angry – and in retrospect, imprudent – letter to the senior officers in which I accused them of lackadaisical handling of a report filed by a local Vietnamese resident who had been stabbed.) My part-time colleague then took over the coordinator's position on a full-time basis. However, in the spring of 1998, she was also fired by the board. The reason given for this dismissal, according to her, was that she was "not taking the CPO in the right direction." In the summer of 1998, she launched a civil suit against the Safer Community Society for wrongful dismissal (with the society being represented by City of Vancouver legal counsel). The next few years were no less turbulent for the Mount Pleasant CPO and its governing body. Between 1998 and 2002, three more coordinators were hired and then were either fired or quit. The original board of directors of the MPSCS resigned en masse and a new board was appointed, with one of the recently fired coordinators being selected as the society's chairperson. During the same period, the CPO moved offices twice, ultimately ending up in donated space located in the Kingsgate Mall.

In 2000, the Mount Pleasant Community CPO, along with most other CPOs, negotiated a more formal partnership with the Vancouver Police Department and was renamed the Mount Pleasant Community Policing Centre (although for the sake of continuity, this book will continue to refer to it as the crime prevention office). On 7 March 2002, the Vancouver City Council renewed the Community Safety Funding Program, which included grants for the crime prevention offices/community policing centres. One of these grants, for $21,000, was provided to the Mount Pleasant office, on the condition that the funds be used for the implementation of Neighbourhood Watch, foot and bike patrols, education and awareness, and child identification programs; that the office must be open at least twenty hours a week with volunteer support; and that a written report regarding volunteer activities was to be submitted by 15 June 2002 (Lee, 2002). In March of 2002, a new coordinator was hired, but by the end of May she was also fired by the board on the grounds that the crime prevention programs required by the City grant were not being implemented. Three days after the firing, however, City of Vancouver legal counsel, in a letter addressed to each MPSCS board member, stated that they considered the firing a wrongful dismissal and advised them that the city would not indemnify the society in the event of another civil suit. In the same month, the Vancouver Police Department Liaison to the Mount Pleasant CPO physically moved out of the office, citing these ongoing problems as well as security concerns (including accusations that letters addressed to the constable were opened by board members). On 24 June 2002, the annual general meeting of the MPSCS was held (on one week's notice), and in a sparsely attended gathering the recently appointed chairperson was re-elected. In an interview for this study, the Vancouver police liaison to the Mount Pleasant CPO character-ized the election as a "crock," due to the short notice provided to members and the chairperson's efforts to "stack" the meeting with friends and supporters.

On 11 September 2002, an administrative report was submitted to the Standing Committee on City Services and Budgets from the direc-tor of social planning and the chief of the Vancouver Police Depart-ment recommending that the City of Vancouver rescind half of the $21,000 grant provided just five months earlier to the Safer Commu-nity Society. The rationale, according to the report, was that it "has not implemented crime prevention programs with sufficient volunteer support and, therefore, has not met the conditions of the grant. They did not provide a written report as per the condition and, furthermore, they were not able to provide a mid-term report, which was required from all CPC's [sic] in the City" (Lee, 2002: 1). The report to the Stand-ing Committee further recommended that the rescinded funds be diverted as a grant to the Vancouver Crime Prevention Society for vol-unteer training activities to be implemented in Mount Pleasant. In a media interview, Mario Lee, a City of Vancouver social planner who wrote the aforementioned report, stated, "They simply don't have enough volunteers," noting that only three volunteers were working at the office when he met with society representatives in the summer of 2002 (Howell, 2002a). Equally devastating for the CPO was the with-drawal of the support and participation of the Vancouver Police Department. According to Inspector Max Chalmers, who at the time was in charge of policing for the Mount Pleasant area, "There wasn't sufficient program delivery that would lead us to believe that our con-tinued association with that non-profit society would bear fruit in the long run" (Howell, 2002a). In a 2 December 2002 media article, Inspec-tor Chalmers was quoted as saying the volunteer base for the Mount Pleasant CPO was almost non-existent (Howell, 2002b). In the same article, the MPSCS chairperson acknowledged that the office, which was now being run by the society's board of directors following the May 2002 firing of the coordinator, had only been open fifteen days in October and November because of the lack of volunteers and the with-drawal of police support. The board's chairperson attributed the prob-lems and impending closure of the CPO to "infighting among the board, police and former volunteers," whose conflicting agendas prevented programs from being implemented. "It makes me feel like the police don't care because if they cared, they would have tried to solve the problem instead of just backing out," the chairperson was quoted as saying (Howell, 2002b). On 12 December 2002, the provincial government officially revoked the registered society status of the MPSCS citing its failure to file annual reports. Finally, on 31 December 2002 the Mount Pleasant CPO was forced by the management of the Kingsgate Mall to vacate its office, effectively ending its existence.

Despite the ongoing problems and eventual demise of the Safer Community Society and the community CPO, local resident groups continued to address crime and prostitution issues in Mount Pleasant. In the summer of 2000, homeowners living around Kingsway between Fraser and Knight Streets began to organize around prostitution and drug problems in that area. With the help of Charles Dickens Elementary School and a local office of the Insurance Corporation of British Columbia, hundreds of flyers were printed in five languages and delivered to area homes advertising a meeting of residents in October of that year. According to one media report, approximately 200 people turned out to the meeting. One of the decisions made by attendees was to hold a rally in the 800-block of Kingsway, a favoured location for prostitution and drug trafficking (Zacharias, 2000). This initiative eventually led to the founding of the Dickens Community Group, which, according to a pamphlet distributed by the group, is made up of a "diverse band of dedicated resident volunteers who work together to make their neighbourhood a better place to live, work and raise their families" and was "initially organized to find workable solutions to a plague of neighbourhood problems stemming from the street level sex and drug trade." Some of the activities undertaken by the Dickens group, according to the pamphlet, include the development of community patrols, street improvement projects, public gardens, garbage clean up, graffiti removal, school anti-vandalism, and "community social events fostering cultural and ethnic cooperation and collaboration." The group also collects information on local prostitution and drug problems, which is then passed along to City Hall and police. In addition, the Dickens group resurrected the confrontational tactics originated by the Shame the Johns campaign, as acknowledged in a 31 July 2002 memo to a senior Vancouver police official by the Vancouver police liaison to Mount Pleasant: "Prostitutes have been in this area for some time and will probably remain ... I have become aware of several incidents where the patrollers are verbally confronting the prostitutes, their customers and some of the other denizens of the area." In January 2002, the Mount Pleasant Business Improvement Association launched the Business Neighbourhood Watch program, with the goal of "improving communication and cooperation between local business owners, the Mount Pleasant Business Improvement Association and the Vancouver Police Department to increase crime prevention awareness and decrease criminal opportunities within Uptown" (*Pleasant Times*, 2003a: 1). Central to this program are Neighbourhood Watch captains – volunteers from local businesses who are responsible for a specific block or area and who are designated as the recipients of criminal or suspicious reports from other businesses in that particular block. In April 2002, members of the Carolina Street Neighbourhood Group were successful in pressuring city authorities to shut down two rental houses on the street that, according to one media source, were "notorious for their eyesore appearances, piles of garbage in the front and back yards, prostitution, drug-dealing and for noisy, wild parties held by a revolving door of tenants" (Pemberton and Ward, 2003). In addition to these neighbourhood-based organizations, a number of government funded child- and youth-centred programs continued to operate in the Mount Pleasant area, including Kids Safe, Parents Together, Kimount Boys and Girls Club, Kivan Boys and Girls Club, Mount Pleasant Family Centre, the Specialized Youth Response Program, and the Grandview Elementary Project.

Summary: Crime Prevention Organizing in Mount Pleasant

Notwithstanding the trials, tribulations, and eventual demise of the CPO and its governing body, Mount Pleasant appears to be fertile ground for organizing residents around crime and disorder problems. In addition to the examples already detailed, this research identified other groups and activities that met with success in mobilizing local residents, including those from demographic groups that typically do not become involved in CCP. These successes (which are examined in more detail in chapter 4) include an aggressive recruitment drive by the CPO that attracted approximately twenty-five new volunteers, many of whom were first-generation immigrants, a child identification program that attracted many immigrant families that spoke little English, and the Vancouver Police Department–initiated Crime Free

Multi-Housing Program that generated a substantial rate of residential participation in two apartment buildings. Accolades for successful community organizing in Mount Pleasant have also come from other sources. In a 31 July 2002 memo, the Vancouver police liaison to Mount Pleasant observed, "The community spirit in this neighbourhood is strong, and the recent efforts here have provided motivation to all the residents in becoming interested in beautifying their area." In their 1994 evaluation of the implementation of the Mount Pleasant community development plan, graduate students in the School of Community and Regional Planning at the University of British Columbia were also impressed by the organization and commitment of local residents:

> From our repeated interactions with the community, it became evident that one of its greatest assets was its commitment to the neighbourhood, and its ability to mobilize residents toward positive action and generate community pride. Some of its recent accomplishments include collaborations between arts and business groups; the creation of a new community crime prevention office; a new neighbourhood house; a community garden; and several street beautification projects. As well, the community was instrumental in stopping a proposed beer and wine store and yet another unsuitably-located special needs residential facility. Moreover, the highly publicized Shame the Johns campaign has ameliorated some of the neighbourhood problems associated with prostitution. (University of British Columbia, 1994: 2)

The authors of this report prod the community to "continue its prolific work as a catalyst and organizer of positive change" (University of British Columbia, 1994: 2).

In contrast to these buoyant observations, the ills of Mount Pleasant have been partially attributed to a *lack* of community action. A 1962 study of the neighbourhood stated that the "Mount Pleasant Community Association has a small membership and almost all present members are elderly. A women's group and the girls' club of this association has dwindled away. The Community Association canvassed the entire Mount Pleasant area in a membership drive and encountered a depressing lack of interest in community activity" (Hicks, 1962: 68). In her history of Mount Pleasant, Smith (1976) writes that years of procrastination by Vancouver City Hall in addressing the problems of Mount Pleasant have resulted in a community "which is itself increasingly apathetic and reluctant to become involved in community efforts." A 1985 report to city council's Community Services Committee also contended that a low level of community participation in public affairs presents a problem in the area (as cited in the *Vancouver Sun*, 1985). A 1989 report by the Mount Pleasant Citizens Planning Committee (1989: 25) concludes that "the Mount Pleasant community has lacked organization and those community groups who did exist were not recognized as contact points for community response." A 1997 interview with a Mount Pleasant resident who also was active in the local Healthy Communities movement said that public apathy among residents was viewed as so endemic in Mount Pleasant that the city-wide Healthy Communities Committee identified it as one of four key issues that negatively affected the health of residents.

These apparently contradictory conclusions regarding the prerequisites for and scope of collective action in Mount Pleasant parallel the findings of this study, which may appear incongruous on the surface, but which can be explained as follows: while there have been numerous instances where residents have successfully mobilized around crime problems, in general, participation has largely been confined to a small, demographically homogeneous group of residents. Conspicuously absent from most CCP groups and activities are those people who make up the majority of the Mount Pleasant population: immigrants, members of visible minority groups, the undereducated, non-professionals, the poor, and renters. The remainder of this chapter empirically documents the research findings underlying this conclusion by examining and estimating the scope and breadth of local participation in collective crime prevention groups and activities in Mount Pleasant.

Gauging Awareness of and Support for CCP Programs in Mount Pleasant

Before attempts are made to estimate the scope of participation in Mount Pleasant CCP programs, it is logical to first establish whether the following assumptions ring true for this neighbourhood: (1) there is a widespread concern over crime and disorder; (2) most residents support the CCP principles and activities carried out by local groups; and (3) most residents are aware of local CCP initiatives. Empirically establishing the existence of these collective action preconditions is imperative for this study because an absence of concern over crime or a lack of awareness of existing crime prevention programs will illuminate the reasons why participation in local crime prevention activities is limited. In other words, if people have little concern over crime, are unaware of local crime prevention programs, or do not support these programs, there is little need to delve any further into why participation is limited.

The conclusion of this study is that the first assumption rings true for Mount Pleasant, while the latter two assumptions are more tenuous and can only be extended to a small proportion of the population. Research carried out for this study reveals widespread concern over crime and disorder among residents. As part of interviews and focus groups with a broad cross-section of Mount Pleasant residents, when asked to rate the most pressing problems facing the neighbourhood, crime was consistently ranked as one of the most significant problems and this concern transcended the demographic characteristics of residents. Expressions of fear over possible victimization was also prevalent, although the level of fear varied widely, mostly along demographic lines (single mothers, seniors, and members of visible minority groups were most fearful of victimization while white, middle-aged professionals and young adult men and women indicated a relatively lower fear of victimization). A high level of concern over crime has also been documented in at least two other studies conducted in Mount Pleasant (Mount Pleasant Citizens' Planning Committee, 1989; Youth Service Canada, 1996). Many residents interviewed for this study also expressed support for the philosophy of community crime prevention, and support the activities carried out by local groups, the CPO, and the police. However, there is a notable variance among residents in their support for the opportunity reduction approaches that dominated the crime prevention agenda in the neighbourhood. Once again, this division appears to be along demographic lines, and socio-economic status, in particular. Those with a lower socio-economic status consistently argued that emphasis should be placed on social problem solving and development–based approaches, such as the creation of local jobs and greater job training opportunities for young adults. Many falling within this group either dismissed the dominant opportunity reduction approaches as ineffectual, expressed concern that this emphasis did not address their needs or concerns, and/or indicated that they felt they were being targeted as possible offenders by the people who carried out these programs. (Upon further prodding, many of those who criticized the opportunity reduction programs confessed that they were unacquainted with the actual programs in operation in Mount Pleasant, and were directing their comments generally towards well known situational programs like Neighbourhood Watch). Higher socio-economic status residents also felt that more emphasis should be placed on community and social developmental approaches, as well as community beautification projects, but were nonetheless supportive of the opportunity reduction approach that had been overwhelmingly pursued by local groups. This difference of opinion and varying support based on socio-economic status reflects and foreshadows major findings of this study regarding the obstacles to a broad-based participation of Mount Pleasant residents in collective crime prevention programs.

The other assumption that cannot be extended to Mount Pleasant is a widespread awareness of CCP groups and activities by local residents. The research discovered that the local concern over crime and the shared support for crime prevention groups and activities among Mount Pleasant residents is not accompanied by a widespread awareness of existing crime prevention groups and activities. Interviews and focus groups with local residents revealed a substantial lack of knowledge of existing crime prevention groups and activities in the neighbourhood. Many who were surveyed during the original research period did not know that the Mount Pleasant CPO existed, despite its high-profile location. Many residents were oblivious to the presence of Neighbourhood Watch programs in Mount Pleasant, including some who lived on streets where a NW program had been implemented. As intimated above, a lack of awareness of existing crime prevention programs was most prevalent among those with a low socio-economic status, new immigrants, and members of visible minority groups. This lack of awareness can be partially blamed on the ineffective outreach and communication strategies of the local crime prevention organizations, which is explored in greater detail in chapter 4.

Participation in Community Crime Prevention Programs

Evidence accumulated through this study indicates that, despite a widespread concern over crime and a strong history of local anti-crime activism, the level of participation in collective crime prevention programs in the neighbourhood is generally low and limited to a small, homogeneous group of residents. (This low level of participation can be partially explained by the lack of broad-based support for the opportunity reduction approaches carried out by most CCP groups, as well as a lack of widespread awareness of local groups and activities. However, as detailed in chapters 3 through 6, the reasons accounting for a low level of participation are much more diverse and complex.) During a 1996 interview, the original coordinator of the Mount Pleasant CPO acknowledged that "very, very few" people in the neighbourhood become involved in local crime prevention programs. Community activists, police officials, and Neighbourhood Watch (NW) captains interviewed for this research also attested to the low level of participation in local crime prevention groups and activities. While there were approximately seventy members of the MPSCS when the original research was conducted, only ten were active. An annual general meeting of the society held in June 1996 attracted only twelve people, even though it was intensively promoted for a month, including the distribution of 4,000 flyers throughout Mount Pleasant East (seventy people did attend a community-wide meeting on local crime problems that was held in the same venue immediately following the annual general meeting). Even those who had assumed a leadership position with the society were not particularly active; board meetings of the Safer Community Society attended by this researcher during the initial research period often had trouble making quorum. The NW program also suffers from a low level of participation in Mount Pleasant. As of July 1997, twenty-three blocks in Mount Pleasant had organized a NW program (there are approximately 250 blocks in Mount Pleasant). By 2004, the NW coordinator for the Vancouver Police Department estimated that thirty blocks or apartment buildings in Mount Pleasant were officially registered with the NW program, although the coordinator admitted that many were "inactive." During a focus group conducted in 1996, NW captains were asked to describe the level of participation on their respective blocks. One captain immediately shouted "very low" and there was general agreement among others present that participation on their block was also low. In a follow-up telephone survey of these captains, the estimated average proportion of homes participating in NW for each block or apartment building hovered around 20 per cent, with a high of 75 per cent of households participating, to a low of zero (not even the captain was involved anymore). The generally low turnout for NW meetings was corroborated through this research: of the fourteen NW meetings attended during the initial and subsequent research periods, the proportion of members that attended was between 20 to 25 per cent (ranging from a low of 10 per cent to a high of 80 per cent).

Participation in crime prevention programs by Mount Pleasant businesses is also low, despite a high level of concern over crime expressed by business owners. A 1996 survey of ninety Mount Pleasant retail businesses, conducted independently of this research, showed that crime was of concern to local business owners: 47 per cent of respondents from local businesses stated that they perceived crime to be on the increase in the area where their businesses were located, compared with 11 per cent who stated it was decreasing, and 15 per cent who believed it had stayed the same. In addition, 69 per cent reported that they had been victims of a crime in the last year; 41 per cent stated that they were aware of existing crime prevention programs in the neighbourhood. The expressed concern over crime and a high rate of victimization does not seem to have spurred significant involvement in local crime prevention programs: only 15 per cent stated that they participated in any collective prevention programs offered in the neighbourhood (Youth Service Canada, 1996). This lack of participation was exemplified by a robbery prevention seminar organized for Mount Pleasant retail businesses by the CPO in 1996. Despite widespread promotion, including the distribution of flyers, telephone calls, and the confirmation to attend from at least thirty businesses, not one person attended the seminar. By April of 2003, more than a year after the Business Neighbourhood Watch was launched by the Mount Pleasant Business Improvement Association (BIA), only twenty-seven of the approximately 400 local businesses had signed up to participate (*Pleasant Times*, 2003b). In an interview with the director of the Mount Pleasant BIA conducted that same year, she conceded that in attempts to mobilize local businesses around crime, her organization "is no more successful that the crime prevention office ... We have great problems getting people out to meetings and AGMs ... This is frustrating given that the BIA does a lot of outreach. We conduct numerous needs assessments of local businesses to cater to their interests."

A community beautification project undertaken by the Mount Pleasant Community CPO serves as a microcosm of how widespread concern over local problems and support for community projects does not necessarily translate into a broad-based mobilization of residents. The CPO organized a mural painting project on an abandoned building on East Broadway, one of the major thoroughfares cutting through Mount Pleasant and Vancouver as a whole. The building had long been an eyesore in the neighbourhood, having been unoccupied for almost ten years. It had not been maintained in any way: windows on the second floor were broken, grass and weeds overgrew its facade, and graffiti adorned the brick exterior. For more than two years, people walking past the derelict building were confronted with the sardonic graffiti greeting "Welcome to Welfare Land," which was crudely spray-painted over the plywood that covered the large, ground-floor windows. The painting of the mural, designed as a patchwork quilt with a banner reading "Celebrate Mount Pleasant," was a highly visible project. The allure of this site (for both the banner painting and the research into local participation) was based upon its prominent location on a busy pedestrian and traffic artery. Throughout the day people walked and drove by the mural as it was being painted. Unsolicited and often enthusiastic support for the mural was provided by those who went by. However, when most passers-by were asked if they wanted to paint a small patch on the quilt, the great majority declined to become involved, despite their stated support of the project. As the afternoon progressed, and the original painters tired, a greater effort was made to involve pedestrians walking by the mural. Eventually, more people did become involved, yet they generally represented the narrow demographic profile of people who typically become involved in local collective action.

Perhaps the worst indictment of the lack of community support for, and participation in, collective crime prevention programs in Mount Pleasant, was the eventual demise of the CPO and the implosion of the Safer Community Society. Despite its ongoing funding shortages and the real threat that the CPO would have to close its doors permanently, facts which were widely publicized by the CPO, its board of directors, and the media (Bula, *Vancouver Sun*, 2 Nov. 1995; *Vancouver Courier*, 7 Feb. 1996; *Vancouver Echo*, 7 Feb. 1996; *Voice*, 7 Feb. 1996; *Vancouver Sun*, 14 March 1996; Howell, 2002a, b), there was little groundswell of support among local residents, let alone a Capraesque financial rescue by community members. During the initial funding crisis of 1995 and 1996, only a minimal effort was made by the board to raise funds (a letter was sent out to neighbourhood residents and businesses). Eventually, it was neither the community nor the board of directors who rescued the CPO from the brink in 1996, but the provincial and municipal governments, which injected $20,000 into the CPO's budget. The Mount Pleasant CPO was eventually forced to cease operations when the city government and police withdrew their funding and support, in part because of the inability of the CPO to attract volunteers. This was intimated in a report to Vancouver City Council recommending that the grant to the Mount Pleasant office be rescinded:

The Community Policing program is a strong communications vehicle between Vancouver Police Department (VPD) and local residents engaged in conducting crime prevention activities. The Community Policing program enjoys the participation of approximately 800 volunteers city-wide. Unfortunately, there are some areas in the city where volunteer participation still needs further encouragement. The Mount Pleasant area could benefit from the availability of more volunteer training programs. Initial conversations with some Mount Pleasant-based community organizations indicate that there is a tremendous amount of interest in seeing the implementation of crime prevention activities in that neighbourhood. The VPD will continue to work with these community organizations and interested citizens in search of a permanent home for anchoring future crime prevention programs. Having volunteers who are appropriately trained is an important first step. (Lee, 2002: 3)

In sum, collective crime prevention groups and activities in Mount Pleasant suffered from a lack of local participation, and, of those who were active, the majority were drawn from a narrow demographic residential base that was not representative of the neighbourhood's population. Of the approximately 24,000 people living in Mount Pleasant, a liberal estimate of those voluntarily involved in an active leadership position in a crime prevention group or activity *at any one time* was between eight and twelve people. (With one or two exceptions, there was a wholesale change between the two research periods in terms of residents who were active leaders.) This small cadre of residents was instrumental in initiating, directing, and sustaining specific crime prevention groups and activities, and, on average, dedicated at least ten hours a month to these responsibilities. During the original research period, those who did not assume a leadership position, but who regularly volunteered at the CPO, was approximately thirty to thirty-five people. By 2002, this number had dropped below ten. Those residents who are sporadically active, such as Neighbourhood Watch captains, those who are intermittent volunteers for the CPO or other crime prevention activities, and those who are members of other local crime prevention groups, number between fifty and eighty people at any one time. "Passive" participants, which include members of a Neighbourhood Watch program or inactive members of other crime prevention groups or activities, total between 300 and 350 people. Finally, there are between 300 and 400 people who may use a specific crime prevention service on a limited basis, such as registering a child as part of Operation

Figure 2.7 A typology of CPP participants and non-participants

Active Leaders	5 to 10 people
Active, regular participants	30 to 35 people
Active, occasional participants	50 to 80 people
Non-active members	300 to 350 people
CP service consumers	300 to 400 people
Non-participants	21,000 people

Identification or making a complaint at the crime prevention office. In short, of the 24,000 people living in Mount Pleasant, a liberal estimate of those at least remotely involved in collective crime prevention activities *at any one time* is between 685 and 875 people (less than 2 per cent). Figure 2.7 provides a typology of the various levels of participation by Mount Pleasant residents in CCP groups and activities.

Conclusion

Mount Pleasant is an inner-city neighbourhood with a diverse mix of people and cultures contributing to its unique character. While it contains a small community of middle-class homeowners, Mount Pleasant East has long been one of Vancouver's poorest and most transient neighbourhoods. It also has one of the highest crime rates in the city, and has long been marred by the inauspicious reputation as "Hooker Central." In this regard, Mount Pleasant East constitutes an example of a disadvantaged neighbourhood that sociologists, beginning with the influential Chicago School of Sociology in the 1930s and 1940s, characterize as "socially disorganized"; that is, an inner-city neighbourhood marked by poverty, inadequate housing, physical deterioration, a large percentage of immigrants, demographic heterogeneity, and a high rate of population turnover. Mount Pleasant East is also typical of neighbourhoods that past studies have identified as infertile grounds for broad-based collective action. Indeed, this study suggests that, like many other disadvantaged neighbourhoods, it has been unable to initiate and sustain a broad-based mobilization of the local population to address crime and disorder problems. At the same time, there is also evidence that Mount Pleasant East residents have launched a number of crime prevention groups and activities that have been successful in attracting support and participation. One attempt to reconcile this apparent contradiction is to acknowledge the rich history and contemporary examples of collective action in the community, but to temper this with the observation that much of the local activism has been undertaken by a small group of dedicated residents. Absent from most of the groups and activities are those Mount Pleasant residents that make up the majority of the population. The following three chapters explore in more detail these observations, with a particular focus on the personal, community, organizational, and structural factors that contribute to the differential participation of Mount Pleasant residents in CCP programs.

PART TWO

Obstacles to Participation in Community
Crime Prevention Programs:
Research Findings, Discussion,
and Analysis

3 Obstacles to Participation and Collective Action at the Individual and Neighbourhood Level

Introduction

Any attempt to identify the factors that impede participation in local collective action must begin by analysing the community and its residents. The objective of this chapter is to identify and explore the impediments to a broad-based mobilization of Mount Pleasant residents around crime, impediments that may stem from their characteristics, attitudes, beliefs, and behaviour at the individual and collective levels. Particular attention is paid to examining and comparing the demographic and socio-psychological characteristics of those who participate and those who do not participate in collective crime prevention groups and activities. These individual characteristics are then extrapolated to the local population as a whole to identify barriers to collective action at the neighbourhood level. The impediments to participation examined in this chapter are not exhaustive; this research has documented an array of factors that can impede an individual's participation in collective crime prevention activities, including a lack of time, more pressing priorities, fear of retribution from offenders, little confidence in crime prevention programs, and apathy, among others. This study does not mean to discount the importance of these factors as contributors to non-participation. Instead, this chapter focuses on those demographic and socio-psychological factors that, according to this study, appear to most strongly correlate with non-participation in community crime prevention (CCP) groups and activities in disadvantaged neighbourhoods. At the level of the individual resident, these factors are low socio-economic status, membership in a first-generation and/or ethnic minority group, and a lack of attachment to the neighbourhood. The most significant obstacles to a broad-based mobilization at the neighbourhood level are low socio-economic status, demographic heterogeneity, a lack of social cohesion, and a high population turnover. Admittedly, if quantitative data were available to measure the correlation between such independent variables as socio-economic status or community attachment, on the one hand, and participation or non-participation in CCP programs, on the other, a statistically significant relationship would probably not emerge; while most CCP participants have a high socio-economic status (relative to the overall population of Mount Pleasant) and express a strong attachment to their community, these same traits are shared by a large number of residents who do not participate in collective crime prevention activities. Instead of trying to draw a correlation between plausible predictor variables of participation or non-participation, this chapter focuses on explaining why and how certain socio-economic and socio-psychological factors serve to promote or obstruct participation in CCP.

Socio-economic Status

Those who are involved in local crime prevention groups and activities are of a generally higher socio-economic status when compared to the Mount Pleasant East population as a whole. To begin with, those who have assumed a leadership position or are most active in local crime prevention groups are generally white-collar professionals. For example, the five (non-police) members of the Safer Community Society's board of directors during the original research period included a lawyer, a credit union manager, a real estate agent, an occupational rehabilitation manager, and a self-employed businessman operating a small janitorial service. These common socio-economic traits became evident in interviews with the leadership of other local groups (and not just those concerned with crime issues). Shame the Johns, the Dickens Group, the Mount Pleasant Action Group, and the Mount Pleasant Neighbourhood Association were all largely founded and led by individuals who can be classified as white-collar professionals. With that said, there is a greater diversity in the socio-economic status and occupations of those who volunteer at the crime prevention office. In general, volunteers at the crime prevention office (CPO) can be classified into four employment categories: (1) professionals (who are in the minority), (2) non-professionals, (3) students, and (4) those who are supported by a supplemental income, such as seniors on a pension or women dependent upon their husbands" income. CCP participants are also better educated than the Mount Pleasant East population as a whole. The initial CPO coordinator estimated that approximately two-thirds of the volunteers between seventeen and thirty-five years of age are either currently college or university students or have some post-secondary education. Of the five aforementioned directors of the Safer Community Society, three have university degrees. Interviews with the volunteer leaders of other local crime prevention groups also indicated that the majority had at least some post-secondary education. The only exception was Neighbourhood Watch (NW) captains; a survey of captains undertaken in 1996 indicated that only 29 per cent had a post-secondary education.

Homeowners are also much more active in CCP groups compared with renters, although among CPO volunteers there is a greater mix of homeowners and renters, as well as younger volunteers who live with their parents. NW programs in Mount Pleasant predominate on streets where there is a large homeowning population: of the twenty-three NW groups that operated in Mount Pleasant during the original period of research, fourteen (61 per cent) were located on streets where single-family dwellings predominated. The remaining nine NW groups were all located in apartment buildings where the majority of dwellings were owner-occupied. In fact, of the thirty-four NW Block Captains in Mount Pleasant surveyed during the initial research period, thirty (88 per cent) indicated that they own their residence. In short, NW programs predominate on blocks or in apartment buildings that are predominately owner-occupied, homeowners make up a substantial proportion of NW members, and the percentage of those in a leadership position (i.e., block captains) who own their dwelling is even higher. In either research period, this study did not find any rental apartment building in Mount Pleasant East participating in the NW program. During the initial research period, two Mount Pleasant apartment buildings had joined the pilot of the Vancouver Police Department–sponsored Crime Free Multi-Housing Program, which involves a NW component. However, for both buildings, the program was initiated and coordinated by two members of the Vancouver Police Department, who devoted considerable time and energy to its implementation. While participation in the program among tenants was high, once the two officers were reassigned, the program was not sustained for much longer in either building.[1] By the time the follow-up research was conducted in 2003, there were no crime prevention programs of any kind operating in the two buildings.

Block captains from Mount Pleasant East who took part in a focus group during the original research period were asked if they saw any difference in the participation rates between owners and renters on their street or in their multi-residential building. All agreed that there was a difference, and, in general, renters tended not to participate. A block captain living in a mixed occupancy building in the northeast corner of Mount Pleasant indicated "pretty good" participation by those who own their apartments, while noting that renters "keep pretty much to themselves and don't get involved." According to a block captain who lived on a street with both owner-occupied and rental houses, "We would probably have greater luck if there wasn't so many damn homes on the block that have been subdivided. We have all these renters who don't get involved because they don't give a damn." One block captain disputed this argument, saying that some renters living in his mixed-occupancy apartment building did become involved when he approached them. "All it takes is a little persistency and the right message," he said. A comparison of participation rates in Mount Pleasant with more affluent communities in Vancouver also provides evidence of the relationship between socio-economic status and home ownership, on the one hand, and participation in CCP activities, on the other. According to the Vancouver Police Department's Neighbourhood Watch coordinator, who was interviewed in 1996, "In communities such as Kitsilano or Kerrisdale," which have a higher level of average personal income and homeownership, "there are definitely more Neighbourhood Watch programs ... I would say that participation is probably higher there as well." The effect that tenure of residence and low socio-economic status play in determining where a NW group is initiated by residents was not lost on one fledgling block captain who attempted to organize his Mount Pleasant apartment building:

> The response was OK I guess. But with the effort I put in. I went and knocked on every door of the building but one of the problems was that it was "Welfare Wednesday," and the last thing people had on their mind was crime prevention. But to answer your question, when I lived in a basement suite on 19th around Clark, which is nice, all houses, I think I was the only renter, and someone organized a Neighbourhood Watch. I mean everybody on the block was there. And everybody was in suits, except me. But when I moved here I said, "This is what I will do here."

But hell, you sure can tell the difference ... I talk to people here and they are supportive, but to get them to come out and do something is like pulling teeth.[2]

(The NW program was never implemented in this building, due in part to the disqualification of the aspiring block captain by police because of his criminal record.)

Participation in NW and other collective crime prevention programs also appears to correlate with the amount of time one has lived in the neighbourhood (which also generally correlates with tenure of residence). Of the twenty-three block captains who participated in a focus group during the original research, sixteen (70 per cent) had lived in Mount Pleasant for five or more years. They also generally agreed most renters involved in the NW program on their block or in their building had lived in the neighbourhood for at least two years. Interviews conducted in 1996 with the leadership of the crime prevention groups most active around that time – the Safer Community Society, the Area Network, the Neighbourhood Association, and the Carolina Street Neighbourhood Group – indicated that the majority had been residents of Mount Pleasant for at least five years.

In short, participants in collective crime prevention programs in Mount Pleasant are disproportionately made up of those who have a higher socio-economic status than the average resident who lives on the east side. Lower-income renters, who make up the majority of the Mount Pleasant East population, are greatly under-represented as collective crime prevention program participants. There are a number of reasons accounting for the lack of participation by those on the lower rungs of the socio-economic ladder. First, according to the coordinator of the Mount Pleasant CPO, the poor are preoccupied with "just surviving." They do not have the time or resources to volunteer "when their priority is to put food on the family table." Poverty can also serve to isolate and marginalize community members, thereby limiting community involvement. This isolation also limits social interaction with higher socio-economic status residents who are active in CCP groups. The poor and middle class live largely separate lives in Mount Pleasant and this limits the opportunities for participation in local groups by the former because recruitment in local groups is often promoted and conducted through existing social networks. Poverty can also undermine an essential prerequisite for participation in local groups and activities: community attachment and a sense of belonging. Interviews and focus groups with low-income residents who did not participate in local CCP programs revealed a profound absence of any attachment, either emotional or financial, to the neighbourhood. Most said that the only reason they live in Mount Pleasant was the relatively low rent or the convenience of its centralized location. Most also indicated that their social networks existed outside of the neighbourhood and that they knew few of their immediate neighbours. In interviews and focus groups, poorer residents also expressed feelings of intimidation by the challenge of participating in CCP groups that are dominated by better-educated professionals.

One single mother on social assistance offered this explanation as to why she does not become more involved in a local initiative to protest crime and problem premises on her street: "It's scary. I don't know what to do. I lock my doors, but no, I didn't become involved in the fight with the Tait houses. I'll leave that for the people who know what they are doing. I never finished high school and you want me to go and work with people who have all these degrees. Forget it ... I know my place. That is why I am in Mount Pleasant."[3] Less educated residents also expressed apprehension about volunteering at the CPO because they felt they simply had no skills to offer. My observations of CPO volunteers reveal that when the poor and undereducated do become involved, some are overwhelmed by the challenges of the tasks asked of them. As a result, they often become frustrated and disillusioned, and abandon their volunteer work.

At the aggregate level, the low socio-economic status of Mount Pleasant translates into a lack of indigenous financial resources, which negatively affects community outreach and volunteer recruitment efforts. It was clear that a reliance on funding from Mount Pleasant residents and businesses would be wholly inadequate to sustain the CPO, and, as a result, the office had to rely almost exclusively on government funding (including a cut of the revenue from government-sanctioned casinos). As detailed in the previous chapter, the absence of a local funding base directly undermined program implementation and outreach by the CPO. The low socio-economic status of the neighbourhood also translates into a shortage of human resources. Compared with higher socio-economic status neighbourhoods, there is a scarcity of educated professionals in Mount Pleasant who have the skills or personal efficacy to assume leadership positions or who work in the legal, financial, or political/government sectors that are conducive to initiating and sustaining a community group. Without a critical

mass of localized expertise or connections, access to (external) economic resources and the levers of political power is greatly inhibited.
While CCP groups and the stability of Mount Pleasant have benefited
from a small group of educated professionals, many that assumed
leadership positions eventually burned out because they had to shoul-
der so much of the work.

The socio-economic heterogeneity of the Mount Pleasant population
may also pose an indirect obstacle to local collective action by undermining the social cohesion of the neighbourhood. A 1989 report by the
Mount Pleasant Citizens' Planning Committee noted that in addition
to the physical divisions created by the major arteries that run through
the neighbourhood, "Internal economic divisions also exist. Such divisions make it difficult for the community to organize and present a
unified voice to City Council and other governments ... Maintaining
the area as an integral unit is critical to the future of Mount Pleasant"
(Mount Pleasant Citizens' Planning Committee, 1989: 23). My research
also exposed palpable tensions and visible cleavages between the more
affluent homeowners and low-income renters. These divisions are
particularly perceptible when blame for local crime problems is ap-
portioned. Mount Pleasant East homeowners participating in focus
groups consistently cited poorer residents of the neighbourhood as the
source of a number of local problems, including crime. When asked
what he felt were the principal causes of crime in Mount Pleasant, one
homeowner on the east side identified "the kids who come from the
poor families around here." He went on to say, "I certainly feel sorry
for them. Many of them live miserable lives. They are poor and on
drugs, they have no future. But the fact is that it is not the homeowners
around here that are breaking into our homes. And that is the reality of
living in a poor neighbourhood like Mount Pleasant: you are going to
have crime because you have a lot of poor people." Another homeowner participating in the focus group was more blunt: "Sure, it is the
white trash that lives here. You see them all the time. I mean on this
street we have nothing but single-family homes, nice homes. But a
block away are a bunch of houses, which are rented out, which are
crack houses, and it is the people who live there that are the problem.
And it is their customers, because before they go there to buy the drugs
they come here to rip us off."

This socio-economic cleavage is also apparent in those apartment
buildings and multi-residential homes that lodge both owners and
renters. Repeatedly, apartment owners interviewed for this study dif-

ferentiated themselves from renters, whom they singled out as the source of crime problems within their building. In two focus groups held with residents who owned their apartments and participated in the Neighbourhood Watch program, many believed that recent break and enters were "inside jobs" committed by renters or accomplices who were provided access to the inside of the building by the renter-occupant. Focus groups and interviews with residents on the more affluent western half of Mount Pleasant also revealed perceptions that local crime problems were an outcome of their proximately to the poorer eastern half. The socio-economic disparity between the western and eastern halves also contributes to a lack of unity and social cohesion for Mount Pleasant as a whole. In the course of this research, it became apparent that residents on the west side of Main Street do not view themselves as part of the same community as those living on the east side. As the original coordinator of the Mount Pleasant CPO put it, "I think the west side of Mount Pleasant ... doesn't really want a crime prevention office because it implies there is a crime problem and they don't want to have one ... I think that, in general, people in Mount Pleasant West would rather not be known as Mount Pleasant. Certainly the realtors don't call it that." One NW captain, who lives west of Main Street, summarized the sentiments of his fellow NW members participating in a focus group when he discussed the differences between the eastern and western halves of Mount Pleasant and the resulting difficulty in forging a common, cohesive identity between the two: "There is nothing in common between the two sides. You just have to cross Main Street and you know you are on the other side of the tracks. That side of Main Street is completely different from this side of Main Street and so are their problems. To try to work with both sides simultaneously won't work because their crime problems are so different and so much worse."

The abundance of low-rent apartment buildings in Mount Pleasant East may also contribute to a lack of social cohesion by encouraging a high population turnover and undermining neighbourhood attachment and local stability. Oscar Newman (1972) argued that apartment buildings, especially tall ones, foster disassociation between dwellings and street activities and promote a sense of alienation from the surrounding neighbourhood and from other residents. This theory was echoed by a senior Vancouver Police Department official who grew up in Mount Pleasant: "I think that apartments do create a loss of community ... When we look at apartment dwellings, it creates more of an isolation type of atmosphere that people live in. And because they don't have a way to communicate with their neighbours they feel that it is them alone ... They don't have a sense of commitment, whereas if you have a block of single-family dwellings where people know each other and the kids play with each other and you can mix and mingle over the back yard fence the topics of problems in the community rise more and you get a better feeling that there are more people with you than just yourself."

Findings from this research suggest that low levels of social cohesion do not stem so much from the vertical height of the building, but the tenure held by occupants. In Mount Pleasant, there appears to be a greater sense of social interaction, integration, community attachment, and social cohesion within owner-occupied buildings compared with rental apartment buildings regardless of their size. This is reflected in the fact that all NW programs in Mount Pleasant have been organized on blocks or in multi-residential buildings with a high proportion of owner-occupied dwellings. One block captain who lives in an owner-occupied apartment building stated, "I think the strata council concept of condominium living builds a stronger sense of community because they are united in one front and that is the well-being of their property, because they have a vested interest in it. Apartment people don't." Local integration and community attachment was notably absent among renters interviewed for this research. These socio-psychological traits, however, are not exclusive to renters. A typical homeowning resident who was not involved in any collective crime prevention activity noted in an interview that she was aware of the NW program on her block but rebuffed any invitations to become a member. Principal among her reasons was the fact that she did not want to become "involved" in the neighbourhood. She stated that she wanted to live in privacy, which should be respected by her neighbours. Thus, while she had enough concern to phone the CPO and file a crime report, her lack of integration into the neighbourhood appears to have obstructed her willingness to become involved in a collective program like NW.

Crime prevention practitioners, community leaders, and police officials interviewed for this research agreed that the transient nature of Mount Pleasant East represents one of the most significant obstacles to social cohesion and successful community organizing. This outlook was echoed in a 1962 study of the neighbourhood that concluded: "The high degree of transience among owners and renters alike, the concomitant lack of social organization, and the notable absence of a sense of identification with the neighbourhood present considerable obstacles to citizen involvement in neighbourhood rehabilitation" (Hicks, 1962: 75). The barrier that constant population turnover presents to successful CCP organizing was articulated by one block captain as such: "My problem is that on one side of the street it is all houses. On the other side of the street, it is all apartment buildings and rooming houses. You talk to them and then a month later or two months later there is somebody new in there." And that, according to one police official, "is why this yuppie base in Mount Pleasant is most involved, because these are the only people who are permanent and who really care. The rest are there for a short time and then move on." When asked about the NW program on her street, another block captain remarked, "Well, we actually got to get it back together because we have had a big turnover in people, a lot of houses have sold lately. And my co-captain has left." The high turnover rate is compounded by the fact that those who take up residence in Mount Pleasant are largely made up of demographic groups who do not traditionally participate in collective anti-crime groups, such as those on social assistance, the working poor, and new immigrants. According to a senior Vancouver police official:

> Because Mount Pleasant is a cheap place to live, it becomes a hot spot for every wave of new immigrants. For example, Somalians [sic] will be coming in the thousands here shortly. And I am sure you don't have anyone representing the Somali population [at the CPO] ... I think these waves of immigrants screw a neighbourhood up big time. Because what happens is that Mount Pleasant had a lot of poor white people and a lot of Native Indians, originally. I am going back ten years. Then we had waves of Hispanic people come in. And once they become established and started finding jobs, they move out of there. So the neighbourhood disappears again. And then another group, the Vietnamese, came in, and now we are getting Somalians in there, and waves of Eastern European immigrants are coming in and they get established and move out. So things are always changing. And the problem with police, like any service provider, is that you never get caught up.

Race/Ethnicity

The vast majority of individuals who participate in CCP groups and activities in Mount Pleasant are second- or third-generation Canadians of European heritage. The racial and ethnic homogeneity is especially apparent among those who are most active and/or have assumed leadership positions within local crime prevention groups. The voluntary leadership of the Mount Pleasant Safer Community Society, the Mount Pleasant Neighbourhood Association, Shame the Johns, the Carolina Street Neighbourhood Group, the Mount Pleasant Action Group, Neighbourhood Watch, and the Dickens Community Group almost exclusively falls into this ethic and racial category. At a meeting of NW block captains held during the initial research period, there was only one visible minority person present among a total of twenty-three people. Meetings among NW participants ob-served as part of this research revealed a similar racial homogeneity. Block captains, including those who have several Asian families on their block, also reported that the majority of participants in their program are white, and lamented the difficulty they encountered in efforts to enlist the involvement of first-generation Asian families. There is somewhat greater ethnic and racial diversity among CPO volunteers, although the number of volunteers from visible minority groups was still disproportionately low compared to their local population size; of the approximately thirty-five people who regularly volunteered at the CPO during the original research period, at minimum thirty are of European heritage. One Mount Pleasant resident who had long been active in local crime prevention groups acknowledged that the membership in such groups is racially homogeneous: "In Shame the Johns, we really tried to get all sorts of people out. Not just white people. When I joined the Safer Community Society, it was the same people from Shame the Johns. And it is the same people who are in Block Watch. It is almost all white!" This is not to imply that people of colour have not become involved in CCP activities and groups in Mount Pleasant; however, the majority of these residents are second- or third-generation Canadians, fluent in English, and thoroughly acculturated. During her tenure at the Mount Pleasant CPO, the original coordinator observed, "There are no people who volunteer who are first-generation Chinese or Vietnamese. And I know this is not right because you only have to look at how many new Chinese and Vietnamese live in Mount Pleasant." This was echoed by a Vancouver police officer long involved in crime prevention in the area: "If you look at the volunteers again, you wouldn't find too many First Nations people, Chinese, Vietnamese, or Hispanic people involved in the programs." In a 1996 interview conducted for this research, the Vancouver Police Department's crime prevention officer for Mount Pleasant noted that, despite determined efforts to involve many ethnic groups in CCP, "there was very little response, especially among the Vietnamese, Chinese, and Hispanic groups." In a 2003 interview, a former Vancouver Police Department liaison to the Mount Pleasant CPO also admitted that the police and the CPO "could not get input from the Vietnamese community."

Community organizers in Mount Pleasant, as well as CPO coordinators in other parts of Vancouver, acknowledged that it is generally more difficult to attract members of visible minority groups, especially if they are recent immigrants. When one CPO coordinator from another East Vancouver neighbourhood was asked about the biggest challenge she faces in the administration of local crime prevention programs, she quickly volunteered that it was "motivating people to become involved, especially [those from the] first-generation Asian community who do not get involved as much in community groups." Another long-time CPO coordinator and community activist from East Vancouver stated, "It took more than ten years to reach out to the Vietnamese community" who generally "did not get involved" in programs such as NW. One event that symbolizes the lack of success in soliciting the participation of the Asian community in collective crime prevention activities was a public forum on crime and safety held in Mount Pleasant on 30 July 1996. Through its intensive and month-long promotion, the Asian community was deliberately targeted for attendance: 4,000 flyers advertising the forum were printed in English, Chinese, and Vietnamese and distributed throughout East Mount Pleasant, including Asian stores and restaurants. Among the approximately seventy people who did attend the meeting, however, there were no representatives of the Vietnamese community, and only one person of Chinese descent showed up.

The lack of participation of the Asian community in CCP programs was reflected in a report examining NW in the City of Richmond, a middle-class suburb just south of Vancouver with a high proportion of middle- and upper-income immigrant Chinese families. The report acknowledges that while almost half of the population of Richmond is of Asian descent, only a small minority have become involved in the community safety program, despite the fact that NW newsletters, pamphlets, and neighbourhood notices are printed in both English and Chinese. The report also concedes that NW has struggled to attract Asian volunteers, and that some of the biggest hurdles facing the program are language and cultural barriers. The report recommends that increased efforts be undertaken to attract more volunteers from minority groups who can make program presentations to their own ethnic groups in their native tongue (*Vancouver Sun*, 1999b; van den Hemel, 1999). The lack of involvement of Asian immigrants in neighbourhood groups and activities is not confined to crime prevention. In a 2003 interview, the director of the Mount Pleasant Business Improvement Association (BIA) said, "New Asian immigrants generally don't get actively involved in the BIA." She did note, however, that "once Asian business owners have been here for ten or fifteen years, they do get more involved."

Despite the generally low participation rate, certain crime prevention functions did attract a significant number of members of immigrant and visible minority groups. For example, on one Saturday at a local mall, the Mount Pleasant CPO, in conjunction with the Vancouver Police Department, set up a kiosk to promote Operation Identification, a program where children are photographed and fingerprinted for identification by police in the event they go missing. This kiosk attracted many first-generation Asian and Hispanic families who spoke little English, even though the event was promoted and conducted entirely in English. (While the participation of ethnic and racial minorities in this program was high, this involvement can be viewed as individualistic crime prevention behaviour because it revolves primarily around the family, without requiring any ongoing interaction or cooperation with other neighbourhood residents.) This research also discovered that members of immigrant and visible minority groups do volunteer in other neighbourhood-based programs. According to the long-time director of the Mount Pleasant Neighbourhood House, many volunteers there are immigrant women and/or of Asian origin, an assessment that was confirmed by my own observations made during my visits to the Neighbourhood House. A senior staff member with the Kivan Boys and Girls Club in Mount Pleasant also described a typical parent volunteer as an immigrant Filipino mother.

Research in Mount Pleasant reveals a number of factors that may account for why there is minimal involvement of racial and ethnic minorities in CCP programs. The most obvious is the language barrier: poor English language skills of many residents and the lack of proficiency in predominant languages other than English among local crime prevention group leaders, CPO staff and volunteers, and the police. When asked about the level of participation of immigrant, ethnic, and visible minority groups in NW, the Vancouver Police Department NW coordinator stated that they "do get involved, but to a lesser extent because of the language problem." A survey conducted among Mount Pleasant businesses, many of which are owned by first-generation Asians, concluded that one of the greatest obstacles to participation in collective crime prevention activities is the language barrier: "The inability to communicate with police and crime prevention offices fosters fear, reluctance, and misunderstanding. Many merchants who expressed an interest in participating in a crime prevention seminar hosted by the police department said it was necessary to conduct it in a variety of languages" (Youth Service Canada, 1996: 15). When asked if the lack of participation by immigrant and minorities transcends language, one NW captain in Mount Pleasant East insisted it is not "culture or nationality," but language that represents the greatest barrier. He cited an example of a Vietnamese family who participates in the program on his block. While new to the country, all family members spoke English "very well," which led him to assert, "I think if we can just get past the language obstacle, then the Vietnamese and Chinese families will become involved. But it is very difficult."

Despite this claim, there is evidence that obstacles to the participation of immigrant and minority groups in CCP programs goes beyond language and may be influenced by the cultural environment of the countries from which they emigrated. Research in Mount Pleasant indicates that much of the social interaction by immigrant members of Asian cultures is largely confined to the family or to their ethno-cultural network. This apparent lack of "external" social interaction may also lead to different perspectives on how local social problems should be addressed. According to one CPO coordinator, "Other cultures may feel that crime is not a community problem. It is a family issue: 'We will deal with it within our family.'" This seems especially true for Chinese residents, whose lives are very much centred on the nuclear family. One CPO coordinator in Mount Pleasant recounted this experience in working with the Chinese community: "I remember talking to a group of Chinese moms, who, when we starting talking about spousal abuse, said to me, 'What has that got to do with anybody else. It is a family matter and that stays within the family, and we don't tell anybody and we would lose face if we did.' And it was quite obvious. I mean a couple of heads turned toward this one woman who admitted a problem. And it was all known but it wasn't something that you dealt with in public."

Another related obstacle to participation that may stem from Asian cultural norms is the assumption that voluntarism or philanthropy does not extend outside the family or one's immediate social network. According to one Vietnamese resident of Mount Pleasant interviewed for this study, "The concept of volunteering is new to Vietnamese. Very little is done unless it contributes directly to the family." In his research into crime prevention organizing in England, Crawford (1997: 186) came across similar obstacles to volunteering among the Asian population, which is illuminated by this quote from a coordinator of a victim/ offender mediation project, who himself is of Asian descent: "I have two volunteers who speak most of the Asian languages. I'm looking for more. I'm looking for Asian, females as well, to come forward. It's hard to recruit them. Very difficult. I remember when I used to do volunteer work they [people from the Asian community] used to ask me, 'Oh, you are doing voluntary work; how much do you get paid?' You know, it's hard do tell them you are doing it for nowt [sic]. It's hard getting people from the Asian community. There is still a lot of development work to be done."

The contention that collective crime prevention is an alien concept to Asian cultures is disputed by the coordinator of the Chinese Community Policing Centre in Vancouver. He cites an old Chinese proverb – which he translates into English as "Neighbours should watch out for each other" – as an example of how such concepts as communalism, local collective action, and informal social control are not foreign to Chinese culture. This assertion is supported by researchers such as Lening Zhang and colleagues (1996: 202) who write, "China is a distinctively 'communitarian' society in which priority is given to the group rather than to the individual. A strong group orientation has been part of traditional Chinese culture for centuries and in recent times," and this means "responsibility for crime prevention and control in China is not reserved for judicial and law enforcement agencies but is distributed across a wide variety of social organizations" (206). Kam Wong (2001) agrees: "Historically and traditionally, functional social control in China was supplied informally and outside of the courts." This resulted from a deliberate state policy to build upon existing natural communal structures, ancient cultural habits, and deeply rooted customary practices. "Hence, although in theory the local magistrates were supposed to be in total control on all matters large and small in rural China, in actual practice, broad police powers were conceded to the local community to be exercised by the family" (210–11). Wong maintains that because of this delegation of powers, the family is at the centre of a communal-based informal social control: "Historically, social control in China was decentralized and organized around natural communal and intimate groups, such as the family and clan," with governmental endorsement and support. "The emperor ruled the state by and through his officials, who in turn governed the people by and through the heads of families and community leaders" (211). While Wong emphasizes that crime control policy and practice in China has long been seen as "a local, indigenous and, above all, family affair," it is very much influenced by Confucianism, which stresses informal forms of social control and order maintenance that builds upon, but extends beyond, the family into the broader community: "Consistent with the above Confucian ideas and ideals, crime prevention and social control in traditional China was realized through indigenous groups starting with the family, which provided the education and discipline for character building, the neighbors, who provided the supervision and sanction against deviance, and the community, which set the moral tone and customary norms to guide conduct. Finally, the state acted as the social control agency of last resort in providing legal punishment for crime, and economic maintenance and social welfare to anticipate civil disorders" (211).

That said, the communal philosophy that some assert is inherent in Chinese culture may lose its potency within Vancouver's multicultural, multi-racial society. One Mount Pleasant resident of Chinese origin, who is active within the local Chinese community, provided this explanation concerning the obstacle his culture may pose to participation in multi-ethnic neighbourhoods: "You have to understand that the Chinese are very inward looking culturally. We will join together, but that is largely internal to the Chinese community. We are hesitant to join in with different cultures, even other Asian people, because of the history of Asian cultures. We can be very suspicious of other cultures, and yes, even racist at times." The coordinator of Vancouver's Chinese Community Policing Centre agrees that suspicion of, or even racist attitudes towards other cultures may be present among some first-generation Chinese residents and may impede their involvement in local collective action. However, he contends that a more significant obstacle to the participation of Chinese residents in groups that involve people from other cultures is the threat of "losing face" in public: "Chinese [people] are not traditionally enthused about active participation, especially in foreign cultures where they are not as proficient. Not because they are selfish or racist, but they are afraid of losing face in the community. If they cannot master the language, they may feel that they may not be seen as competent or may make mistakes. Losing face is a very big shame for Chinese families, especially the father because Chinese families are very paternalistic."

A suspicion of other cultures or the fear of losing face in public may not only serve to limit the communal sentiments of Chinese immigrants within a multi-ethnic neighbourhood. It may also bolster the primacy of the family as far as safety and crime prevention activities are concerned. This research does provide some evidence that crime prevention activities and messages emphasizing the family – such as the aforementioned Operation Identification program, which is geared towards protecting children – do appeal to Asian families, especially when compared to more neighbourhood-oriented collective programs such as NW, Shame the Johns, or the CPO. As Wong (2001) points out, while the family-based social ties that form the foundation for informal social control may extend beyond immediate blood relatives to networks of kinship groups and clan members, it does not necessarily extend to outsiders, especially those from other cultures. This may be especially true and understandable within American and Canadian cities, where early Chinese immigrants were subject to endemic prejudice, violent racism, and legislative disenfranchisement at the hands of the larger white population.[4] Their expulsion from "white" society led to the establishment of the ubiquitous "Chinatown," which helped fuel an insular cultural identity and obviously slowed their lack of integration into the broader North American urban mainstream. What's more, within these "Chinatowns" were dozens of organizations that were formed along political, economic, familial, language, regional, philanthropic, and even criminal lines. Together, these ethnic enclaves and restricted-membership organizations bound Chinese immigrants together by limiting contact with outsiders and by promoting interaction and association primarily within the confines of the Chinese community (Chan, 1983; Uslaner and Conley, 2003).

While it can be argued that the third- and even fourth-generation Chinese Canadians have been thoroughly acculturated into Western society, and are thus more amenable to public participation, Greater Vancouver's Chinese community continues to be made up of a large proportion of new immigrants, many of whom emigrated from Hong Kong. This latest wave of immigration to Canada, which began in earnest in the early 1990s as the 1997 handover of Hong Kong to China became imminent, resulted in the creation of new, highly insular Chinese communities in Greater Vancouver – the biggest in the suburb of

Richmond – that have become so large, so self-sufficient, and so wealthy that there is little necessity or incentive for these new immigrants to learn English, conduct business with, or take part in civic organizations outside of their ethnic community. Moreover, according to Lau and Kuan (1995), public participation by Chinese immigrants from Hong Kong may be limited due to that city's characteristics. Specifically, the communal principles that are inherent in the Confucian philosophy and applicable to the rural villages of Mainland China have been diluted by Hong Kong's mass urban-skyscraper society. Describing Hong Kong Chinese as "attentive spectators," Lau and Kuan make the case that political participation and civic activism by Hong Kong residents was low even before its takeover by Communist China.

Another cultural factor that may serve to obstruct participation in local collective action, which is especially prevalent among immigrants from countries in Asia, Latin America, and the former Soviet Union, is trepidation towards the state and suspicion and even fear of police. Khan (1993) writes that in many developing countries, people live in a "culture of silence" that stifles broad political participation. This is especially problematic for community crime prevention, because, as this research discovered, many immigrants associate crime prevention programs with the government and the police specifically. The majority of immigrants in Mount Pleasant came from countries with ignominious human rights records, such as China, Vietnam, Cambodia, Honduras, Guatemala, Somalia, Iran, Romania, and Russia. In many of these countries, to become involved in a group with an overtly political agenda could mean severe repercussions from the state. Moreover, in many of these countries, the police are often the state's tools of persecution and are notoriously corrupt. The reluctance of immigrants to approach "the authorities" in North America may also be exacerbated out of concern that it may jeopardize their tenuous or even illegal immigration status (Meeker and Dombrink, 1988; Herbst and Walker, 2001). There is evidence that many new immigrants in Vancouver continue to fear and distrust the police and resist involvement in any collective action that questions the policies of the state or may involve contact with the police. According to one police official long involved in CCP in Mount Pleasant:

> They [immigrants from repressive countries] simply don't trust the police and there is no reason to think that the first generation are going to overcome that notion ... Dealing with the government seems to be the last

thing that they would want to do. I think that is a huge obstacle for policing. And how do you deal with hundreds of years of cultural background, and how do you deal with the types of society that they are used to living in where they come from, where policing is an entirely different story, where they come from areas where they are not democratic societies, where the power of the police has been overbearing and sometimes controlling. To get them to come out of that cultural difference ... how to crack that market is really tough ... I think whether it is the police department trying to do it, or the community trying to do it, those cultural boundaries are so hard to overcome.

Another senior police official adds:

They all come from the old country where they are used to the police being the biggest gang in the neighbourhood. Once they start learning how we [the Vancouver Police Department] operate, they become a lot more open. But they don't think of the police as somebody who will help them. They may know individual policemen who will help them, and that is how they operate. If they can't get hold of that guy, they won't talk to anybody.

This suspicion of police is not restricted to new immigrants, of course. The media and the scholarly literature continue to be replete with stories of poor relations between police and visible minority groups – in particular, the black community – due to perceptions and realities of police racism, discrimination, profiling, brutality, and so on. It has also been demonstrated consistently that members of minority communities are more hostile towards and fearful of the police than whites. Studies dating back as far as the 1960s concur that African Americans in particular evaluate the police more negatively than white Americans (see Davis and Henderson, 2003). It is easy to discern how such distrust can obstruct the participation of visible minorities in crime prevention programs, especially when police are involved. As Thacher (2001: 783) points out in his study of community policing in Knoxville, Tennessee, despite intensive efforts by police to promote participation in planning sessions around a crime control plan and proposed Community Advisory Committees (CAC), the black community was greatly underrepresented, which "offers one example of how perceptions of harassment can limit an otherwise successful effort to develop community partnerships":

This process turned out hundreds of community participants for the annual planning sessions and created a steady group of about three dozen people who attend monthly CAC meetings. It had difficulty expanding the small base of participation among blacks despite extensive efforts by CAC leaders to reach out to minority neighborhoods, however. Many police and community leaders attribute this failure to general feelings of distrust between Knoxville blacks and the [Knoxville Police Department], and surveys at the time confirmed that this distrust was substantial (Lyons & Scheb 1998). Thus in Knoxville, widespread difficulty building partnerships among blacks may have had as much to do with general issues of police-community relations as it did with the specific interactions between police and individual would-be partners.

Finally, racial and ethnic heterogeneity at the neighbourhood level can also potentially undermine the essential social cohesion preconditions necessary for local collective action, community crime prevention, and informal social control. Merry (1981) was one of the first to observe that racially heterogeneous neighbourhoods are often more difficult to organize around crime prevention compared to those that are racially homogeneous. The argument that racially heterogeneous neighbourhoods are difficult to organize is supported by evidence collected at the block level in Mount Pleasant: streets where the population is racially and ethnically heterogeneous have significantly fewer Neighbourhood Watch programs. This racial and ethnic heterogeneity appears to undermine collective action at two levels. First, streets with a heterogeneous population include racial and ethnic minorities, such as the Chinese or Vietnamese, who traditionally do not become involved in CCP due to both cultural and linguistic factors.[5] Second, the racial and ethnic heterogeneity of a street's inhabitants undermines the existence of binding forces such as a common language, a shared culture, or inter-cultural social interaction. A lack of interaction and cohesion among different racial and ethnic groups in Mount Pleasant is exacerbated by the fact that some groups are historical adversaries. For example, there have been decades and even centuries of animosity between the ethnic Vietnamese and Cambodian communities as well as between the ethnic Vietnamese and Chinese communities. According to the original coordinator of the Mount Pleasant CPO, "There is a lot of fear between the communities and it is xenophobic as much as anything else. And that is in all directions."

In sum, based on the Mount Pleasant research, belonging to an ethnic/racial minority group, especially if one is a new immigrant, is strongly related to non-participation in CCP. By itself, race or ethnicity is a weak explanatory variable in accounting for participation or non-participation in CCP groups and activities. Obstacles to a greater participation of first-generation racial minorities appear to be rooted in a number factors, most of which are contextualized by the predominately white, Anglo-Saxon culture, and, to a lesser extent, the multicultural environment of Mount Pleasant. These obstructing factors include a lack of English language skills; predisposing cultural traditions, norms, and values; a lack of acculturation and local integration (including an absence of social networks outside the family or ethnic community); and a suspicion and mistrust of other cultures, the police, the larger criminal justice system, and, by association, local prevention groups and activities. At the collective level, the ethnic and racial heterogeneity of Mount Pleasant may obstruct a broad-based mobilization because it inhibits the essential prerequisites of social interaction and social cohesion. A 1999 newspaper article (Skelton, 1999), summarized below, provides an erudite assessment of the obstacles facing police and community crime prevention organizers in Vancouver in their efforts to solicit the support and active participation of immigrant members from Asia and other parts of the developing world:

> Vancouver Police and RCMP officials admitted that while it is difficult to know how often crime incidents go unreported, they suspect many new immigrants don't report crime – even serious crime – because of language barriers and bad experiences with police in their home country. "We have had cases where individuals have been reluctant to go to police because of their previous experiences," said Chris Friesen, director of settlement services with Vancouver's Immigrant Services Society ... One of the biggest problems police face is the experiences immigrants – especially refugees – have had with police in their home countries. In several parts of Asia, such as Hong Kong and Taiwan, corruption is widespread and officers are often in the pocket of organized crime. And in some countries in Latin America, Africa and the Middle East, police are the enforcers of a brutal authoritarian regime. Either way, many immigrants don't believe that police can protect them. "The credibility of police officers is not that great. [Immigrants] bring their bad experiences to Canada," said Constable Gary Law, a Chinese-speaking RCMP officer in Richmond who was born in Hong Kong ... Even more than distrust, police in the Lower Mainland face a formidable language barrier in serving new immigrants. The 1996

census shows that about 380,000, or 20 per cent, of the 1.8 million people living in Greater Vancouver speak a language at home other than English or French. (Almost a third of the population, 593,000, has a foreign mother tongue.) More than one third of those living in Richmond speak a foreign language at home – primarily Chinese. Yet on a force of almost 200, Richmond has only about 12 to 15 members who can speak Cantonese or Mandarin, Laurie said. About 10 officers can speak Punjabi, Urdu or Hindi; only two speak Korean and only one Japanese.

The Social Psychology of CCP Participation and Non-participation

The Mount Pleasant case study suggests that CCP program participants share common socio-psychological traits, which, for this study, refer to attitudinal, behavioural, and cognitive patterns that are formed in relation to one's immediate social environment and that can influence one's behaviours and actions within that environment. While there are many personal reasons why people choose or are motivated to become involved in CCP groups and activities, this research focused on two major schools of thought that have dominated the debate over which socio-psychological factors are most strongly related to participation (summarized in chapter 1). The first argues that personal and contextual salience of crime is the most important factor that influences citizen involvement in collective anti-crime measures; that is, participation stems directly from victimization experiences, fear of crime, perceptions of neighbourhood crime problems, and area crime rates. The second school of thought proposes that collective responses to crime are more significantly related to an individual's (emotional and financial) attachment to and integration within their neighbourhood.

The Personal and Contextual Salience of Crime

Research in Mount Pleasant indicates that many CCP participants have at least a moderate level of concern over crime or have been victimized in the recent past. When interviewed as part of this study, members of the board of directors of the Safer Community Society cited specific crime problems, in particular prostitution and drug trafficking, as issues that compelled them to become active. NW block captains and CPO volunteers also indicated how concern over local crime problems was a factor in influencing their decision to become involved in these respective organizations. One block captain recounted how he and his neighbours had become distressed about a house on their street that had "considerable" prostitution and drug trafficking activity: "When the crime and noise became unbearable a few of us talked to our neighbours, who agreed that we must do something to address the crime in the neighbourhood." Previous victimization also appears to be a factor that influences one's decision to initiate or join a NW program. Over half of the twenty-three block captains interviewed for this study stated that they had been victims of a property crime at least once in the last five years. One Vancouver police liaison to Mount Pleasant suggested that it is the *threat* of crime that represents the most significant inducement for people to become involved in collective crime prevention activities. He cites an example of how the publicity of a suspected paedophile living in one East Vancouver neighbourhood galvanized residents in a collective effort to expel him from the area.

Among the few members of visible minority groups who participated in CCP programs during the research periods, concern over crime emerged as the dominant factor that motivated involvement. In a focus group involving local Chinese mothers, one woman stated that crime had been a part of her family's life in both Hong Kong and Mount Pleasant, and that the only way to combat it was through "the family and the neighbourhood." For Chinese and Vietnamese residents especially, concern over crime and an attachment to community (in this case, their respective ethnic communities) are intertwined as motivating factors. In a rare instance of an unsolicited offer to participate in CCP programs, a young, first-generation Vietnamese man approached the coordinator of the Mount Pleasant CPO and voiced a serious concern over crime within the local Vietnamese community. It also became clear that he was motivated by his desire to better the lives of other Vietnamese immigrants when he cited four other examples of volunteer work he had pursued in his ethnic community in Vancouver.

Interviews and focus groups with CCP non-participants reveal that this cohort shares the same level of concern over crime, fear, and victimization as participants. Non-participants interviewed for this research consistently ranked crime and poverty as the most pressing problems facing Mount Pleasant and expressed a personal concern over the threat of victimization. Concern was highest among women, many stating they were afraid to walk around their neighbourhood alone at night. During one focus group with non-participants, most of whom were female, two young women indicated that they had been propositioned by men who perhaps mistook them for prostitutes, yet they still did not take part in any local anti-prostitution initiatives. Non-participants also experienced similar levels of victimization relative to participants. While many non-participants expressed concern over and fear of crime, however, most indicated that they pursued only individualistic crime prevention activities.

Community Attachment, Social Interaction, and Social Cohesion

Besides the issue of crime, one factor that previous studies indicate is strongly related to participation in CCP groups and activities is an individual's attachment to the neighbourhood in which he or she lives. The relationship between community attachment and involvement in CCP programs is quite evident in Mount Pleasant; members of local crime prevention groups and CPO volunteers consistently expressed and displayed a strong affection for the neighbourhood. When CPO volunteers were asked in interviews and focus groups why they donated their time to the office, a common response was a desire to help the community in which they lived. Neighbourhood attachment was also visible when examining the responses to a question on the Mount Pleasant CPO volunteer application form. While concern over crime was most often the primary response to a question that asked why an applicant wanted to volunteer at the CPO, this concern was often couched in terms of a desire to safeguard his or her community. In fact, those who indicated a desire to help their community outnumbered those who cited personal safety as a motivation to become involved. Answers that indicated personal and family safety as motivating factors were often imbued with a desire to safeguard their community. One reply on the CPO volunteer application form that epitomizes the interrelationship between concern over crime and attachment to community was the following: "I have lived in Mount Pleasant from [*sic*] over ten years. I want to do all I can to make Mount Pleasant a better place to live for me and my children. That means fighting the drug dealers and prostitutes."

This infusion of crime concern, personal safety, and community attachment was also found among members of NW. During a focus group with NW members, one resident indicated that her family became involved in the program because "I am sick and tired of the crime in my neighbourhood. I am sick of seeing the prostitutes around my kids' school. This is our neighbourhood, not the prostitutes' and the pimps' and the drug dealers'. It is like what was said before: it is our neighbourhood and we have to do something to take it back from them." A 2003 survey of volunteers at the Hastings North Community Policing Centre, located in the poor north-east corner of Vancouver, documented similar responses. In one open-ended question that asked survey respondents their "purpose for volunteering" at this crime prevention office, twenty of the thirty-seven responses alluded to "helping community," compared to the second highest plurality of seven responses, which was the need for experience to join the Vancouver Police Department. Only six respondents cited safety issues, while four expressed a desire to gain volunteer experience. In another (close-ended) question that asked respondents what was important to them when volunteering at the Hastings North office, the single largest frequency of responses was "community involvement" (30), followed by "crime prevention" (20), "programs" (20), "experience" (12), "training" (18), and "policies" (12) (Teixeira, 2003: 6).

As indicated in the previous chapter, community attachment also appears to be strongly related to tenure of residence. Mount Pleasant homeowners who were interviewed indicated a significant level of neighbourhood attachment and social interaction with other residents. The causal relationship between home ownership and involvement in local collective action suggests that community attachment is not exclusively emotional in nature, but also financial. A positive correlation between local financial investment (i.e., home ownership), commitment to community, and participation in CCP groups and activities was succinctly articulated by a senior Vancouver Police Department member (and a former Mount Pleasant homeowner): "One of the other aspects of it is a financial aspect ... In Mount Pleasant, the homeowners have a vested interest because they are putting dollars into property there. So if the area is perceived to be unsafe, their dollars are worth less than the initial ones they put in. The renters, on the other hand, if the area is perceived to be unsafe and not a good place to live, are benefiting because the rents are lower and they don't care because if it gets too bad they just move out." Interviews with CPO volunteers who are renters revealed that they generally share two characteristics with homeowners. First, they are relatively longer-term residents of Mount Pleasant (all had lived in the neighbourhood for two or more years), and, second, they expressed a strong emotional attachment to the community. One CPO volunteer exhibited both attributes when she emphasized how much she "loved" Mount Pleasant and had lived in the neighbourhood (as a renter) for over ten years. In short, an individual's time spent living in the neighbourhood may be as strong a determinant of local social integration (and hence participation) as tenure of residence.

One indication that an individual's involvement in local crime prevention groups and activities stems from a sense of belonging and commitment to his or her community is the finding that many CCP participants in Mount Pleasant are also involved in other local volunteer groups and activities. As documented in the previous chapter, studies suggest that an individual's participation in CCP programs is part of a broader proclivity for volunteerism. This is especially true of the leadership of crime prevention groups; the recent history of Mount Pleasant activism reveals that a small number of residents are actively involved in different community organizations. During a focus group with the board of directors of the Safer Community Society, all five volunteer members stated that they were involved in at least one other local non-profit group. One board member even received a City of Vancouver award for his volunteer work with various local groups and causes. Interviews with the CPO's unpaid staff also indicated involvement in more than one community group. In a focus group with eight CPO volunteers, six indicated that they volunteered for other non-profit groups, including a crisis hotline, the Neighbourhood House, the Mount Pleasant Community Centre, and a women's shelter, to name just a few. (The one exception to this general rule are those younger volunteers who donate their time at the CPO as part of a policing career path and who indicated that they did little other volunteer work.) During an interview, one indefatigable seventy-year-old CPO volunteer stated that she was active in four other local groups in Mount Pleasant. She expressed a strong attachment to her neighbourhood, having owned the same home for more than thirty years. Moreover, she made it clear that she did not volunteer in the CPO or participate in the local NW program out of a fear of crime, stating that she often walked alone around the neighbourhood at night. This volunteer provides further evidence that participants in collective crime prevention are often motivated, not exclusively by a concern over crime, but for more emotive reasons, in particular attachment to their neighbourhood.

Based on the above findings, a causal (and linear) relationship appears to exist between three variables: socio-economic status (in particular, home ownership), attachment and commitment to the local community, and involvement in two or more voluntary groups (including crime prevention groups). However, the influence that home ownership has on community attachment and participation in local groups begs the following question: Why do the majority of Mount Pleasant homeowners decline to take part in local CCP programs? Through focus groups and interviews, socially integrated, middle-class homeowning residents rationalized their lack of participation in collective CCP groups and activities through one or more of the following explanations: (1) time constraints, (2) little faith in the impact of collective crime prevention activities, (3) disagreement with the particular focus or strategies of existing groups or strategies, (4) a reliance on personal, individualistic crime prevention measures, and/or (5) a lack of awareness of existing groups and activities. In interviews and focus groups with low-income renters living in Mount Pleasant, many provided similar rationales for not participating in local crime prevention programs, but also expressed a further justification not articulated by homeowners: a lack of attachment to the neighbourhood and little desire to interact with their neighbours and other community members outside of their existing and well-defined social network. This finding suggests that if an individual resident is not socially integrated or does not have an emotional attachment to his or her community, there is less chance he or she will become involved in collective crime prevention activities, regardless of the level of concern over crime.

At the community level, the lack of local attachment and social interaction apparent among Mount Pleasant residents with a low socioeconomic status indirectly undermines CCP groups and activities because it weakens social cohesion at both the block and neighbourhood level. Within Mount Pleasant, NW programs and other crime prevention groups are more prevalent on those blocks and in those multi-residential buildings where there is a high level of social interaction and cohesion. During one focus group, block captains agreed that the NW program exemplified the cohesiveness and "high level of contact" among those who took part in this program. All block captains participating in the focus group indicated that they recognized most of their neighbours, and half stated that they talked to at least one of their neighbours on a weekly basis; approximately one-third stated that they had socialized with their neighbours outside the NW program by hosting barbecues, house-sitting for a neighbour, or contributing to a garage sale held among houses on the block. One focus group participant commented that it was "not uncommon for neighbours on the street to tell other neighbours when they were going away for the weekend ... and to keep an eye on their house." A block captain summed up the local social cohesion and informal social control as such: "This block has actually been quite friendly. That is one thing I like ... We have been watching out for each other and each other's kids right from the start. You know, like I yell at their kids and they yell at mine, and so on and so forth."

Those areas of Mount Pleasant that have a high level of social cohesion are generally restricted to streets or multi-residential buildings with a high proportion of homeowners and/or long-term residents, and as such are in the minority. This research suggests that those areas with a high proportion of low-income renters have the lowest level of social interaction and cohesion. It is no coincidence that there are no NW programs on these blocks or in these apartment buildings. One NW captain, who lived in a rental apartment building in Mount Pleasant East, blamed her lack of success in mobilizing residents on the negligible social interaction and cohesion in the building, remarking in an interview, "How can you get people to work together when they don't even want to talk with each other?" There is much evidence to suggest that Mount Pleasant as a whole suffers from a lack of local social cohesion, which is caused by a number of interrelated factors that have been identified in this chapter: widespread poverty, social isolation and exclusion, a lack of community attachment and belonging among much of the population, a high rate of population turnover, and demographic heterogeneity (including adversarial relations between different demographic groups). Individually, each of these factors constitutes a significant obstacle to social cohesion. Together, they form what one long-time Mount Pleasant resident called "an impenetrable force that will always stop any semblance of internal community." It is this lack of social interaction and cohesion at the aggregate level that helps undermine the collective action foundations so essential to CCP.

Conclusion

Participants in collective crime prevention groups and activities in Mount Pleasant are drawn from a narrow base of neighbourhood residents who can be generally characterized as white, middle-class, long-term homeowners with a strong attachment to their neighbourhood and who are often involved in a number of volunteer-based groups. This profile is particularly true of NW block captains as well as the leadership of local crime prevention groups. A meeting held in the summer of 2003 and spearheaded by the Dickens Group – which is made up of residents who live around the Charles Dickens Elementary school in Mount Pleasant East – served as a microcosm of the typical characteristics of crime prevention activists and participants. The meeting was held in a local church to address accusations that the minister was accommodating local prostitutes by providing food and shelter. The majority of the twenty-six people who attended were white (the exception was two first-generation Asian males and one Hispanic male who had lived in the neighbourhood for twenty-two years). Almost all were between thirty-five and fifty years of age. Sixteen of the participants were male and ten were female. With the exception of four people, all were homeowners. A little over half of those in attendance stated that they had participated in at least two other events sponsored by the Dickens Group. While it was clear that they were highly concerned over the threat posed by a potential influx of prostitutes, most of those who spoke at the meeting prefaced their comments by noting the length of time they had lived in neighbourhood and/or their strong attachment to the neighbourhood.

The characteristics that predominate among individual participants in collective CCP programs can also be extrapolated to the block level. Those blocks or apartment buildings that have been the most successful in organizing a Neighbourhood Watch program or collectively protesting against street prostitution, drug trafficking, or problem premises have a high proportion of owner occupation and a strong sense of social cohesion. In an interview for this study, a Vancouver Police Department member who served as a liaison to Mount Pleasant observed that, in general, "white middle-class neighbourhoods" are more prone to become involved in CCP activities and NW specifically. In a training session held for prospective block captains, one participant discussed the socio-economic and racial homogeneity of the residents of the owner-occupied suites in her building. The Vancouver police officer present at the meeting replied that this building would probably be "easy" to organize. In this respect, the Mount Pleasant case study reflects the findings of other research that suggests CCP groups and activities predominate in middle-class, demographically homogeneous neighbourhoods, due, in part, to the essential prerequisites for collective action that this homogeneity appears to provide (such as social interaction, cohesion, and shared values and norms).

Disproportionately absent from most CCP groups and activities in

Mount Pleasant are those people that make up the majority of the neighbourhood: immigrant members of visible minority groups, the undereducated, non-professionals, the poor, and renters. What appear to be missing in most non-participants are those demographic and socio-psychological factors that drive an individual's involvement in local collective action. The social psychological traits underlying CCP program participation appear to be a mixture of crime concern and neighbourhood attachment. The fact that non-participants display similar levels of crime concern as participants suggests that attachment to one's neighbourhood is the key factor in transforming an individual's concern into action. In turn, local attachment and commitment appear to be highly dependent upon such variables as socio-economic status (in particular home ownership) and the duration of time someone has lived in the neighbourhood. Socio-economic status may be the single most important constitutive element of participation in collective crime prevention groups because it appears to strongly influence such socio-psychological determinants of participation as local integration and neighbourhood attachment. In other words, socio-psychological variables that correlate with participation, such as social interaction, local integration, and an attachment to the neighbourhood, appear to stem from such socio-economic predictors as above-average income, professional employment, post-secondary education, and home ownership. Non-participants generally lack the socio-psychological characteristics that motivate people to become involved because they lack the appropriate socio-economic status. A linear progression of motivating factors underlying participation – which links socio-economic characteristics, socio-psychological underpinnings of participation, and involvement in local activism and volunteerism in a causal fashion – is depicted in figure 3.1.

As the conceptual model in figure 3.1 proposes, an individual is less likely to become attached and committed to a neighbourhood if he or she does not have some emotional and/or financial stake in that neighbourhood. Long-term residency and affective emotional and financial investments in a neighbourhood are often contingent upon home ownership, which, in Vancouver's expensive housing market, is very much dependent upon a certain level of socio-economic achievement. In Mount Pleasant East, the majority of residents cannot afford to buy a home, and this serves to weaken the attachment and commitment to a neighbourhood that is so essential in promoting participation. The demographic and socio-psychological factors that obstruct an individ-

Figure 3.1 The linear relationship between socio-economic factors, socio-psychological factors, and participation in community crime prevention activities

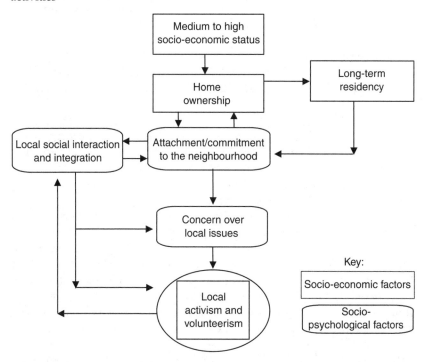

ual's participation in CCP activities are manifested at the aggregate community level. Transience, widespread poverty, and ethnic, racial, and socio-economic heterogeneity are all traits that characterize Mount Pleasant. In turn, these factors contribute to the low level of social cohesion and obstruct broad-based collective action. As bluntly stated by a former coordinator of the Mount Pleasant CPO in a 2003 interview: "The community is so diverse; between the desperately poor, drugged-up prostitutes and immigrants on the one hand and the nouveau yuppies on the other, they just don't see eye-to-eye." The relationship between obstacles to participation at the level of the individual resident and the community is provided in table 3.1.

In the case of Mount Pleasant, the correlation between socio-economic status and participation holds true even when intervening variables, including socio-psychological variables, are controlled. Using

Table 3.1 Individual and collective obstacles to participation in CCP

Variables	Individual	Collective
Demographic	Mobile renter	Transient population
	Ethnic/racial minority	Ethnic/racial heterogeneity
	New immigrant	Widespread poverty
	Low socio-economic status	
Socio-psychological	Lack of social integration	Low level of social interaction,
	Lack of local attachment	cohesion, and informal social
	Lack of local commitment	control

home ownership as the constant variable, there are CCP participants in Mount Pleasant who are socially integrated and committed to their community who do *not* own a home. However, in general these participants possess socio-economic attributes shared by most other participants, such as post-secondary education and a professional occupation. But this does not account for the fact that most Mount Pleasant homeowners do not participate in CCP programs, which limits the ability of socio-economic status to exclusively predict participation in CCP. The inability to draw an exclusive causal relationship between any single variable and participation or non-participation in CCP leads to an important conclusion of this chapter: participation and non-participation at the community level are influenced by a complex interaction of many different demographic variables, socio-psychological factors, and opportunity structures.

It is much more difficult to assemble a typical profile of those who do not participate in CCP programs. Because non-participants constitute the vast majority of the Mount Pleasant population, this sizeable faction is replete with representatives from all demographic backgrounds. Indeed, the majority of Anglo-Saxon, middle-class, professional, long-term, homeowning, socially integrated residents in Mount Pleasant do not participate in most collective crime prevention activities. However, as described above, most conspicuous in their absence from CCP groups and activities are the more marginalized residents who make up the majority of the Mount Pleasant East population. Low participation rates in Mount Pleasant CCP programs are not unusual when placed in the context of community organizing in poor and mixed status neighbourhoods. As Louis Wirth (1938: 213) writes, "The older areas of cities are inundated by restless, migrant, heterogeneous assortments of people who are strangers to one another and to the areas in which they find temporary abode, in which they fail to take root, and for which they feel no responsibility because they are neither owners of property nor share in the traditions of the community." This has great relevancy for Mount Pleasant and efforts to mobilize residents around crime prevention and other local social problems. Yet, as this study argues, obstacles to participation stem not only from the characteristics and behaviour of residents and the community as a whole, but also from crime prevention groups and the structure of advanced Western societies. Indeed, the poverty and resulting lack of social cohesion that contributes to crime and community apathy can ultimately be traced to broader political economic forces and institutions that are external to neighbourhoods such as Mount Pleasant. The following chapters examine obstacles to participation at these organizational and structural levels.

4 Organizational Obstacles to Participation in Community Crime Prevention

Introduction

In contemporary western societies, local collective action and social movements are less and less the result of a spontaneous galvanization of shared interests and more likely the product of arduous planning and coordination of existing or fledgling groups (Piven and Cloward, 1977; Rich, 1980; Checkoway and Zimmerman, 1992; Diani, 1992; Fisher, 1993; Tarrow, 1996; Della Porta and Diani, 1999; Clary and Snyder, 2002; Passy, 2003). This is no different when the issue of concern is crime; research shows that community organizations and their leadership are critical to the successful mobilization of neighbourhoods around crime and community safety (Skogan, 1990; Bennett, 1995; Yarwood and Edwards, 1995; Donnelly and Majka, 1998). By the same token, community crime prevention (CPP) groups and programs have also been held accountable for low levels of participation (Roehl, 1984; Forst and Bazemore, 1986; Skogan, 1988; Rosenbaum, 1988b; Bennett and Lavrakas, 1989; Grine, 1994; Bennett, 1995; Miller, 2001; Thacher, 2001). In other words, a low participation rate in local crime prevention groups and activities is not simply a function of community characteristics, but may also stem from program implementation voids and deficiencies. The objective of this chapter is to identify and examine those obstacles to a broad-based mobilization of Mount Pleasant residents that can be traced to weaknesses and voids in local crime prevention groups and programs. This analysis is particularly significant given that a central inquiry of this study is to determine whether the immobilization of disadvantaged neighbourhoods around crime prevention is the result of theory failure or program implementation failure (or both).

Because the Mount Pleasant Crime Prevention Organization (CPO) and the Safer Community Society constituted the primary vehicles for mobilizing neighbourhood residents around crime prevention during the period covered by this study, they form the principal (although not exclusive) focus of this chapter. A critical analysis of crime prevention organizing by local crime prevention groups is not meant to be an indictment of these groups or their leadership.[1] Instead, the goal of this chapter is to deduce general lessons on organizational impediments to local participation in CCP programs from this case study. To that end, this study found that the main organizational obstacles to a broad-based mobilization of residents around crime prevention included weak, inappropriate, and ineffectual community outreach and communication; an absence of strong, stable, and active leadership; and inadequate resources. This chapter also recognizes and documents the intermittent organizing successes realized by CCP groups within and outside of Mount Pleasant. Based on these observations, the chapter concludes by tendering important principles of successful crime prevention organizing.

Community Outreach and Communications

For the purposes of this study, "community outreach" encompasses efforts intended to raise awareness of, support for, and participation in local crime prevention groups and activities, while "communication" encompasses both the message and the medium through which the outreach and substantive crime prevention programs are "marketed" to community residents. Crime prevention practitioners and police interviewed for this study agreed that outreach and communication are pivotal factors in promoting participation in CCP groups and activities and can potentially overcome some of the impediments to mobilization that are rooted in the social environment of Mount Pleasant and similar neighbourhoods. Coordinators from other Vancouver CPOs that enjoy a high rate of community participation were also of the opinion that outreach and communication are essential, and if planned and implemented effectively can engage those who traditionally do not become involved in collective crime prevention activities. These sentiments were succinctly articulated by the first Vancouver Police Department constable appointed as a crime prevention liaison for Mount Pleasant: "Without a doubt. It [communication] is very important. You see big differences in some communities because the way they [crime prevention groups] deliver their crime prevention message is effective. If we can't talk to them about crime prevention and invite them to get involved, then we will never reach them. It is like anything; you need to advertise."

This research found that a lack of appropriate and effective outreach and communication by the Mount Pleasant Safer Community Society and the CPO constituted the most significant organizational impediment to a broad-based mobilization of local residents. One of the most prevalent problems appeared to be the lack of emphasis placed on promoting the office and its programs among neighbourhood residents. The result was that few people in Mount Pleasant were aware of the CPO and its programs, and even fewer people used its services or participated in the crime prevention activities offered. Among the CPO's voluntary leadership and paid organizers there appeared to be a lack of appreciation of the importance of active community outreach. Instead, the emphasis was placed on establishing the CPO in a high-profile location, which was then expected to draw people into the office and crime prevention programs (a "build it and they shall come" mindset that is emblematic of the community mobilization model's implant hypothesis). This strategy was acknowledged by an original Safer Community Society board member who was involved in establishing the CPO in its original location: "We were willing to pay the high rent for the office because it was in a high-traffic location. We thought it was important to make the office as visible as possible and that was where much of our early energy went into. But I do agree that we were so proud of ourselves after getting the office going and putting up our big blue sign, that we probably did not spend enough time going out into the community. We naively thought they would flock to us, which of course they haven't."

While establishing the CPO in a highly visible location can rightfully be seen as a promotional tool in itself, the minimal outreach efforts during its initial years of operation limited the impact of this strategy. There appeared to be no coherent plan with respect to the development and implementation of outreach and communications. There was little promotional material on the CPO and its programs that could be distributed to residents, and the stock crime prevention literature that was made available to all Vancouver CPOs sat in the office with minimal efforts to distribute it to homes. The absence of an outreach strategy was aggravated by the limited resources, time, and support available to the original CPO coordinator (and subsequent coordinators) who had to carry out a number of responsibilities – program development and implementation, coordinating volunteers, fund-raising, liaison with police – that left little time to plan and carry out an outreach campaign. This dilemma was recognized by a senior Vancouver police officer who was involved in establishing the Mount Pleasant CPO: "The Society rented a very high-profile storefront. However, that storefront was too expensive and [the coordinator] spent half her time trying to raise funds to pay the rent, which detracted her from crime prevention duties. A visible storefront is important. However, if it takes away from important community outreach, then it doesn't have the means to make people in the community aware of the CPO and pull people into to use it ... A CPO is more than just a storefront; the challenge is going to be to get out there and stop expecting people to come in here." CPO coordinators were also hampered by the lack of assistance from volunteers as well as from Safer Community Society directors and members. Most CPO volunteers had neither the skills nor the inclination to conduct outreach programs. In addition, society directors, many of whom were experienced local activists, rarely became involved in the day-to-day activities of the CPO, including outreach and promotion.

Outreach to Marginalized Groups and Individuals

Community outreach by the Safer Community Society and the CPO was especially lacking in relation to those demographic groups that make up the majority of the neighbourhood, but which are generally absent from collective crime prevention initiatives, such as the poor, renters, immigrants, and racial minorities. While socio-economic, linguistic, and cultural factors do serve to impede the participation of these segments of the local population in CCP programs, as obstacles to participation they were compounded by the indiscernible or ineffective outreach by the CPO and the Safer Community Society. With a few exceptions,[2] there were no specific strategies or concerted efforts to reach out to and involve individuals from first-generation ethnic minority groups. For the most part, services provided through the CPO were not available in any language other than English (although some of the Mount Pleasant CPO coordinators did enjoy intermittent success, through intensive outreach, in recruiting volunteers who did speak Mandarin, Cantonese, and Vietnamese). A survey of Mount Pleasant retail businesses (Youth Service Canada, 1996) documented a concern among minority ethnic proprietors that the crime prevention literature was not in their native language, and, as such, they were unable to understand it. While promotional literature was increasingly made available in other languages, such as Spanish, Chinese, Korean, and Vietnamese, there were little efforts to actively disseminate this literature. What's more, the promotional impact of this literature was weakened because the translation from English was literal without much regard to appropriate themes or messages that would appeal to the cultural backgrounds of different ethnic groups. One Chinese resident interviewed for this research stated that the Chinese-language brochure for Neighbourhood Watch (NW) was translated literally from the English version, and its message emphasized the need to look out for one's neighbours as opposed to protecting families, which he suggested would have greater appeal to Chinese residents. In fact, the medium and the message for the minimal outreach and communication that was undertaken by the CPO was standardized regardless of the "target market." Few efforts were made to tailor the standard crime prevention messages or programs to the needs or cultural context of different demographic groups in the neighbourhood.

Moreover, the substantive crime prevention programs emphasized by the CPO may have also undermined any promotional impact vis-à-vis traditional non-participants because of their lack of appeal to the needs and priorities of marginalized groups. There was little emphasis placed on ascertaining the needs and desires of neighbourhood residents generally, let alone those of new immigrants, minority groups, or poor single mothers, and the CPO generally failed to research such important issues as crime and victimization rates, pressing problems (criminal or otherwise) facing specific areas or local groups, the unique needs or desires of different demographic groups, or the types of programs required to address these problems, needs, or desires. Opportunity reduction programs, in particular NW, were the primary crime prevention vehicles offered by the CPO to local residents. However, given the instrumental messages that stress surveillance, territoriality, protecting one's assets, and reporting suspicious people or activities, NW and similar situational approaches appeal primarily to socially integrated, middle-class homeowners who have assets worth stealing (which helps to explain why this demographic group is so over-represented among NW participants). NW is less appealing to, for example, the first-generation Chinese or Vietnamese family who is less integrated into the neighbourhood, or the poor single mother who owns few assets and may be more concerned with keeping her children out of gangs. In short, the CPO's community outreach and substantive crime prevention programs were indecorous to the needs, desires, or cultural background of the majority of Mount Pleasant residents. According to one CPO coordinator in a neighbouring community, there is little wonder why participation in CCP programs in disadvantaged, mixed-status neighbourhoods like Mount Pleasant is low: "Did anyone ask [neighbourhood residents] whether they thought Neighbourhood Watch was a good idea, the program itself? Did anyone ask them what they thought should be used in the community to reduce crime? Did anyone ask them whether a CPO would be an effective tool to do so? Probably not. I know that people organizing out there weren't asking any [questions]. So what happens is that a bunch of white men get together and figure out the best thing to do and then they say [to the community]: 'Come on guys you have to get involved.'"

The role that weak, nonexistent, and ineffectual outreach and communications play in inhibiting resident participation in CCP programs has been documented in other studies. Based on research in eight American cities, Grine (1994) attributed low levels of participation in community policing programs on poor communication and information dissemination by police. Communication failures by crime prevention groups were also blamed for a high rate of cynicism among the poor and ethnic minority residents about the benefits of local crime prevention programs in the Tees Valley of Britain (Safe in Tees Valley and the Home Office, 2003). A survey of nearly 1,000 residents found that less than a third of residents from minority ethnic groups could recall any crime prevention campaign, compared to one in two who classified their ethnicity as "white British." "These findings represent a tremendous challenge," said the program director of the crime prevention group, Safe in Tees Valley. "If we expect members of ethnic minorities to improve their security by changing their behaviour, then we have to reach them with the right prevention message, delivered in the right way" (British Broadcasting Corporation, 2004).

The argument that low levels of participation by minority ethnic groups is due to poor outreach, as opposed to cultural or linguistic factors, may be substantiated by examining the participation of first-generation Chinese residents in crime prevention activities in other Vancouver neighbourhoods. The coordinator for the Chinese Community Policing Centre was quoted in the media as saying they have "excellent participation" by local Chinese residents in different programs. He notes there is a "steady traffic" of Chinese immigrants through this office because they "have nowhere else to go" (*Vancouver Sun*, 10 April 1999a). In a 1997 interview for this study, the same coordinator stated that the lack of available services in Chinese languages in Mount Pleasant limits the use of the CPO by local first-generation Chinese residents. The Chinatown office is successful, in part, because the demographic characteristics of its staff and volunteers reflect their constituency. This is not the case with the Mount Pleasant CPO or its governing body. In fact, the absence of substantive programs and community outreach that caters to marginalized groups in Mount Pleasant may partially stem from the fact that most paid and unpaid staff of the CPO, as well as the its board of directors, are unrepresentative of the neighbourhood's diverse population. As a result, the crime prevention programs and communications stressed by the Mount Pleasant CPO primarily reflect and appeal to the needs and values of a narrow, homogeneous group of residents. As one former coordinator of the CPO put it, "The poor are never represented on the board" of the Safer Community Society, and "It is not really a community office when it only serves one part of the community." This was echoed by a senior Vancouver Police Department official: "The people who are on the board or steering committees are not representative of the community fully ... When it comes time to call out the troops, to really get things going, they only go to people who they know will share their interests." These observations contribute to a major thesis of this study (detailed in chapter 6), which is that traditional, opportunity reduction programs, such as NW, have become a means by which middle-class homeowners and neighbourhoods nurture a group identity, based on shared demographic characteristics. In turn, this common, self-nurtured identity may serve to (intentionally and unintentionally) exclude those who do not share similar characteristics.

Police Communication with Neighbourhood Residents

Communication problems are not confined to citizen-based crime prevention groups. The Mount Pleasant case study also reveals problems in the nature and scope of communication that takes place between the Vancouver Police Department and neighbourhood residents, which may also serve to inhibit participation in community policing and CCP programs. One of the most significant problems that became apparent in the course of the research was that communication between neighbourhood residents and the police was largely unidirectional. Residents would make crime and nuisance reports to the CPO, which were then referred to the police. However, on a consistent basis, there was little or no feedback from the Vancouver Police Department to the CPO or the reporting residents.[3] This is a significant problem because a central objective of community policing is to increase the two-way flow of information between the police and community members (Sherman, Milton, and Kelly, 1973; Trojanowicz, 1986). The lack of two-way communication became a considerable source of frustration among some Mount Pleasant residents, who would report a crime or suspicious activity to the CPO and then receive no reply from either the office or police. CPO coordinators were equally frustrated because they also received little feedback from police, and as such were unable to provide residents with information. During an interview, one NW member typified this frustration: "They [police] tell you to call 911 when you see someone suspicious, and you give your name and number to the [911] operator, but you never know if they catch someone because they never call you back. And you know that we have been dealing with this drug house on our street for years, and we have been calling police for years about it, but it is business as usual there and I have no idea what the police are doing, if anything. At least they should keep us informed. I don't think that is too much to ask." Local businesses also remonstrated about the unidirectional communication with police. As part of a crime prevention survey of retail businesses in Mount Pleasant, some respondents stated that they were not provided with a follow-up by police after reporting a crime. The authors of this study wrote that respondents "felt it was important to know what the case developments were, even if there were none" (Youth Service Canada, 1996: 15).

The frustration expressed by reporting residents stems from a lack of awareness about what action, if any, is taken by police to address a specific crime or disorder problem. This frustration increases when there is a perception that no action has been taken. Based upon the Mount Pleasant case study, there are generally two consequences that result from this frustration. In some instances, it translates into a reduction or even a cessation of crime or suspicious activity reporting, which undermines the essential "watch and ward" aspect of opportunity reduction programs such as NW. At the other extreme, this frustration may translate into a greater commitment to and participation in local crime prevention activities, which at the extreme may border on vigilantism. In one example, a local NW captain repeatedly aired his aggravation over the perceived lack of effort by police to combat prostitution and drug trafficking on his block. He finally intensified his own crime prevention efforts by initiating a one-man neighbourhood bike patrol (without the sanctioning of the police or the CPO), which included intervening in open-air drug deals. In short, research in Mount Pleasant suggests that the lack of two-way communication between police and neighbourhood residents can contribute to frustration, hopelessness, and apathy on the one hand, or vigilante activities on the other, both of which impede positive collective crime prevention behaviour.

Communication problems were particularly acute between the Vancouver Police Department and members of racial minority groups in Mount Pleasant. Despite an earnest effort to recruit police candidates from the different ethnic and visible minority groups that represent Vancouver's diverse multicultural population, as well as the establishment of a Diversity Relations Unit, the Vancouver Police Department continues to be overwhelmingly white and unilingual. As with the local crime prevention groups, the fact that the makeup of the police in Vancouver does not reflect the multicultural and linguistic diversity of its constituency hinders their relationship with ethnic minority groups, which can serve to limit crime reporting by these groups or participation in community-based crime prevention activities. The coordinator of the Chinese Community Policing Centre stated in a media interview that despite the important conduit his office plays between the Chinese community and police, he concedes it is not a long-term solution for policing immigrant communities. It would help, he said, "to have the police force more reflect the immigrant factor ... But that will take a long time" (*Vancouver Sun*, 1999a). In an interview conducted for this research, the coordinator acknowledged that the inability of most Vancouver Police Department members to converse in the language of many of the ethnic communities is an "obvious" impediment to their crime reporting and CCP group participation. However, he also noted that communication problems go beyond language and may be manifested in the inability of police officers to understand the cultural norms of minority groups. For example, gestures of respect or disrespect can be communicated through simple body language. Nonverbal communication problems between police and marginalized groups can also arise due to the fear and trepidation that immigrants, especially those from countries with repressive human rights records, have towards police. This research indicated that similar verbal and non-verbal communication problems are evident in the relationship between police and other marginalized groups, such as the mentally ill. In a focus group session held with mentally ill adults in a Mount Pleasant group home, one of the topics raised was their relationship with police. Despite their general praise for the Vancouver Police Department, an uneasiness was articulated by focus group participants towards police officers, and much of this anxiety stemmed from their interactions with police in crisis situations. Of the eight people involved in the focus group, every participant attested to witnessing the physical restraint of another mentally ill person by police (which was unanimously and ardently condemned). As a result, they often associate police with these highly stressful and adversarial encounters, which in turn contributes to their negative image of police and their intimidation at the sight of a uniformed officer. As one focus group participant stated, "Sick people get very disturbed when they see a uniform."

Leadership

Like any organization, the leadership of a CCP group represents one of the most important determinants of its success, including the extent to which it can mobilize the local population (Toumbourou, 1999). This axiom becomes apparent when examining the numerous anti-crime groups that formed in Mount Pleasant, many of which benefited from strong and dedicated leadership. As one long-time resident said during a 1997 interview, past crime prevention groups, such as Shame the Johns, were effective because of their determined leadership: "We benefited because we had strong leaders, people who were committed, bright, energetic, and could motivate people around the prostitution issue. They knew how to reach people and how to get them involved. That is why Shame the Johns and the other [anti-]prostitution groups before it were so successful. And that is why now there is such a void. Most of these people either left or just sit around and depend on [the coordinator of the Community Crime Prevention Office]."

Research for this study confirms this latter observation; a lightning rod for blame over the failure of the CPO, and its negligible levels of community support, was the leadership of the Mount Pleasant Safer Community Society. One of the earliest of the CPO coordinators stated candidly: "The board is quite apathetic, and those members who are competent and energetic have their own political agendas." This accusation was repeated by a Vancouver Police Department manager, who sat on the first elected board of the Safer Community Society: "It is not an activist board. It is not a particularly politically astute or politically active board ... It is not a lack of talent, but it is a lack of focus and direction." Personal interviews conducted in the summer of 2003 with Vancouver police officials, former and current Mount Pleasant community activists, and crime prevention organizers from other parts of the city, generated similar criticisms of the different board of directors that governed the society and the CPO. The executive director of a province-wide crime prevention organization laid much of the blame for the problems experienced by the CPO on the leadership of the last board, arguing that there were too many "narrow self-interests" among directors, who were working "too much as individuals" and not as a collective. She also cited poor relations between the directors and the various CPO coordinators, who had been cycled through the office, as well as a poor relationship with the Vancouver Police Department. She believed that "the board had no overall direction" because "each board member had their [sic] own priorities." The director of the Mount Pleasant Business Improvement Association partially blamed the failure of the CPO on its "inadequate leadership," stating that board members and some coordinators were "ill equipped," lacking crime prevention and community organizing skills. Each board member, as well as selective coordinators, had their own special interests and there was "no common guiding direction." The CPO lost sight of "why they were there," and had difficulty finding a "galvanizing issue" that is critical to mobilizing a community. She added that board members were not fully representative of the community and as a result only reached out to a small proportion of residents. The relationship between the CPO and the Vancouver Police Department became increasingly strained, and, after a while, responsibility and accountability to the community "went out the window." A former Vancouver Police Department liaison to the CPO accused one chairperson of being more concerned with "blowing his own horn," while other directors of the society were "more concerned with their own personal issues." Everyone on the board "was creating their own little kingdom," and they actively opposed and quickly fired coordinators who did not strictly adhere to their agenda.

The leadership weaknesses persisted throughout the eight years covered by this research, regardless of the composition of the board's personnel. While the original directors of the Safer Community Society were largely drawn from those active in the anti-prostitution battles of the early and mid-1990s, this board did not display the same level of activism of its precursor groups. As directors, few of them spearheaded crime prevention projects or undertook any community outreach. Most of their activism was confined to attendance at monthly board meetings that dealt primarily with administrative matters. The demise of the CPO was greatly hastened by the (in)actions of the final chairperson. During her short tenure, the society had its legal status revoked by the provincial government (due to its failure to file an annual report), the City of Vancouver rescinded a grant it had provided for crime prevention projects (because the CPO failed to implement required programs, had an insufficient number of volunteers, and was closed too frequently), and the Vancouver Police Department ceased all cooperation with the CPO and the board. In a 2 June 2002 memo to her superiors that precipitated the cessation of this formal association, the Vancouver Police liaison to Mount Pleasant recommended: "The police should dissolve the partnership with the office and restart. Mt P has a very bad name, and we run the risk at the AGM that a sneaky move will be pulled. Even with one or two of them, they can do damage. As long as it remains the safer society, no one will want to be involved. People from Mt P call Collingwood office daily to report concerns that they won't speak to our office about. At the front of our office, there is supposed to be a 'public book,' including the minutes and the treasurers reports, which anyone can access as it's a non-profit organization. Needless to say, we don't even have this report."

Financial Resources

Like most other organizations in the public, private, or NGO (non-governmental organization) sectors, CCP programs require adequate resources to prosper. The level of support for and participation in local crime prevention activities is also affected by the level of resources available to community groups. Throughout its life, the Mount Pleasant CPO was engulfed in one fiscal crisis after another, which directly and indirectly affected participation in its crime prevention programs. As mentioned, the lack of funding *indirectly* affected participation because CPO coordinators were constantly preoccupied with fundraising duties, which diverted them from community outreach as well as program development and implementation. The coordinator of the Collingwood CPO stated in a 1996 interview for this research: "About

75 per cent of my time is spent on fund raising, not on crime prevention." Meetings of a coalition of Vancouver crime prevention offices
that I attended during the original research period were dominated by
discussions about fund-raising. Funding shortages also *directly* weakened community outreach and communication efforts by the Mount
Pleasant CPO. There were few funds available to develop programs, to
solicit volunteers and program participants, to promote the office and
its programs, or to produce and translate promotional literature. The
lack of funding forced the original coordinator to reduce her hours to
part-time, further limiting her ability to conduct community outreach.

Organizational Success Stories

Despite the difficulty local groups encountered in their efforts to engage
the support and participation of Mount Pleasant residents in crime prevention, during the eight-year period covered by this research there
were instances where local organizers met with success in rallying
neighbourhood residents.[4] These examples include the following:

- A program entitled Operation Identification, which photographs
  and fingerprints children for easy identification by police should
  they go missing, was set up in the Kingsgate Mall in 1995 and
  attracted many families, including numerous immigrant families
  that spoke little English.
- An aggressive recruitment drive by the CPO in 1996 attracted
  approximately twenty-five new volunteers, many of whom were
  first-generation Canadians who had emigrated from such countries as China, Vietnam, Cambodia, Philippines, Guatemala,
  Turkey, Poland, and Romania.
- In 1997, a meeting was held to discuss the installation of a green
  belt on a Mount Pleasant street. This meeting, which was initiated
  by a small group of neighbours living on the affected streets, was
  attended by forty people, which should be considered an excellent
  turnout given the limited number of homes immediately affected
  by the proposed green belt.
- As part of the Crime Free Multi-Housing Program, meetings
  among residents were held in two apartment buildings in Mount
  Pleasant and both realized impressive turnouts. In one building,
  every household signed up for NW, and eighteen out of thirty-
  seven households turned up for the initial meeting. In the second

building, the managers estimated that approximately 75 per cent of the households showed up to the initial NW meeting.

- On an annual basis over a number of years, a group of Mount Pleasant residents planned and implemented a local beautification project called "Banners on Broadway." Individualized banners were designed, painted, and then attached to lamp standards along one the major thoroughfares cutting through the neighbourhood. Interviews and participant observation research revealed enthusiastic community involvement, including participation by the children and parents of low-income and immigrant families.

- In 2002, the Mount Pleasant CPO hired a new coordinator, who recruited a number of new volunteers, many of whom were from segments of the local population that typically did not become involved in local groups, including young adults, renters, first-generation immigrants, and members of visible minority communities.

- According to a senior official with the Mount Pleasant Neighbourhood House, they have never "had a problem attracting community support and local participation." Participant observation research for this study corroborated this claim; the Neighbourhood House has been very successful in attracting a broad base of volunteers who are local residents. Program participants and volunteer staff are made up of a large number of women, including single mothers and immigrants from visible minority groups. The Neighbourhood House has staff and volunteers that allow clients to be served in a number of different languages, and many of the paid staff members began as program participants or volunteers.

Crime prevention offices in other Vancouver communities have also enjoyed success in attracting and sustaining the support and participation of their constituents, including those neighbourhoods with demographic characteristics and crime problems similar to Mount Pleasant. A description and analysis of the success enjoyed by four such CPOs is provided below.

Successful Crime Prevention Organizing in Other Vancouver Communities

By the summer of 2003, ten crime prevention offices were in operation in Vancouver. This was less than half the total that existed at the pinnacle of the CPO's proliferation in 1997. While these remaining offices benefited from a formal partnership with the Vancouver Police Department (which resulted in a change of name from Community Crime Prevention Office to Community Policing Centre), these ten offices also survived, in part, because they have been successful in attracting and sustaining the support and participation of their constituencies. In terms of community support and local participation, some of the most successful Community Policing Centres (CPC) include those located in the communities of Collingwood-Renfrew, the West End, Strathcona, and South Vancouver.

Collingwood Community Policing Centre

As of the summer of 2003, the Collingwood CPC was serving the south-central and south-eastern portions of Vancouver, including much of Mount Pleasant East. The population falling within this jurisdiction is demographically diverse, while the average income of residents is slightly below that for the city as a whole. Founded in 1995, and originally called the Joyce Street Crime Prevention Office, the Collingwood CPC was the first community-based crime prevention facility to be opened in Vancouver. During an interview in the summer of 2003, the coordinator estimated the office had more than 100 active volunteers, the majority of which were either young people who wanted to be police officers or seniors (residents in the thirty to fifty age range are underrepresented, according to this coordinator, "because they do not have the time to volunteer"). Also represented among the volunteers are members of the Aboriginal and Asian communities. The success the Collingwood CPC has enjoyed in attracting volunteers and program participants is due to a number of reasons. It has more than ten years of activism with the community and a history of strong and stable leadership. The office was founded by a group of long-time community activists, and it has had the same coordinator since its founding. Board members, who are required to volunteer at the CPC, are also active in the neighbourhood. The office undertakes regular needs assessments of the local population and then responds to these needs through appropriate programs and activities. The CPC actively recruits volunteers, including those from outside the community (such as university students), and recognizes the contribution by volunteers and program participants (including awards). Acknowledging the challenges in mobilizing low-income and diverse communities, the coordinator preaches patience: the success this office has enjoyed in attracting volunteers and program participants in recent years is partially the result of its reputation, which "takes a while to be built up." Certain demographic groups, such as new immigrants and residents of social housing, have been more difficult to engage, and outreach to these groups require more time, labour, and patience compared to that required to enlist the more affluent, integrated members of the neighbourhood.

The coordinator cited the example of the local Vietnamese community, which "took over ten years to reach." One Vietnamese volunteer started donating items to the office "and then kept coming back." This volunteer ended up translating anti-marijuana grow-op pamphlets for the local Vietnamese population. Marginalized groups will become involved in CCP groups and activities, this coordinator insists, if their concerns, desires, and problems are addressed; organizers must ignore the demographic characteristics of individuals and "treat everyone the same regardless of race and socio-economic status." For this coordinator, the most critical variable in determining participation in CCP programs is "whether people care about their community." The key to working with and retaining volunteers in the CPC is "to keep them busy" and to provide them with tasks at their skill level, but which will also allow them to learn and build new skills. The Collingwood CPC is also successful because the office is "more than crime prevention ... we are also involved in skills development, job search, community development ... We often forget the human side. We need to help build human capacity." The CPC also benefits from a positive working relationship with the Vancouver Police Department (although not without the "occasional disagreement"), and has strong support – financial and otherwise – from the local business community. This includes rent-free space in a well-resourced, highly visible, and accessible storefront office donated by a local real estate developer.

Hastings North Community Policing Centre

This CPC serves the north-eastern portion of Vancouver, which is one of the poorest and most ethnically diverse parts of the city. The coordinator of this office estimates there are approximately sixty-five active volunteers, with seventy-five to eighty in total. As part of a survey of Hastings North CPC volunteers (Teixeira, 2003), one question asked respondents to rate their experience at the office since they began volunteering. Of the forty-one survey participants, thirty-two answered that they were "very satisfied," while eight responded that they were "somewhat satisfied." While this CPC does have volunteers from the Asian community, including one that provides translation services and another that volunteers on a weekly basis, the coordinator admits that Chinese volunteers are under-represented relative to their population size. He believes that most people serve as volunteers or participate in a specific crime prevention activity because of their attachment to the neighbourhood or concerns over specific crime problems (or both). Some of the volunteers first came into contact with the CPC by making a complaint or filing a crime report. In an interview, the CPC coordinator and a board member cited a number of reasons why they have been successful in attracting volunteers and program participants. These reasons included intensive outreach and communications ("not as much as we want, but we try ... lots of advertising and word of mouth'), strong partnerships with other local groups and agencies (including business groups, community groups, schools, and the police, all of which help promote the office), listening to different groups within the community and then "figuring out what they want and catering to those needs," an emphasis on positive messages in their communications ("instead of promoting fear of crime, our message is that you should get involved in the community to help your community"), and an active board of directors that is "very community-oriented," "very experienced in local affairs," and "very good at working with police." According to the coordinator, "a strong board is crucial" to the success of a CPC, as are the "personalities of the leaders" of crime prevention groups, which is "a big factor" in why some crime prevention offices fail and some succeed.

Another ingredient in the success of this CPC is its volunteer-centered approach: volunteers are provided tasks that are appropriate to their skills and needs ("our responsibility is to meet their needs; in some cases we meet out volunteers needs more than they meet our needs"). For both volunteers and the community as a whole, the philosophy of the CPC is to "focus on capacity-building," which involves nurturing an "accumulate skill-set in the community" by providing volunteers and CCP participants with "the skills to do much of the work." Volunteers are also encouraged to "come up with ideas on how to raise money, or about specific [crime prevention and community beatification] projects." This CPC places particular emphasis on community beautification and graffiti clean-up projects, because there is something "magical" about these projects that attracts people. As the coordinator put it, "There is a real beginning and an end ... There are tangible results and feelings of accomplishment among volunteers. You can see tangible results. People need to see tangible results for their efforts." Citizen patrols are also coordinated by the CPC, which makes sure these volunteers are given "something active to do while patrolling," such as conducting informal safety audits, identifying graffiti and vandalized property, and checking licence plates for stolen cars (volunteers are provided with micro-computer Palm Pilots that contain police information on stolen cars). "Again, this gives people a sense of accomplishment. They are active and not just walking around."

Davie Street Community Policing Centre

The community served by the Davie Street CPC is known as the West End. While the community is small spatially, it has one of Canada's highest population densities, most of whom are renters living in one of the many high-rise apartment buildings that dominate the local land-scape. The population is largely Caucasian and middle class, with small Asian and Hispanic communities and many young professional couples that work in the neighbouring downtown core. There is also a large gay and lesbian community in the West End. At the time of my visit in 2003, the CPC was located in a visible office on Davie Street, one of Vancouver's busiest pedestrian, shopping, and dining destinations, in office space donated by (and attached to) a retail outlet of a large drugstore chain. There is a wide diversity in the ages of the 108 people who volunteer at the office, according to the volunteer coordinator – from younger people who want to become police officers to seniors who have lived in or around the neighbourhood for decades. The volunteer base is reflective of the local population: most are renters and there are a few volunteers from visible minority groups, although, as the volunteer coordinator stated, "It is not that difficult to get volunteers from different ethnic groups," and Korean volunteers are over-represented relative to their local population size. The fact that this office has a position dedicated to volunteers speaks volumes about the importance placed on recruiting and accommodating the unpaid staff of the office as well as other program participants. For the volunteer coordinator, his main job is to "make sure the volunteers are made to feel appreciated and valued" (which includes an annual volunteer appreciation dinner where a Volunteer of the Year award is presented). The visible and convenient location of the office on a street with heavy pedestrian traffic, combined with its consistent office hours, contribute to the frequent use of the office by neighbourhood residents. This CPC also benefits from a history of activism around crime issues in the neighbourhood, including a pioneering community-based anti-prostitution group that began in the 1980s.

While much of the population is made up of renters, a demographic that traditionally does not lend itself to a strong sense of community, this is offset by a population that is racially and socio-economically homogeneous, and includes a large professional middle class and a cohesive gay and lesbian community. The volunteer coordinator also noted that the office has many volunteers from the gay and lesbian community, especially following the 17 November 2001 murder of West End resident Aaron Webster by four males, a crime police labelled as gay bashing. A public meeting held to discuss the murder, and the larger issue of hate-inspired violence against the gay and lesbian community, attracted more than 200 people (XTRAWest, 2003) and was a prime recruiting opportunity for the CPC. The volunteer coordinator stated that many gay and lesbian residents use this CPC because they believe they will be treated fairly and sympathetically by its civilian and police staff. The relationship between the CPC and members of the gay and lesbian community was also bolstered by the appointment of Canada's first transgendered police officer as the Vancouver Police Department liaison to this office. In general, participation rates in local crime prevention activities are high, although the volunteer coordinator lamented the lack of support for a park watch program (only one person volunteered). Community outreach is undertaken by the CPC on an ongoing basis and includes a monthly newsletter, advertising activities that focus on specific crime priorities, and exposure through the local media. Some campaigns target certain demographic groups, such as gays and lesbians or residents of multi-residential buildings, focusing on crime issues of particular concern to them. Through its outreach and crime prevention activities, the office has garnered a positive reputation in the community and the CPC has received support from other local groups and businesses (CPC posters were evident on the windows of a number of local businesses as I strolled down Davie Street before my visit to the CPC). The volunteer coordinator also spoke highly of the "very active" board of directors and a committed staff.

South Vancouver Community Policing Centre

The South Vancouver CPC serves the south central and south-eastern portions of Vancouver, which are historically working-class areas and today are largely made up of middle- and lower-middle-class residents. In addition to its traditional Caucasian population, South Vancouver has long been home to a large Indo-Canadian population (which is now made up of first, second, and third generations) as well as a large Asian population (primarily Chinese and Vietnamese, many of which are new immigrants). The CPC is located in a strip mall on a major thoroughfare and is highly visible, due in part to its large blue electric sign that simply reads "Community Policing." According to the CPC coordinator, the office has approximately 160 volunteers, including a "hard core" group of sixty to eighty people. The volunteer base is diverse and includes business people, students, homemakers, and retirees, many of which have been "volunteering at the office for a number of years." The volunteer base also includes "lots of immigrant families." Commitment and attachment to the local community is a key factor in influencing the decision to volunteer at the CPC, according to the coordinator, although people "also get involved because of a specific crime issue." The coordinator credits the "healthy, positive dynamics in this office" where "we have lots of fun" (this was confirmed by one Indo-Canadian volunteer who was making phone calls to local businesses during my visit and who described the CPC to me in glowing terms). Ongoing outreach and communications target existing crime prevention participants such as NW block captains, "to make them feel important and needed." As the coordinator put it, "These people are essential, so we must keep in constant contact." Emphasis is also placed on reaching out to visible minority and immigrant residents. To this end, the office is staffed with volunteers who speak the dominant languages of the neighbourhood, pamphlets are available in different languages, and workshops have also been held specifically for the local Vietnamese, Hispanic, and Indo-Canadian populations.

The South Vancouver CPC also reaches out to international students, the outreach and communications stressing a positive message ("we get in their face constantly ... but in a nice way"), which is "as personalized as possible" (including personal contact by the CPC coordinator or police officers). This personal contact is particularly important, because, in the experience of this CPC coordinator, many community members who use the services of or volunteer at the office hear about it through word of mouth. The volunteer base, including board members, is reflective of the demographic diversity of the neighbourhoods served by this CPC, which "helps with promoting the office among different racial and ethnic groups through word of mouth." The Coordinator estimated that in 2002, the CPC organized 132 events, including many beautification projects such as an annual garbage clean-up and a graffiti removal project that attracted more than 200 volunteers. This wide variety of situational crime prevention and community development programs helps to increase the visibility of the office, while appealing to different needs, interests, and priorities of community members. The CPC also provides incentives to encourage participation and such community beautification; for example, local businesses that keep their area clean are rewarded with cedar planters, plaques, or flower boxes. The coordinator also stressed that this CPC pays "close attention to our volunteers," making sure "their time spent at the office is meaningful" and assigning tasks and responsibilities that "bring benefits to volunteers," such as improving their work skills. The CPC has benefited from considerable stability among its leadership: both the coordinator and Vancouver Police Department liaison have been at the office for several years. The coordinator cited leadership as a key factor in attracting volunteers and program participants, and she stressed that CPC coordinators must be prepared to "invest a lot of time" in reaching out to and working with volunteers. Success in attracting volunteers and program participants is also the result of nurturing a strong working relationship with other local community groups, businesses, and the Vancouver Police Department.

The Five Oaks Neighborhood Improvement Association

Donnelly and Majka (1998) report on a case study that may very well represent one of the most successful community organizing efforts documented in the crime prevention literature. When crime problems began to intensify in Five Oaks, an inner-city, multi-racial neighbourhood in Dayton, Ohio, more than 400 residents attended a community meeting to address these problems. Donnelly and Majka attribute the high turnout to the efforts of the Five Oaks Neighborhood Improvement Association (FONIA), a multi-issue group that was well known and respected by local residents and city officials, and which had in place a ready communication network, a strong leadership cadre, and an existing membership base that was used to recruit other residents through existing social networks. As part of an intensive outreach and communications strategy, "dozens of volunteers 'walked 'n' talked' every block in the neighbourhood, knocking on almost 1,800 doors, explaining the purpose of the meeting, and inviting residents to attend." A neighborhood newsletter, which is hand-delivered on a monthly basis to all households, played up the meeting, and "a [reminder] postcard was mailed to every household ... This amounted to three contacts in the two weeks prior to the meeting" (198). FONIA also emphasized a decentralized approach to the community's role in addressing local crime problems. Organizers divided the neighbour-hood into numerous "mini-areas" and then selected captains for each, who used the same "walk 'n' talk" process to invite residents to attend a meeting in their mini-area. Relying on deliberative dialogue tech-niques, each mini-area meeting discussed a proposed action presented by an external consultant at a previous community-wide meeting, focusing on how it affected their area. Another community-wide meet-ing was eventually held, wherein issues and concerns discussed in each mini-area meeting were presented, with a view to arriving at a community-wide action plan. More than 300 residents attended.

While primarily concerned with safety issues, FONIA moved beyond the strict situational-based approach to crime prevention rec-ommended by the consultant, and instead adopted a more develop-ment-based philosophy that emerged from the mini-area meetings. Based on this resolution, committees of community members were established to deal with issues that were viewed as the causes of crime and other local problems, including those concerned with housing, the physical environment, residential support services, security, social and recreational programs, and organizational development. Despite the large turnout at the various community meetings, Donnelly and Majka (1998) note that the audience was still disproportionately made up of white homeowners. To ensure better diversity, FONIA amended its constitution to require greater representation from the diverse popula-tion on the board from each mini-area. In addition to effective commu-nity outreach and micro-level organizing, FONIA's success was also due to its long-standing external linkages. In particular, the neighbour-hood group was able to secure support and resources for its commu-nity safety initiatives from a sympathetic municipal government that had in place structures and resources that encourage citizen partici-pation. FONIA also benefited from the genuine commitment of local residents to a healthy, inclusive, and racially diverse neighbourhood (Donnelly and Majka, 1998).

Discussion and Analysis: Organizational Success Stories

These case studies provide some insight into the organizational factors required to successfully mobilize (disadvantaged) neighbourhoods around crime prevention. Each of the aforementioned cases benefited from competent leaders who reached out to a broad array of residents through ongoing, intensive, and, in some circumstances, specially tailored communications and programs, and through personal and multiple contact that appeals to both crime concerns and community attachment.

Outreach and Communications: Intensive, Varied, Personal, and Appropriate

One common element in all of the successful cases was effective outreach and communication by organizers. Communication with the target population was frequent, the mediums used were varied, personal contact was often stressed, and measures were taken to ensure that both the medium and the message were appropriate to the target population. In most of the successful attempts at organizing residents around crime problems in Mount Pleasant, the target population was personally contacted on multiple occasions using several mediums. Prior to a meeting of Mount Pleasant NW block captains, in which the turnout was particularly high, each captain received one letter and two telephone calls from the organizer of the meeting. The high turnout for the green belt meeting in Mount Pleasant was due in part to its exhaustive promotion by the principal organizer, who knocked on doors, distributed flyers, telephoned residents, and mailed advertisements. The overflowing attendance at two meetings held in apartment buildings as part of the Crime Free Multi-Housing Program was due in part to the effort of two charismatic police officers and the respective building managers who personally invited each resident. Successful outreach efforts also involved communication mediums and messages that were appropriate to the target population. "Appropriate communications" means that the message appeals to and addresses the concerns of the target population. Some examples include taking into account education and literacy levels, linguistic and cultural backgrounds, crime concerns, previous victimization, and the level of local integration and neighbourhood attachment. Those who successfully organize residents are familiar with the demographic makeup, concerns, and needs of the target population, and this allows them to develop an appropriate communications strategy. Taking into consideration cultural and language differences is one example of developing an appropriate communications strategy, as the coordinator of the Collingwood CPC stated: "We went into neighbourhoods marking property. The Chinese people would not even talk to us at the door. So we sent Chinese volunteers to talk to them and explain to them what we were doing. And they didn't have a problem with it. That is exactly how you do it. You try to match up your target clientele with your volunteers ... The first thing is that you must have volunteers that speak the language and know the culture of the different ethnic groups in the community."

It may be that language is of secondary importance in attracting first-generation residents if other essential organizing strategies are pursued. For example, certain crime prevention projects in Mount Pleasant were conducted exclusively in English, yet they experienced a high rate of participation by residents who barely spoke the language. This success was due, in part, to the presence of other vital organizing elements, including intensive and appropriate communications, micro-level organizing, strong leadership, and activities that appealed to family-centred, first-generation Asian parents.

Micro-level Organizing

Another common denominator in most of the successful mobilization efforts was a numerically small and spatially concentrated target population. Within Mount Pleasant, the Carolina Street Neighbourhood Group, the Crime Free Multi-Housing Program, and the green belt project all targeted a small, spatially concentrated group of residents. In contrast, an ambitious community-wide outreach effort that involved distributing more than 4,000 flyers throughout Mount Pleasant East met with a disappointing attendance at the promoted event. Concentrating on a limited and spatially confined area facilitates an intensive, personal, and ongoing outreach effort by a limited number of organizers that could not be realized with a larger population. It also allows organizers to appeal to the shared interests, space, and concerns of residents living on a particular street or in an apartment building, thereby promoting social cohesion among the targeted population. Research into local social movements also reveals the importance of organizing a spatial community at the block level. Small citizen groups, according to Fowler, McCalla, and Mangione (1979), are much more effective crime prevention vehicles than large neighbourhood-, city-, or region-wide organizations. Some researchers suggest that the traditional concept of "neighbourhood" has less meaning to residents than the "micro-neighbourhood" represented by a small group of houses, one or two blocks, or an apartment building (Gans, 1962; Lee, 1968; Marans, 1976; Perkins et al., 1990). Micro-level organizing also facilitates personal contact between residents and local organizers (Mulberg, 1976). According to Perkins and colleagues (1990: 90), there are several reasons why the block is an important organizational focus for CCP: its boundaries are less ambiguous to local inhabitants; residents are more likely to know one another; neighbours share common concerns that affect their neighbourhood; social interaction, social cohesion, and informal social control are more likely to flourish in a face-to-face setting; and the small settings allow for a more intensive recruitment effort by community organizers.

A Focus on Volunteers and Program Participants

As discussed, one of the most time-consuming and demanding responsibilities facing local organizers is attracting and working with volunteers. Each of the coordinators of the aforementioned CPCs attested to the considerable time they spend planning, coordinating, and supervising office volunteers and organizing local residents. Moreover, it is clear that each of these offices places the utmost emphasis on valuing their volunteers and even contributing to their personal development. The coordinators make sure the work provided to volunteers is at their physical and intellectual level, while helping to enhance their skills (especially for volunteers who were younger or have minimal education or work skills); they nurture a positive environment and express their appreciation for the work done by volunteers (including awards), and they encourage volunteers to recommend crime prevention or fund-raising activities and/or to provide their views concerning the operation of existing programs.

A Diverse Range of Community Programs and Services

With some exceptions, community groups that achieved success in attracting and sustaining the participation of local residents offered a wide variety of programs and services. Not only are situational crime prevention programs offered (which address the immediate crime concerns of residents), but each of the aforementioned CPCs implement popular community beautification and development activities (which cater to those with a strong sense of local attachment). At the very least, offering a diverse range of programs and activities maximizes community participation by appealing to a broader range of interests, concerns, and needs. In addition, these CPCs assess the interests, concerns, and needs of the local population, and then design programs to address them. A manager with the Mount Pleasant Neighbourhood House believes their success in attracting a broad base of volunteers and program participants is "because we serve everyone" in the community, including the provision of services that are in high demand such as daycare, legal aid, after-school programs, and employment preparation. In other words, not only are a broad range of services and programs offered, which can appeal to a diverse range of community members, but these programs and services address the day-to-day needs of community members, which is particularly important in disadvantaged neighbourhoods.

Networking and Inter-organizational Relationships

The successful CPCs also benefit from an ongoing relationship with other organizations, including community groups, businesses, and the Vancouver Police Department. These relationships are important for both program implementation and community outreach. Positive relationships with businesses can also result in much needed financial and in-kind donations.

Strong and Stable Leadership

Underpinning all of the aforementioned attributes of successful local organizing is enthusiastic, competent, experienced, and motivating leaders who are known and respected by community members. The importance of leadership becomes clear when juxtaposing the Mount Pleasant case study against its more successful counterparts, where the coordinators and board members stood out as effective organizers skilled in crime prevention, community organizing, working with volunteers, and collaborating with the police and other groups. As importantly, there is a level of stability within the leadership of these CPCs that was sorely absent in the case of the Mount Pleasant CPO, although the importance of leadership was also apparent in the examples drawn from Mount Pleasant. The lead organizers of the green belt project and Banners on Broadway both have a background in community activism, are well-liked and respected by other residents, and are known for their dedication to improving the neighbourhood. In the case of the green belt project held in Mount Pleasant, the principal organizer confined his outreach to a few blocks surrounding the proposed greenway; his communications were personalized, frequent, and varied; and he was familiar with the concerns of other residents. According to one participant who attended a meeting on the green belt project, "This meeting is a success because of [the organizer]. It was his efforts, and it is because people around here know him and like him for what he has done for the neighbourhood. That is why you see so many people out tonight." For Foster and Hope (1990), research into crime prevention within multi-residential buildings demonstrates that effective leadership is essential in organizing tenants. This was reflected in the implementation of the Crime Free Multi-Housing Programs in two Mount Pleasant apartment buildings. One reason accounting for the substantial turnout at the initial meetings was the buildings' resident managers, who in each case were respected and liked by the tenants. The building managers were also supported by two Vancouver Police Department patrol officers who had long worked with the manager and were well known and seen as credible by tenants. These successful programs stand in contrast to an attempt to start a NW program in another building in Mount Pleasant with similar demographic characteristics and crime concerns. While approximately 300 people lived in this latter building, only eight attended the initial NW meeting. Despite the involvement of the same police officers, the most visible difference may have been the building manager, who maintained a low profile, was not a particularly dynamic leader, nor did he display much enthusiasm or commitment to the crime prevention program being implemented in the building.

Conclusion

The evidence presented in this chapter strongly suggests that when identifying the various factors limiting participation in CCP groups and activities, crime prevention groups must often look inward. In the case of the Mount Pleasant Safer Community Society and the CPO, the primary self-imposed obstacles to a broad-based mobilization of residents were weak, inappropriate, and ineffectual community outreach and communication efforts, leadership voids and weaknesses, and inadequate resources. The funding problems, leadership voids at the board level, and the constant turnover of coordinators meant that the CPO was plagued by instability, which undermined the development and implementation of effective community outreach and crime prevention strategies. The result, according to one former coordinator, was that the office was "too preoccupied with its own survival and not focused on the needs and desires of [its] clients."

The list of organizational deficiencies documented in this chapter is not exhaustive, nor does it suggest that these problems are common throughout the universe of crime prevention groups. Using the Mount Pleasant case as a point of reference, it can be argued that organizational impediments to participation in CCP groups can be traced ultimately to the leadership of these groups. The evidence indicates that throughout its life, the Mount Pleasant CPO was saddled with inadequate leadership at the governance level, which permeated all aspects of its operations. The final years of the CPO read like a Shakespearean tragedy. It was saddled with a chairperson and board of directors that appeared to be ill-equipped to govern the office and which hastened its demise. These leadership woes also directly affected local participation: the internal environment of the CPO was so poisonous in the end that community residents expressly avoided the office. While these failings are certainly in the extreme, they draw attention to the importance of leadership in the effective operation of local crime prevention programs and how a breakdown in leadership can contribute to a lack of community support and participation. Of those board members who agreed to be interviewed for this research, there was some personal acceptance of the problems experienced by the CPO. But this self-professed culpability was accompanied by an apportioning of blame to what they saw as the true underlying causes of the lack of community support and the demise of the CPO – factors, they argued, that were beyond their control – in particular, a lack of sufficient (government) funding and an absence of support by the police, municipal and provincial governments, and community residents. The importance of leadership in CCP organizing and program implementation is further substantiated when examining examples of successful crime prevention organizing, drawn from Mount Pleasant and other communities in Vancouver.

Admittedly, the leadership woes afflicting the Safer Community Society and the CPO, especially during its final years, were extreme, and it is beyond the scope of this research to account for why other crime prevention offices in Vancouver also ceased to operate. That said, by 2000 it had become evident that the total complement of twenty-one CPOs in existence in Vancouver could not be sustained financially or politically, especially given their dependence on government funding. The death knell began to ring loudly with the 2001 election of a conservative provincial government that was strongly committed to cutting government spending. By the summer of 2003, only ten crime prevention offices had endured. Those that continue to operate and receive support from the City of Vancouver and the Vancouver Police Department appear to have the following attributes working in their favour: they maintain an active and vibrant community presence; implement a number of crime prevention and community development projects; are strongly supported by local residents, businesses, and police; and have a large and active volunteer base. (These factors are particularly applicable to the CPCs that existed in the largely middle-class neighbourhoods of Collingwood, the West End, South Vancouver, and Marpole/Oakridge.) Additional factors that appear to have played a role in determining which CPOs survived were the geographical or ethnic constituency served by the office. Those offices that served the high-risk downtown core and surrounding neighbourhoods (Granville Downtown South, Grandview-Woodland, Hastings Street North, the Downtown Eastside), and those that served large "ethnic" populations (the Chinatown CPC) or more vulnerable populations (the Native Liaison Policing Centre), appeared to have been favoured. While Mount Pleasant was certainly needy enough, the apparent lack of community support for the CPO and its leadership problems conspired to ensure that it would not receive the government and police support necessary to survive.

While it can be argued that the fate of the Mount Pleasant Safer Community Society and the CPO were in large part determined by its organizational problems, this conclusion is not intended to intimate a direct and exclusive causal relationship between organizational weaknesses and levels of participation that operate in a vacuum. Rather, as emphasized throughout this book, obstacles to a broad-based participation of neighbourhood residents in CCP programs are a mix of numerous factors and forces that are internal to a community (e.g., population characteristics, the leadership of CCP groups), but also external (such as government support and the prevailing political economy). No single factor can be held exclusively accountable for the problems that disadvantaged neighbourhoods encounter in mobilizing residents around crime prevention, although, as argued in the next chapter, the obstacles at the community and organizational levels can be linked to broader structural factors within advanced Western societies.

Despite the difficulties involved in disentangling the respective impact of the various factors that obstruct the mobilization of disadvantaged neighbourhoods around crime, the success stories presented in the latter half of this chapter may help address two questions posed at its beginning: (1) Can strong leadership and effective community outreach overcome those obstacles to participation that are rooted in the deleterious social environment of disadvantaged neighbourhoods? and (2) Are the failures of CCP groups and activities in disadvantaged neighbourhoods the product of theory failure or implementation failure? In regard to the first question, it can be inferred from the examples of successful crime prevention organizing that obstacles to participation that derive from the population characteristics of disadvantaged neighbourhoods can be overcome through strong and effective leadership. These organizational success stories corroborate Hope's (1995) contention that when comparing the participation of individuals from different socio-economic groups, the privileged will become involved in CCP on their own, given their stake in the community. The less privileged will also become involved, although a much more concerted effort must be made to attract them and sustain their participation. The juxtaposition of the Mount Pleasant CPO case study against the examples of the surviving CPCs appear to support the thesis that it is implementation failure, and not theory failure, that is most at fault for the "immobilization" of disadvantaged neighbourhoods around crime. In other words, the community mobilization theory (and implant hypothesis) can be applied to disadvantaged neighbourhoods and potentially result in local support and participation as long as these programs are accompanied by strong leadership, effective outreach and communication, appropriate crime prevention and community development strategies and activities, sufficient resources, and support by the state and police.

While the community mobilization theory may be safe (for now), an examination of both the weaknesses and successes of local crime prevention organizing in Vancouver suggests that CCP theory has paid too much attention to *outcomes* (e.g., prevention of crime and disorder problems), at the expense of *processes* (i.e., collective action, community organizing and outreach, leadership, etc.). The findings of this study suggest that when community groups focus their efforts on crime prevention outcomes, without a commensurate emphasis on the processes for involving residents in a community safety program, there is an increased risk of failing to effect a broad-based mobilization of residents. As detailed in part 3 (chapters 6 and 7), to be truly successful in organizing disadvantaged populations, crime prevention theory and practice must place greater emphasis on process.

5 Structural Obstacles to Collective Action Crime Prevention

Introduction

Tim Hope advises that when considering the factors that contribute to the effectiveness of Community Crime Prevention (CCP) programs, one must make the distinction between two dimensions along which these programs operate. The first is the "'horizontal' dimension of social relations that exist among individuals and groups who share a common residential space." The second is the "'vertical' dimension of social relations that connect local institutions to sources of power and resources in the wider civil society." Hope (1995: 23–4) believes the two are equally important in combating crime at the local level. Yet, while "the principal mechanisms for maintaining local order may be expressed primarily through the horizontal dimension, the *strength* of this expression, and hence its effectiveness in controlling crime, derives in large part from the vertical connections that local residents have with the power and resources" that are beyond neighbourhood boundaries.

The previous two chapters examined obstacles to participation in CCP programs as they are manifested horizontally; that is, within Mount Pleasant. This chapter focuses on the vertical dimensions of these impediments, obstacles that are beyond the boundaries of Mount Pleasant and which can be traced to broader structural forces. Drawing upon theories and hypotheses exploring the impact of modernity and the political economy on the control and prevention of crime (Skogan, 1990; O'Malley, 1992; Hope, 1995; Crawford, 1997, 1998; Garland, 1996; 2001; Taylor, 1999; Young, 2001; Pavlich, 2002), this chapter applies a critically oriented framework to the Mount Pleasant case study to investigate whether obstacles to participation in CCP in this neighbourhood can be linked to broad structural forces, and if so, how. While acknowledging the difficulties in empirically establishing a direct and causal relationship between macro-structural conditions and localized issues and phenomena, this chapter nonetheless makes the argument that the personal, community, and organizational obstacles identified in the previous two chapters can be linked to institutions and forces that are external to disadvantaged neighbourhoods such as Mount Pleasant. The structural obstacles to collective action in disadvantaged neighbourhoods are the product of various aspects of modernity, including a global, national, and local political economy that spatially concentrates poverty, crime, and community apathy, a culture of individualism, a positivist-inspired purposive rational approach to local problem solving, and the historical discontinuities and contradictions of the post-war (welfare and neo-liberal) state.

This chapter argues that modernity, and the post-war political economy in particular, has helped forge the preconditions for and spatially concentrates crime and criminality, while severely limiting the ability and the political will of the state and civil society to mount effective off-setting interventions. Politico-economic structures and forces at the global, national, and local levels contribute to crime by fuelling socio-economic disparities and concentrating poverty and other criminogenic preconditions with certain neighbourhoods and/or groups. Other characteristics of modernity, such as the formation of mass urban society and a pervasive culture of individualism, is said to contribute to the loss of social cohesion at the local level, which is so critical to collective action and community crime prevention. The rise of the welfare state in post-war period has meant that government institutions increasingly assumed an almost exclusive responsibility for ensuring public safety, thereby undermining traditional community-based approaches to crime and other social problems. While the mercurial rise of neo-liberal ideologies in the 1980s promulgated community crime prevention as part of a governance strategy that sought to dismantle the welfare state and promote individual responsibility and community self-reliance, governments of this ideological mindset also diminish the role of civil society in controlling crime through their reluctance to mitigate the effects of the politico-economic forces that help give rise to and spatially concentrate the prerequisites of crime, criminality, and community immobilization in certain neighbourhoods and communities.

The remainder of this chapter expands on these hypotheses by exploring how structural forces associated with modernity have served to undermine the necessary preconditions for collective action crime prevention, especially in disadvantaged neighbourhoods. As intimated above, it is exceptionally difficult, if not impossible, to empirically establish a causal relationship between modernist and political economic forces at the structural level, and the highly individualized and idiosyncratic reasons why the majority of Mount Pleasant residents do not participate in CCP groups and activities. Not only is there considerable debate and controversy over the existence of certain contemporary developments, such as the claim that late modern societies have become bereft of community or civic engagement. But the methods available for cross-sectional ethnographic research (or any research design for that matter) are ill-equipped to scientifically measure whether such structural developments and trends have taken place at the local level, let alone isolate the impact they have had on the dependent variable of CCP participation. The linkages drawn between the largely theorized structural forces and the research findings from the Mount Pleasant case study should be interpreted more as hypotheses than conclusions. With this said, there is considerable evidence the prevailing political economy of advanced Western societies has greatly contributed to a spatial segregation within urban centres based on socio-economic status (and, to a lesser extent, race and ethnicity), helping to create neighbourhoods where the conditions that promote poverty, marginalization, crime, and apathy are highly concentrated. As this and numerous other studies have documented, it is within these unfavourable environments that CCP programs are least likely to take root.

The Political Economy of Crime and Crime Prevention

Politico-economic impediments to the mobilization of neighbourhoods around crime are shaped by an incestuous combination of and relationship between market forces and political decisions that are external to, and beyond the control of, most neighbourhoods. The post-war political economy has helped forge the structural preconditions for spatial concentrations of crime, criminality, and community immobilization in most larger urban centres by fuelling socio-economic disparities and the spatial amalgamation of poverty and other social problems within certain neighbourhoods and/or groups. Census data and numerous other studies show that the wealth of most Western nations is held by a shrinking number of individual and corporate elites, the gap between the rich and the poor has been widening, urban centres have become segregated along socio-economic lines, and poverty has become ever more concentrated in certain neighbourhoods and communities.

U.S. Census figures indicate that income inequality between the rich and the poor has increased since 1968, with its sharpest rise beginning in the 1980s. Since 1968, an escalating share of total household income has been disproportionately concentrated among those in the highest-income quintile: 49.1 per cent in 1994 (up from 42.8 per cent in 1968). During the same period, the share of aggregate income for the middle 60 per cent dropped from 53.0 to 47.3 per cent; and for the bottom 20 per cent, from 4.2 per cent to 3.6 per cent. In other words, by 1994, the top 20 per cent of American income earners garnished almost half of the country's personal wealth, compared to the bottom 20 per cent of Americans who held less than 4 per cent of that wealth. Further, the average income of households in the top quintile grew from $73,754 in 1968 to $105,945 in 1994 (a 44 per cent increase). For the same period, the average income in the bottom quintile grew from $7,202 to $7,762 (an 8 per cent increase) (Weinberg, 1996: 1–2). In the United Kingdom, according to studies conducted for the Joseph Rowntree Foundation, average incomes grew by about 40 per cent between 1979 and 1995. For the richest tenth of the population, growth was between 60 and 68 per cent. For the poorest tenth, the growth was only 10 per cent (before housing costs) and falls to 8 per cent (after housing costs). "Even with recent falls, overall income inequality in the UK was greater in the mid-1990s than at any time since the late 1940s" (Hills, 1998). The Commission on Social Justice (1994: 28, 29) in the United Kingdom concluded that the "bottom half of the population, who received a third of our national income in 1979, now receive only a quarter" (as cited in Taylor, 1999: 15). The result of these developments for Great Britain, according to Jones-Finer and Nellis (1998: 38), is that "there has been an increasing polarization of income and wealth at the local level," producing a greater spatial segregation between the poorer and more affluent areas and a growth in concentrated poverty in urban areas. A Statistics Canada report released in April 2004 found that the income growth realized during much of the 1990s was also concentrated among the country's high-income earners. While the top 10 per cent of Canadians saw their income increase by between 5 and 10 per cent, the poorest 10 per cent of families in most cities saw their income fall during the 1990s (Statistics Canada, 2004a; Galloway, 2004). Statistics Canada also confirmed the ongoing processes of socio-economic segregation in most large Canadian cities; poverty has become more spatially concentrated while the income gap between richer and poorer neighbourhoods has increased. In Toronto, for instance, median family income in the poorest 10 per cent of the city's neighbourhoods amounted to $32,900 in 2000, up 2.6 per cent from 1980. In the richest 10 per cent of neighbourhoods, it was $92,800, an increase of 17.4 per cent. In 1980, 6.1 percent of neighbourhoods in twenty-seven metropolitan areas of Canada were designated as "low-income" (where more than 40 per cent of families make less than the Statistics Canada–designated low-income cut-off). This proportion fell to 5.5 per cent in 1990, doubled to 11.8 per cent in 1995, and then fell to 5.8 per cent by 2000. The Statistics Canada study also documented that many large urban centres have a single or multiple cluster of low-income neighbourhoods surrounding relatively affluent downtown cores (Statistics Canada, 2004a; Galloway, 2004). DeKeseredy et al. (2003: 7) report that in 1991, over one-third (1,364) of all Canadian census tracts with a population of 1,000 or more met the criteria required to qualify as a "distressed neighbourhood," which is one marked by a high poverty rate among individuals, a high proportion of total household income coming from government transfer payments, a low proportion of the fifteen- to twenty-four-year-old population attending school full time, a low percentage of the male population fifteen years and over with full-time employment, and a high percentage of single-parent families. Corroborating the growing gap between the rich and poor in advanced Western nations are the United Nations indexes of development and poverty. For example, while Canada is fourth on the United Nations" 2004 human development index (out of 177 countries), it is twelfth (out of seventeen countries) on the human poverty index for rich countries (United Nations Development Programme, 2004: 139, 147). The juxtaposition offers a sobering look at how wealth is spread. The most egalitarian of the seventeen developed countries are all in northern Europe. The least egalitarian are all English-speaking countries. In the United States, 17 per cent of all households have an income less than half the median after-tax income for the country. Australia, at 14.3 per cent, is second worst, and Canada, at 12.8 per cent, is third worst, only slightly worse than Italy, Britain, and Ireland (Little, 2004).

Hills (1998) cites several factors that have contributed to the growth in income inequality in the United Kingdom between the late 1970s and early 1990s, including increased wages for those with specific technological skills and qualifications; the declining importance of unions and minimum wage protection; a rise in the number of "workless" households, which was greater than the rise in overall official unemployment rates; an increase in the number of single-parent households; a polarization between families with no income provider and those with two-income earners; and the linking of government benefits to inflation, which meant those who receive government transfers on an ongoing basis automatically fell further behind the rest of the population when overall incomes rose. The contemporary trends in income inequality and the spatial concentration of poverty have ultimately been blamed on the process of economic globalization (White, 2000), which has resulted in the export of manufacturing jobs from developed countries to lower-income regions and countries, and an increase in minimum-wage jobs in the former. This has been accompanied by a "post-Fordist" environment that has transformed the sphere of production and consumption. For Jock Young (2001: 29), "this shift from Fordism to post-Fordism involves the unravelling of the world of work where the primary labour market of secure employment and 'safe' careers shrinks and the secondary labour market of short-term contracts, flexibility, and insecurity increases, as does the growth of an underclass of the structurally unemployed." The income gap and poverty rate has also increased as governments in advanced western societies have cut social welfare benefits to the poor (White, 2000). This neo-liberal ideology is symbolized by a single line in the ninety-three-page election platform for the Republican Party prepared for the 2004 American elections: "The taxation system should not be used to redistribute wealth or fund ever-increasing entitlement and social programs" (as cited in Toner and Kirkpatrick, 2004).

These trends and developments, according to Young (1999: 20), are propelling Western nations towards a "dystopia of exclusion," where "the poor are isolated in inner-city ghettos, in orbital estates, and in ghost towns where capital originally led them then left them stranded as it winged its way elsewhere, where labor was cheaper and expectations lower." In their analysis of income and poverty trends in the United Kingdom, Jones, Finer, and Nellis (1998: 38) write, "Generally, two aspects of the resulting 'new poverty' seem common: a widespread failure of entry into the primary labour market for low-skilled and otherwise disadvantaged youth – which has consequences for their present and future capacities to sustain independent living, family formation and public participation – and a spatialized concentration of poverty, characterized by the increasing likelihood for the poor to be living in close, residential proximity to those of a similar income level." This spatial concentration of poverty and accompanying "exclusionary society" has not gone unnoticed by some governments. The Social Exclusion Unit, which was established by the Labour government with a mandate to integrate disadvantaged and marginalized communities into the mainstream, had this to say about British society in a 1998 report: "Over the last generation, this has become a more divided country. While most areas have benefited from rising living standards, the poorest neighbourhoods have tended to become run-down, more prone to crime, and more cut off from the labour market. The national picture conceals pockets of intense deprivation where the problems of unemployment and crime are acute and hopelessly tangled up with poor health, housing and education. They have become no go areas for some and no exit zones for others" (Office of the Deputy Prime Minister, 1998: 4). In the foreword to the same report, Prime Minister Tony Blair alluded to the concentration of poverty within council estates: "Over the last two decades the gap between these 'worst estates' and the rest of the country has grown. It has left us with situation that no civilised society should tolerate ... It shames us as a nation, it wastes lives and we all have to pay the costs of dependency and social division" (2). For Pitts and Hope (1997: 37), "while the tendency for low-income groups to become economically marginalized may be a structural feature of the globalizing, post-Fordist economy, the degree to which they are allowed to become socially excluded is arguably a political decision."

The politico-economic forces that operate at the global and national levels ultimately reverberate at the local level. The deleterious environment of poor, high-crime neighbourhoods are heavily influenced by broader political, economic, and social forces, especially when these forces converge to concentrate poverty and further socio-economic inequalities, and promote social exclusion at the local and regional levels (Movenoff, Sampson, and Raudenbush, 2001). Skogan (1990: 173) believes that the global-national-local politico-economic nexus is essential to understanding both crime and crime prevention, "because many features of life in city neighbourhoods are shaped in important ways by essentially political decisions. These decisions are made by governments and large institutional actors such as banks, insurance and utility

companies, and real-estate developers. The causes of disorder problems as well as their solutions lie in part in what these powerful players
decide to do. Many neighbourhoods plagued by disorder have lost out
as a result of past politics." Hope (1995: 72) agrees, writing that the
operation of urban markets, primarily in housing and employment, is a
crucial context for both the causes of local crime problems and for community-based responses: "Changes in the dynamics of the urban market, in which individual communities are located, thus have a major
impact on their levels of crime and disorder, mediated by the employment and housing opportunities available to both current and prospective residents." Housing markets tend to differentiate people,
reinforcing social division through segregation according to class,
income, and race (Harvey, 1985), and this concentrates the poorest segment of the population and the social disorganization prerequisites for
crime and disorder, often in older, inner-city neighbourhoods. In short,
the "concentration of social dislocation in specific neighbourhoods is
itself merely a product of the distortions of the housing market intro-
duced by state involvement, which simply concentrates crime-prone
individuals together" (Pitts and Hope, 1997: 38).

Indeed, crime rate statistics, national victimization surveys, and
scores of other studies show that crime is unevenly distributed within
cities, with crime rates generally the highest in poor, inner-city neighbourhoods. According to the U.S. Office of Juvenile Justice and Delinquency Prevention (1996), most of the serious violent juvenile crime in
the United States is concentrated in a relative handful of neighbourhoods. The same neighbourhoods have homicide rates twenty times
higher than the national average (Sherman, Shaw, and Rogan, 1995).
For Lawrence Sherman (1997a: 35), the entire rationale for the federal
politics of crime prevention in America is largely "driven by the
extreme criminogenic conditions of these relatively few communities
in the U.S., areas of concentrated poverty where millions of whites and
an estimated one-third of all African-Americans reside." Pitts and
Hope (1997: 38, 40) write that in Great Britain, city-wide inequalities in
crime seem to be mirroring the spatial economic redistribution, with
patterns of crime reflecting "the emergent distribution of the new poverty in Britain." British Crime Survey data for fiscal year 2004/05
showed that one-third of all recorded crime took place in just forty
"High Crime Areas." Although the survey results showed the number
of recorded offences recorded in these high-crime areas fell by a greater
percentage than the rest of England and Wales between 2003/04 and

2004/05, the authors acknowledge that poverty at both the individual and neighbourhood levels still positively correlates with the rate of property crime. Households with an annual income of less than £5,000 were more likely to have experienced at least one burglary in the past year, compared with households with higher incomes and England and Wales as a whole, while neighbourhoods with a high level of "physical disorder" were also at a greater risk of property crime (Nicholas et al., 2005: 52–3).

In their study for Statistics Canada (2004c), entitled *Neighbourhood Characteristics and the Distribution of Crime in Winnipeg*, Fitzgerald and colleagues examined crime data at a neighbourhood level in this prairie city through a combination of statistical analyses and crime mapping. The findings indicate "that crime was not randomly distributed across the city in 2001, but rather was concentrated in the city centre and highly correlated to the distribution of socio-economic and land-use characteristics." Approximately 30 per cent of reported property crime occurred in 7 per cent of neighbourhoods, while 30 per cent of reported violent crime incidents occurred in 3 per cent of Winnipeg's neighbourhoods. The results of the study "point to significant differences in the characteristics of high- and low-crime neighbourhoods. For instance, high-crime neighbourhoods were characterized by reduced access to socio-economic resources, decreased residential stability, increased population density and land-use patterns that may increase opportunity" (Fitzgerald, Wisener, and Savoie, 2001: 22). This leads the authors to conclude, "After taking into account all other factors, the level of socio-economic disadvantage of the residential population in a neighbourhood was most strongly associated with the highest neighbourhood rates of both violent and property crime" (8).

In sum, concentrated in poor, inner-city neighbourhoods, such as Mount Pleasant East, are a multitude of adverse factors that simultaneously promote crime and criminogenic conditions: unemployment (especially among young males), poverty, a lack of jobs, instability, a transient population, weak local institutions, family breakdown, a lack of social cohesion and informal social control, the absence of a positive socializing environment and positive role models for children and youth, violence, an easily attainable drug supply, and a relatively large substance-abusing population. The problems that plague Mount Pleasant stem from a local environment that has been forged by economic transformations, much of which were external to the neighbourhood, that have transpired since the end of the Second World War. In her brief history of Mount Pleasant, Smith (1976: 92) succinctly captures how the neighbourhood fell victim to forces and developments that were beyond its control: "The story of Mount Pleasant has been a continual struggle for attention and self-control. Originally situated between a developing central business district and New Westminster, Mount Pleasant, instead of developing an autonomous community character, remained a neighbourhood caught between. The community became a transit centre, controlled by external big-business decisions."

Most important were changes that occurred in Vancouver's labour market over the last forty years. This predominantly working-class neighbourhood suffered from the combined processes of a deindustrialization of Vancouver's economy, the relocation of industry from the inner-city to the suburbs and beyond, the centralization of office space in the downtown core, and the gradual re-zoning of Mount Pleasant and surrounding lands, from industrial to residential. The result was the export of industries and low-skill jobs from Mount Pleasant (Randall, 1983). Combined with an influx of immigrants who took menial, low-paying jobs, many of the remaining unskilled workers were displaced from Mount Pleasant industries, contributing to a surplus of labour in the area. Unemployment, poverty, and the increased impoverishment of the neighbourhood, especially on the east side, ensued. As industry and jobs left Mount Pleasant, so did many of the middle-class families, who retreated to the suburbs. Absentee owners bought up residential properties at discount prices, subdivided homes, and offered cheap rent, attracting an even greater number of poor residents. The decline in the local formal economy of Mount Pleasant East was accompanied by an unyielding growth in an illicit economy that revolved around prostitution, illegal drugs, property crime, and the fencing of stolen goods. Drug trafficking and prostitution flourished out of apartments and houses rented by negligent and sometimes complicit property owners, while local informal social control dissipated due to a downward cycle fuelled by unemployment, poverty, prostitution, drugs, physical deterioration, and other crime and disorder problems.

The political economy that helps shape inner-city neighbourhoods and their crime problems also influences their capacity to collectively mobilize around such problems. The Mount Pleasant case study reflects other research that suggests community-based responses to crime are difficult to organize effectively in disadvantaged neighbourhoods due to a social and economic environment that undermines the preconditions necessary for a broad-based collective action (see chapter 1). As Donnelly and Majka (1998: 190) write, many inner-city neighborhoods where the problems of street crime and disorder are most prevalent, "have undergone significant changes including the loss of the industrial job base, population decline, shifts in ethnic composition, and increasing concentrations of poverty which have affected the ability of residents to address the myriad problems their communities face including the increase in crime and disorder." A comparative analysis of Vancouver communities shows that participation rates in collective crime prevention groups and activities positively correlate with the overall socio-economic status of the community. During an interview, one coordinator of the Mount Pleasant crime prevention office (CPO) cited an example of how upper-middle-class neighbourhoods in Vancouver, such as Kitsilano, have proven to be more fertile ground for mobilizing community members around crime prevention. In particular, she noted how the Kitsilano CPO coordinator spoke to a Rotary Club meeting and "walked out with 55 new Neighbourhood Watch [NW] captains." This was a recruiting achievement the coordinator had never enjoyed in Mount Pleasant: "Well it is not going to happen here. Like ever. I can't imagine, I can't envision a situation where I can walk into a room and come up with 55 Neighbourhood Watch captains. There are just not those kind of commitments." The greater success enjoyed by NW in more affluent parts of the city was corroborated by the NW coordinator for the Vancouver police: "I think there is more participation [in NW] in the West [the West Side of Vancouver] simply because it is a more stable community. They have lived there for years, they know their neighbours. They are not as transient. They have more sense of community."

Evidence that seemingly contradicts the supposed correlation between a neighbourhood's socio-economic status and the level of participation in CCP programs is provided by comparing the mobilization of Mount Pleasant East and the more affluent West End of Vancouver around their respective prostitution problems. The level of organization in both neighbourhoods were largely commensurate. Both had active anti-prostitution groups made up of local residents that targeted streetwalkers and their johns (the tactics used by the Mount Pleasant group were modelled on those used in the West End). Both neighbourhood groups also intensively lobbied police and government for greater enforcement. Thus, on the surface there is little evidence to suggest that politico-economic factors impacted significantly on the mobilization of these two different neighbourhoods in combating street prostitution. However, this inference is tempered by the finding (detailed in chapter 2) that the participants of the Mount Pleasant anti-prostitution groups had more in common demographically with residents of the West End than they did with most of the population of Mount Pleasant East.

Studies showing that people with moderate or high socio-economic status more frequently participate in collective crime prevention initiatives suggest to Skogan (1989) that "there is considerable evidence of a class bias in the opportunity structure created by the distribution of avenues for participation in collective efforts against crime." The class bias has led Rich (1980) to argue that a reliance on voluntary organizations to achieve public goals generally places poor, disorganized neighbourhoods at a severe disadvantage to middle- or upper-income neighbourhoods. The political economy of crime and crime prevention is such that the structural preconditions that help concentrate crime and disorder problems also deprive these same neighbourhoods of the economic and political resources necessary to combat these crime and disorder problems. This lack of internal resources and political influence prompted John Flint (2002: 253) to point out a basic weakness in community crime prevention theory. "Demands for communities to take responsibility for incidences of disorder is built on the premise that it is an inherent capacity of all communities to mobilize their own resources of social control." However, "the resources required to regulate social order are not evenly distributed across communities in cities and high crime areas suffer the most chronic lack of these resources." Adam Crawford (1998: 263) concurs: "Rendering communities responsible for their own safety, regardless of the context in which responsibility has to operate, fails to acknowledge the powerful dynamics created by the commodification of security or to address the relative distribution of social and economic disadvantage, including safety from crime. Communities, groups and individuals are not equally able to protect themselves against crime." Of paramount importance to Flint, Crawford, and others is the recognition that more affluent communities have greater access to political power, expertise, and resources compared with disadvantaged neighbourhoods. In their research examining the relationship between fear and participation in CCP programs, Lewis and Salem (1981: 414–15) found, "Neighborhoods with political power, for example, appeared more capable of addressing local problems than did those without it; and this capacity often appeared to contribute to diminishing fear ... The power to react

Table 5.1 Neighbourhood socio-economic status, crime rates, and 1997/98 CPO funding

	Downtown Eastside	Mount Pleasant	Renfrew-Collingwood	Kitsilano
Average household income (1996 census)	$17,200	$37,703	$44,559	$72,563
# of offences (Jan. to June 1997)	4,563	2,541	N/A	2,158
Population (1996 census)	16,275	23,695	41,780	36,580
Crime rate (Jan. to June 1997)	380.25	112.23	N/A	62.50
1997/98 CPO funding	$22,500	$25,000	$25,000	$22,500

Sources: Statistics Canada, 1997; Vancouver Police Department, 1997; City of Vancouver, 1997; Downtown Eastside Residents Association, 1997.

to community problems either was derived from well-established political connections or stemmed from the efforts of active community organizations." Simply put, "Collective efficacy does not exist in a vacuum. It is embedded in structural contexts and a wider political economy that stratifies places of residence by key social characteristics" (Sampson et al., 1997: 919).

This study found that while Vancouver is no different than most other North American cities in that certain neighbourhoods are more affluent, better resourced, and more politically connected, the assumption of a level playing field among different Vancouver neighbourhoods seemed to be inherent in some crime prevention polices adopted by the city government. In the summer of 1996, a public meeting was held between city staff and CPO coordinators to discuss the establishment of the government-financed Community Safety Fund. During the meeting, I asked city officials whether the allocation of funding would be based on need, taking into consideration factors such as the crime rates and socio-economic status of neighbourhoods. A City of Vancouver social planner responsible for the funding program replied that, in general, poor inner-city communities are given priority in social program funding by the city. However, when examining the 1997/98 fiscal year financing provided to CPOs from a joint municipal/provincial fund, there is little indication of such prioritizing. Table 5.1 provides data for four communities in Vancouver: two low-income, one medium-income, and one high-income. It shows that the two neighbourhoods of Vancouver with the lowest socio-economic status and the highest crime rates received roughly the same amount of crime prevention funding as those medium- and high-income neighbourhoods (which had lower crime rates).

The same city planner stated that the funding allocation decision also took into consideration such factors as how "established" the CPO was, the level of support it received from the community, and the amount of funding it received from other sources. Yet, the equal disbursement of funds across the different communities seems to have ignored the fact that some CPOs, like those in Renfrew-Collingwood, South Vancouver, and the West End, had office space donated to them by private sector firms, thereby eliminating one of the costliest monthly expenses. During the original research period, the Mount Pleasant CPO paid $1,230.50 a month in rent.[1] The city official cautioned that this was the first year of funding the CPOs through this joint provincial/municipal program and that different factors might be taken into consideration in the future. A review of funding provided to CPOs in subsequent years, however, reveals that crime rates or the socio-economic status of neighbourhoods continued to be ignored in funding decisions. In 2000, for example, grants to CPOs in middle-class neighbourhoods such as South Vancouver ($20,000), Renfrew-Collingwood ($21,800), and the West End ($19,000) were largely the same as the funds provided to poorer, more crime-ridden neighbourhoods, such as the Downtown Eastside ($20,000), Mount Pleasant ($21,800), or Strathcona ($19,000) (Lee and Lemcke, 2000). The city's decision to provide equal funding to CPOs located in neighbourhoods with different socio-economic standings ignores both the widely varying neighbourhood crime rates and the great disparity in indigenous resources and mobilization potential of different neighbourhoods that arise from the inter-neighbourhood socio-economic disparities. At the same time it propagates the incorrect assumption that levels of expertise, organization, and access to political power and economic resources are similar among different neighbourhoods. As one Mount Pleasant Safer Community Society board member put it, "Program funding is not based on need, it is based on the communities' capacity for grantsmanship." Communities like Kitsilano, with their lawyers and other professionals, have the expertise and resources to make better application for funding, regardless of their need. We don't have nearly this type of expertise in Mount Pleasant."

The differential access that neighbourhoods have to political resources and power in Vancouver is illustrated by a comparison of the anti-prostitution efforts in the West End and Mount Pleasant. During a personal interview, a past leader of the Mount Pleasant anti-prostitution movement argued that the neighbourhood inherited its prostitution problem because of the ability of the West End residents to place pressure on the municipal and provincial governments to evict prostitutes from their neighbourhood. "They [West End organizers, police, and city government] knew that they could never get rid of prostitution. So the next best thing was for them to move it into poor communities like the Downtown Eastside or Mount Pleasant." Critics of the government response to the prostitution problem in the two neighbourhoods cite the extraordinary legal strategy undertaken by the provincial government to rid the West End of its problem; what ultimately drove many of the street workers from the community was a warning from the provincial government that some fifty prostitutes would be compelled to leave by a civil injunction, enforceable by police, if they continued loitering in the area. The city and the province declined to embark on similar measures for Mount Pleasant. As one Mount Pleasant anti-prostitution group leader stated in a 1996 interview for this study: "When push came to shove, the city and the province really went to bat for the West End. Why? It is obvious, because that is where the votes are and where the money is ... One of the original organizers of [Shame the Johns, in the West End] eventually became a city councillor ... You are not going to see either government go to that extreme for Mount Pleasant." John Lowman (1992: 8, 9) notes that the provincial government's rationale for refusing to use the threat of civil injunctions against prostitutes in Mount Pleasant was because of an ongoing federal commission into prostitution.

The differing levels of internal resources and political connections, combined with the greater capacity for more affluent neighbourhoods to organize around crime problems, may also skew the allocation of existing public resources into those areas. According to Crawford (1998: 247), "This has been the experience of neighbourhood watch in the UK and USA, where schemes – more easily established and maintained in wealthier neighbourhoods – draw more heavily upon police resources, in order both to set them up and service the demands generated by them. Perversely, this acts to suck public resources towards those places which least need them and those people most capable of protecting themselves." The unequal capacity of neighbourhoods to mobilize around crime, based on their socio-economic status, may have the net effect of redistributing crime prevention programs and other related resources from those who are worse off to those who are better off (Schneider, 1987; Skogan, 1988). As Bennett, Fisher, and Lavrakas (1986: 3) note, "the tendency for residents of racially homogeneous and higher socio-economic status communities to participate more frequently could result in additional concentrations of resources and services in communities which do not have the most need for those resources or services." Middle- and upper-class neighbourhoods are better organized, and, according to Skogan (1990: 157), "it appears that the government and foundation funds that are available for community mobilization efforts are usually scooped up by a few aggressive and well-organized neighbourhoods, while most languish without support."[2] Washnis (1976: 3) argues that higher-income communities have also proven much more successful in demanding and receiving better police cooperation and protection: "In more stable areas where preservation of the neighbourhood is honoured, police usually take a deeper interest than in other areas, and they engage in intensive campaigns to get residents to secure their homes and act as the 'eyes and ears' for police." There is evidence suggesting that affluent neighbourhoods do not necessarily have to exert the effort to demand better police protection. They simply purchase crime prevention, policing, and security services. As one senior Vancouver Police Department official put it, "We have the downtown core where we have probably the densest population in the City of Vancouver with the least sense of community than anywhere in Vancouver because they are all vertical communities. However, we have the businesses down there realizing that unless the city streets are safe the businesses are affected and people won't come and live where they want them to take advantage of them. So what they have done is say, 'Hey, it's in our best interest to assist the community here.' And they supplied the offices and it is the police that have to drive any involvement."

The ability of more affluent neighbourhoods to purchase crime prevention and security services is not restricted to *public* policing. The same police official stated that as far as crime prevention and security are concerned, the empowerment of upper-income communities is directly related to their ability to purchase *private* policing services: "I think when you say that people in Shaughnessy[3] feel more empowered because of their financial or political ties, they feel more empowered because if they want more policing, then they hire it. And I am not talking about public police, but they hire private police to look after their things for them. If people in Mount Pleasant want more policing they have to lobby for it and try pressure tactics." The trend that has seen more affluent neighbourhood hide behind the protection of locked gates and private security contributes to what Anthony

Giddens (1998: 103) calls "two forms of exclusion." The first is "the exclusion of those at the bottom, cut off from the mainstream of opportunities society has to offer. At the top is voluntary exclusion, the 'revolt of the elites': a withdrawal from public institutions on the part of more affluent groups, who choose to live separately from the rest of the society. Privileged groups start to live in fortress communities, and pull out from public education and public health systems."

The Loss of Community and the Decline in Civic and Political Participation

Within crime prevention theory, the essential resource to be mobilized in the battle against crime is the sociological concept of "community." Traditional CCP theory is fundamentally reliant on the notion that neighbourhoods are or can become cohesive entities complete with a common identity, shared goals, and a high rate of social interaction and community attachment (Crank, 1994: 336–7; Young, 2001: 31). At the level of the individual resident, participation in local crime prevention programs appears to be contingent upon one's attachment and commitment to the neighbourhood in which one lives, while, at the neighbourhood level, collective action is said to be dependent upon a strong sense of social cohesion among the local population. The primacy of local social cohesion in CCP theory is not surprising. This quest for community has become a universal aspiration for many social theorists, practitioners, and policy makers dealing with the ills of modern society. As Wilson (1976: 65) observes, unlike such words as "state" or "government," community rarely seems to be cast in a disparaging light. The notion of a community-based approach to crime prevention speaks to the highest ideals of civic life and civil society, while evoking such appealing metaphors as democracy, neighbourliness, and small-town morality. The almost universal homage paid to the ideal of community is surpassed only by the frequency of the eulogies that lament its passing. For both critics and supporters of modernity, it has become fashionable to grieve the inexorable loss of community. Forrest and Kearns (2001: 2128) write that advanced western societies display "all the hallmarks of a loss of cohesion, including social disorder and conflict, disparate moral values, extreme social inequality, low levels of social interaction between and within communities and low levels of place attachment." The basis for these arguments dates to the late nineteenth century, when, during a time of unparalleled urban growth and industrialization, influential social theorists such as Ferdinand Tonnies, Emile Durkheim, and Georg Simmel wrote that as society became increasingly urban, industrialized, and specialized, relationships based on informal and personal interactions became strained and replaced by legalistic and impersonal relationships. While allowing for fuller development of the individual, modern urban society provides for weaker, more superficial ties between individuals, leading to social fragmentation and jeopardizing socially cohesion. As industrialization progressed and cities grew, there was great concern that the sense of community that allegedly abounded in pre-industrial society would disappear altogether. This proposition was sustained in the first half of the twentieth century by sociologists at the University of Chicago who believed that as the urban population increased in size, density, and heterogeneity, neighbourhood residents became less socially engaged with one another and thus less integrated in and attached to the local community (Wirth, 1938; Shaw and McKay, 1942). The result is that in modern society, "social ties are characterized as being weak, communal ties as being scarce," and community has "decayed, if not declined into oblivion" (Leighton, 1988: 353).

Lamentations over the loss of community in modern society have been accompanied by similar accusations that civic engagement has declined. For Robert Putnam (1995, 1996), there has been an associated deterioration in social cohesion, "associational activity," civic engagement, and political participation in the United States. He cites various pieces of evidence to support his thesis: the ever-declining voter turnout in U.S. elections beginning in the early 1970s; social surveys that he argues document a decline in the number of people who attend public meetings or political rallies, are members of local organizations, or volunteer for a political party; surveys that report a steady decline of feelings of trust and confidence in governments and politicians; and surveys which show that the proportion of Americans who socialize with their neighbours more than once a year has slowly declined. Based on this and other evidence he asserts that "by almost every measure, Americans' direct engagement in politics and government has fallen steadily and sharply over the last generation, despite the fact that average levels of education – the best individual-level predictor of political participation – have risen sharply throughout this period. Every year over the last decade or two, millions more have withdrawn from the affairs of their communities. Not coincidentally, Americans have also disengaged psychologically from politics and government over this era." Robert Bellah and colleagues (1991: 49–50) agree, observing that Americans have become increasingly disengaged from the political process due to widespread cynicism and outright distrust of government and politicians. Instead of trying to challenge and even fix dysfunctional and unrepresentative state institutions, Americans have fallen into a "palpable malaise" when it comes to public institutions.

In Canada, the ongoing reduction in voter turnout for federal elections has been cited as one indication of the decline in civic and political participation in this country. Elections Canada figures show that 60.9 per cent of eligible voters headed to the polls to vote in the 2004 federal election, down from the previous low of 61.2 per cent set in 2000. While a comparison of the elections in 2000 and 2004 reveals a 5.3 per cent increase in the number of votes cast (the first increase in more than ten years), the "apparent turnout has again declined" (Chief Electoral Officer of Canada, 2004: 84). The decline in voter turnout between the 2000 and 2004 elections is a continuation of a trend beginning in the 1990s when the turnout for federal elections was less than 70 per cent of eligible voters (for much of the century, the turnout of eligible voters has generally been above 75 per cent). According to information compiled on the Elections Canada web site, the turnout for the federal election on 28 June 2004 was lower than in any other federal election since the first one held in 1867.[4] The evidence is somewhat more ambiguous on whether Canadians' altruism and participation in community groups and civic affairs has declined. According to survey research by Statistics Canada (Hall et al., 1997; Hall, McKeown, and Roberts, 2001), voluntary activities by Canadians increased by 40 per cent from 1987 to 1997 (26.8 per cent of Canadians reported that they volunteered in 1987 compared to 31.4 per cent in 1997) but then decreased from 1997 to 2000 (27 per cent reported that they volunteered in 2000). Interestingly, the greatest decrease in the volunteer rate was among those with a university degree (from 48 per cent to 39 per cent). The report concludes that an increasing number of voluntary hours are being contributed by a declining number of Canadians (Hall, McKeown, and Roberts, 2001: 32). There was no change in the proportion of Canadians that were involved in "civic participation": 51 per cent of respondents reported that they belonged to at least one civic organization in 2000; the same percentage reported in 1997. Once again, however, a comparison of the two surveys revealed a decline in civic participation by those with a university degree (from 74 per cent to 67 per cent) and those reporting household incomes of $100,000 or more (from 73 per cent to 63 per cent) (Hall, McKeown, and Roberts, 2001: 49). Thus, a significant finding of these surveys is that the greatest decline in volunteering and organizational membership was among those with a higher socioeconomic status – demographic groups that generally are over-represented in volunteer and civic activities.

Putnam (1996) considers many possible "culprits" for the loss of civic and political engagement, including "busyness" and time pressure, economic hard times (or, according to alternative theories, material affluence), residential mobility, suburbanization, the movement of women into the paid labour force and the stresses of two-career families, disruption of marriage and family ties, changes in the structure of the American economy, the disillusion with public life that was brought on by Watergate and the Vietnam War, the counterculture revolt against authority in the 1960s, and the growth of the welfare state, as well as technological changes, in particular the introduction of television and the Internet. Many social critics have heaped the blame for the loss of community on a culture of individualism, which ultimately can be traced to the ideology of liberalism that originated with the writings of the British philosopher John Locke, who, as part of his opposition to authoritarianism, argued that the intelligence and reasoning abilities of people elevated the individual to a superior position over the collective and the state. Writers on the "Far Right," who view communalism and the welfare state as the principal instruments that repress the liberties, rights, self-determination, and the creative potential of the individual, propelled Locke's ideas of liberalism and anti-authoritarianism into a more pervasive ideology of individualism, whereby the rights and liberties of the individual supersede those of the collective (see Rand, 1943, 1957). For critics, however, the rising tide of individualism has fermented a culture that has loosened the sinews that bind civil society, while leading "to the preponderance of frivolous rights and the deterioration of the sense of social responsibility" (Horvath, 1998: 144).

The dependence of CCP theory upon the assumption of a communal citizen, or at the very least the inner potential of neighbourhood residents to conjure up sentiments of communalism, ignores how individualism, consumerism, materialism, and free market relations, all of which reached new heights with the neo-liberal reign of the 1980s, have replaced the communal citizen with the individualistic, self-fulfilling, self-interested, economic animal. According to Lewis et al.

(1988: 137–8), this assumption is the "fatal flaw" in the theory of community crime prevention. "They feed our desire for attachment and community, but offer a faulty program to bring us together. They fail to change the institutions which breed our individualism." By assuming the communal citizen, collective crime prevention theories fail to appreciate how individualism has shaped responses to the crime problem. George Kelling (1987: 92) contends that the impact of individualism means that the underlying concepts of community and informal social control proposed by Jane Jacobs in the early 1960s are no longer applicable: "Street life since the observations of Jacobs in the early 1960s has been characterized by an erosion of reciprocity. Streets have become stages for the drama of what Wilson (1983) has called 'the psychology of radical individualism and the philosophy of individual rights.' This era has emphasized individual liberty over communal security, privilege over responsibility, self-expression over restraint, and egalitarianism over meritocracy."

Wesley Skogan (1990: 18) states that America's "strong orientation toward individual rights rather than collective responsibilities" has limited the potential effectiveness of community crime prevention efforts because it suppresses the sense of "duty" that helps spur involvement in community safety initiatives. According to Young (2001: 34), in the face of this perceived loss of community, the challenge for community crime prevention is how to "maintain order amongst lightly engaged strangers." While CCP theorists and practitioners preach collective action, the rational, economic citizen views the risks of crime individualistically, which promotes individualized security precautions. Johnston (2001) cites British Crime Survey data, which shows that between 1992 and 2000 there was a marked increase in the percentage of households with security devices: households with burglar alarms rose from 13 per cent to 26 per cent; double deadlocks, from 61 per cent to 75 per cent; window locks requiring keys, from 52 per cent to 75 per cent; and light timers or sensors, from 22 per cent to 50 per cent.

Others reject the view that there is less social cohesion in modern society, arguing that every period of western civilization has been described by scholars and other pundits, haunted by reminiscences of a prior golden age, as the watershed when community was lost. Flint (2002: 250) points to the 1750 treatise, *Discourse on the Arts and Sciences,* by the French philosopher Jean-Jacques Rousseau, who decried the harmful effects of modern civilization and wrote despairingly that "We have no longer a citizen amongst us." The current claims of a decline in socially cohesive communities and civic engagement have also been refuted by other studies. According to Warren Freidman (1998), even the poorest segments of America's population continue to have a rich array of formal and informal associations. He cites the work of John Kretzman and John McKnight, who found a wealth of citizen associations in the poor, African American community of Grand Boulevard, Chicago. The 319 associations they identified included religious, social, cultural, neighbourhood improvement, senior, youth, advocacy, and political groups (1474). Using the same U.S. General Social Survey data that Putnam relied upon, Guest and Wierzbicki (1999: 109) confirm a general decline in neighbouring from the 1970s to the 1990s, but provide assurances that it is not particularly steep, and that neighbouring "continues to be an important activity for a sizeable segment of the population." Philippe Lyet (1998) views the volunteer situation in France as "dynamic," when measured by the enthusiastic participation of volunteers and growing numbers of volunteer-based organizations. In their study of women's civic groups in rural Australia, Coakes and Bishop (1998: 250) enthusiastically write, "The number of voluntary organisations within rural communities is staggering; towns with fewer than 5,000 people can have as many as 100 local community organisations." In two British studies, Lockwood (1999) and Hall (1999) found that there is only equivocal evidence for a decline in civic engagement in the United Kingdom (as cited in Egerton, 2002: 604). Arguments that civic engagement has declined are also forcefully contradicted by the proliferation of contemporary social movements in the past fifty years, including those organized around civil rights, women's equality, migrant workers, sexual preference, the environment, and peace, among other causes. The contention that local organizations are in decline also contradicts the proliferation of community crime prevention groups and activities since the early 1980s. Even Robert Putnam (1996) cites Neighbourhood Watch as a "notable exception to the general decline in social connectedness over the last quarter century," although he also accurately notes that most NW groups are not totally driven by communities, and instead have emerged from programs arduously promoted and sponsored by government agencies. Moreover, as documented in chapter 1, the NW program has not been without its own participatory problems, which include a generally low membership, difficulty in initiating NW programs in those neighbourhoods that most need them, and the challenge of sustaining the active participation of residents in NW programs that have been implemented.

This latter point provides an appropriate segue to juxtapose the contentions that Western societies have experienced a loss of social cohesion against the central dilemma faced by CCP: the inability of crime prevention programs to mobilize disadvantaged neighbourhoods. Notwithstanding the debate over whether there has been a decline in localized social cohesion in urban centres, there is a significant body of theory and research, summarized in chapter 1, demonstrating that nowhere is social cohesion, community attachment, and civic engagement more tenuous than in poor, heterogeneous neighbourhoods. This lack of social cohesion constitutes a major obstacle to mobilizing poor communities around CCP initiatives. Admittedly, it is difficult to substantiate whether there has been a historical loss of community in Mount Pleasant, let alone establish a linkage between this highly theorized trend and the lack of participation in CCP programs. However, there is evidence that individualistic crime prevention measures largely outstrip collective initiatives in the neighbourhood. In focus groups and interviews conducted in 1996, NW block captains living in Mount Pleasant consistently stated that in the previous five years, they have enhanced security in their home and also attest to an increase in "target hardening"[5] measures among residents living on their block. The most frequently mentioned forms of security were the installation of alarms, fortified locks and door frames, and window bars. Many of the block captains indicated that it was during this same five-year period that participation in their NW program was low and/or decreasing. A comment by one exasperated block captain succinctly represented the frustration expressed by focus group members: "It's like I am competing with alarms. I see people on my block installing alarms and ... putting up fences or whatever, and when I ask if they want to join NW they say no. I don't understand it." An observation of retail businesses in Mount Pleasant also reveal an extensive use of individualistic security measures, such as window bars, fortified-steel window and door shutters, closed-circuit video cameras, and security mirrors.

Long-time residents of Mount Pleasant interviewed for this study offered contradicting views on whether there had been a loss of social cohesion in the neighbourhood. Regardless, there was almost universal agreement among research participants that relative to many other parts of Vancouver, Mount Pleasant is a less cohesive neighbourhood. This research suggests that this lack of social cohesion stems primarily from the dominant characteristics of the neighbourhood, in particular a transient population, poverty, and demographic heterogeneity. One Mount Pleasant resident who has lived in the same house on the east side for more than twenty-five years was resolute in his belief that the neighbourhood has lost a sense of cohesiveness, which has stemmed from its highly transient population: "Things have just gotten worse – the crime – and you look around the neighbourhood: houses are run down and falling apart because the owners, who live on the west side, don't care. And the people who live there don't care because they are only renters. When I first moved here from Italy, everyone in the neighbourhood owned their own home and it was different. People knew each other and helped each other out."

This argument should also be placed in a historical context. For decades, the Mount Pleasant East landscape was characterized by owner-occupied, single-family dwellings. Since the 1970s, many of these homes were converted into multiple-occupant rental dwellings. As documented in chapter 3, those streets that are the most resistant to crime prevention organizing have a high proportion of renters, which impedes social interaction, local integration, and social cohesion. One senior police official who grew up in Mount Pleasant and eventually became responsible for supervising its policing put it as such: "I grew up in that area [Fraser and Broadway], and when I grew up [during the 1950s and early 1960s] there wasn't that big base of transient population; it was all single-family dwellings. And there was a very strong sense of community. What you've got there now ... is a transient population where research even shows that people who are apartment dwellers have difficulty in even identifying who their next door neighbour is because they never see each other. There is no open space where people can walk around and recognize each other." Another long-time Mount Pleasant resident, who also serves as an amateur historian for the neighbourhood, agrees with this observation but places the blame squarely on a culture of individualism that has undermined community and created barriers to local collective action: "People don't seem to want to get involved anymore. And it is because of the prevailing culture. We live in a culture which no longer places emphasis on community or even family, but it is on the individual. Just look at all the baby boomers who in the sixties were setting up local area councils in Mount Pleasant. Now all they care about is paying off their house and getting ready to retire."

Many have written that the sense of community has not been lost, it has just lost its mooring in the local neighbourhood. Social networks are now city-wide, national, and international in scope and increasingly virtual thanks to the advances in telecommunications and the Internet in particular. As Forrest and Kearns (2001: 2129) note, "it would seem that as a source of social identity, the neighbourhood is being progressively eroded by the emergence of a more fluid, individualised way of life" that is defined, in part, through social, cultural, and communicative connections that transcend the neighbourhood. For Pantoja and Perry (1998: 225), the spatially defined community has been weakened because "modern people come and go, meeting their needs in different institutions of the total society." The community functions of mutual support, social control, and socialization that were once met in the neighbourhood are now being satisfied elsewhere, through other institutions. What is significant about this trend, according to Jock Young, is the "way in which people through the various media can share experiences and identity despite the separation of physical distance." This is not to deny the importance of locality, as "people after all must live somewhere." But it does point to the "diminution" of the local community as a central medium for personal and collective identification, belonging, and interaction (Young, 2001: 35).

The displacement of neighbourhood-based identification, interaction, and cohesion by the "extra-spatial" community, however, has significant implications for community crime prevention. Most property crime and collective crime prevention programs are acted out in real time and space, in neighbourhoods and streets and homes and apartment buildings. These so-called extra-spatial communities contribute little to the neighbourhood-based collective action imperatives of community crime prevention. The observations that community has been transformed and "liberated" from the local area in the form of cohesive ethnic, racial, or cultural communities (Leighton, 1988) also does not bode well for the cohesiveness of heterogeneous neighbourhoods such as Mount Pleasant. A preferred identification with ethnic and racial communities over the neighbourhood-based community may be symptomatic of a larger obstacle to local social cohesion that has emerged as a major finding of this study: the formation of highly segregated, self-sufficient, and often mutually antagonistic "communities" that are self-defined primarily along demographic lines. According to Hancock and Matthews (2001: 111), "rather than seeing a movement towards the ideal of 'community' we appear to be witnessing the emergences of new groupings and forms of neo-tribalism centred around temporary forms of solidarity and political organisations."

Research in Mount Pleasant East indicates that this neo-tribalism is especially pronounced among the small homogeneous group of middle-class homeowners who dominate local crime prevention groups and who may obstruct participation in local collective crime prevention programs because they consciously or unconsciously exclude those who do not fit into their shared demographic identity.

In sum, it is beyond the scope of this study to take sides in the contentious debate over claims that there has been a historical loss of community in developed societies. Nor does the Mount Pleasant case study provide sufficient evidence to determine whether there has been a decrease in local social cohesion. While this debate is certainly pertinent to better understanding the obstacles that impede local collective action, what is most critical for this study is to determine (1) whether there is a causal relationship between social cohesion and the capacity of a neighbourhood to organized around crime prevention (the Mount Pleasant case study suggests this relationship does palpably exist), and (2) the extent to which there is a sufficient level of social cohesion in Mount Pleasant to provide a foundation for a neighbourhood-wide, broad-based mobilization of residents (the findings of this study argues there is not).

The Purposive Rationality of Community Crime Prevention

The epistemology underlying the theory and practice of CCP is "purposive rationality," a term coined by Jürgen Habermas (1973) to denote a system of meaning proposed by scientific rationalism, the origins of which can be traced to the emergence of the scientific method of inquiry around the seventeenth century. In forever changing how we view, understand, and manage the world and all its physical and social parts, the scientific method also fundamentally changed social problem solving by emphasizing empirical data gathering, testing and analysis, functional and technical reason, objectivity, rational planning, and instrumental action. By formulating its interventions based upon etiological theories of crime (Jacobs, 1961; Newman, 1972; Cohen and Felson, 1979; Brantingham and Brantingham, 1981; Wilson, and Kelling, 1982; Felson, 1987; Clarke and Cornish, 1985; Skogan, 1990; Farrington, 1994), and through a reliance on strategic planning models (Feins, 1983; Geason and Wilson, 1998; Plaster and Carter, 1993; Linden, 1996; Sherman et al., 1998), crime prevention theory and practice are predicated on the grounds of, and indeed assert their legitimacy through, scientific inquiry and knowledge. As a result, the field of crime prevention has not escaped the purposive rationality that has come to characterize efforts to control crime in advanced Western societies. The rationalization of crime control and the criminal justice system has led to a "New Managerialism" philosophy, characterized by an actuarial approach in which crime control policies are fashioned through objective, scientifically derived risk assessments (Bottoms, 1995). Crawford (1998: 248) cites the *Crime and Disorder Act* in the United Kingdom as being "infused with a managerialist philosophy" that is "output-fixated and driven by performance measurement." For Garland (2002: 17–18), crime control in late modernity is embedded with an "economic rationality," incorporating an analytical language of risks and rewards, efficiency, and cost-effectiveness.

The actuarial and risk management foundation of the opportunity reduction approach to crime prevention is built on the Rational Choice Theory of criminal acts, which proposes that offenders make rational choices in the course of their work (Clarke and Cornish, 1985). Through this theory, the traditional criminological characterization of the biographical offender has been replaced with a polar opposite, the abstract and universal "abiographical" criminal, the "rational choice" actor (O'Malley, 1992). This theory assumes that the rationally minded malefactor follows a logical process in the course of committing criminal acts: setting objectives, exploring alternatives, weighing the risks and potential costs of each option, and then committing an offence when the benefits outweigh the costs. In order to counter the rational offender, situational crime prevention also stresses rationality, and, because responsibility is placed in the hands of the citizenry, citizens are encouraged to adopt a mindset as rational and logical as that of the offender. This security-conscious, crime-preventing *"homo prudens"* is a "rational, self-interested individual, unfettered by any moral compass or super-ego controls – a consumer who is alert to criminal opportunities and responsive to situational inducements" (Garland, 2002: 23).

The crime prevention strategies undertaken by rational actors begin with the establishment of objectives (e.g., a reduction in crime and disorder), and are then followed by the development of technical solutions and instrumental propositions with which to achieve these objectives (e.g., surveillance, NW, environmental design, etc.). The theoretical propositions of community crime prevention, and the community mobilization model in particular, are epitomized by technical solutions that attempt to "engineer" community (Nelson, 1976: 34), while social cohesion, collective action, and informal social control are sold to the public on the basis of logic and efficiency (O'Malley, 1992: 255). An observation of opportunity reduction programs in Mount Pleasant, in particular NW, reveals an underlying purposive rationality. The NW program is applied to different Mount Pleasant streets with little modification of its original theoretical suppositions. Manuals and pamphlets circulated to NW members and prospective members begin by describing crime as occurring when a motivated offender and an undefended space or victim intersect. The prescriptive watch and report role of the citizenry then flows from this theoretical premise. In Vancouver, the technocratic crime prevention didactic has been displayed by police officers who train NW block captains or who attend NW meetings. Observations of meetings held with Mount Pleasant residents, for example, reveal that many police officers focus overwhelmingly on the technical aspects and instrumental strategies of NW, such as the surveillance function, calling 911, target-hardening, and property-marking.

The application of this purposive rational approach to crime prevention in Mount Pleasant may have repercussions for a broad-based mobilization of its residents. First, as documented in previous chapters, many residents of Mount Pleasant are more concerned with their day-to-day survival and many do not even have assets worth stealing, yet they are encouraged to become involved in crime prevention efforts for either instrumental or purposive reasons (e.g., protecting one's assets). Second, as Lewis et al. (1988: 124) suggest, collective action, social cohesion, and informal social control develop out of attachments that are *not* rational. Rather, they are *emotional* with origins in the tribal sentiments that predate modernity. In other words, an emphasis on technical solutions to social problems may contribute to the inability of collective crime prevention initiatives to take root in disadvantaged neighbourhoods because they may not have the capacity to invoke the necessary emotional response that is critical to participation in local collective action. This argument is supported by the evidence gathered through this study. Participation in CCP programs in Mount Pleasant is not exclusively determined by instrumental interests, such as concern over crime or victimization. Instead, a common trait that separates participants from non-participants is that the former are characterized by their emotional attachment to the neighbourhood. Yet, the crime prevention messages emanating from the

Mount Pleasant CPO or the police stress issues of crime and promote the adoption of technical and instrumental methods.

That said, police officers, CPO coordinators, block captains, and other crime prevention organizers in Mount Pleasant have emphasized the affective-emotional aspects of CCP initiatives to potential participants, stressing the need for increased communal responsibility, social interaction, and social cohesion, while appealing to residents' sense of local integration and attachment. However, while collective action, social interaction, and cohesion are communicated to Mount Pleasant residents, this message is often instilled with instrumental overtones (i.e., collective action as a means to prevent crime). The result is that social interaction, collective action, and community building are sold and redefined as efficient, instrumental tools to combat crime problems rather than pursued for their own merits (Crawford, 1994: 508).[6] According to Nelson (1976), attempts to artificially create social cohesion may actually undermine a sense of community because "help" and "care" have become institutionalized, impersonal, budgeted, and controlled to the point that people begin to feel like objects to be manipulated. Even if these emotional appeals to community are sincere, they may fall largely upon deaf ears in disadvantaged neighbourhoods where local social integration and community attachment among residents are limited to a few. Lewis et al. (1988: 124) claim that appeals to pre-modern sensibilities, like social interaction, integration, and local cohesion fail to resonate in an age (i.e., modernity) and in neighbourhoods (e.g., Mount Pleasant) where such sentiments no longer seem to be cherished. As documented in numerous studies, the ability of CCP to take root in neighbourhoods is very much contingent on the pre-existence of social cohesion, social interaction, community attachment, and the local integration of residents. However, these important prerequisites are largely absent in poor, mixed-status neighbourhoods like Mount Pleasant East. As such, messages that stress the solidary and communal incentives for participation in local crime prevention programs tend to appeal mainly to a small group of middle-class, locally integrated homeowners.

The State and Crime Prevention

Since the end of the Second World War, the nature and scope of the state's role in crime control in advanced Western societies can be divided into two halves. The first period persisted to around the early

1970s, when the state's jurisdiction over crime was unchallenged which, along with the overall expansion of the welfare state, fuelled the steep growth of the criminal justice system. The second period was characterized by an ever-expanding role of non-state actors in crime control, including the private sector, the voluntary sector, and community groups. The developments in this second period is an explicit reflection of the limitations of the state in controlling crime, the need for partnerships among all relevant sectors of society, and the importance of assuming a more proactive, preventative approach. David Garland asserts that the latter two elements are part of a broader "responsibilisation strategy" of governance in the post-war period, whereby the central government devolves responsibility for crime prevention on to non-state organizations and individuals, while persuading them to act appropriately. The intent is for the state to "act upon crime not in a direct fashion through state agencies (police, courts, prisons, social workers, etc.) but instead by acting indirectly, seeking to activate action on the part of non-state agencies and organisations" (Garland, 1996: 452). A devolution of responsibilities to individual citizens, families, neighbourhoods, communities, schools, and employers is a recognition that the state can no longer be the exclusive guarantor or provider of safety or security (McEvoy, Gormally, and Mika, 2002). Instead, it is a partner or facilitator that helps steer, guide, and regulate rather than row (Rose, 2000: 323–4). This decentralization is a reflection of the rise of a neo-liberal ideology in many advanced western societies that advocates a smaller role for the state in society, and, more pointedly, "the dismantling of the welfare state and its perceived perpetuation of a culture of dependency" (Crawford, 1997: 299). Community crime prevention coalesces perfectly with this neo-liberal ideology through their shared advocacy of individual responsibility and self-reliant communities. George Pavlich (2002: 104) believes these right-wing beliefs helped propel the ascendancy and currency of crime prevention because "the political logic underlying community crime prevention derives from an advanced neo-liberal discourse that has substantively eroded the previously dominant 'social welfare' governmental rationalities" and which instead valourizes the free market, individual initiative, moral self-responsibility, and community self-reliance as the most effective means to solving (local) social problems.

Despite this philosophy and the delegation of crime prevention responsibilities to civil society, it can be argued that the state undermined the capacity of the poorest, most crime-ridden neighbourhoods to take on these new responsibilities. The overwhelming responsibility the welfare state assumed over crime control for much of the twentieth century – whereby members of the public were viewed as passive recipients of law enforcement and broader criminal justice services – robbed local neighbourhoods of the capacity to mobilize around local crime problems due to their dependence on and subservience to the criminal justice system (Lofland, 1983; Shonholtz, 1987; Boostrom and Henderson, 1988; Garofalo and McLeod, 1989; Skogan, 1990; Garland, 1996). While the neo-liberal state advocated, encouraged, and funded a greater role for local communities in crime control – which began in earnest during the early 1980s, a period of great ascendancy for both crime prevention and neo-liberal governments – a number of contradictory governance priorities and processes came into play that further diluted the collective action capacity of (disadvantaged) neighbourhoods. In particular, the ongoing withdrawal of the neo-liberal state from progressive social welfare policies, combined with economic policies that hastened the spatial concentration of poverty and its concomitants within certain neighbourhoods, not only helped fuel crime problems in these locales, but undermined their capacity to mobilize around local social problems (Skogan, 1990; Hope, 1995; Donnelly and Majka, 1998). In their critique of the crime control policies of both the Conservative and New Labour governments in England, Zedner and Lacey (2000: 158) draw attention to the "successive governments whose policies have taken away power and resources from local communities" but have "encountered a particular need to appeal to the existence of 'community' in the face of increasingly unmanageable consequences of social policies that celebrate the individual and denigrate the social." The coherent triumvirate of right-wing crime control policies – tough sanctions for offenders, situational crime prevention, and zero tolerance policing – also ignores the underlying developmental needs of poor communities that are so essential to local organizing, empowerment, and problem solving. Instead, in their calls for community mobilization, neo-liberal governments favour a "communitarian" approach (Etzioni, 1993) that narrowly stresses the moral duty of individual citizens and communities to address local problems. What's more, this neo-liberal crime control triumvirate ostensibly targets property crimes typically committed by the poor, the underprivileged, and racial minorities, which, according to David Garland (1996), contribute to a criminology that serves to divide communities between the so-called "criminal class" and the law-abiding citizen. And, as argued throughout this book, this criminology hampers an inclusive, broad-based mobilization of mixed status and disadvantaged neighbourhoods because it can be exploited by crime prevention activists, participants, and criminal justice officials who cultivate community safety programs that exclude based on demographic characteristics.[7]

Moreover, while conservative governments promoted CCP as part of a philosophical doctrine that advocated a decreased role of the state and a greater emphasis on individual responsibility and community self-help, the state's criminal justice apparatus continued to expand. This expansion was fuelled largely by the growth of the corrections system, which, in turn, was the result of the incarceration of a greater number of offenders for a longer period of time, itself a direct offshoot of the punitive approach that is paramount in the neo-liberal crime control philosophy. For Crawford (1997), crime prevention would continue to be a poor cousin to an increasingly punitive crime control agenda that was focused on the detection, apprehension, and punishment of offenders. This get-tough approach to crime and offenders, which is symbolized by the so-called three-strikes laws that are in effect in many American states, has culminated in what David Garland (2001) calls the "penal-welfare state." In addition, while conservative governments espoused a smaller role for the state, and a greater role for communities, government agencies, such as the police, found it difficult to relinquish control over crime issues to communities (McPherson and Silloway, 1981; King, 1988; Marx, 1989; Walker and Walker, 1993; Garland, 1996; Pavlich, 2002).

In short, since the end of the Second World War, the overarching role and influence of the state in community crime prevention have been marked by philosophical discontinuities, policy contradictions, and a schizophrenia that has helped to undermine the ability of disadvantaged neighbourhoods to mobilize around crime. The remainder of this section will apply the aforementioned arguments to the Mount Pleasant case study, with particular emphasis on how the impact of the welfare state and the reluctance of state agencies to relinquish control over crime issues at the local level have undermined the capacity of the community to effectively mobilize around crime prevention.

The Criminal Justice System and the Welfare State

A defining characteristic of modernity is the interventionist role the state has assumed in society and the economy. The aftermath of two world wars, the Great Depression, and the advent of Keynesian fiscal policy, all propelled an unprecedented intervention of the state in the market economy and the broader welfare of society during the postwar years. While governments in most Western countries assumed the responsibility for ensuring public safety prior to the Second World War, in the past fifty years the growth and intractability of the state-run criminal justice apparatus has been explosive.

In historical terms, the state's monopoly over crime control is a relatively recent phenomenon, and stands in contrast to centuries of human civilization where responsibility for local safety was in the hands of the citizenry. Pre-civilized tribal villages, according to Tom O'Connor (2006), were thought to have "a rudimentary form of law enforcement (morals enforcement) derived from the power and authority of kinship systems, rule by elders, or perhaps some form of totemism or naturism. Under kin policing, the family of the offended individual was expected to assume responsibility for justice by capturing, branding, or mutilating the offender." Stansfield (1996: 190) notes, "During the agricultural era policing was a community responsibility." This meant that villages reproduced order through part-time volunteers who were recruited from within the community (Critchley, 1972). Beginning around the tenth century, English law required every commoner to be a member of a "tithing" – literally, ten people – which was generally organized on a village-by-village basis. Members of the tithing conducted patrols and were responsible for bringing to the court's attention any crimes committed by its members. The "tithingmen" had to respond to the "hue and cry, or call to arms, whenever someone needed to be apprehended" (O'Connor, 2006). The tithing also acted as a pledge for the behaviour of its members, guaranteeing that offenders within their immediate group and jurisdiction would be delivered to feudal lords for disposition. Each member of a tithing was bound to undertake a "frankpledge" – an oath "that they would not engage in illegal behaviour" (Alsford, 2005). This oath was a symbol of the informal social control that guided the conduct of members of English feudal villages. In 1285, King Edward I proclaimed the Statute of Winchester, which, among other things, codified into law the requirement that all villages in the kingdom adopt a system of surveillance and policing that relied primarily on the sort of citizen-based cooperative practices that had been emerging across England (Lab, 1997). This royal order formalized the "watch and ward" system, which required all able-bodied men to take turns guarding the gates and patrolling the town at night. For Shonholtz (1987: 46), community responsibility prior to the industrial revolution went beyond policing. Individuals and groups turned to community and religious institutions for the settlement of many types of conflict and the promotion of common social values. Thus, policing, crime prevention, and the broader notion of civic justice relied on social ties that existed naturally within the community and emanated from one's communal responsibilities. Crime prevention, community safety, and civic justice were understood to be a community undertaking, outside of and separate from the more narrow responsibility of the state's exercise of formal control, which in fact was not directed towards criminal acts that occurred between private citizens, but was meant to maintain obedience and loyalty to the monarchy, and, to a lesser extent, the church (Lab, 1997: 2).

As societies became more urbanized and complex, the state increasingly supplanted localized informal social control with formal methods of social control developed, imposed, and enforced by state institutions. Legislation, such as the Statute of Winchester, heralded the beginning of this slow, but steady, transition that led to the appointment of "Shire-reeves" and paid constables to carry out policing responsibilities and culminated in the creation of the London Metropolitan Police in 1829, which itself signalled the start of a new era where policing and community safety became the responsibility of the state and police agencies would serve as society's principal instrument of crime control. Throughout the next 150 years, the criminal justice system became more and more entrenched, while police agencies became increasingly reactive, centralized, preoccupied with the narrow responsibilities of law enforcement, and estranged from the communities they served. The sprawling urban city required the need for the patrolling police car, which physically (and symbolically) removed police from communities, and made the walking "beat cop" almost extinct. By the early 1970s, with the crime rate skyrocketing throughout North America, it became apparent that the formal criminal justice system could no longer exclusively control crime, and the pendulum swung back to a greater role of the public in addressing local crime and disorder problems. This led to the fundamental assumption of CCP that the state would relinquish part of its responsibilities for the *proactive prevention* of crime to the community.

Some have argued that the mercurial rise of the criminal justice system has wholly eclipsed and usurped the community-based system of informal social control that had been in place for centuries (Lofland,

1983; Shonholtz, 1987; Boostrom and Henderson, 1988; Garofalo and McLeod, 1989; Skogan, 1990; Garland, 1996), which may help to explain why CCP programs have failed to take root in many neighbourhoods. This hypothesis is part of a larger argument over how the interventionist role of the welfare state in the twentieth century undermined civil society, communal responsibility for local problems, and an active political discourse among citizens (what Habermas calls the "public sphere"). A strong and secure community derives from primordial relations that stress a politicized populace, which is defined, not through the relationship between the citizenry and the state, but by relations and discourse within the populace itself. However, the welfare state shifted political discourse from the realm of political society (i.e., between citizens) to a discourse between the citizenry and the state. In other words, the rise of the welfare state replaced the political community and civil society with an asymmetrical relationship between the state and an increasingly passive populace. A centralized approach to addressing public issues risks the creation of an apathetic and depoliticized population because of the subservience and dependence engendered in individuals and entire communities by a paternalistic, controlling state. The theorized result is that the community-based imperatives of crime prevention have fallen victim to a citizenry that has become highly dependent upon the state for its security. According to Skogan (1990: 171), citizens in modern societies became more dependent upon the state than they did on their neighbours for their well-being and security. As a result, they "rely on formal mechanisms for settling disputes, and on formal control institutions for protection – ways of making and imposing decisions that are backed by the coercive power of the state." Shonholtz (1987: 46) believes that the expectations and social norms that motivate people to undertake civic responsibilities have atrophied in the wake of continued professionalization of nearly all social services. "The result of this transition has been to take – or perhaps to steal – from citizens a broad range of social responsibilities and initiatives leaving many communities, citizens' groups and individuals feeling more alienated, isolated and dependent." For Boostrom and Henderson (1988: 58), the state occupies the central position in defining the nature and extent of public problems such as crime, and therefore exercises "ownership" of the problem and its solutions. Gilling (1997: 142–143) writes that even during the mid-1980s, when crime in many Western countries had reached its highest level since the 1960s, "private citizens were not necessarily any more inclined than before to see themselves as responsible for its prevention. Indeed, given the heavy emphasis on law and order policies, and the propaganda that is an inevitable part of the professional aspirations of criminal justice agencies, this 'dependency culture' was as not surprising as it was contradictory with crime prevention policy."

Research in Mount Pleasant suggests that the primacy of the state and the police in preventing crime and disorder is uncontested by much of the local population. The dependence of community residents upon police intervention is also evident in non-criminal matters, such as public nuisances or grievances between neighbours. One senior Vancouver Police Department officer interviewed for this study remarked that, through the philosophy of community policing, police agencies contributed to this culture of dependency. In his opinion, "selling" the concept of community policing to the public "more or less convinced people that the police could do so many more things than they thought possible. Our call load has just gone up astronomically and people came to rely on us more and more ... whereas before they tried to settle some of their own problems, they ignored some things that would naturally go away. We sold a bill of goods which placed an inordinate demand on our services to the point where what we had going was not working particularly well ... The public per se came to expect that the police could do it."

One result of this increased dependency on the police may be a questioning of the legitimacy of community-based approaches to crime and disorder problems as carried out by private citizens unless they are initiated, or at least supported, by the police. Based upon observations in Mount Pleasant, the presence of a police officer seemed almost mandatory to establish the legitimacy of a crime prevention activity in the eyes of residents invited to attend an event. I observed a number of people who, upon entering the community CPO, immediately asked for a police officer, and when they were told one was not present, quickly turned and exited without even broaching their concern with the volunteers working the front counter. Despite the presence of the civilian CPO coordinator at NW meetings, questions from residents were often not forthcoming until a police officer was present. One block captain, who was unsuccessful in her attempts to initiate a crime prevention program in her apartment building, stated in an interview that a significant impediment was the lack of police involvement in the fledgling program. She concluded that residents will not become involved in NW based solely on the cajoling of fellow community members, but will respond enthusiastically if there is some indication of police involvement. She pointed to a second meeting that was much better attended by residents in her apartment building compared to an initial meeting, "and the only difference was that the invitation to attend in the second attempt included a business card" of the local Vancouver Police Department crime prevention officer. "It goes back to the concept of authority," she remarked. "You can't change people's attitudes towards crime prevention if you don't have a sense of legitimate authority behind it."

An evaluation of the Neighbourhood Watch program in the Greater Vancouver suburb of Coquitlam came to the conclusion that successful implementation, among other factors, was closely linked to "whether the police enter an area and offer such a program" (Consultation Centre, 1987: 2). Daniel Gilling (1997: 144–5) attributes the remarkable rise of Neighbourhood Watch within this "culture of dependency" to the fact that it is administered and sanctioned by police agencies. Yet, despite the message that emphasizes the crucial role for local residents in this program, Gilling argues that police "still have not managed to convincingly penetrate the widespread expectation that the criminal justice system is primarily responsible for crime control" (162).

The increased reliance on the government to address social problems in disadvantaged neighbourhoods transcends crime. In Mount Pleasant, the role of the state in local social control is evident in the myriad of government services and agencies, which is one reason why Mount Pleasant continues to attract poor families or immigrants. Elementary schools in Mount Pleasant no longer simply educate children, but also provide food and nourishment, daycare services, adult education, and family counselling. During an interview, one police officer noted that parents in Mount Pleasant seem increasingly reliant on the police to assume duties once exclusively the domain of the family: "I don't know how many times I have been called to a house where the parents have lost total control of their kids. And then they expect us to supervise them or punish them. I'm sorry but I don't have time to be a babysitter. That is not my job. If parents around here were more responsible parents then we wouldn't have to deal with so many youth problems."

In their book, *The Community Justice Ideal*, Todd Clear and David Karp (1999: 38) write that informal social control may be irreparably diluted by the formal social control exercised by the state and its agents. When agents of the state become the key problem solvers, they might be filling a void in community. However, "once a function is being performed by one party it becomes unnecessary for another to take it on. It is plausible to think of the formal agent of the state as supporting the social control processes of community life, but it is perhaps just as accurate to think they take them over. Weak informal control systems are gradually replaced by the stronger formal social control processes: parents expect police or schools to control their children; neighbors expect police to prevent late night noise from people on their street; and citizens expect the courts to resolve disputes ... informal control systems may atrophy like dormant muscles, and citizens may come to see the formal system as existing to mediate all conflicts." One coordinator of the Mount Pleasant CPO provided a cogent summary of how the interventionist role of the state has undermined collective action in Mount Pleasant when she stated, "The problem is that years ago the government said that it would do everything and people just decided not to do anything for themselves."

State Control over Crime Prevention

In addition to *indirectly* undermining participation in crime prevention by eroding an engaged and active citizenry, the state may also *directly* undercut participation through its reluctance or inability to relinquish control over crime issues. While CCP theory emphasizes a subordinate or partnership role for the state in local crime prevention, studies in the United States and Britain indicate that most CCP programs are planned, funded, administered, and controlled by government agencies. According to Gary Marx (1989: 503), since the early 1970s, CCP models in the United States have been funded and guided by federal agencies, organized and implemented by police forces, and evaluated by government policy makers and academics. This led him to characterize most CCP programs as "top-down outside expert model[s]." King (1988) criticizes the centralizing tendencies within crime prevention initiatives in Great Britain where the Home Office maintains a direct control over funding and the broader policy agenda. Likewise, in his analysis of the Labour Party's crime prevention policies, Pavlich (2002: 120) says that communities are provided with a "dubious managerial 'freedom'" to choose from a list of crime prevention programs prioritized by the government, while the latter retains "control over important funding decisions" and monitors "the entire process through protocols, accountancy and evaluation." For David Garland (1996: 454), crime prevention is part of the neo-liberal strategy of "governance-at-a-distance," which simply represents another mode of exercising power. Under this new crime control model, the state does not diminish or become merely a nightwatchman. On the contrary, it retains all its traditional functions and takes on a new set of coordinating and activating roles, which "leaves the centralized state machine more powerful than before, with an extended capacity for action and influence." Indeed, the reluctance of the state, and police agencies in particular, to share control over crime prevention and policing may stem from the perception among police agencies that to give up absolute control over crime issues would be to compromise their power within society, not to mention a potential reduction in their resources. Police agencies have come under considerable criticism for failing to relinquish greater control over local crime issues and for failing to live up to the ideals of community policing, which emphasize a decentralization of decision-making power to communities (McPherson and Silloway, 1981; Marx, 1989; Garofalo and McLeod, 1989; Walker and Walker, 1993; Garland, 1996; Fielding, 2001; Miller, 2001; Pavlich, 2002). In their guidelines for citizen participation in community policing prepared for the Canadian government, Walker and Walker (1993: 18) put it quite simply: "A crucial question to ask regarding community policing programs is, how far the police are willing to go to share their authority with the citizen? At first glance, the answer would appear to be not very far at all."

The centralized control that the state and police agencies exercise over local crime prevention projects has also been cited as a factor limiting citizen participation. In their critique of the U.S. Federal Community Anti-Crime Program, McPherson and Silloway (1981: 153–155) contend that a top-down approach to crime prevention may hamper community participation because the legalistic "conceptualization of the crime problem and crime prevention program at the federal level serves to limit the range of problem alternatives that would be considered in local programs." Programs formulated by governments and police and then "sold" to community groups "may not be the ones the community would freely choose and as a result citizens may decide not to get involved." Lisa Miller (2001: 168) concludes that a low level of participation by African-American residents in a "Weed and Seed" crime prevention program in a Seattle neighbourhood may have stemmed from their perceptions that the lead organizers (mostly from federal and state government agencies) were out of step with their priorities and preferred strategies. The results of her study "highlighted the ways in which the original program reflected the priorities of national crime control agendas and local law enforcement goals more than a genuine interest in community revitalization and involvement." According to Garofalo and McLeod (1989: 337), NW does not appear to be effective in preventing crime, mobilizing residents, or building community because "most are not emergent, in the sense of being devised and initiated by residents on their own." The authors discovered in their survey of NW programs in the United States that the police usually play the lead role in organizing, educating, training, and motivating residents. "In short, Neighbourhood Watch is generally not something created by residents in an area to meet their self-defined needs; rather it is a set of predefined rules, procedures and structures that the residents can either adopt or reject. As such, one may argue that the extensiveness of police involvement in forming and managing Neighbourhood Watch programs is detrimental to the process of citizens developing their own solutions to their problems" (341). For Pepinsky (1989:461), a primary problem with NW is that it turns management of neighbourhood activity over to outsiders: the police. "It offers few opportunities for sustained interaction among residents. Those constrained to rely more heavily on having community matters handled by outsiders – here the police – can be expected to find themselves more isolated from other community members in the process." The strategic approach of NW has also been criticized as being impotent in arousing greater participation because an active involvement of the citizenry is discouraged through the inherently passive nature of their "observe and report" function. In training sessions of prospective NW captains and members conducted by the Vancouver Police Department, which I attended as part of this study, great emphasis was placed on the public's role as "the eyes and ears" of police, and prospective NW members were consistently cautioned by their police instructors against taking any direct action, other than calling 911. (During one NW training session, a Vancouver Police Department member also emphasized that the role of the CPO is simply to refer complaints to the police.) While safety is of paramount concern in discouraging direct intervention in a criminal act, this passive watch and report function may nonetheless dissuade a more active role of neighbourhood residents in designing and implementing crime prevention programs. According to Garofalo and McLeod (1989:

337), "potential NW participants are not really asked to exercise a great deal of additional social control; they are asked to be more active in initiating social control by the police. While these messages may help to entice adoption of NW by people who are wary of making time commitments, it is not the kind of message that stimulates people to devote a great deal of effort to the solution of neighbourhood problems." Moreover, while the police stress the use of the 911 emergency system by local citizens, this system has become overloaded, which delays police response time and can further erode citizen confidence and participation in NW.

Despite criticisms concerning the control exercised by police over NW and other crime prevention initiatives, shortly after the Mount Pleasant NW was founded, the Vancouver Police began to share responsibility for coordinating the local NW program with the CPO. The coordinator of the CPO was delegated responsibility to help residents with the implementation process, to organize meetings with and train block captains and members, and to arrange for a police presence at block meetings. Despite the shared responsibilities, however, NW remained the property of the Vancouver Police Department, which had exclusive jurisdiction over approving block captains and groups, and relieving block captains of their duties, if necessary. Thus, despite the shared responsibilities over NW in Mount Pleasant, the CPO had to adhere to the strict rules and regulations in the administration of the program that were set by the Vancouver Police Department. One attempt by a Mount Pleasant CPO coordinator to modify the program to adapt it to local apartment buildings was frustrated by police officials, who would not sanction any modifications. Moreover, by 2003 the implementation, coordination, and training functions of the NW program were once again centralized back in the Vancouver Police Department. In a 2003 interview, the NW coordinator for the Vancouver police stated that this centralization was necessary because there was a lack of consistency in how the CPOs administered the program, including the fact that some were actively involved in the NW program while others were not.

In general, the Vancouver Police Department had only a minor role in the genesis and proliferation of CPOs in Vancouver, most of which were truly community-initiated. Almost all were planned and founded by community groups, and enjoyed considerable discretion in developing and implementing programs. Each office was run by an independent non-profit society that raised money, solicited volunteers, and hired staff. Notwithstanding the support from the Vancouver Police Department, as well as start-up capital and program funding from the municipal and provincial governments, for much of their existence the CPOs were largely autonomous with regard to the Vancouver Police Department and the two levels of government. Despite the largely hands-off approach of the police and local government, however, funding from the municipal and provincial governments became critical to the survival of the CPOs.[8] This government funding has also been at the heart of an acrimonious debate that has centred around two main issues: (1) the quantity of funding provided to the CPOs, and (2) the extent to which the funding would have strings attached. While the former issue was at the fore of most discussions and disputes between the CPOs and the provincial and city governments, the latter was equally contentious due to concerns that government funding would allow them to exercise control over the CPOs. One particular episode provided some evidence of the potential control that the municipal government wielded over the CPOs through its funding power. In the summer of 1996, a report was prepared by the city manager recommending that the city provide *program* funding to CPOs, and not *core* funding for operating expenses, such as rent and the coordinator's salary, which was the preference of the CPOs' staff and directors. As one coordinator complained during a meeting with the city manager, an implication of program funding is that it allows the municipal government greater leverage over the terms of crime prevention activities implemented by the CPOs. This coordinator noted that program funding could potentially inhibit CPOs from undertaking political action that may be directed towards the local government, such as lobbying for or protesting against government programs or bylaws. In addition, CPO coordinators complained that the process that led to this City Council decision was highly exclusionary: the report was prepared with little input from the CPOs or their governing boards and it was distributed to the CPOs only ten days prior to its presentation to City Council for approval, leaving the coordinators with little time to prepare a response or consult with neighbourhood residents. In one meeting with the coordinators, the assistant city manager not only declined to reach a compromise with them on the substance of the report, but refused to defer its tabling before City Council, as requested by the coordinators. The report was approved by City Council on the recommendation of the assistant city manager despite the objection of the CPO coordinators.

While the municipal and provincial governments are instrumental in funding the CPOs, this research gathered no evidence that these governments interfered in or tried to influence the policies, programs, or day-to-day operations of the offices, although in later years government grants provided to some CPOs were conditional on certain criteria being met (Lee, 2000). Similarly, while the Vancouver Police Department worked closely with the CPOs, there was little evidence that they attempted to control the crime prevention agenda in Mount Pleasant or any other community (at least during the initial years of the CPOs). In their ongoing cooperation with the Mount Pleasant CPO, the Vancouver police provided the Safer Community Society and the coordinators great latitude in planning, implementing, and leading specific crime prevention programs. As the years passed, however, the relationship between the CPOs and the Vancouver Police Department became more formalized, with the police exerting increasingly more control and influence over the offices. Most significantly, in 2000, "Operating Agreements" between the CPOs and the Vancouver Police Department were put in place. As part of these agreements, police liaisons were officially assigned to each CPO and many of the offices became known as "Community Policing Centres" (complete with the Vancouver Police Department logo affixed to the front window or sign). The operating agreements also included the provision that "CPO activities must be sanctioned by the local Neighbourhood Patrol Officer" (as cited in Lee and Lemcke, 2000). In September 2000, a memo was sent to Vancouver City Council recommending "a strict assessment be in place before the development of a Community Policing Centre is initiated" (Lee and Lemeke, 2000). The need for this assessment was due to the perception that CPOs were proliferating at an unfettered pace.[9] Responsibility for conducting these assessments was vested in the Vancouver Police Department, thus giving police the power to determine whether a new crime prevention office could come into being.

The most overt attempt by the Vancouver Police Department to control neighbourhood crime prevention agendas crystallized in April 2003, when the chief constable presented a proposal entitled *Revised Community Policing Centre Model* to the Vancouver Police Board. This report recommended that the Vancouver Police Department manage and staff seven of the 10 remaining community policing centres with two officers and a coordinator employed by the Department. In addition, the report proposed that the elected directors of the community policing centres be replaced with community advisory groups that would be appointed by the chief (as cited in Lee and Goddard, 2003). A 23 June 2003 memo to the Standing Committee on City Services and Budgets from the chief of police and the director of the city's Social Planning Department acknowledged that this "proposed new model" differed "significantly from the existing model" (Lee and Goddard, 2003: n.p.). This memo did not hide the fact that this new model allowed the Vancouver Police Department to "influence the development and success of the CPCs" in part through the "integration of the community policing centres model into Vancouver Police Department operational and strategic planning" (Lee and Goddard, 2003: n. p.). In an interview conducted in 2003 with a local newspaper, Chief Jamie Graham said the rationale for the new model was due to "substantial dissension" about whether the community policing centres were effective in their current structure. As well, he said, whenever there was some kind of difficulty at a community policing centre, it was never clear who was in charge. He promised that under this new system the community policing offices would be provided with more stable policing financing and therefore would not be subject to the whim of fundraising (Bula, 2003). The June 2003 memo also acknowledged that "the community feedback received at two public meetings clearly indicated community concerns with this proposal," which "dealt for the most part with the need to clearly recognize a community role in any new model" (Lee and Goddard, 2003).

These concerns were also reported in a newspaper article, which noted that the plan to "dramatically change" the current community-based control and governance of the community policing centres had

> sparked anger, dismay and, in some cases, outright refusal to turn over assets and operations to the police department as proposed. "It seems as though what you're really doing is asking city council to establish police sub-stations," said Eileen Mosca of the Grandview-Woodlands community policing office. "We do not believe the community will be a true partner. And we do not believe that turning over our furnishings and assets to the Vancouver Police Department, firing the two people from our neighbourhood who work at the office, and dissolving our board would serve our community." She said her board has decided that, even though its office was one of those selected under the new police plan to keep its operations, albeit under the management of the department, it will continue to operate on its own and will not hand over its operations to the police. South Vancouver representative Gabriel Yong and Collingwood's

Chris Taulu said the same, while Elaine Barbour of Hastings North said her board will take the same position if police do not accept its suggestion that the report be taken back and revised. "Our community donates $37,000 in money and time," she said. "Our partners have said they will not contribute to the new model." While a few offices welcomed the plan, saying it would help provide citizens with more services, many more questioned the effectiveness, cost and motives of the police proposal. Critics also said it destroys any sense of a real partnership between the community and police. (Bula, 2003)

In the face of this defiant opposition, Chief Graham retreated from his proposal. Emphasizing that the plan to replace the CPOs' elected directors with Vancouver Police Department-picked advisors would undermine each community's ability to shape policing priorities in their areas, Jim Deva, vice-president of the Davie Street CPO, was quoted in the media as saying. "I don't want to advise ... I want to work as a partner to solve problems. I don't think its community policing without an elected board" (*XTRAWest*, 2003).

Conclusion

The Mount Pleasant case study provides some tentative empirical evidence supporting the hypothesis that obstacles to a broad-based mobilization of disadvantaged neighbourhoods around crime can be causally linked to structural conditions. Of most significance are the politico-economic forces that create within neighbourhoods, like Mount Pleasant, the ecological preconditions for crime, criminality, and disorder, while undermining a collective efficacy necessary to deal with these and other local social problems. As Lawrence Sherman (1997a: 35–6) puts it, the principal reason CCP programs have failed in disadvantaged neighbourhoods is that "such programs are too weak to make a difference in the underlying structural conditions." He adds:

The causes, or at least the risk factors correlated with serious crime, are basic and interconnected, while the [crime prevention] programs are superficial and piecemeal ... Community prevention programs address none of these causes of community composition and structure, which in turn influence community culture and the availability of criminogenic substances like guns and drugs ... Ironically, a central tenet of community prevention programs has been the empowerment of local community leaders to design and implement their own crime prevention strategies. This philosophy may amount to throwing people overboard and then letting them design their own life preserver. The scientific literature shows that the policies and market forces causing criminogenic community structures and cultures are beyond the control of neighbourhood residents, and that "empowerment" does not include the power to change those policies. (Sherman, 1997b: 58–9)

Hope (1995: 24) agrees, writing: "The paradox of community crime prevention thus stems from the problem of trying to build community institutions that control crime in the face of their powerlessness to withstand the pressures toward crime in the community, whose source, or the forces that sustain them, derive from the wider social structure." The structural barriers to local collective action in disadvantaged neighbourhoods find expression through the demographic, sociopsychological, and organizational obstacles discussed in the previous two chapters. Obstacles at the neighbourhood level, such as poverty, transience, instability and a lack of social cohesion, collective efficacy, and informal social control, are at least partially the product of politico-economic forces that create and perpetuate impoverished, high-crime neighbourhoods. These same structural forces help ferment organizational obstacles by limiting the indigenous resources of poor neighbourhoods necessary for successful community organizing. Traditional CCP theory and practice ignore these structural forces, and, instead, are preoccupied with the technical fine-tuning of collective opportunity reduction strategies that appeal largely to the needs and values of the middle class.

In highlighting the inability of local crime prevention programs to invoke a broad-based mobilization of disadvantaged neighbourhoods, this study critiques the application and applicability of traditional CCP theory to these environments. However, this critique does not automatically lead to the unequivocal rejection of the community mobilization or implant hypothesis for disadvantaged neighbourhoods, especially in light of the successful crime prevention organizing case studies presented in chapter 4. This brings us to the question of whether the difficulties encountered by CCP programs in mobilizing poor neighbourhoods should be attributed to the voids and weaknesses of its theoretical underpinnings or to program implementation failures. Reflecting on the myriad of impediments to collective mobilization documented in this and other studies, one should dismiss any attempt to wholly or unilaterally blame the immobilization of disadvantaged neighbourhoods on either CCP theory or program implementation failure. The sheer variety of, and interrelation between, factors at various levels that serve to obstruct the mobilization of disadvantaged neighbourhoods around CCP ensures that no single variable, concept, or theory can be held exclusively responsible. Taken together, the past three chapters have emphasized that the determinants of participation and non-participation are not simple, unilateral, or mutually exclusive; they are the product of a complex interaction of many factors at the personal, community, organizational, and structural levels.

That said, some program implementation failures can be traced, in part, to theory failure, and, more specifically, the inapplicability of traditional CCP theory and approaches to disadvantaged neighbourhoods. There are two basic theoretical deficiencies in relation to the essential community mobilization prerequisites of CCP. The first is that CCP theory has paid little attention to its collective action processes – it has overwhelmingly emphasized *outcomes* (e.g., crime reduction) while ignoring or at least downplaying the essential *processes* (i.e., empowering and mobilizing poor neighbourhoods) needed to achieve these outcomes. This is both a fatal and a bewildering void given the vital importance that collective action and community organizing assume in CCP theory, and the community mobilization hypothesis in particular. A second deficiency of traditional CCP theory is the incorrect assumption that society is pluralistic and that all communities have similar characteristics, problems, needs, and access to political power and economic resources. In its suppositions regarding the indigenous capacity for neighbourhoods to mobilize around and solve crime problems, traditional CCP theory neglects to factor in the disparities that exist between advantaged and disadvantaged communities. Poverty, crime, and the social prerequisites for local collective action are unevenly distributed throughout societies and within cities. The concentration of poverty and related social problems in certain neighbourhoods has nurtured a spatial and interpersonal inequality of crime and victimization, while negatively influencing the ability of these neighbourhoods to collectively address these problems.

Yet, CCP theory is implicitly premised upon a pluralist view of the world that sees power and the distribution of public and private resources as the product of competition between relatively symmetrical groups. In both crime causation and crime prevention, traditional theories of CCP do not take into account the unequal access that different neighbourhoods have to political power or economic resources. By failing to critically examine the role of power in society, traditional CCP theory and strategies overlook the fact that social roles and entire communities are formed, defined, and circumscribed by relationships of (politico-economic) power. By presuming an existing social consensus within a pluralist society, traditional CCP theory remains severely bound by the apparent belief that the strategies and goals of community crime prevention are universally shared. In stressing consensual relations, and by ignoring the asymmetrical power relations between different communities and between socio-economic classes within mixed status neighbourhoods, the idea of a universally applicable approach to crime prevention that is implicit in traditional CCP theory ignores both inter- and intra-community conflicts. This is a significant oversight because, not only do these conflicts tend to favour more affluent populations and neighbourhoods, but the real and perceived intra-community conflicts that take place between different demographic (and more specifically socio-economic) groups within heterogeneous disadvantaged neighbourhoods are a significant obstacle to social cohesion and an inclusive, broad-based mobilization.

The opportunity reduction approach that dominates CCP theory and practice also fails to promote a broad-based mobilization of disadvantaged neighbourhoods because it is explicitly geared towards stable, ethnically homogeneous middle- and upper-income populations and neighbourhoods. This broad situational approach ignores the root causes of crime and the basic developmental needs of marginalized individuals, groups, and entire neighbourhoods while overlooking structural forces that concentrate crime, criminogenic factors, community lethargy, and other social problems in certain neighbourhoods. What's more, the technical, utilitarian, and actuarial praxis of situational crime prevention has drawn away from any moral analysis that focuses on the social causes of crime. "Pragmatism and efficiency" have replaced normative or moral purposes, and, consequently, there is only limited space in CCP theory for principles of civil rights, social justice, or democracy (Crawford, 1994: 513). Opportunity reduction models view crime not as a social, political, or even a moral problem, but as a technical problem that can be resolved through technical methods. According to Matthews and Pitts (2001: 6), a major attribute of the "new managerialist" approach to crime control is its capacity to turn "political and moral decisions into administrative and technical ones." For Pat O'Malley (1996: 190), crime has increasingly been understood, not as a matter of personal and social pathologies in need of correction, but as a set of risks that are predictable and manageable. This risk management approach is tied to a neo-liberal ideology that ignores the links between "crime, social deprivation, and social justice" (O'Malley, 1996: 197–8). Opportunity reduction approaches to crime prevention emphasized in the risk society (Beck, 1992) are unconcerned with the "attainment of 'good' normative ends such as justice, equality or equity," and instead are preoccupied with simply protecting people from "the ubiquitous hazards of daily life" (Johnston, 2001: 964).

The inadequacies of pluralist, reform-oriented, and technically preoccupied crime prevention theories in mobilizing disadvantaged neighbourhoods expose the need for an alternative paradigm that addresses the interrelated theoretical and epistemological voids and weaknesses in CCP programs and practices as applied to these locales. A reconceptualized and refocused CCP theory must first address the lack of attention given to the essential processes of community crime prevention, in particular its collective action and citizen participation underpinnings. Chapter 6 takes an initial step to understanding crime prevention as collective action and its inability to initiate and sustain a broad-based mobilization by examining CCP through concepts, theories, and research dedicated to collective action, social movements, and citizen participation in local problem solving. Second, a reconceptualized CCP theory must recognize and address the asymmetrical nature of power relations within advanced Western societies and the shared root causes of crime and community apathy. Chapter 6 fills this void in CCP theory and practice by outlining a critically oriented approach to mobilizing poor neighbourhoods that attempts to overcome the impediments at the individual, neighbourhood, and organizational levels. These critically oriented theories are built on a politico-economic perspective that views the causes of crime and the obstacles to successful crime prevention organizing as social, political, and economic in nature, which can best be addressed through development-based strategies that strive to transform disadvantaged neighbourhoods into cohesive, healthy, safe, caring, inclusive, and politically empowered communities.

PART THREE

Reconceptualizing and Refocusing
Community Crime Prevention

6 Community Crime Prevention as Collective Action

Various forms of community crime prevention are interpreted not only as applications of criminological theory but also as complex pieces of socio-political action that also have a defining ideological and ethical character.

T. Hope, "Community Crime Prevention," p. 22

Introduction

Although firmly predicated upon collective action and citizen partici-pation, community crime prevention (CCP) scholarship has generally failed to learn from and incorporate concepts, theories, and research concerned with collective behaviour, citizen participation, community organizing, and social movements. Because of this neglect, there have been no concerted attempts, theoretically or empirically, to examine CCP as a form of collective behaviour. This is unfortunate, for the jux-taposition of collective behaviour and social movement scholarship against CCP has the potential to help foster a better understanding of the latter, including those factors that promote and obstruct participa-tion in collective crime prevention activities. This chapter fills this void by exploring the dominant characteristics and theories of collective action, social movements, and citizen participation and then applying this analysis to the theory and practice of CCP, and the Mount Pleasant case study specifically. The ultimate goal of this chapter is to facilitate a greater comprehension of the factors that impede participation in CCP programs and the obstacles to a broad-based mobilization of disadvan-taged neighbourhoods around crime.

Collective Behaviour and Social Movements: An Overview

Although it continues to be ill-defined and conceptually vague, the sweeping sociological concept of collective behaviour can be broadly defined as an unstructured form of social behaviour operating through informal, ad hoc groups of people. At the risk of simplicity, collective behaviour is fundamentally characterized by two interdependent elements: it is emergent in nature and operates outside the dominant cultural and political norms and institutions of a society. Collective behaviour is emergent in that it appears, diffuses contracts, or changes form suddenly and unexpectedly (Marx and McAdam, 1994: 11). Not only does collective behaviour involve emergent *structures,* but it is defined by emergent *norms.* Turner and Killian (1993: 8) characterize collective behaviour as "those forms of social behaviour in which usual conventions cease to guide social action and people collectively transcend, bypass, or subvert established institutional patterns and structures." When faced with a shared problem that cannot be solved by the established social, cultural, political or economic institutions, people interact and consider alternative solutions – often pursued outside traditional political institutions and processes – and out of this "meaning-creating process" a new norm emerges to guide the actions of the assembled collective (Curtis and Aguirre, 1993: 1).

The terms "collective behaviour" and "collective action" have often been used interchangeably, but the latter should be viewed as a subcategory of the former. Collective behaviour is an omnibus sociological category that attempts to denote how people act and behave in group settings, which can include such spontaneous and fleeting group settings as crowds, mobs, and riots. Collective action refers more specifically to the actions of a group or network that generally takes place outside of normal political channels, and which is oriented towards achieving a shared social, economic, political, or cultural goal or interest (Oliver, 2003: 198). Collective action is also associated with some form of change-oriented (or change-resistant) process that challenges (or supports) established political or economic policies, practices, or institutions. Community organizing, social movements, public demonstrations, civil disobedience, revolutions, and terrorism can all be considered forms of extra-institutional collective (political) action.

Conceptually, social movements constitute an even more specific form of collective action and can be defined as an emergent collective of people united by and voluntarily mobilized around a common belief, a common ideology, and often a common group identity, that is focused on a specific issue, and who together try to achieve certain goals that promote or resist change in society, relying, in part, on non-institutional forms of political action and influence. Like collective behaviour in general, social movements materialize out of a high degree of engagement and interaction of people with little or no assistance from dominant political institutions (Olson, 1965; Turner and Killian, 1993; Fisher, 1993; Marx and McAdam, 1994). While many social movements embody emergent norms and extra-institutional characteristics, they are often formally organized and structured; are often ongoing, rather than ephemeral; are known to eventually work with or within established political institutions; and pursue very specific goals oriented towards social reform or change. Indeed, social movements, such as those organized around labour, civil rights, women's equality, peace, sexual orientation, and the environment have been major agents of social change in the twentieth century.

Participation (and Non-participation) in Collective Action and Social Movements

The issue of public participation (also referred to as citizen participation, community involvement, or civic involvement) is an essential part of, and an enduring question in, the study of collective behaviour, but also of civil society and governance. Public participation refers to the voluntary involvement of people, either individually or as part of a formal or informal collective, in the issues, processes, and/or goals of public life (Arnstein, 1969; Verba and Nie, 1972; Conge, 1988; Checkoway, 2003). Citizen participation can take many forms: engaging in the formal political process; volunteering for charities; participating in a neighbourhood group or a social movement; or involvement in fraternal, leisure, or sports organizations, to name a few. In general, the principal modes of citizen participation are classified into four categories: volunteering, financial donations to charities, participating in civic associations, and political participation (Verba and Nie, 1972; Reed and Selbee, 2001; Hall et al., 1997, 2001).

Public participation is seen as a necessary foundation for a vibrant, healthy, well-functioning society and is idealized as both a means to an end and as an end in itself. As a means to an end, public participation protects the interests, liberties, and rights of people; bolsters democratic processes and institutions; forces government programs to meet the needs of the population or certain groups; guards against government and corporate authoritarianism and abuses; redistributes power and resources in society; and helps address social problems. Citizen participation is also viewed as an end it itself, and is said to foster personal empowerment, skills development, self-determination, social networks, and collective efficacy. The virtues of citizen participation are linked to Robert Putnam's concept of "social capital," which consists of institutions, relationships, and other features of social organizations that make up a vibrant and stable civil society. Central to social capital are connections and relationships among individuals, such as networks, bonds, norms, reciprocity and trust, that facilitate coordination and cooperation for mutual benefit and enable participants to act together to pursue shared objectives. Putnam, Leonardi, and Nanetti (1993: 90) extol the benefits of participating in civic organizations because it inculcates cooperation as well as a sense of shared responsibility for collective endeavours. The philosophy of communitarianism (Etzioni, 1995), whereby civil society takes ownership of the many social welfare responsibilities and tasks carried out by the state in the post-war years, is also explicitly built upon citizen participation and civic engagement, (Lab and Das, 2001). Exponents of social capital and communitarianism agree that communities and societies with a high degree of civic engagement produce "an interlocking and mutually reinforcing set of values, norms of behavior, civic engagement, and cooperative behavior that constitute a virtuous circle," resulting in a society that is more engaged, equal, trusting, happier, self-fulfilled, and prosperous (Uslaner and Conley, 2003: 332). In short, the "good society" can only be restored if individuals are integrated into a web of communal responsibilities, reciprocal obligations, and civic participation (MacLaughlin, 2002: 89).

Factors Relating to Participation in Collective Action

Despite the controversy summarized in the previous chapter over whether civic participation has declined in recent years, it has nonetheless been well documented that most people do not volunteer their time for civic organizations or charitable groups and avoid participation in collective action, especially that which entails political protest (Olson, 1965; Lipsky, 1969; Salisbury, 1969; Garnson, 1975; Henig, 1982; Muller, 1990; Stoecker, 1990; Clapper, 1995; Williams, 1995; Marsh, 1999; Munk, 2002). In their analysis of how civic engagement is distributed among the Canadian population, Reed and Selbee (2001) show that there is a small group of individuals who are responsible for the majority of "contributory efforts": 6 per cent of Canadian adults account for 35 to 42 per cent of all civic involvement. The authors refer to this group of individuals as Canada's "civic core." Similarly, a study by Statistics Canada found that, in 2000, the top 25 per cent of donors contributed 82 per cent of the total dollar value of charitable contributions (Hall et al., 2001: 9). The concentration of charitable giving, volunteerism, and social activism among a small group of people is reflected in other surveys and studies from other countries (Allardt et al., 1958; Perkins et al., 1990; Della Porta and Diani, 1999; Miller, 2000; Clary and Snyder, 2002).

Given these findings, a principal dilemma facing social movements and local collective action "is the oft demonstrated fact that, when it comes to problems facing society, people's attitudes typically outreach their actions." In other words, "many more people support the idea of volunteerism as a way of tackling society's problems than actually enter into service as volunteers, and many more people endorse the values of participating in the political process than actually exercise their right to vote" (Clary and Snyder, 2002: 581). This conclusion leads Wharf-Higgens (1997: 277–8) to ask, if "participation is such a good thing, why don't more people participate?" Researchers have attempted to explain this phenomenon of differential participation by identifying and examining factors that *motivate* people to participate in the public realm, as well as independent variables that merely *correlate* with the dependent participation variable. To a lesser extent, factors associated with non-participation have also been the topic of research and theorizing. The remainder of this section summarizes the literature that examines factors influencing an individual's decision to participate (or not participate) in collective action and social movements. In doing so, these variables are grouped into the following categories: (1) demographic factors, (2) socio-psychological factors, including concern over or identification with a certain cause or issue, (3) the immediate social environment, (4) organizational factors, and (5) the structural context. For each of these categories, theories and research findings on participation in collective action are summarized and then applied to help explain participation and non-participation in collective crime prevention generally and the Mount Pleasant case specifically.

Demographic Factors

The two (overlapping) demographic variables that most studies have used to predict participation in social movements are socio-economic status and educational level. The research shows that the two strongly correlate with civic engagement and participation in collective action, social movements, and civic organizations specifically (Milbrath, 1965; Piven, 1966; Hyman and Wright, 1971; Huckfeldt, 1979; Gittell, 1980; Perkins et al., 1990; Prokopy, 1998; Marsh, 1999; Greenberg, 2001; Hall et al., 1997, 2001; Nihei, 2003). According to Booth (1972: 34), "The evidence from empirical research on the effects of socio-economic status as well as other social rank characteristics points in the same direction: healthy, middle-aged, highly-educated, native born, white collar, and upwardly mobile members of the labour force belong to more formal voluntary groups than persons in other categories." For Vasoo (1991: 4), the leadership of local social movements is a microcosm of the influence that socio-economic status holds over participation: "It appears that the leadership in grass-roots organisations has a higher percentage of involvement of people with professional and technical background, than any other occupational status ... What appears to be more significant is that there is an under-representation of neighbourhood leaders with lower socio-economic status."

Of all the socio-economic variables, education appears to correlate most strongly with public participation (Berelson, Lazarsfeld, and McPhee, 1954; Campbell et al., 1960; Verba and Nie, 1972; Miller and Shanks, 1996; Nie, Junn, and Stehlik-Barry, 1996; Putnam, Leonardi, and Nanetti, 1993; Putnam, 1995; Verba Schlozman, and Brady 1995; Hall et al., 1997, 2001; Clary and Snyder, 2002). A national survey conducted for Statistics Canada indicates that volunteering generally increases with the level of education; 19 per cent of volunteers have less than a high school education compared to 39 per cent who have university degrees. The rate of membership in civic and charitable organizations also increased with education; over 67 per cent of those with university degrees were members or participants, compared with 40 per cent of those who did not complete secondary school (Hall et al., 2001). High levels of education and socio-economic status work together to promote participation in a number of ways. Verba et al. (1995) and Hauser (2000) found that education helps establish what Egerton (2002) calls the preconditions for "effective citizenship," which include a privileged social and economic position, access to cognitive and civic skills and resources, and a conducive environment. A review of the literature dealing with public participation by Louis Penner (2002) suggests that better educated people have the kind of jobs that allow them more time to devote to their volunteer activities. He also believes that "people from upper social economic classes (e.g., better educated people) may be more willing to volunteer because this provides them with a way to give some additional meaning to their lives. That is, they need something beyond their jobs to make them feel fulfilled" (457). Hauser (2000) also notes that civic organizations and political parties tend to target educated citizens in their efforts to mobilize support and participation. In contrast, those with a low socio-economic status are generally less educated, which militates against transforming one's concerns and grievances into action and participation (notwithstanding some very famous exceptions to this rule). The poor generally have less personal efficacy; they lack sufficient resources and political power; their social environment and networks do not support volunteerism, participation in civic groups, or political activism; and/or they are estranged from the educated, middle-class core that makes up many civic or political groups. Piven (1966) identifies several characteristics of the "urban lower class" that makes public participation less likely. People with a low socio-economic status are overwhelmed by concrete daily needs that detract from any concern with community issues; they have little belief in their ability to affect the world in which they live; they frequently lack the knowledge and information to enable them to scrutinize social policy; and they have fewer leadership capabilities, organizational skills, and professional skills.

Other studies have shown that socio-economic variables may have limited power in predicting who participates in collective action and social movements, although these studies tend to be in the minority. In their research into local groups protesting toxic waste contamination, Masterson-Allen and Brown (1990: 485) note that "this movement is unique," in part because of "the social composition of its adherents – chiefly working and lower class people, as opposed to the middle and upper class individuals normally motivated by environmental concerns." Similar results were found by Byron Miller (2000) in his analysis of the peace movement in the Boston area. He writes that "although the peace movement is generally characterized as a white, middle-class movement, the support of this constituency could not be taken for granted" (xi). "Indeed, the cases studied here tend to undermine common generalizations about the peace movement being an innately white, well-educated, middle- and upper-middle-class movement" (171). Smith (1975) argues that social background loses much of its power in predicting participation in voluntary associations when intervening attitudes, personalities, and situational variables are controlled statistically. Wandersman (1981) concludes that socio-economic status may be less relevant to participation in social movements than one's relationship to the community, length of residence, or even marital status.

The Mount Pleasant case study confirms research that posits a positive correlation between socio-economic status and participation in social movements and local groups. As detailed in chapter 3, socio-economic characteristics such as above-average income, post-secondary education, and home ownership positively correlate with other essential predictors of participation in CCP programs, including social interaction, integration, and community commitment. However, the fact that most middle-class residents of Mount Pleasant refrain from participating in collective crime prevention groups or activities diminishes the ability of socio-economic status to exclusively predict participation in local crime prevention groups and activities.

Socio-psychological Factors

Functionalist theories of social movements, which focus on the shared grievances and perceived deprivations that are emergent prior to and during the rise of a social movement, suggest that collective action is triggered by societal strain and mediated via social "uprootedness" and anomie (Smelser, 1963) or frustration and fear (Gurr, 1970). Classical functionalist accounts of collective behaviour – which can be traced to European thinkers such as Gustave LeBon, Pasquale Rossi, and Sigmund Freud who had written about "crowd psychology," "collective psychology," or "group psychology," all of which stressed the irrationality and abnormality of the crowd – treat collective action and participation in it as a form of irrational behaviour (Rule, 1989). Participants are thought to be emotional, irrational, backward, marginal, alienated, and easily manipulated (Marx and McAdam, 1994: 11). In 1920, *The Behaviour of Crowds* was written by Everett Martin, who regarded the crowd as highly susceptible to the simultaneous release of repressed, socially forbidden impulses. For Martin, the crowd simply consisted of "people going crazy together" (as cited in Turner and Killian, 1993: 6). As part of the strain theory of collective action, Smelser (1963) viewed social movement participants as excitable, emotional, and regressive social isolates. Kornhauser (1959) writes that social movements provide "substitute communities" for those alienated, marginal members of society who are, disproportionately, drawn to activism. Feuer (1969), in his study of the free speech movement at Berkeley, attributes the participation of male students to unresolved emotional conflicts directed at their parents.

While these pathology-based theories have been largely discredited, the connection made between the social environment and psychological preconditions for collective action has influenced contemporary functionalist theories of collective action. A defining feature of "aberrant" collective behaviour is that it results from social stimuli, occurs outside established institutions, and does not follow prevailing social norms. Smelser's Strain Theory proposes that collective action occurs under situations of structural strain in the values, norms, and motivational systems of a society. Social movements are a response to major disruptions in the normal functioning of society that are an inevitable product of the modernization process. For Smelser, rapid social change that produces disruptions, such as economic depressions, urbanization, and industrialization, serve as a potential trigger for collective action by introducing serious strains into society that become manifested in widespread feelings of uncertainty and anxiety. Social movements arise as a way for people to collectively cope with these feelings (Marx and McAdam, 1994: 78) and occur when conditions of strain have arisen, but before public resources have been mobilized (or are inadequate) to deal with the source of the strain (Smelser, 1963; Turner and Killian, 1987).

Early functionalist accounts that view participants of collective action as pathological and irrational social pariahs clearly cannot be used to understand CCP participants. However, an argument can be made for the relevancy of some aspects of Smelser's Strain Theory to CCP at both the macro- and micro-societal levels. The emergence of the CCP philosophy in the late 1960s and early 1970s in North America has been attributed to the dramatic rise in the urban crime rate, which to some social theorists was the result of a potent mix of modernization, urbanization, demographic trends, emergent counterculture norms, and structural economic shifts. When examined in light of Smelser's Strain Theory, the increased crime rate can be viewed as a societal strain (or at least a symptom of a more fundamental strain) that heightened uncertainty and anxiety, in turn providing the impetus for the emergence of community-based approaches to crime control. Moreover, this philosophy appeared, not only because of rapid social change, but also as a response to perceptions that existing institutions and public resources were inadequate to effectively control the source of the strain. The application of Strain Theory to CCP participation is also relevant to the micro level. The Mount Pleasant case study suggests a strong correlation between personal concern over crime and participation in collective efforts. Specific crime and disorder problems, such as street prostitution or "drug houses," raised the anxiety level of some neighbourhood residents, which provided the impetus for the emergence of local crime prevention groups. This societal strain among Mount Pleasant residents was aggravated by their perception that the local and provincial governments and police were not adequately responding to these problems. While Strain Theory has some validity in helping to explain the emergence of local CCP groups, it cannot explain why many Mount Pleasant residents, who share the same level of concern over crime with CCP participants, do not become involved in collective crime prevention programs.

As the 1960s drew to a close, functionalist accounts of collective behaviour were being challenged by new theories contending that successful social movements were less contingent on pathologies and emotions and better explained as the outcome of an instrumental mobilization of resources by rational, politically astute, and purposeful people. Resource Mobilization Theory (RMT) emerged as an alternative to the functionalist school and advances the idea, first proposed by Clark and Wilson (1961), Olson (1965), Gamson (1968), Oberschall (1973), and Shorter and Tilly (1974), that protest is the continuation of orderly politics by other means. Because protest grows out of the ongoing political process, it need not be irrational. Instead, social movements are made up of a collective of like-minded, rational thinkers strategically striving to maximize their power through both institutional and extra-institutional means. The decision to participate in collective action is also highly rational, based on an instrumental cost-benefit calculus (McCarthy and Zald, 1977; Oberschall, 1973) whereby participants try to minimize personal costs of participating while maximizing the benefits (Berk, 1974). Individuals who base their decision to become involved in collective action on whether it will help them achieve personal goals are following what Wood and Jackson (1982: 36) call the "rational calculation approach" to participation.

This cost-benefit, decision-making approach to participation was also of concern to Mancur Olson who, in his 1965 book, *The Logic of Collective Action,* explored the issue of "free-ridership," which raised the question: Why would individuals participate in collective action when they can benefit regardless of whether or not they participate? (a question very relevant to community crime prevention). His answer is that one's participation in collective action is determined by a range of highly personalized incentives. These incentives, according to Clark and Wilson (1961) are purposive or solidary in nature. Purposive incentives are the substantive outcome sought by collective action; that is, activism grows out of strong attitudinal support for the values and goals of the movement or organization. For example, Miller (2000) refers to a number of studies showing that peace activists demonstrate a sincere concern and/or commitment to nuclear disarmament. In her study of participants in the community health care movement, Wharf-Higgens (1997: 201) observes that involvement served the needs and "concentrated interests" of health care professionals and providers, who were the predominant participants, while it generally failed to ignite the interest of those with "diffuse interests" (the general public). For Hinkle and colleagues (1996), support for and agreement with a particular cause may not be a sufficient attitudinal foundation for engagement in extra-institutional political action. What may be a more meaningful precursor are perceptions of the effectiveness of these actions. In other words, as one explores the costs and benefits of participation, a more significant issue is whether one sees such actions as having an impact. Dennis Chong (1993) writes that participation is maximized when it appears that the movement has sufficient popular support to be politically effective. In contrast to purposive motivations, solidary incentives derive, not from the goals of the collective action, but from the act of participation, the process or experience of involvement and association (Hirschman, 1982). Principal benefits stemming from this solidary incentive include socializing; friendships; the expansion of social networks; feelings of belonging to a group; the status resulting from membership, fun, and conviviality; and an identity that is gained by individuals through group membership.

In addition to solidary and purposive incentives, potential participants may also be motivated by material incentives, which are the provision of some good or service (or the means to obtain them) that will benefit the participant personally (such as skill development and career preparation), or collectively (such as equal rights, a safer community, or a decreased threat of nuclear war) (Rubin and Rubin, 1992). Horvath (1998) refers to research showing that disarmament activists have frequent worries or concerns about the threat to themselves and their families from nuclear weapons and nuclear power, suggesting that their activism is partly motivated by self-protection concerns.

Bloom and Kilgore (2003: 437) believe that altruism and self-interest are connected in that many of the volunteers they studied derived a great deal of personal satisfaction and fulfilment from helping those in need and were motivated by their experiences of privilege from having grown up with middle- or upper-middle-class backgrounds.

In the context of the Mount Pleasant case study, the material, self-interested incentives for participation in CCP groups and activities are particularly apparent among younger volunteers at the crime prevention office (CPO), many of whom indicated that they were motivated to donate their time by a desire to advance their studies or pursue a career in the criminal justice system. The achievement of solidary goals also appear to be an incentive for participation in CCP programs among those interviewed, who indicated the importance of group membership for social interaction and a sense of usefulness and belonging. In addition, the purposive incentive for participation in CCP is exhibited in Mount Pleasant in those program participants who stated that they are motivated by their concern over crime, while voicing their support for the principles and objectives of crime prevention. Alternatively, some of the leaders of the anti-prostitution groups lacked the purposive motivation to become involved with the Safer Community Society due to their disagreement with its broad goals and strategies (they preferred a continued focus on prostitution exclusively). The instrumental and utilitarian approach of (situational) crime prevention theory also appears to be consistent with a Resource Mobilization Theory interpretation of CCP participation: situational crime prevention is premised on theories of the rationally minded offender and encourages the equally rational, self-interested, crime-preventing subject, "a consumer who is alert to criminal opportunities and responsive to situational inducements" (Garland, 2002: 23). This rationalist perception of membership in CCP groups was recognized by Skogan (1990: 46), who considers participation as a function of both opportunity and purposive calculations: "Few people will be inclined to participate if there are no available opportunities or if they judge the prospects of successful community organization in their neighbourhood to be poor." The Mount Pleasant case study does not provide sufficient data to explore the extent to which participants and non-participants weigh the pros and cons of joining Neighbourhood Watch or another local crime prevention activity. However, according to Tim Hope (1995: 51), "a purely rational-choice" approach to studying participation in CCP programs would suggest that, were individuals to make a personal cost-benefit calculation, "they would, in many circumstances choose *not* to participate." For Hope, a decision not to participate is likely under four conditions. The first occurs when "the perceived costs or risks of voluntary participation outweigh its apparent benefits" (e.g., "poor residents of high-crime neighbourhoods have few personal resources to donate to voluntary activity, feel they may face considerable risk in contacting neighbours whom they perceive to be dangerous," and may have little personal or financial stake in the neighbourhood). The second is "where neighbourhood commitment has opportunity costs" such as when participation may distract from efforts that might otherwise be spent pursuing other activities. The third is "where marginal additions of participation are perceived not to produce commensurate reductions" in the risk of victimization. The fourth is "where 'free riding' obtains the benefit of safety at little or no cost to the individual."

Many of these calculated reasons for avoiding participation in CCP programs were articulated by Mount Pleasant residents. Although the rationales were highly diverse and varied, many indicated, both implicitly and explicitly, that they were sceptical about the ability of these crime prevention initiatives to have any impact, they had neither the time nor the resources to dedicate to the cause, they had little personal or financial commitments to the neighbourhood, or they feared retribution from local drug traffickers. Few of the non-participants directly stated that their decision to avoid joining local CCP groups was based on a belief that they could get a "free ride" from the crime prevention groups and activities. Indeed, the generally held belief among non-participants that the impact of local CCP groups and activities on crime was negligible appears to negate any perception of the potential for a free ride.

Another socio-psychological variable that research causally links to participation in local collective action and social movements is feelings of personal empowerment and efficacy. Wharf-Higgens (1997) reports that people who participate in community organizations often feel more empowered or have a greater sense of control than non-participants prior to becoming involved. They have a strong belief in their personal abilities and volunteer their time when they believe they can make a difference (indicating a connection between socio-psychological traits, such as personal empowerment, and purposive incentives, like the probability that the social action will be successful or have an impact). Peter Horvath (1998) cites numerous studies suggesting that disarmament activists have a high level of self-efficacy and a belief in their personal ability to contribute to achieving the goals of their cause. His research also indicates that feelings of personal efficacy and empowerment increase one's interest in social and political issues. Research into citizen participation suggests that feelings of personal efficacy positively correlates with one's level of education (Verba et al., 1995; Egerton, 2002; Clary and Snyder, 2002; Hauser, 2000), again indicating the strong causal relationship between socio-economic status and other variables that correlate with citizen participation. In her study examining participation in community health groups, Wharf-Higgens (1997: 201) observes that most of the participants interviewed were professionals with a high level of education, as well as experience in previous or concurrent volunteer community initiatives or professional efforts, which "gave them a repertoire of skills and knowledge that they could draw on to contribute effectively, such as skills that enabled them to run a meeting, write briefs, speak in public, facilitate group discussions, interpret research, and absorb a great deal of written material." Some research also suggests that personal empowerment may encompass, not only self-perceptions of personal power and control, but a sense of connectedness to others. Lenski (1966) proposes that "status inconsistency" is a significant socio-psychological obstacle to participation. Individuals who have (or believe they have) inconsistent or "unequally evaluated status" (i.e., a lack of confidence or personal efficacy especially in relation to others) are often exposed to disturbing experiences in social encounters and react to these experiences by withdrawing from certain forms of social interaction, such as participation in voluntary organizations. Huckfeldt (1979) also finds that undereducated people who live in "high-education" neighbourhoods are more than 20 per cent less likely to get involved than low-educated individuals living in low-education neighbourhoods. In other words, "high status environments encourage high status individuals, but discourage participation among low status individuals" (587). These observations are confirmed by the Mount Pleasant case study. High-status, personally efficacious individuals are more likely to predominate in CCP programs while low-status individuals are discouraged from participation due partially to a lack of personal efficacy, which is compounded by their intimidation of the high-status CCP participants.

    Finally, one's sense of local belonging, integration, and community attachment has also been posited by some to be an important antecedent to public participation. In his research into peace movements in Boston, Miller (2000) notes that participants expressed strong attachments to the cities and neighbourhoods in which they lived. Miller (2000: 21) also cites the research of Rebecca Smith, who points to the role of "place identity" in her examination of neighbourhood activity in Minneapolis. She contends that participation in a local group is tied not only to high levels of home ownership, education, and income, but also to a strong sense of place.

In sum, unlike the arguments put forth by classical functionalist theories of collective action, more recent research views the archetypal participant in collective action as a politically astute, personally empowered, rational thinker, who is socially integrated with a strong (local) social network, and is relatively well versed in social and political issues (Milbrath, 1965; McCourt, 1977; Carr, Dixon, and Ogles, 1976; Perkins, et al., 1990; Marx and McAdam, 1994; Wharf-Higgens, 1997; Horvath, 1998; Coakes and Bishop, 1998; Della Porta and Diani, 1999; Miller, 2000; Clary and Snyder, 2002; Passy, 2003). In contrast, those individuals who are less socially integrated, have smaller local social networks, abstain from interacting with fellow neighbours, and have little attachment to their neighbourhood are more apt to avoid voluntary group participation.

Social Environmental Factors

Public participation is not determined solely by one's demographic traits or socio-psychological disposition, nor does this decision-making process take place in a social vacuum. It can also be influenced by external stimuli (Huckfeldt, 1979; Kenny, 1992). Researchers have long argued that the social, cultural, political, and economic environment, at the local, regional, and national levels, can influence one's level of civic engagement. As Coakes and Bishop (1998: 255–7) succinctly state, "Some environments may be supportive, while others may be more rigid, autocratic, and controlling." The social composition of a neighbourhood is often seen as an important factor in influencing participation in local collective action and the capacity of a community to effectively mobilize. As with CCP, some studies examining local social movements conclude that the more homogeneous the population of a neighbourhood, the more likely it can be successfully mobilized (Lenski, 1966; Michelson, 1970; Shorter and Tilly, 1974; Perkins et al., 1990; Marston and Towers, 1993).[1] Homogeneity also indirectly contributes to the essential prerequisites for collective action in that it contributes to social cohesion among potential participants. A study into block associations by Perkins et al. (1990) indicates that participation is positively associated with levels of social cohesion at the neighbourhood level. Conversely, neighbourhoods that are demographically heterogeneous have a more difficult time in mobilizing residents. Marston and Towers (1993) found neighbourhood movements in American Sunbelt cities that are fragmented along class, race, ethnicity, and geographic lines tend to be the most difficult to organize.

One's social network is also an important influence on the decision to become civically engaged. People seem more likely to join a cause or organization if they are connected to others who are sympathetic or active in that cause or organization. Family members, friends, or neighbours who are civically engaged informally transmit norms and values that translate participation into a social obligation. A survey of the civic participation of the "DotNet Generation" (those born after 1978) suggests that "adult actions can and do have a significant impact on the degree of engagement of young people. Having good role models at home makes a big difference; young adults who often heard political talk while growing up are much more involved in a host of activities. Having volunteer models at home made a big difference in DotNets' civic and political engagement" (Pearson and Voke, 2003: 10). It is through these interpersonal linkages that potential participants develop a certain vision of the world, are exposed to certain information, are subject to implicit and explicit social pressures, and acquire the skills and desires necessary for participation in collective action (Della Porta and Diani, 1999: 112–13). Social support and positive affirmation from others help to influence people to become involved in addressing social issues and problems, especially in controversial or highly politicized causes (Chavis and Wandersman, 1990). Clary and Snyder (2002) refer to several studies suggesting that before people decide to volunteer they are exposed to both explicit and implicit kinds of social pressures. The greater these pressures, the more likely the person is to volunteer. These social pressures can be transmitted through kinship ties, where there is a family history of activism, civic involvement, or volunteering (Greenberg, 2001), or through extra-familial networks that transmit similar expectations and influences (Marwell, Oliver, and Prahl, 1988; McAdam, 1994; Tarrow, 1996; Della Porta and Diani, 1999). Della Porta and Diani (1999) point to an "impressive body of research relating to collective action on different issues and in different countries" that has "confirmed how important [interpersonal] networks are for the recruitment of activists and the mobilization of supporters." Social networks "intervene in the early stage of the participation process" through a "socialization function" that creates an initial disposition to participate while creating channels through which people are connected with an opportunity to participate (Della Porta and Diani, 1999: 117). For Marx and McAdam (1994: 90–91), the "social structural factors" that most influence participation include the extent of an individual's social integration and interaction, contact with activists, and membership in an organization (from which an individual is recruited for other causes). Diani (1995: 71–2) discovered in his analysis of environmental activists in Milan that 72 per cent had joined their current organization via their social networks (as cited in Della Porta and Diani, 1999: 113). Passy (2003: 23) refers to research demonstrating that many of the African American activists involved in the civil rights movement during the 1950s and later were recruited from the membership of Baptist churches.

The Mount Pleasant case demonstrates that at both block and neighbourhood levels, the social environment influences individual participation in crime prevention programs. One sees two distinctive social environments in this demographically heterogeneous neighbourhood, each of which, respectively, promotes or discourages participation. The first social environment consists of white, middle-class, socially integrated homeowners who are committed to their neighbourhood. Those blocks that have a large proportion of residents with these characteristics are more apt to act collectively when faced with a local crime problem. This social environment is crucial in spurring participation in local groups and activities through a positive feedback loop: group-based norms are informally transmitted to those residents who share these demographic characteristics, values, and social networks. Research in Mount Pleasant also indicates that CCP participants are drawn from existing networks (a block, an apartment building, friends, an existing organization, etc.) and are stimulated to become involved by being exposed to others who participate and by sharing demographic characteristics and prevalent (middle-class) group norms and values that encourage participation. The second social grouping is made up of members of visible minority groups, immigrants, transient renters, and those with a low socio-economic status. For these residents, there is less stimulation to participate because they are around people who exist in a social environment that generally discourages local civic engagement. While coexisting in the same neighbourhood, these two social groupings and environments may as well be living worlds apart. Rarely do individuals from either group traverse their demographic boundaries through sustained social interaction. The result is that a recursive process operates in each socio-demographic environment, encouraging (although not always successfully) members from one group to participate while discouraging the other. Thus, demographic factors are critical to understanding how social networks and the larger social environment in which one lives influence participation in CCP programs. The demographically homogeneous networks used as the primary recruitment basis for CCP groups in Mount Pleasant inevitably result in a similar homogeneity among CCP group participants. Conversely, the heterogeneity of Mount Pleasant East limits the extent to which demographically defined social networks can overlap or interact to provide for an inclusive, broad-based mobilization of residents.

Organizational Factors

Consistent with Resource Mobilization Theory, research into local social movements shows that organizational variables are often key to mobilizing people (Alinksy, 1971; Piven and Cloward, 1977; Rich, 1980; Checkoway and Zimmerman, 1992; Rochon, 1993; Clary and Snyder, 2002; Passy, 2003). Effective organizations and their leaders stimulate public interest, motivate individuals to become active, bring individuals and like-minded organizations together, help synthesize norms and values to create a cohesive group identity, provide a vision for the group, mobilize necessary resources, and sustain participation. Hinkle and colleagues (1996) place great importance on the ability of organizers and organizations to translate sympathetic values and norms among potential participants into membership and action by helping to nurture personal identity in a shared group context. Developing "a sense of identification with the grassroots organization may be of particular importance to effective grassroots organizing." Such activities as "team building, development of group cohesion, and increasing perceived social support within a grassroots movement may prove effective in enhancing identification with the consequent effect of further strengthening the favorability of members' attitudes toward the political issues and processes at hand" (49). Other important organizational determinants of participation in a volunteer-based group include the nature of its goals (Perlman, 1979; Staples, 1984), its structure and communications (National Federation of Settlements and Neighborhood

Centers, 1968), the division of labour, and leadership (Rich, 1980; Delgado, 1993). Active recruiting can also influence one's decision to participate. A survey in the United States found that many youth who volunteer became "involved because someone else encouraged them, or they were recruited by a group" (Pearson, and Voke, 2003: 11).

According to RMT, what is fundamentally important in the emergence and success of social movements is not necessarily social problems, which are omnipresent, but the ability of organizations to mobilize resources and participants (McCarthy and Zald, 1977). This is no different in the field of crime prevention where opportunity structures and the availability of resources greatly influence a community group's capacity to respond to crime and disorder problems (Podolefsky and Dubow, 1981). In her examination of crime prevention in the English town of Merseyside, Lynne Hancock (2001) found that the ability to secure resources, particularly paid and volunteer human resources, was regarded as being essential for inviting and sustaining participation of local residents. For some observers, organizational success is especially contingent upon the ability of local crime prevention groups to access political resources, including political institutions beyond their neighbourhood borders. In their research into the mobilization of neighbourhoods around crime and disorder, Lewis and Salem (1981: 414–15) found that "the community's political and social resources appeared to constitute the prime mediating force between the perception of crime and other neighborhood problems and the subsequent expression of fear. Neighborhoods with political power, for example, appeared more capable of addressing local problems than did those without it; and this capacity often appeared to contribute to diminishing fear ... The power to react to community problems either was derived from well-established political connections or stemmed from the efforts of active community organizations."

As detailed in Chapter 4, organizational variables, and leadership in particular, were cited as important factors in sustaining or hindering participation of Mount Pleasant residents in CCP groups and activities. When the local anti-crime movements were most successful, during the early and mid-1990s, they were characterized by strong and energetic leadership. In contrast, during the period of research, the leadership was inconsistent, fractionalized, less active, and at times lacking experience and expertise, which directly and indirectly contributed to low participation levels. While concern over crime exists throughout Vancouver, it is those communities that have strong and efficacious organizations and leadership that have been most successful in attracting and sustaining community support and participation. RMT also highlights the influence of external institutions, in particular those of the state, in supporting and frustrating social movements and community groups. This is particularly relevant to CCP where support by governments and police is crucial in ensuring adequate resources, technical support, and legitimacy for local groups and the CPO. Limited government funding and the lack of financial support from the neighbourhood were factors that restricted the efficacy of the Mount Pleasant CPO in its efforts to mobilize the local population and implement crime prevention programs. The withdrawal of government funding and police support, combined with the revocation of free office space in the Kingsgate Mall, were the final nails in the coffin of the CPO and the Safer Community Society.

Structural Factors

The previous chapter presented arguments linking structural forces to a decline in civic engagement. There are equally pervasive counterarguments that attribute various aspects of modernity to a growth in civic engagement and the rise of social movements. These include increased levels of welfare, universal education, greater racial tolerance, the growth of the middle class, and increased equality for women and visible minority groups (Inglehart, 1988). On the other hand, critics of modernity (which always seem to outnumber proponents, at least among scholars) have at various times blamed industrialization, individualism, positivism, bureaucratization, urbanization, and the welfare state as structural impediments to greater civic engagement, collective action, and local social cohesion. The argument is that these structural forces have resulted in a decline in local social cohesion, a breakdown in traditional communal values in favour of individual rights, the fermentation of society, alienation, marginalization and social exclusion, and the centralization of power in large government bureaucracies and corporations. The dilemma, according to Pilisuk, McAllister, and Rothman (1996: 15, 19), is that modernity and the post-Fordist milieu have exacerbated the need for grass-roots community activism, but it has also created new impediments, the most significant being (1) a decline in the supportive capabilities of communities, (2) the fact that local problems are more frequently the manifestations of global causes, (3) the concentration of unaccountable transnational power, (4) the remoteness of information about power in the social structure, (5) the centralized domination of symbols of legitimacy, and (6) the disempowering effects of the mass media.

For Etzioni (1968), the "societal guidance model," by which public affairs are managed and controlled by the welfare state and corporate interests, has robbed society of a political populace and undermined civil society's democratic power over and input into important issues. Apathy arises from a deep dissatisfaction with oligarchic modes of participation; people are unwilling to participate in a political process that is viewed as increasingly elite-directed, hypocritical, dishonest, and corrupt, and which assign a subordinate and passive role to the general populace (Segatti, 1990). A culture of individualism, materialism, and personal self-fulfilment has overtaken communalism and has moved North American society "from politics to self-examination" (Lasch, 1979: 43), which is incompatible with a political commitment and public responsibility to the broader civic interest (Bell, 1976; Lasch, 1979; Bellah et al., 1985). Contemporary society has nurtured an imbalance between individual rights and social responsibilities; people constantly express a strong sense of entitlement – that is, a demand that the community and the state provide more services and strongly uphold individual rights – but have lost their sense of civic responsibility (Etizoni, 1995). The scientific legacies of the Enlightenment – purposive rationality, technical reason, and positivism – has led to technical and functional preoccupations that have the potential to destroy the epistemological and motivational foundations of a critical, communicative, democratically based culture. Jürgen Habermas writes that modern society is characterized by a dialectic of control that has configured our "lifeworld" so that only purposive rationalities, such as the concern for technique, strategies, and tactics are paramount. The ideological limitations of the positivist approach are that fewer and fewer topics become issues for political discourse among the general population. Alienation is the inevitable result as society becomes unresponsive to the individual, and rational administration becomes possible only at the expense of democracy (Habermas, 1973).

The assumption of a pluralistic society is viewed as a fallacy as evidence continues to mount concerning the inequitable distribution of wealth and the gap between the rich and the poor, the powerful and the powerless. Those neighbourhoods and communities most in need of development and collective empowerment are the least able to organize due to a lack of resources and power and a concomitant concentration of poverty and hopelessness (Gittell, 1980; Heller et al., 1984; Perkins et al., 1990; Fainstein and Fainstein, 1993; Clapper, 1995). In their study of participation in social movements in New York and London, the Fainsteins (1993: 67) argue that "whatever the theoretical merits of citizen participation, it is a practical strategy within a political economy subject to severe market constraints."

Those who critique the modernity critics argue that not enough attention or respect is paid to the power of human agency. Regardless of structural forces at the global or national level, the nature and potential of citizen action is still determined at the local level. As Smith (1989: 355) notes, people are not merely passive recipients of these structural economic and political conditions.

Summary: Factors Related to Participation and Non-participation

The factors influencing (or obstructing) participation in collective action are complex, myriad, and highly individualized. The list presented in this chapter is admittedly incomplete, although it does reflect some agreement that appears to exist among researchers as to the key factors that motivate, facilitate, and inhibit public participation. A review of the literature indicates that public participation, and the capacity of groups of people to mobilize around social problems, must be viewed as the product of a combination of factors at the individual, community, organizational, and structural levels. At the individual level, a combination of a potentially large number of interconnecting motivating and facilitating factors (a mixture that is highly unique to each individual) must be in place to transform latent interests, concerns, norms, and values into action. Participation in collective action, and the motivation and capacity of people to mobilize, are also influenced by the relationship and interaction between environmental conditions at the global, national, and local levels, and by demographic and socio-psychological characteristics at the level of the individual member of society. As part of their compromise position in the debate between structuralism and human agency, Fisher and Kling (1993: xvi–xvii) propose that local social movements are the result of a combination of forces at local, regional, national, and international levels: "We think grass-roots mobilizations are the product of and are deeply affected by the international transformation of the global economic base and its mediation through national/local political contexts and peoples' everyday actions and activism." Examining community crime prevention as local collective action validates Fisher and Kling's compromise position: while local contexts and variables do spawn differences in the ability of neighbourhoods to mobilize around crime, national and international politico-economic forces play an influential role in determining which neighbourhoods have the necessary prerequisites to successfully mobilize around crime.

Rosenstone and Hansen (1993) state that any analysis of collective action must consider an individual's demographic characteristics, resources, interests, and values in combination with the "strategic mobilization" practices of organizers and the broader political system that acts to encourage and discourage, to varying degrees, the participation of different demographic groups (as cited in Hauser, 2000: 558). In demarcating factors that affect the likelihood of local collective action, Henig (1982: 203) points to contextual and situational factors of the neighbourhood and those beyond the neighbourhood's boundaries. The neighbourhood situational factors refer to the leadership and mobilization strategies, while the neighbourhood contextual variables relate to the wealth, stability, and homogeneity of the population as well as the existence of local organizations. The situational factors external to a neighbourhood include the political traditions and culture of the city, while the external contextual factors are the city's openness to participation in specific decisions as well as their strategies.

Louis Penner (2002) maps out a conceptual model that hypothesizes the cognitive process and determining factors that lead to an individual's initial decision to volunteer, as well as those factors that sustain participation. His predictive model emphasizes the causal interaction between an individual's demographic and socio-psychological characteristics, situational variables (historical events), social environmental variables (social pressure), and organizational variables. The historical context can greatly influence a person's decision to volunteer (he cites data showing that in the first few days after the 11 September 2001 terrorist attacks, the number of people who offered to volunteer for different charities almost tripled). These situational factors, however, are less influential when compared with immediate social environmental factors, in particular "volunteer social pressure," which is a potential volunteer's subjective perceptions of how significant others feel about him/her becoming a volunteer and his/her motivation to comply with these feelings. An individual's decision to volunteer can also be explained in part by connecting three other sets of variables: demographic, dispositional, and organizational. The most important demographic variables are age, income, and education. The three "dispositional variables" are (1) pro-social personal beliefs, values, and tendencies, (2) pro-social personality, which concerns personality traits associated with pro-social thoughts, feelings, and behaviours, and (3) volunteer-related motives, which are the personal reasons why a person decides to volunteer. Penner's model asserts that the dispositional variables directly influence both the likelihood that a person will be the target of social pressure to become a volunteer and the decision to volunteer itself. The organizational variable that influences the decision to volunteer include the attributes, practices, reputation, and values of the group for which the volunteering is performed.

When compared against the research that focuses on the myriad combination of factors related to participation, relatively fewer studies have directly examined factors related to non-participation, including obstacles to collective action at the local level. Reasons accounting for non-participation are usually posited as a corollary of those factors related to participation. Classical functionalist theories would argue that those who decline to become involved are not sufficiently excitable, emotional, irrational, alienated, or easily manipulated. Strain Theory intimates that non-participants do not experience sufficient strain to propel them into action. Contemporary functionalist perspectives, such as RMT, suggest non-participants are rational decision-makers who have declined to join because of their perception that the costs of participation outweigh the benefits (or similarly, as the free-ridership hypothesis would propose, non-participants believe they can reap the benefits of collective action without actively taking part). RMT would also suggest that obstacles to mobilization result from a lack of organizational resources necessary to transform concerns and grievances into action or the inability of organizers to sufficiently offer or communicate to potential participants the solidary, purposive, or material benefits of becoming involved. Gittell (1980) contends that a low level of participation in social movements within disadvantaged communities can be partially attributed to the inability of organizers to address issues of direct concern to powerless groups.

Klandermans and Oegema (1987) cite three broad reasons why people may not participate in a mass demonstration: lack of sympathy for the movement, not being the target of organizers, and a lack of personal motivation to become involved. In his analysis of the Participatory Rural Appraisal approach to rural development, Kumar (2002: 316) classifies obstacles to participation into three categories: a centralized political system that is not oriented towards people's participation, administrative structures that are control-oriented and "hardly provide significant space to local people to make their own decisions and to control their resources," and social obstacles "which include a mentality of dependence, domination by the local elite and gender inequality." Using social movement theory to clarify some of the barriers that can prevent people from becoming active participants in community-based development projects, Prokopy (1998) discusses one project in a village in northern Thailand that was successful at facilitating participation among financially stable men, but could not invite similar levels of involvement from women or the poor. He postulates four reasons why women were not active participants: they did not see how they might benefit from active participation in many of the available community groups, they believed the projects had a low probability of success, they had to overcome more costs than the men to participate, and the non-governmental organization working in the village had not framed its messages in a way that made sense to them. In their comprehensive attempt at identifying obstacles to public participation in development projects, Botes and van Rensburg (2000) provide the following list: the paternalistic role of development professionals (professional experts often dominate decision-making and manipulate, instead of facilitate, development processes); the inhibiting, centralizing, and controlling tendencies of the state; selective participation (often it is the most visible and vocal, wealthier, more articulate, and educated groups that are allowed to be partners in development without attempts to identify less obvious partners); "hard-issue bias" (technological, financial, physical, and material issues are perceived as being more important for the successful implementation of projects than the "soft issues," such as community involvement or decision-making procedures); an overemphasis on "the development product" (without sufficient attention to "the right approach or process"); and corruption and "gatekeeping" by local elites.

CCP as a New Social Movement: Collective Identity and the Politics of Exclusion

This final section of this chapter examines CCP through an analytical framework that has been used to understand contemporary social movements. New Social Movement (NSM) analysis is not so much a systematic theory as an attempt to identify common characteristics in significant social movements that have arisen in the post-war era. Influenced by such European writers as Alberto Melucci (1980), Alain Touraine (1985), and Claus Offe (1985), NSM analysis arose out of the perceived limitations of Marxist theories in explaining widespread social and political movements in post-industrial societies. As Barbara Epstein (1990: 45) points out, Marxism has no way of accounting for movements that involve issues that transcend class politics, such as the "defence and construction of identity (as in the gay and lesbian movements), the critique of personal life and gender (as in the women's movement), or the effort to realize a utopian vision of community (as in the direct action movement)." In fact, the "new" in the New Social Movement school of thought is an attempt to differentiate modern social movements from "old" movements inspired by Marxist-Leninist doctrine and reflected in socialist revolutions and the labour movement. In these classical movements, economic and political deprivation were the primary sources of group formation, and whether it was union organizing within the workplace or in working class neighbourhoods, people were mobilized around class-based issues.

Social movements that emerged in advanced Western societies in the post-war era materialized around a myriad of issues that were largely divorced from class relations and the workplace. The common bonds of participants are found in diffuse social statuses and cultural issues – such as gender, sexual orientation, ethnicity, or race – and are ultimately about such issues as lifestyle, values, identity, human rights, civil rights, respect, and personal autonomy. One of the common elements of contemporary social movements is the emergence of a new or formerly weak dimension of identity, with participants mobilizing around sentiments of belonging to a differentiated (and often mistreated) social group that involves a struggle in which members can feel equal, powerful, respected, and valued. According to Melucci (1980, 1985, 1989), grievances are inextricably linked with a social identity and NSMs emerge in defence of this identity: "What individuals are claiming collectively is the right to realize their own identity: the possibility of disposing of their personal creativity, their affective life, and their biological and interpersonal existence" (Melucci, 1980: 218). In speaking of identity, one is referring to the means and processes by which social actors recognize themselves, and are recognized by others, as part of a broader group. Thus, the search for one's personal identity in a group context is viewed as a crucial motivating factor among participants. Through an empathy with and allegiance to the grievances, norms, values, and interests of a larger group to which they identify and feel a sense of belonging, the identity construction of group participants provides a coherent meaning to the lives and experiences of the individual (Della Porta and Diani, 1999: 85). In other words, through the construction of identity, contemporary social movements also help construct meaning for their participants (Klandermans, 1993). The very existence of a social movement indicates that there are differences regarding the meaning of some aspect of reality, and, for Melucci (1992), social movements represent the arena in which social actors are engaged in a struggle for the construction of meaning, especially as it is tied to the own personal and group identity.

Viewed through the lens of NSM analysis, anti-crime groups in Mount Pleasant, especially those that pursue opportunity reduction approaches to crime prevention, can be seen as internalizing a collective identity. Not only is there a shared ideology among participants (the need to address crime and disorder by community members through collective action and the reconstitution of a spatially defined, cohesive community), but this homogeneous group of CCP participants are guarding their collective identity as a neighbourhood generally, while asserting and protecting their identity as a minority group within Mount Pleasant (i.e., white, middle-class, law-abiding, locally integrated, homeowners). Thus, unlike other NSMs such as the gay and lesbian movement, which deconstructs and destabilizes traditional conceptions of identity (Gamson, 1995), CCP supports the "traditional mainstream" identity as rooted in localized, middle-class, cohesive communities made up of nuclear families. For Mount Pleasant CCP group participants, shared ideology and collective identity coalesce into a search for, and a reconstruction of, meaning that is found in such middle-class values as safety, security, neighbourliness, and a sense of community. In short, this search for (or struggle over) identity is central to CCP groups in Mount Pleasant. It is their identification with and protection of their neighbourhood and their community that forms participants' ongoing social construction and reassertion in the group context.

While contemporary social movements are not concerned with the relationship between labour and capital – nor are they directly concerned with economic redistribution – the social base of most contemporary social movements is often class-specific; they are middle-class movements, with their core membership dominated by well-educated, middle-class professionals (Offe, 1985; Merkl, 1987). According to Eder (1995: 29), "The middle classes have become the most dynamic element in the modernization of modern society – they have proven to be an important carrier of collective mobilization, thereby fulfilling a social role ascribed to the lower classes by traditional theory." Middle-class professionals have come to dominate contemporary social movements, not because they feel they are the most grieved or powerless or are the strongest proponents of advancing a particular cultural identity, but because they possess the essential prerequisites for civic engagement. For Bagguley (1992), the middle class provides the key social resources for mobilization within Western societies. Not only are CCP participants overwhelmingly from the middle class, but opportunity reduction crime prevention programs also bear a relation to class-based roles in western societies (although not in the Marxian sense, where one's identity is defined by one's relationship with private capital). Research in Mount Pleasant suggests that opportunity reduction crime prevention programs pit individuals and blocks with higher socio-economic status (CCP group participants) against those with low socio-economic status (who are perceived as the source of crime threats). In turn, most situational CCP programs incorporate a class bias that emphasize opportunity reduction programs that either target the poor as offenders or fail to appeal to their crime prevention needs. This serves to exclude the poor and marginalized from participating in such groups, partially by the nurturing of an exclusionary group identity that forms around the narrow demographic (mostly socio-economic) characteristics of CCP group participants.

For Crawford (1994), crime prevention within middle- and upper-income neighbourhoods is grounded in social conflict that involves the policing of, and interventions against, certain individuals and groups outside of and "below" that neighbourhood. The territoriality promoted by opportunity reduction programs like Neighbourhood Watch is imbued with a xenophobia that emphasizes the alien nature of outsiders, often overlaid by class-based and racial overtones, and the threat that they pose to their neighbourhood and its values (including property values). The opportunity reduction approach to crime, according to Boostrom and Henderson (1983: 28–9), emphasizes the sanctity of private property and the responsibility of those with a stake in maintaining private property to police those who have no such stake. Therefore, "this model reinforces the power of those who own property in our capitalist social structure and reinforces the traditional suspicion and fear they feel towards the propertyless." An analysis of CCP organizing in Mount Pleasant substantiates those arguments that local movements can be examined in light of the conflict between class-based social groupings played out in spatial terms at the neighbour-hood level. Crime prevention programs predominate on those blocks with a high proportion of owner-occupied dwellings. Home-owning CCP participants interviewed for this study expressed a general suspicion of renters living in their neighbourhood or building, who, it was argued, were the causes of crime and instability in the area. In interviews and focus groups, Neighbourhood Watch (NW) members in the more affluent portions of Mount Pleasant, west of Main Street, blamed their high property crime rate on their proximity to Mount Pleasant East. Focus groups held with NW members living in apartment buildings just west of Main Street discussed the hazard of living so close to Mount Pleasant East, which one person typically characterized as "a very poor community with a very big drug problem." Another added, "While we don't have the drug or prostitution problems here, we have to deal with the runoff from the other side [of Main Street]." Even within Mount Pleasant East, NW members who lived on more affluent streets intimated that crime and crime prevention in their neighbour-hood is class-based. During focus groups and interviews, block captains on streets with a predominately middle-class, homeowing population expressed concern that their block was surrounded by poorer residential neighbourhoods. Even within apartment buildings that contain both renters and owners, block captains instructed members to be particularly vigilant against specific renters and their associates, who they suspected were responsible for victimizing apartments and cars in the building.

Organizing around crime prevention by middle-class homeowners in Mount Pleasant is partially built upon, not only a real and perceived threat to their personal security emanating from their poorer neighbours, but also an ongoing fear over the impact that crime and the reputation of Mount Pleasant as a crime-ridden neighbourhood will have on their property values. To some extent, the Mount Pleasant case study supports the "British Theory of Housing Classes" (Rex and Moore, 1967; Rex, 1971; Saunders, 1978), which argues that local collective action results from class cleavages and conflicts that are structured around the ownership and control of domestic property and tenure-based divisions in residential neighbourhoods (i.e., homeowners versus renters). Participation in CCP groups in more affluent neighbourhoods is higher, not only because the residents have more to lose in the event of a property crime, but because they have been able to clearly identify an "enemy," which, according to Saul Alinsky (1971), is an important ingredient in the successful mobilization of communities.

In sum, an examination of anti-crime groups in Mount Pleasant through the analytical framework of NSMs suggests that, while such groups are not organized directly around identity, such as the gay, civil rights, or women's movements are, it can be proposed that these CCP groups and their participants have gradually nurtured a group identity, based on shared socio-demographic characteristics, and, more specifically, on liberal middle-class norms and values. It is the protection of this identity as a spatial and demographic community that forms participants" ongoing social construction and reassertion of meaning in the group context. The protection of this identity is almost literal, in the sense that this group coalesces around safety and security, which involves protecting themselves and their assets. Moreover, these groups emerge from real and perceived threats that are seen as external to their demographically defined social identity. This nurtured identity may intentionally or unintentionally exclude those who do not share similar characteristics, and thus do not fit into this common demographic identity. Opportunity reduction CCP programs are largely based on an inherent conflict between social groupings that revolves around socio-economic cleavages, especially as they are manifested in the interrelated politics of identity, crime, and crime prevention (e.g., the propertied middle class as victims versus the poor as offenders). This conflict between social groups is played out in spatial terms at the neighbourhood level through crime and opportunity reduction crime prevention programs, which are largely carried out by the middle class to defend themselves, their property, and their shared identity. It is no wonder that some crime prevention scholars refer to community-based situational crime prevention as the "community defence model" (Hope, 1995; Graham, 1995).

This conclusion exposes an ominous side to situational crime prevention and the sociological concept of the community. One must remember that a community is an association of people who form a collective identity around what its members share or perceive themselves as sharing, and how this group identity differentiates them from those (outsiders) who are not members (Suttles, 1972: 51; Crawford, 1997: 154). Given the inherent defensive logic of situational crime prevention, when communities construct their boundaries around concerns and anxieties about crime, a "defensive exclusivity" emerges, which means that communities may increasingly come together less for what they share in common and more for what they fear in common (Crawford, 1998: 264). Community defence strategies embody an assumption about the relationship between offenders and a defended community. Offenders are viewed primarily as outsiders against whom the community needs to defend itself. Hence, this vision tends to assume an "us versus them" attitude that feeds into, and is reinforced by, the existence of an "ideology of unity" (Crawford, 1999: 516). This argument coincides with the interpretation of identity-based new social movements by Della Porta and Diani (1999: 87), who say that while "collective action cannot occur in the absence of a 'we' characterized by common traits and a specific solidarity," equally indispensable to this group identity is the identification of the "other." The construction of identity therefore implies both a positive definition of those participating in a certain group, and a negative identification of those who are excluded. As Gordon Bazemore (2000: 225) notes, African Americans have particular reason to be suspicious of the terms "justice" and "community" because criminal justice in the United States has historically meant "just us," while in some parts of the country "community justice" was synonymous with lynching.

In their analysis of the English town of Macclesfield, Girling and colleagues (2000: 108) report on how residents view crime threats as emanating from outside the town. While conducting research in neighbouring Presbury, these researchers discovered a high level of fear about offenders who were from outside their community and a widespread sense that the town needed to be defended from these threats. However, the authors argue that the intensity of these worries suggests that this was not just about protecting one's possessions. It was people's sense of what Presbury ought to be that was at stake, that their expectations of quaintness, orderliness, and tranquillity were endangered by the prospect of crime and disorder. "The existence of incivility seems to threaten people's ideals of the 'English village' and undermines the possibility that people can and have found – in the midst of a general moral decline – a safe and orderly place in which you know your children are going to mix with other decent children." For Crawford (1997: 159–60), the symbolic embodiment of danger is often represented through the unknown and the alien "other." He rightly points out that despite the research indicating that "much violent offending takes place with familiar and the familial relationships" (163), the figure of the ominous "stranger" permeates most people's perception of where the greatest danger of interpersonal crime and violence lies. Crawford refers to a study in a racially heterogeneous inner-city neighbourhood in the United States conducted by Sally Merry (1981: 223) who concludes: "Danger encompasses the fear of the stranger, the morally reprehensible, disorderly, or culturally alien person, and the anonymous member of a hostile and threatening social category." Or, as Crawford (1997: 270–1) states, "A sense of danger may arise from antagonisms, both real and symbolic, between groups which emerge from class, gender, and cultural differences." Further, "this insider/outsider dichotomy which community safety can foster, taps deep-seated fears about social identity and otherness, particularly given the tendency of crime to bifurcate the 'rough' from the 'respectable.' Given the anxieties that crime evokes, it can feed fears. The external threat, whether actual or imagined, can become both the reason for, and the means of sustaining 'community.' In such a context, the collective identity that emerges can become idealized, all-pervasive and rigid, the perfect conditions condition for intolerance to breed" (Crawford, 1998: 245–6).

The implications of the exclusionary identity formation engendered by situational crime prevention is particularly profound for demographically heterogeneous neighbourhoods such as Mount Pleasant because it contributes to divisions and obstructs the development of a truly inclusive, socially cohesive community. Crawford (1997, 1998, 1999) warns that in seeking to construct communities around crime, we may be creating parochial and exclusive neighbourhoods and social groupings with intolerant values. The "tendency of 'crime' as a category to bifurcate the 'normal' (law-abiding individual) from the 'pathological' (criminal) has serious implications for the formation of community boundaries, around distinctions between 'insiders' and 'outsiders,' as well as the nature and practice of actual community involvement" (Crawford, 1997: 200–1). Beckett (2001) argues that people are much more likely to embrace punitive and exclusionary solutions to crime problems when the source of those problems is perceived to emanate from "others" and "outsiders." In this sense, traditional theories of (situational) crime prevention, along with zero tolerance policing, three-strikes laws, and other excessively punitive strategies, are part of a new criminology that David Garland (1996: 460) argues is built upon "essentialized differences": "It is a criminology of the alien other which represents criminals as dangerous members of distinct racial and social groups which bear little resemblance to 'us.' It is, moreover, a 'criminology' which trades in images, archetypes and anxieties, rather than in careful analyses and research findings – more a politicized discourse of the unconscious than a detailed form of knowledge-for-power."

A criminology that is based on "essentialized differences" promulgates punitive strategies that incorporate characterizations of offenders as "'predators,' 'career criminals,' 'sex beasts,' as 'evil,' 'wicked,' or members of an 'underclass,'" each of which are suitable enemies "for a ruling culture stressing family values, individual enterprise, and the limits of welfarism" (Garland, 1996: 460). In her indictment of the zero tolerance polices pursued in New York City, and championed by former mayor Rudolph Giuliani, Sophie Body-Gendrot (2001) contends that the blame for social and urban decay was shifted away from the economic and political elite and onto those who are often the most marginalized and vulnerable: "Rather than indict capitalists for capital flight, landlords for abandoning buildings or public leaders for a narrow retrenchment to class and racial self-interest, Mayor Giuliani preferred to point to homeless people, panhandlers, prostitutes, squeegee cleaners, squatters or unruly youths from racial minorities as the enemies of the quality of life (918)." Therefore, the dual dangers of the community defence model, and this new criminology as a whole, are that communities become increasingly defensive, paranoid, bifurcating, and exclusionary, while blame is shifted away from the social and politico-economic causes of crime. As a result, according to Jock Young (2001: 31):

> The criminal underclass, replete with single mothers living in slum estates or ghettos, drug addicts committing crime to maintain their habit and illegal immigrants who commit crime to deceitfully enter the country (and continue their lives of crime in order to maintain themselves), have become the three major foci of emerging discourses around law and order of the last third of the twentieth century. These types can be summed up as the welfare "scrounger", the "junkie" and the "illegal." This triptych of deviancy, each picture reflecting each other in a late modem portrait of degeneracy and despair, comes to dominate public discussion of social problems. As the discourse develops, their ontologies become distinct and different from "normal" people, their social norms absent or aberrant, their natures frequently racialised and rendered inferior. Crime, a product of our society, becomes separated from the social structure: it is viewed as a result of distinct aetiologies, it embodies differing values, it emanates from distinct and feared areas of the city.

Conclusion

One benefit of examining CCP through the lens of collective behaviour and public participation scholarship is that it fosters a better understanding of how collective action materializes and of the factors related to participation and non-participation therein. The Strain Theory of collective behaviour would indicate that CCP groups emerge from a shared societal strain: a heightened concern among neighbourhood residents over crime combined with their perceptions that the state is unable to address these problems unilaterally. RMT views CCP groups as the product of an instrumental mobilization of rational-thinking actors who attempt to advance their concerns through calculated efforts that are both institutional and extra-institutional. RMT also underlines the utmost importance of internal and external resources, including government funding, in actuating concerns and emergent norms into local crime prevention programs. The application of NSM analysis is particularly fruitful in identifying obstacles to a broad-based mobilization of heterogeneous neighbourhoods, such as Mount Pleasant. Through this school of thought, CCP can be viewed as a largely middle-class phenomenon that coalesces around and asserts a group identity based on shared demographic characteristics that may also consciously or unconsciously exclude those who do not share these demographics, thereby impeding a broad-based mobilization of residents around crime prevention.

The Mount Pleasant case study also reflects the research into local collective action and public participation, which asserts that the ability of neighbourhoods to mobilize effectively is influenced by a myriad of interrelated factors at the individual, neighbourhood, organizational, and structural levels. Based on a juxtaposition of research examining participation in CCP groups and activities (including the Mount Pleasant case study) with collective action, social movement, and public participation scholarship, figure 6.1 provides a conceptual map of the various layers of forces and factors that influence an individual's decision to participate in, and the ability of neighbourhoods to mobilize around CCP programs. This conceptual map also highlights the causal relationship between the various levels of influencing factors. Structural factors at the global and national levels set the broad politico-economic and socio-political environment for neighbourhood action. Socio-political factors, such as the extent to which strong participatory democratic institutions and processes exist, help determine whether

Figure 6.1 A conceptual map depicting the causally interrelated factors and forces that influence public participation and the mobilization capacity of neighbourhoods around crime

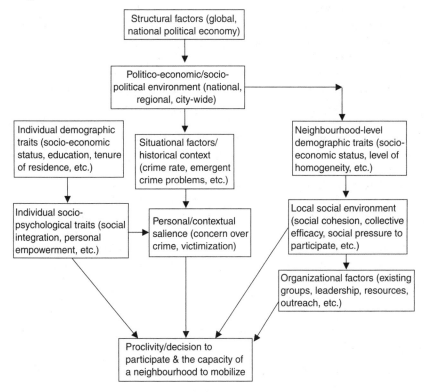

the national and local environment is conducive to promoting civic participation and political protest. The political economy helps determine the aggregate demographic factors at the neighbourhood level (e.g., socio-economic status), which in turn are highly influential in determining the existence of the essential preconditions for local mobilization (i.e., social cohesion, collective efficacy, social pressure to participate, etc.). The neighbourhood's aggregate, demographic traits, and the social environment also influence whether there will be an effective organizational structure or capacity (e.g., groups, leadership, resources, etc.) that can recruit potential participants and ensure a successful mobilization of the local population. This conceptual map also indicates that an individual's demographic characteristics (e.g., socio-economic status, level of education) greatly influences one's decision to participate, which is often mediated through the individual's socio-psychological characteristics (e.g., social integration, personal empowerment, and efficacy). Finally, structural forces also help dictate the nature and scope of crime and disorder problems in a society and within individual neighbourhoods, which can impact on the extent to which the personal and contextual salience of crime (e.g., concern over crime, personal victimization) influences one's decision to participate in CCP programs.

Implicit in the conceptual map illustrated in figure 6.1 is the understanding that while many in society may internalize purposive concerns, interests, and values that can motivate them to participate in the public realm, unless there are sufficient facilitating factors (at the individual, organizational, social, environmental, and structural levels) that can push and pull people into action, a propensity to become involved may simply lie dormant. The "push" factors can be grouped into two categories: those that *motivate* an individual to participate (e.g., purposive, solidary, material incentives) and those that *facilitate* an individual's decision to become more active and involved (e.g., post-secondary education). These push factors are essential because they provide individuals with the personal resources and traits that research indicates are critical precursors to public participation. A high socio-economic status, and educational achievement in particular, appear to foster greater social interaction and integration at the local level, greater social and technical skills, and greater personal empowerment and efficacy, as well as a better knowledge and understanding of salient issues. A high socio-economic status may also instil in participants a greater sense of civic duty and social responsibility (cynically referred to as liberal guilt), which promotes greater personal self-fulfilment, self-satisfaction, and meaning in the lives of volunteers, donors, and activists. Another important category of "facilitating push factors" is the social environment. A history of activism, volunteerism, and participation in one's family, one's social network, or one's neighbourhood can help translate concerns into action through social pressure or by providing the essential opportunity structures, connections, and recruitment links to civic organizations and activities. Research suggests that organizational variables can be the most important "pull" factors in influencing citizen participation. Volunteer-based organizations or networks are successful in recruiting and sustaining participation if they have strong, motivational, stable leadership; if they carry out appropriate and effective outreach and communications; if they are sufficiently resourced; if they can demonstrate they are conducive and sympathetic to the interests, concerns, norms, and values of potential participants; if they can provide (and communicate) appropriate and attractive purposive, solidary, and material incentives; if they serve as a vehicle to help nurture personal identity and self-fulfilment within a group context; and if they value their members, volunteers, and/or participants.

Overshadowing and influencing both the push and pull determinants of participation is the broader structural setting, which helps establish the essential prerequisites of participation: the socio-economic status of individuals and entire groups of people, the level of personal and collective efficacy and empowerment within social groupings and neighbourhoods, and the level of political connections and economic resources necessary for groups to take action. Thus, participation in collective action, and the motivation and capacity of people to mobilize, is contingent upon the relationship and interaction between macro-structural forces at the national and global level, on the one hand, and micro-sociological forces at the local level (the socio-economic status and collective efficacy of neighbourhoods, as well as the socio-economic status, personal empowerment, and level of social integration of individuals).

Decades of research into collective behaviour also buttresses our understanding of the obstacles to participation in CCP groups and activities by showing that all forms of collective action suffer from low levels of participation, that participation in the public realm is concentrated among a small number of activists and volunteers, and that disadvantaged neighbourhoods and marginalized populations are often the most difficult to organize. Based upon the juxtaposition of the findings of the Mount Pleasant case study with a review of the literature into collective behaviour and public participation, table 6.1 compares the characteristics of participants in collective crime prevention initiatives in Mount Pleasant with those of the majority of the local population, who are disproportionately under-represented in these collective initiatives.

Despite the gloomy prognosis that collective action research portends for enticing a broad-based mobilization of poor neighbourhoods around crime, the same research does offer one optimistic conclusion: two categories of variables that are influential in motivating and facili-

Table 6.1 Characteristics of CCP program participants and those who are disproportionately under-represented (based on Mount Pleasant population)

Predictive Variables	Participants	Disproportionately Absent
Demographic characteristics	White, middle-class, educated, stable, long-term, homeowner	Ethnic/racial minority, immigrant poor, undereducated, transient, renter
Socio-psychological characteristics	Socially active and integrated, high level of personal efficacy, strong sense of social attachment and integration	Little social interaction or local integration, lack of belonging, lack of personal efficacy
Purposive incentives	Concern over local crime; participate to protect oneself, family, personal possessions, and property investments	Concern over crime, personal and family safety best ensured through individualistic measures
Solidary/affective emotional factors	Commitment to one's neighbourhood, a desire for social interaction, belonging, fostering identity in a group context	Little commitment to one's neighbourhood, low level of local social interaction or integration
Rational calculations	A belief that crime prevention group will reach goals and personal participation will lead to personal and group goals	Little belief in the ability of the group to reach goals, participation will not lead to personal or group goals
Social environment/ Opportunity structure	Association with social network and organizers, status consistent with other (potential) participants	No association with social network or organizers, status inconsistency
Organizational factors	Awareness of existing groups, affinity with group goals, strategies and messages	Awareness of existing groups, but no affinity with group goals, strategies and messages

tating public participation – personal variables (socio-economic status and socio-psychological traits) and organizational variables (leadership, communications, etc.) – are not static. Interventions can be made to influence these variables in a way that may bolster public participation and local collective action. While there is no easy solution to raising the socio-economic status of an individual or neighbourhood, it can be an attainable goal if the political will and leadership exists. Research also shows that organizational factors are key to promoting participation in local problem solving. The potential impact on participation and collective mobilization that can be realized through a sufficiently resourced organization staffed with capable and motivational leadership is great, even in the absence of a favourable socio-economic environment and politico-economic climate (although efforts to enhance the socio-economic status of community members, and the community at large, will also augment the organizational capacity by increasing local resources and fostering a pool of residents from which indigenous organizers and leaders can be drawn).

Ideally, efforts to remove the obstacles to participation and collective action must also address the structural factors that help forge the deleterious socio- and politico-economic environment within disadvantaged neighbourhoods. The application of collective behaviour and public participation scholarship to crime prevention, and the Mount Pleasant case study in particular, indicates that the difficulties encountered in organizing disadvantaged neighbourhoods is not simply confined to crime prevention. This problem is common among poor and marginalized communities regardless of the issue that collective efforts are organized to address. The widespread nature of this "community immobilization" problem draws attention to the crucial role that structural factors play in obstructing the mobilization of disadvantaged neighbourhoods and lends credence to the argument that theoretical prescriptions and real efforts to mobilize poor communities around CCP must transcend crime and traditional opportunity reduction approaches to crime prevention. Instead, CCP theory and practice must incorporate prescriptions and processes that address (or at the very least acknowledge) the broader social, political, and economic structural forces that help give rise to crime, community apathy, and other problems that plague poor neighbourhoods. These critically oriented, development-based prescriptions are presented in the final chapter.

7 Crime Prevention through Community Development: An Integrated, Critically Oriented Approach to Local Organizing

Introduction

The consistent difficulties that collective crime prevention programs have encountered in summoning a broad-based mobilization of disadvantaged neighbourhoods calls into question the assumptions, tenets, and epistemologies of traditional community crime prevention (CCP) theory as they are applied to these neighbourhoods. The objective of this final chapter is to refocus and reconceptualize the normative aspects of community crime prevention for disadvantaged neighbourhoods, emphasizing prescriptions that may be able to provide a more efficacious basis upon which a widespread and inclusive mobilization of residents can be realized. The recommendations presented in this chapter directly address and attempt to overcome the obstacles to public participation in local problem solving documented in this study as well as other relevant research. A refocused CCP model strives to overcome the shortcomings of traditional crime prevention normative theory, in particular the lack of attention given to such essential process-oriented prerequisites of the community mobilization model as collective action, citizen participation, social development, and community building. As importantly, this reconstituted model discards the erroneous assumption, inherent within traditional CCP theoretical models, of a pluralistic society characterized by symmetrical power relations whereby all neighbourhoods have similar characteristics, problems, needs, and access to political power and economic resources. Instead, this reconceptualized model of CCP organizing views the causes of crime and the obstacles to crime prevention and community action as social, political, and economic in nature. As such, at the core of this alternative model is a critically oriented, development-based approach that attempts to ameliorate the impact of the shared structural causes of spatially concentrated poverty, marginalization, powerlessness, crime, and civic disengagement. In doing so, it supplies process-oriented prescriptions and essential prerequisites that attempt to satisfy the political, economic, and social imperatives necessary to mobilize poor communities. To this end, the broad prescriptive framework for this chapter is made up of an interdependent combination of a *politico-economic stratagem*, which seeks to redistribute and re-centre political and economic resources and power within local communities; a *social and community development approach*, which strives to lift the poor and the disenfranchised from the detrimental conditions that works to exclude them from the public decision-making process; and an *affective-emotional, community building appeal* that attempts to nurture local social integration, interaction, cohesion, collective efficacy, and an inclusive common identity for those who live in disadvantaged and mixed-status neighbourhoods.

The politico-economic foundation for this critically oriented approach to CCP organizing is the dichotomy Hope (1995) presents regarding the horizontal and vertical dimensions along which crime prevention programs operate. Traditional CCP theory operates almost exclusively along the horizontal dimension, emphasizing the technical aspects of program implementation, but ignoring the structural impediments to collective action within poor neighbourhoods. And as Sherman (1997b: 67) counsels, "Further experimentation with different 'vertical' tactics may be needed to find out if community mobilization or other methods to affect decisions external to the local community can change such decisions in ways that cause local crime prevention." One such theoretical experiment is the application of a critically oriented framework to community (crime prevention) organizing that is built upon the recognition of how the political economy of advanced Western societies helps to create and (spatially) concentrate inequalities and disadvantages. The Mount Pleasant case, as well as other research, suggests a causal linear relationship between the dominant politico-economic institutions and forces at the global, national, and local levels; the affluence and power of neighbourhoods; the nature and scope of local crime and disorder problems; and the capacity of neighbourhoods to organize around such problems. As such, the point of departure for a critically oriented approach to CCP organizing is found in measures that simultaneously recognize the interrelationship between the prevailing political economy and local social and community development. While it is unlikely that changes can be brought to bear on the influential global and national politico-economic forces, the potential does exist for a community development approach that simultaneously addresses the common underpinnings of spatially concentrated poverty, underdevelopment, crime, and community immobilization. This culminates in an approach I call simply "crime prevention through community development." This critically oriented developmental approach attempts to address local problems as they are rooted in both the vertical and horizontal dimensions along which poor neighbourhoods are shaped.

A theoretical foundation for this critically oriented model of CCP organizing is John Friedmann's (1987) idea of "the recovery of the political community," which involves a greater decentralization of resources and decision-making powers to (disadvantaged) neighbourhoods. The prescriptions presented in this chapter engender an integrated, holistic approach that combines idealistic politico-economic strategies that operate along the vertical relations of power through a greater decentralization of resources and power, with pragmatic developmental and organizing approaches that are concerned with horizontal relations within a community and an attempt to address program implementation failures. The model advocated in this chapter is a more radical and development-based version of David Blunkett's (2003) "civil renewal agenda," which strives towards an "active citizenship" (empowering and creating opportunities for people to define and take on the problems in their communities), "strengthened communities" (helping neighbourhoods form and sustain local groups, activities, and community participation), and greater "public partnerships" (between community and governmental organizations in the planning and delivery of public services).

Despite its idealistic overtones, this chapter recognizes that there will always be factors that create and spatially concentrate disadvantage, inequality, and social exclusion. While social and community development is paramount to tackling the shared preconditions of poverty, crime, social exclusion, and neighbourhood immobilization, one must accept that these problems will not go away any time soon. Therefore, short-term community organizing and building must be implemented that caters specifically to those neighbourhoods where these problems are most pronounced. This must include strategies that address those situational factors that research suggests are crucial to local collective action and problem solving in any neighbourhood: strong and effective leadership within the context of inclusive community-based organizations, a sense of local belonging and commitment, a high level of individual and collective efficacy, greater social interaction and cohesion among neighbourhood residents, and the nurturing of a collective neighbourhood identity that transcends demographic differences. The utopian nature of this alternative model is also tempered with the realization that many will continue to refrain from participating in collective action and resist civic engagement for countless reasons. Even if the standard of living was raised for those living in poverty, a high socio-economic status is not a guarantee that people will automatically become more civically engaged. The goal of a reconstituted theory of CCP is not to *fully* mobilize disadvantaged neighbourhoods around crime or other related problems, as this would be almost impossible, but to ensure a more broad-based, inclusive movement that is representative of the diverse population of disadvantaged and mixed-status neighbourhoods. Particular emphasis is placed on increasing the opportunity structures for the involvement of those who are under-represented in civic affairs and who are insufficiently served by the political and economic institutions of advanced Western societies.

In short, the CCP model presented in this chapter attempts to balance, within a holistic framework, critically oriented, idealistic, long-term, development-based theories that aim to extract greater power and resources for poor neighbourhoods with short-term, pragmatic, and empirically informed local organizing and community-building strategies. These two broad areas of foci will also interconnect by operationalizing abstract, critically oriented theories into tangible, pragmatic strategies. And while the shortcomings of purposive-rational approaches to CCP are avoided, the normative prescriptions presented in this chapter do not reject completely such traditional approaches. A critically oriented, developmental approach must work alongside, accommodate, and complement traditional, opportunity reduction crime control strategies, including law enforcement. Thus, in its efforts to mobilize disadvantaged neighbourhoods, this holistic CCP model tries to bridge the instrumental with the affective-emotional, the idealistic with the pragmatic, the long-term with the short-term, and the structurally deterministic with the vast potential of human agency. It also attempts to strike a balance between individual rights and liberties with social responsibilities and collective security.

The theories and strategies proposed in this chapter have been constructed to address the obstacles to organizing disadvantaged neighbourhoods documented in the Mount Pleasant case study (chapters 3 to 5), as well as other research concerned with participation in community crime prevention programs (chapter 2), and collective action and social movements more generally (chapter 6). The strategies are also informed by successful community organizing gleaned from the research conducted in Vancouver and other locales (chapter 4). In addition, this critically oriented community development model borrows from disciplines that are concerned with local collective action, civic engagement, and the empowerment of poor communities, such as social, community, and economic development, local organizing, systems theory, social movements, urban planning and design, restorative justice, social learning, deliberative public dialogue, and participatory action research, among others. This chapter also strives towards the progressive strategies and objectives idealized for crime prevention and the criminal justice system by critical criminologists[1] and left realists, such as developing communities with binding social relations and supportive local networks (Einstadter, 1984; Pepinsky, 1991; Michalowski, 1992), a democratization of policing (Michalowski, 1983), and a greater participation of marginalized groups in determining and carrying out criminal justice polices (Taylor, 1981). The theories and strategies presented in this chapter endeavour to integrate CCP into a broader change-oriented, grass-roots movement that adheres to and reinvigorates the principles of direct democracy by increasing the meaningful participation of marginalized individuals, groups, and neighbourhoods in decisions that affect them. Indeed, this alternative model ultimately sets its sights beyond crime. Its intent is to help nurture the capacity of disadvantaged neighbourhoods to mobilize around any and all issues, endeavouring to address the common structural and situational causes of concentrated apathy, crime, poverty, marginalization, and other deleterious aspects of poor neighbourhoods.

The remainder of this chapter details this vision of a critically oriented, community development approach to CCP in disadvantaged neighbourhoods. The essential and interconnected philosophies, principles, and strategies of this model can be summarized as follows: (1) social, economic, and community development at the local level; (2) a decentralization of resources, political power, and decision-making control to neighbourhoods, while nurturing democratic principles, equality, and justice at the community level; (3) micro-level organizing that transforms existing passive crime prevention programs (e.g., Neighbourhood Watch) into action-oriented cells that are networked with one another; (4) face-to-face, deliberative, and undistorted dialogue as the primary means of communication and organization; (5) fostering and strengthening local social cohesion, social capital, and a shared identity and meaning among residents of disadvantaged and mixed-status neighbourhoods – including strategies to diffuse cleavages between different groups – while recognizing and accommodating diversity and even inter-group conflict; (6) a partnership approach that emphasizes mutual learning and empathy, and ensures greater symmetry in power relations between disadvantaged neighbourhoods and police, as well as between neighbourhoods residents; (7) the nurturing of strong local leadership and community organizations, the focus of which transcends crime; and (8) an activist state that supports, transfers resources to, and helps build capacity in disadvantaged neighbourhoods to address crime and other local problems, without usurping local control and decision-making.

Social and Community Development

Appeals to participate in local collective action in poor neighbourhoods will continue to be limited unless they are preceded or accompanied by social and community development strategies that instil in these neighbourhoods and their residents the essential prerequisites for collective action and public participation. A community development approach to CCP is premised on research that establishes a positive correlation between socio-economic status, at both individual and neighbourhood levels, and some of the most important prerequisites for civic engagement: personal and collective efficacy, an awareness and understanding of salient issues, a financial stake in a neighbourhood (i.e., home ownership), as well as local social integration, attachment, and cohesion.

A development-based approach has the potential to ameliorate within individuals and neighbourhoods the common causes of poverty, criminality, and civic disengagement, as well as a broad range of antisocial and dysfunctional behaviours. The developmental basis underlying this crime prevention model advocates greater public and private investments in disadvantaged neighbourhoods, while emphasizing a comprehensive array of programs and services encompassing prenatal care; early childhood and adolescent development (academic and behavioural); and the education, gainful employment, and empowerment of adults. Particular emphasis must be placed on programs and resources targeting the most vulnerable families, such as young, single, undereducated mothers living in poverty. These programs must benefit children and young people *indirectly* by fostering a more positive and nurturing social environment (e.g., poverty alleviation, supporting good parenting practices and a stable family, adequate housing, community beautification, strong local schools, etc.) and *directly* by fostering resiliency within and "protective factors" surrounding an at-risk child (e.g., good nutrition, remedial tutoring, physical activity, social and life skills development, etc.). Developmental programs must also benefit older youth living in disadvantaged environments by encouraging a positive socialization process through meaningful education, leisure, recreation, job training, and employment opportunities. In his review of crime prevention practices in North America and Europe, John Graham (1995: 17) cites seven basic forms of social developmental interventions for disadvantaged families: (1) preventing teenage pregnancy, (2) the provision of prenatal and post-natal services, (3) providing education and guidance for parenthood, (4) providing pre-school education for the children of disadvantaged parents, (5) providing support for families under economic and psychological stress, (6) preserving families by avoiding the removal of a child into care, and (7) preventing youth homelessness. Similarly, Irvin Waller and Daniel Sansfaçon (2000) identify the following development strategies as most promising when intervening in the lives of at-risk children, youth, and their parents: pre-school and after-school remedial programs to increase the cognitive and social abilities of children and youth; increasing support and assistance to parents; home visitations by professionals to help improve the parenting skills of young, single, low-income mothers; strengthening the social and life skills of children and young people; providing incentives to youth and adults to complete secondary studies by offering educational and financial assistance; improving the self-esteem and social integration capacity of children and young people; organizing school and after-school educational and recreational activities; and working with families of first-time young offenders.

A crucial aspect of any development approach, whether it is aimed at children, youth, or adults, is ensuring that effective and innovative educational opportunities are available and accessible locally. As documented in the previous chapter, research has also shown that education correlates with civic engagement, indirectly (by raising one's socio-economic status and personal efficacy) and directly (by providing the cognitive capacity to learn about and understand complex civic issues). Greater public resources must be invested in creating and expanding schooling and educational opportunities for children, young people, and adults in disadvantaged neighbourhoods. A range of measures should be implemented to assist schools in fully integrating at-risk children and youth: persistent truants, academic under-achievers, impulsive violence-prone children, bullies, their victims, and the social isolates. Schools serving disadvantaged neighbourhoods should be provided with specialized reintegration programs to entice dropouts back into school and teams of teachers trained to work with special needs students should be made available to these schools (Graham, 1995: 27–8). The Positive Action Through Holistic Education (PATHE) project is one example of an innovative and comprehensive approach to education for at-risk children and youth. The PATHE project consists of a partnership approach among students, teachers, parents, school administrators, educational experts, and community members, who review, revise, and implement positive changes affecting a school's curriculum, disciplinary policies, and overall environment; diagnose and strengthen school-wide academic weaknesses and truancy problems through innovative teaching techniques; provide special academic and counselling services to pupils with learning disabilities or behavioural problems; implement innovative pedagogical techniques, such as active and group learning; work to improve the sense of community and school attachment among students, teachers, and parents; promote an active role for parents in the education of their children; and help students in their transition from school to post-secondary education, job training, or the labour market (Graham, 1995: 28; Gottfredson, 1990).

Greater opportunities must also be created for adult education, with particular emphasis on reaching out to those who have dropped out of school, those who have little or no post-secondary education or marketable skills, and post-release offenders, as well as under-educated immigrants and refugees. According to Guy Henson, the first director of the adult education division for Nova Scotia during the late 1940s, adopting a holistic approach to adult education provides an ideal vehicle to enable people to take on responsibilities of citizenship, by supplying them with the methods and tools necessary to participate in issues that affect their everyday lives. For Henson, adult education has an obligation to provide more than simple vocational skills; it should also work to enhance civic engagement, build community solidarity, and initiate community-based programs (as cited in Welton and Lecky, 1997). Research also shows that the aggregate level of education of neighbourhood residents is strongly linked with the level of economic development so essential to an active and healthy community. According to a Statistics Canada (2004a) study, "investment in human capital," such as education and skills training, is three times as important to economic growth over the long run as investment in physical capital. This suggests that a priority for local economic development is investing in the education of the local population. In targeting at-risk populations through education, flexibility must be emphasized to accommodate different learning styles, schedules, speeds, and encumbrances of potential students (Stukas and Dunlap, 2002). Subsidized and free education and job training opportunities should be provided to disadvantaged populations. Alternative and flexible distance-education mediums, such as television and the Internet, should be enhanced and subsidized for underprivileged children, youth, and adults. Civics classes should be offered for all ages and should connect community involvement activities to student educational goals (Stukas and Dunlap, 2002). For Pantoja and Perry (1998: 233), essential to social and community development is a process of education that allows people to analyse and understand forces that create and sustain the conditions that may exclude them from opportunities in mainstream society, as well as their own assets, strengths, knowledge, and skills, which they can rely on to further their own development as well as that of the community in which they live. One example of an applied, experiential education philosophy that contributes to both a personal self-awareness and community development is participatory action research (discussed later in this chapter).

Employment-based programs that provide a job, job training, or work experience have been viewed as the most important social developmental strategies for older youth and adults who are at risk of chronic unemployment, offending, or have been convicted and are in the process of reintegrating into society. A legitimate job not only removes the necessity to revert to crime for income, but it can also promote pro-social behaviours, further social integration, and help expand positive social networks. The Canadian Criminal Justice Association (1989: 386) provides the following employment-based recommendations for at-risk youth and adults: secondary-school dropouts should be provided with opportunities to acquire the skills necessary to obtain and retain gainful employment; job training programs should be available to disadvantaged youth; economic policies should be developed to reduce long-term employment, and to provide fulfilling alternatives for those who are unemployed; and employers in the private and public sectors should put in place special employment entry programs for disadvantaged youth. Efforts to rescue neighbourhoods with concentrated poverty also requires supporting local economic opportunities and reviving local labour markets. This community economic development approach includes promoting small business opportunities (through no- or low-interest loans and technical help for local entrepreneurs), attracting companies to a neighbourhood (through no- or low-interest loans or tax relief), establishing business cooperatives among residents, and setting up local entrepreneurial and job training centres.

When pursued in the context of this critically oriented framework for action, community (economic) development is not simply concerned with advancing the socio-economic status of local residents or the neighbourhood as a whole. For Rubin and Rubin (1992: 10), community development is intended to achieve five goals: (1) the improvement of the quality of life of community members as a whole, through the resolution of shared problems; (2) a reduction in social inequities caused by poverty, racism, sexism, and so on; (3) exercising and preserving democratic values, as part of the process and outcome of community organizing and development; (4) personal self-development and efficacy; and (5) social cohesion. For Robin Ersing (2003: 261–2), empowering communities to achieve such developmental goals (or any goals) entails three principles: capacity-building, collaboration, and community action. The first principle involves "building the competence or capacity of local residents and groups," which means "identifying the knowledge, talents, skills, and social networks of individuals, groups, and local organizations." Second, opportunities must be created for residents and local organizations to collaborate in resolving problems and effecting positive social change by harnessing the assets, skills, and resources of individuals and groups. The third principle "is the use of advocacy or social action as change strategies" that develop or shift power to those who are marginalized and do not participate in local policy- and decision-making processes. For Ersing, a vital community empowerment goal is to reduce the dependence of poor neighbourhoods on external institutions and actors that traditionally play a major role in addressing local problems in these locales (2003: 261–2). More specifically, Pepinksy (1989: 469) asserts that CCP programs and philosophies must work to empower community members to manage their own affairs. Thus, central to a community development approach to crime prevention is empowering underprivileged groups or neighbourhoods to achieve greater political and economic self-sufficiency and independence.

Community Building, Decentralization, and the Recovery of the Political Community

To better ensure that the intertwined goals of community development, empowerment, self-sufficiency, and independence can be achieved in disadvantaged neighbourhoods, a critically oriented approach to crime prevention advocates that political power be recentred back within civil society – ultimately to the neighbourhood. This is what planning theorist John Friedmann calls the reclamation of the spatial community as the central social, political, and economic organization of society. For Friedmann (1987: 343), it is this "recovery of the political community," complete with decentralized control of public resources and decision-making power that can best provide the foundation for a truly democratic and just polity, while strengthening citizen involvement in, and public accountability for, social problems such as crime. This philosophy embodies a return to the roots of civil society where communities were largely self-reliant and not dependent upon a paternalistic state (Friedmann, 1987). The ultimate goal is the flourishing of a "fully realized direct democracy," which is characterized by political equality, where citizens" preferences count equally in a representative process; deliberation, where competing arguments are presented and given careful consideration in small, face-to-face group discussions; and participation, where a significant proportion of the affected population is engaged in public affairs equally, sincerely, and thoughtfully (Fishkin, 1995: 34). A critically oriented approach to crime prevention contributes to the realization of these lofty goals by setting its sights beyond merely addressing crime at the local level. Rather, attention is shifted to the vertical dimensions of power. No longer can CCP programs in disadvantaged neighbourhoods afford to be exclusively concerned with the delivery of crime prevention services. They must also pursue the decentralization of economic and political resources and decision-making power.

Explicit in a critically oriented, development-based approach to crime prevention is decentralization, the implications of which are two-fold. First, at the societal level, this approach involves a diffusion of power and control over public policy decisions and resources from the state to local neighbourhoods. Second, at the local level, it involves dispersing control and decision-making power among as many community members as possible. The decentralization of power and resources is based on the assumption that disadvantaged neighbourhoods can be more successfully organized if they are given greater direct control over issues and problems affecting their lives, as well as sufficient resources to address these issues. For Jim Lotz (1997: 18), "Community development is about redistributing power and resources. It is a political process, not simply a tool or technique for calming people or rubbing raw the sores of discontent." Lyons, Smuts, and Stephens (2001: 1245–6) believe that community empowerment is highly dependent on decentralizing control and decision-making to civil society, whereby a community gains increased power concerning its own affairs and destiny. Radical planning theorists Grabow and Heskin (1973: 109) write that for people to be truly free, they must participate in decisions that affect their lives, which necessitates their involvement in public decision-making. To accomplish this, "Society must be reorganized so that the maximum number of decisions possible can be within the effective reach of as many people as possible." Relying on a metaphor of biological evolution to depict the importance of decentralized decision-making, Grabow and Heskin declare that complex, diversified organisms survive while single-cell organisms perish. This metaphor parallels a line of reasoning for decentralized decision-making, which is premised upon the internal complexity of systems, made by General Systems Theory. As systems grow larger and more complex, ways must be found to improve planning, coordination, and control over a multitude of activities that belong jurisdictionally, functionally, and geographically to different subsystems, but which satisfy a common set of objectives (Churchman, 1968; Boothroyd, 1994).

Within the last thirty years, there has also been some incremental decentralization of criminal justice decision-making power, principally through the development and implementation of community crime prevention, community-oriented policing, and community justice models. Neighbourhood residents have being given more say in the referral, treatment, and punishment of offenders through restorative justice (Galaway and Hudson, 1990; Umbreit, 1994; Classen, 1996;

Bazemore, 2000) and community prosecution and corrections programs (Pearce and Olderman, 1995; Weinstein, 1998; Boland, 1998). Notwithstanding these important precedents, the decentralization of the criminal justice system in most Western countries has been piecemeal and incomplete; control over local crime control decisions and resources is still largely concentrated within the state. A critically oriented approach to crime prevention advocates that the decentralization of the criminal justice system be increased in its depth, breadth, and speed in order to address what Adam Crawford (1997: 259) calls the continued "democratic deficit in crime control." For Taylor (1981: 121), the "democratization of the criminal justice system" is achieved by promoting political action at the local level and by increasing representation of the disenfranchised in policing, courts, and corrections, thereby creating a system that is "authentically responsible to popular demands for justice and social defence." By inviting a greater say in criminal justice institutions, policies, and processes, faith in the system may grow, thereby encouraging greater participation. At the very least, there must be a greater decentralization of policing decision-making power and resources to communities, which will go a long way towards fulfilling the unrequited normative aspects of community policing. This could include establishing joint police-community committees at the neighbourhood level to foster ongoing problem-solving partnerships, and, more importantly, facilitate the sharing of decision-making power over local policing and crime prevention policies and programs. At the operational level, community policing/crime prevention offices should be established and provided with significant decision-making, administrative, policy, and budgetary autonomy from centralized municipal police executives. These offices should be jointly staffed by police and community members and can be governed by the aforementioned committees. Neighbourhood groups should also be given the powers to conduct periodic reviews of policing and crime prevention operations to ensure that their local needs, priorities, and goals are met.

A decentralization of public power and resources must transcend crime control and criminal justice issues, and be extended to governance in general. Numerous experiments that decentralize and delegate political power to local neighbourhoods have been implemented in cities and countries throughout the world. In North America, one of the notable pioneers, according to Walsh (1997) is Seattle, where thirteen district councils were created "in which the city's more than two hundred neighbourhood groups communicate with each other." These district councils, to which any community organization or businesses can belong, are directly involved in setting priorities for the city's annual operating budget. The city's Department of Neighborhoods assists the councils with their work and staffs neighbourhood service centres, which are organized along these district council lines and which function as mini city halls. The city of Saint Paul, Minnesota, has seventeen neighbourhood district councils, all of which are funded by the city. The councils are directly involved in the city's capital budget process and provide advice and direction to the local government on capital improvements for their respective neighbourhoods. Because neighbourhood residents "directly elect district council members, the councils provide an effective way for citizens to influence decisions affecting their neighbourhoods" (46). Notwithstanding these innovations in the decentralization of political power, a critically oriented approach to community development goes beyond these measures and demands that the state transfer greater resources to needy neighbourhoods and civic organizations for social, political, and economic development. In this sense, decentralization and community development must be connected to just and redistributive economic and social policies. One indirect way this can be accomplished is for governments to provide a two- or three-dollar tax deduction for every dollar donated by an individual or corporate taxpayer to a charitable organization (Nelson, 1976: 68).

Complementing the diffusion of power and resources from the state to neighbourhoods is the devolution of decision-making power among as many community members as possible. This horizontal decentralization is especially important within demographically heterogeneous neighbourhoods to counter the tendency of what Adam Crawford (1998: 244–5) calls a "moral authoritarianism" whereby one dominant group or interest is able to impose its values upon all others. Thus, central to the principles of decentralization at the local level is a robust and inclusive democratic decision-making process that protects against the dangers of authoritarianism or monopolization by any one particular group (which in the case of Mount Pleasant is the small cadre of middle-class homeowners). A democratized and decentralized system of decision-making must simultaneously overcome asymmetrical power relations within a neighbourhood, while ensuring a voice to those who traditionally have been silenced and rendered powerless.

This neighbourhood-level decentralization imperative is supported

by the Mount Pleasant case study and research examining local collective action, which shows that organizing success is often maximized
when focused at the block level (see chapter 4). In fact, decentralization
within a neighbourhood might best be achieved through the type of
small, local action groups envisioned by John Friedmann (1973; 1987).
By stressing a localized base, these small groups provide the foundation for a bottom-up, decentralized control over local issues and problem solving (Freidmann, 1987: 275). The tenets that underlie these
action groups include self-organization around interpersonal relations
based on shared space and common concerns, flexibility in adjusting to
local conditions, personal interaction that emphasizes face-to-face dialogue and the deliberative discussion of issues in a supportive environment, and a linkage with other local groups. These block-level action
groups could build upon, expand, and revitalize the passive, apolitical
Neighbourhood Watch (NW) program as the cellular backbone of an
activist, decentralized, and democratic neighbourhood where residents
discuss, deliberate, strategize, and then act in tandem with other
blocks to address local problems. These spatially finite, task-oriented
action groups would counter the vagueness of the existing NW format
which, according to McConville and Shepherd (1992: 5), has "a diluted
clarity" with regard to its purpose and the obligations of its members.
Indeed, one of the greatest dilemmas faced by NW programs is sustaining the active participation of members, and this problem is partially due to the passive function ascribed to its membership. The
action groups can also potentially operate as local vehicles for the
implementation of "restorative justice" models to deal with criminal
acts and offenders that affect their neighbourhood, thereby encouraging greater participation of community members in the administration
of justice. The adaptation of local action groups for restorative and
community justice purposes not only facilitates the decentralization of
criminal justice powers from the state to local neighbourhoods, but can
be charged with mediating and resolving disputes between community members (Michalowski, 1983: 2).

In addition to taking on problems at the block level, these action
groups should be brought together into a larger, neighbourhood-wide
collective that can address issues at the community level. These block-
level action groups, and the broader neighbourhood coalition, should
also forge a working relationship with a variety of other local groups
with the goal being the creation of a broad-based coalition that links
crime prevention groups with other link-minded organizations, includ-

ing neighbourhood associations, community development groups, ethnic communities, anti-poverty groups, trade unions, environmental groups, and local businesses, among others. These networked linkages should be both horizontal (i.e., groups from the same neighbourhood or community) as well as vertical (e.g., partnerships with corporations, universities, politicians, and state agencies). The latter is particularly important in efforts to access economic resources and political power that exists outside of neighbourhoods.

Decentralizing decision-making power also means that local communities must assume greater responsibility for information gathering and knowledge accumulation and application. In his 1956 book, *An Introduction to Cybernetics*, organizational theorist W.R. Ashby proposed his Law of Requisite Variety, which postulates the need to make the information processing capability of an organization comparable and compatible with the information presented by the system on which the exercise of control is sought. In other words, to control instability in a system, the variety in the regulatory or control process must correspond to the variety in the system that is being regulated. The decentralization of information processing inherent in a systems approach to public policy and local problem solving is premised on the assumption that the world is becoming more and more complex, and this complexity within social systems cannot be managed exclusively from the centre (i.e., the state). Rather, solutions lie "in improving our collective information processing capabilities so that we can become more effective in managing ourselves" (Boothroyd, 1994: 150). According to Sietrov (1989: 218), systems theorists "should create not a theory of development, but a theory of self-development, not a theory of guidance, but a theory of self-guidance, for the object of general systems methodology represents a self-developing, self-regulating, self-guiding system." Order in society is not achieved through centralized pre-programming, but by a dynamic process of give and take of plans, demands, and responses that is steered through the information processing capacity of a system.

Informed by Ashby's law, local crime and disorder issues must be viewed as complex social problems, which cannot be controlled exclusively from the centre (i.e., the state, the police, or a few community leaders). A critically oriented approach to crime prevention compels neighbourhoods to demand greater access to information controlled by the police and other criminal justice agencies. Information such as crime rates, dangerous offenders, and policing priorities and strategies should flow openly and be shared with neighbourhoods on a periodic and regular basis (while ensuring that the confidentiality of some police operations, the due process rights of the accused, and the privacy of victims and others are protected). Information would be collected, analysed, disseminated, and interpreted with all the end-users in mind, and disseminated as widely as possible throughout the neighbourhood so that residents have a sound basis upon which to make decisions. A study by Kuttschreuter and Wiegman (1997) found that information meetings held for citizens on residential burglary led to an increase in the knowledge, expectations, and participation of community members in the implementation of prevention measures. One theoretical premise of Crime Prevention through Environmental Design is that the plentiful use of signage, especially in high-risk areas such as underground parking garages, increases safety, while decreasing fear and anxiety among users of that space. The dissemination of information from police and civilian crime prevention leaders to neighbourhood residents should be made through a number of different mediums, including phone calls, bulletin boards, flyers, newspaper ads, the Internet, e-mail, and personal contact. The aforementioned action groups can also constitute a crucial medium for the distribution of information to all community members. Most important, residents should be given the chance to hear this information personally through public meetings to which all residents are invited. These meetings should provide information on current crime problems in the neighbourhood, emphasizing those reported by neighbourhood members, the action that has been taken, and the impact of this action. These meetings should also be used to assess and provide input into broader policing and crime prevention strategies as well as specific problems. Ultimately, these meetings must contribute to the goal of increased community input and local control over policing and community safety priorities and policies, and, as such, would be part of a larger process of action-oriented strategizing by the community, in partnership with police and other relevant state agencies. One process that can help combine the principles of information dissemination, decentralized control, and community action would begin with an invitation to all community members to attend a meeting with police and/or other relevant government officials. Information can then be taken away from the meeting by residents where it can be discussed and deliberated upon separately by the aforementioned block-level action groups. All of the groups (or their representatives) would then be reassembled to compare notes and to discuss and prepare a coordinated community response, which then would be presented to police at a subsequent community-wide meeting. It would be at this meeting that (hopefully) some resolution and/or action plan could be formulated.

In a democratic systems approach to local problem solving, information must flow openly; be widely shared; and be collected, analysed, disseminated, and interpreted with the end-users of the information in mind (Boothroyd, 1994). Moreover, community members cannot just be the passive recipients of information presented by police or other government agencies; they must also be actively involved in collecting, analysing, and using information as a basis for action. This means that community members and local organizations must be empowered to, and have mechanisms in place to, define their problems and gather and analyse information that can be then used to solve these problems. Simply put, if neighbourhoods are to develop and implement strategies to address local problems, they must not only have adequate information, but they must also have control over the collection of information and its application at the local level. In the past decade, a number of opportunities and tools have been created to encourage and help neighbourhood residents collect information at the local level to contribute to their crime prevention efforts, including safety audits and victimization surveys (Metro Action Committee, 1989; The Women's Action Centre, 1995).

A critically oriented theory of crime prevention expands on these important data collection and planning tools by promoting a Participatory Action Research (PAR) approach that is intended to combine research, social investigation, local knowledge and experience, education, and collective action by community members to address local issues or problems (Hall, 1981: 7, as cited in Yeich, 1996: 113). PAR is predicated on two main principles: the democratization of the information gathering and knowledge accumulation process and positive social change (Todhunter, 2001). The word "participation" represents a decentralizing and democratizing thrust in social research that recognizes the value of a number of key partners in generating useful knowledge to address public issues and social problems. The core researchers and decision-makers are in fact those who are affected by the issue or problem and have ultimate control over how to intervene. The participatory aspects of the research planning and data-gathering process is meant to contribute to a more informed decision-making process. Unlike traditional scientific approaches to local social problem solving – where state technocrats or professional researchers define the process, collect and analyse the data, and generate knowledge – the community's interests are identified and defined as the starting point. Community members also determine the focus of knowledge generation, data collection and analysis, and the action that must be taken to manage, improve, or solve their problem situation (Todhunter, 2001). The "action" component of PAR asserts that the research is intended to directly address local issues or problems, and, in a more radical sense, to make a contribution to social change that is based on the desires and direct involvement of group participants. When research is carried out by people affected by local issues or problems, they become engaged in a "collective, self-reflective enquiry." Through the acquisition and control of knowledge, understanding, and indigenous problem solving, this enquiry contributes to their own empowerment (Todhunter, 2001). Thus, PAR facilitates the education of local residents (as people gather and analyse information about a problem or issue), fosters collective action (as people work together to gather information and learn that they share the same problem), and promotes capacity- and community-building (as people work to solve the problem collectively) (Rubin and Rubin, 1992: 156). Guided by a philosophy of participatory action research, community development and safety policies and programs would be researched, planned, organized, and implemented by the block-level action groups individually and/or as part of the broader neighbourhood coalition. Police, other criminal justice officials, and professional researchers would serve as technical consultants. The results of the research conducted at the block level by the localized action groups can then be collated as part of a larger, comprehensive action plan for the neighbourhood as a whole. A PAR approach to safety audits or other crime prevention research goes beyond gathering information on situational factors or symptoms of crime; it investigates a combination of political, social, and economic underpinnings of crime and other community problems, while identifying and exploring the links between the local and the external; that is, the relationship between local problems and broader political and economic forces.

The Social Learning Praxis

Central to the process and goals of participatory action research, and the broader principles of decentralized information gathering and knowledge development, is the concept of social learning. While the accumulation of scientifically based knowledge is the hallmark of a positivist-inspired, rational planning approach to crime and other local problems, one must recognize that knowledge is also derived from experience. A community development approach to crime prevention repudiates an all-consuming reliance on scientific methodology and calls for greater attention to local knowledge and life experiences as an important basis to inform local problem solving. A fundamental premise of social learning is that knowledge grows from, and is informed by, sustained practice. Social learning is an ongoing dialectical process where existing understanding (theory) is enriched with lessons drawn from experience, "and the 'new' understanding is then applied in the continuing process of action and change" (Friedmann, 1987: 81). Because CCP is fundamentally a community-based approach to local problem solving, it must be recursive and iterative, constantly being informed through the process of social learning, primarily by neighbourhood residents, but also involving state officials and other professionals.

Social learning theory is predicated on the writings of John Dewey, the American philosopher, who strongly advocated "learning by doing." All valid knowledge, declared Dewey, comes from experience, by which he means the interaction between people and their physical and social environments. "The plans which are formed, the principles which man projects as guides of reconstructive action are not dogmas. They are hypotheses to be worked in practice, and to be rejected, corrected, and expanded as they fail or succeed in giving our present experience the guidance it requires" (Dewey, 1958: 189). The pioneering work of John Dewey continues to be reflected in new and innovative pedagogical approaches to education, which can be applied as part of community development efforts. "Active learning," for example, advocates techniques that help students learn through greater active engagement with the subject matter and associated themes. Experiential learning is meant to "shape knowledge individually as mediated by personal experience" (Weimer, 2002), which is accomplished by connecting and translating a student's own experiences and observations with abstract subject matter (concepts and theories). The experiential learning cycle consists of four systematically interrelated stages: (1) the immediate or concrete experience of the individual (2) is used as the basis for observations and reflections (3) which are then assimilated and distilled into an existing or new hypothesis, theory, or concept (4) from which new implications can be drawn, tested, and then used as a guide in creating new (learning) experiences (Barr and Tagg, 1995). Like participatory action research, social learning is an attempt to fuse theory (knowledge) with practice (action) (Friedmann (1973, 1979, 1987). Not only must theory be informed by action, but it must be developed by those collective actors who are directly executing this action. As Daly (1978: 200) notes, "To be relevant, social and urban planning theory must be developed by those who are ultimately affected by it in order for it to have validity. One is either a participant in the process by which knowledge is developed, or one is an object of it." Social learning is an important part of a decentralized polity and an active political community because it promotes the view that local problem solving needs to draw on materials from the everyday life of local communities. Invaluable to the design and planning of local problem-solving strategies, is the knowledge of community members, which Vadhansinhdhu (1995) characterizes as technical, descriptive, explanatory, prescriptive, subtle, dynamic, scattered, and holistic. If neighbourhoods are to be more than the mere object of crime prevention theories, then they must participate in the process of theorizing, which is informed by participatory action research as well as personal and collective experiences, and then refined and validated through application and experimentation.

CCP theory must incorporate the principles of social learning by including a greater reliance on local knowledge and experiences. Despite the myriad of studies attesting to the failings of CCP in disadvantaged neighbourhoods, traditional crime prevention theories and programs have changed little in the last few decades; they have remained largely static, relying on suspect epistemologies, faulty assumptions, and worn approaches that have failed to mobilize those most in need of community safety initiatives. One reason accounting for the theoretical failings and stagnant models of CCP is that this field has been controlled by a cabal of professionals, including government officials, local organizers, and researchers. A social learning approach to community development and safety avoids the synthetic, rigid, never-changing, "cookie cut-outs" that are endlessly imposed on poor, high-crime neighbourhoods by dominant theories or external actors. Instead, what must be stressed are organic, evolving, and highly individualized interventions that are unique to each neighbourhood (and block or building), and are derived from the practical experiences of local residents and refined through a recursive process. Crime prevention plans should be continually shaped by cumulative knowledge garnered from application and experimentation. In turn, the localized knowledge and individualized theory of crime prevention and community safety would be continuously derived from and enriched by experience and practice. If opportunity reduction approaches to crime prevention are unsuccessful in mobilizing poor communities or addressing local crime problems, as research has shown to be the case, then the traditional assumptions and theories must be modified or discarded based on the lessons learned from implementation failures and the experiences of local participants. Community development and safety initiatives must emphasize an approach that takes the life experiences of individual residents and entire communities, in particular concern over local social problems and an acute awareness of how to address these concerns. It would then combine these experiences with the knowledge gained through the participatory research process and put into action through specific crime prevention and community development measures. In keeping with the principles of decentralization, the iterative process of social learning would be reflected in the work of the small, action groups.

Police agencies can also mediate the theory and practice of crime prevention by becoming learning organizations, which, according to William Geller (1999: 3), is an organization that is continually expanding its capacity to evolve by capitalizing "on its own and others' experiences – successes as well as failures – to continually hone strategies, tactics, operations, and networks of collaborators" in order to "serve and strengthen their communities more effectively, more efficiently, and more legitimately" (2). Geller urges police departments to constantly reflect and evaluate their strategies by institutionalizing an internal research and development function and to encourage collaborative brainstorming and creative, multidisciplinary, critical thinking that invites reflection, questions traditional assumptions, and approaches and promotes imaginative problem-solving techniques. As importantly, police become learning organizations by listening to those they serve and by incorporating the experiential knowledge of residents and entire communities into policing and crime prevention strategies (Geller, 1999). This mutually didactic relationship between police and the public encourages an efflorescent partnership where the processed, technical knowledge of the police officer is fused with the local, personal knowledge of the resident, and "both are fused with action through an unbroken sequence of interpersonal relations" (Friedmann, 1987: 394).

Nurturing Social Cohesion in Disadvantaged and Mixed-Status Neighbourhoods

An essential element in the aforementioned theories and strategies is community building, which entails efforts to transform a spatial grouping of people (a neighbourhood) into a locally based, socially cohesive network of neighbours who are bound by enduring personal ties and networks, a shared identity and common goals, a high level of social interaction, and a sense of wholeness (a community). Community building is central to crime prevention organizing, at the very least because research has shown that neighbourhoods with a well-developed sense of social cohesion and collective efficacy are more likely to successfully mobilize around local problems. Some of the essential "domains" of social cohesion, according to Forrest and Kearns (2001: 2129) are the existence of common values and objectives, participation in civic affairs, informal social control, tolerance, respect for difference, social solidarity, reductions in wealth disparity, acknowledgement of social obligations and willingness to assist others, strong social networks, a high degree of social interaction, and place attachment. Similarly, strong activist communities are contingent upon trust and reciprocity among members, part of what Robert Putnam and colleagues (1993, 1995) refers to as "social capital." Without sufficient social cohesion or capital, neighbourhoods are deprived of a strong foundation upon which development strategies and vibrant community organizations can be built and sustained. A community development approach to crime prevention recognizes the vital importance of building, reviving, and sustaining social cohesion and social capital within disadvantaged neighbourhoods as a foundation for local collective problem solving and the broader goals of a healthy, self-governing, politically efficacious community.

As detailed in the previous chapter, the two most important organic prerequisites for a socially cohesive neighbourhood appear to be demographic homogeneity and a relatively high socio-economic status. The great challenge is to foster social cohesion and social capital in neighbourhoods that suffer from both demographic heterogeneity and a low socio-economic status. Because demographic homogeneity within disadvantaged neighbourhoods is not achievable, nor is it desirable, social and community development represents the most effective way to nurture local social cohesion. However, given that the developmental process is often long term in nature, the need to nurture social cohesion in the absence of such socio-economic advancement remains. Social interaction, in particular, positive interpersonal communications and face-to-face dialogue, has long been seen as a principal means by which local social cohesion is developed. One of the most effective (and enjoyable) ways to foster interaction and dialogue at the local level are neighbourhood-based social gatherings, commonly referred to as block parties. As Walsh (1997: 46) writes, "celebrating the concept of living together" as neighbours and enjoying one another's company is a successful way to highlight the importance of community. Block parties give neighbours a chance to meet one another in a relaxed social setting and can be conveniently held in backyards, parks, schools, and community centres, or on the street. A block party comes in just about any shape or size and avoids any formal businesslike pretensions of traditional community organization for the sake of a party or carnival-like atmosphere. Neighbourhood social gatherings can come at the end of a community development activity, such as a meeting, a block clean-up, a beautification project, or a garage sale (Dobson, 2005), and can be used to continue community building efforts. Potluck dinners promote cooperation, coordination, and sharing; games for children, youth, and adults can integrate exercises that build trust and teamwork; and in multicultural communities, social gatherings create the perfect opportunity to learn about different cultural traditions, thereby diffusing racial, ethnic, or religious stereotypes and divisions.

Modifications to the physical environment have also been touted as a way to promote social interaction and cohesion. Architectural as well as urban planning and design theories propose that the built and physical environment can be designed to influence social behaviour, which include fostering emotional attachments to a locality, defining the character and identity of a neighbourhood, and encouraging social interaction and cohesion. According to Emily Talen (1999), the home and neighbourhood design philosophy called "new urbanism" attempts to build a sense of community through the careful design and integration of private residential space with surrounding public space. Social interaction is promoted by designing residences in such a way that people are encouraged to get out of their houses and out into the public sphere. One way this is achieved is by limiting private space: lots and setbacks are small, houses are positioned close to sidewalks, and porches that face onto the street are encouraged. Personal space is, in a sense, sacrificed in order to increase the density of acquaintanceship and the nurturing of a "vigorous community spirit." As far as density and scale are concerned, a sense of community can be promoted through small-scale, well-defined neighbourhoods with clear boundaries and a natural centre (preferably an inviting public space). When smaller scales are juxtaposed with increased residential density, face-to-face interaction is further promoted. High-density town centres are an integral part of a new urbanism that promotes commercial viability and a revived public realm. Streets also have an overt social purpose in new urbanism, and are designed to accommodate the pedestrian, to encourage street life, and to increase social encounters among residents. Public space is used for similar goals: neighbourhood gathering places are encouraged, emphasizing parks and civic centres. Mixed land use is also emphasized because when a place of residence is combined with places to work, shop, or recreate, it encourages a more holistic, self-contained community. A mixture of housing types also encourages random personal contact between people of different social classes (Talen, 1999). Proper design can also be used to "create identity and a sense of pride for fragmented neighbourhoods," writes urban planner Sherry Plaster (2002: 19–20). For Plaster, the design imperatives of "placemaking" include the use of names (which provide a sense of local identity), aesthetically pleasing functional features (e.g., clocks, parks, sidewalks, lighting, community rooms, transit stops, etc.), signage (for information and identification), landscaping and public art works (which increase the aesthetics of a locality), and historical landmarks (which link residents to a neighbourhood's history). Charles Dobson (2005) suggests that a distinctive community identity or "expression" can be achieved through such physical design features as community-made signs and markers that define a neighbourhood's boundaries (residents in Seattle name their neighbourhoods, and then help design colourful street signs to mark the boundaries), community-made signs that assert a strong sense of informal social control (residents of one Vancouver street have hand-painted signs that identify the street and ask motorists to slow down and watch for children playing), the use of streets as a community blackboard (in another Vancouver project, residents seeking a park painted a mural showing their ideas on the street surface, which then became a forum for public discussion), and the painting of wall murals or banners to hang from lamp standards (these can beautify a neighbourhood, invite social interaction during its creation, achieve an artful representation of a neighbourhood and its diversity, and promote a sense of personal aesthetic achievement, local belonging, and attachment among participants).

Nurturing a Collective Identity and Shared Meaning within a Heterogeneous Population

Efforts to develop local social cohesion and social capital can also be advanced by nurturing a shared identity among local residents. For Etzioni (2003: 226), a cohesive community has two characteristics: first, "a web of affect-laden relationships among a group of individuals that often crisscross and reinforce one another," and second, "a measure of commitment to a set of shared values, norms, and meanings, and a shared history and identity, in short a particular culture." As detailed in chapter 6, contemporary social movements are characterized by a shared, collective identity among participants (Melucci, 1980). In turn, this collective identity builds upon and feeds into "shared meaning," which Marris (1982b: 56) defines as the emotional attachments underlying a common cause, a collective identity, or a social movement which (potential) participants can aspire to or identify with. This sense of shared meaning or purpose is critical to collective action, according to Hoch (1984: 90, 91), because it provides a motivating purpose and a consciousness that is emotionally driven and is shared by the collective.

As discussed in the previous chapter, collective identity and shared meaning is a defining element of crime prevention groups in Mount Pleasant, due largely to the homogeneity of their membership and their common (middle-class) values and goals. Given this, the objective of a community development approach to crime prevention in heterogeneous, disadvantaged neighbourhoods is to promote an inclusive collective identity that transcends demographic differences. This means finding common ground between homeowners and renters, between different ethnic groups, between the professional and the labourer, between the conservative and the radical, between the police officer and the neighbourhood resident, and even between the victim and the offender. This is not an easy task to say the least. However, a community development approach to crime prevention acknowledges and builds upon the interpersonal and inter-group conflict that exists within mixed-status neighbourhoods such as Mount Pleasant. The same cannot be said for traditional CCP theory. Because of its fundamental assumption of a pluralistic society, the community mobilization model within traditional CCP theory fails in mixed-status neighbourhoods because it does not recognize that, internally, such neighbourhoods are an assemblage of competing groups (Grine, 1994: 460). Hence, in ignoring inter-group conflict, traditional CCP theory has no strategy to accommodate and build upon such conflict for community development and safety purposes. In pursuing the goals of community building, heterogeneous neighbourhoods must tolerate, accommodate, and build upon differences and even conflict between individual residents and groups (Allen and Cars, 2001: 2207).

As Adam Crawford writes, mutual recognition of differences is a preferable premise for community building, as opposed to a forced, reluctant, or tenuous consensus, which hides conflicts below the surface and often seeks to manage opposition by unaccountable and undemocratic means, leaving differential power relations unchallenged and unregulated, and potentially excluding and alienating large swaths of the local population (1997: 291, 311). The community building challenge for heterogeneous neighbourhoods is how best to "mediate competing claims" and negotiate local conflict in a socially constructive manner that forges the connections that link, rather than separate, people and groups (291). The importance of "diversity, disagreement, and constructive conflict negotiation" should be pursued with the goal of exposing and managing difference "within the context of a common interest and public purpose" (297). For community safety to hold back the dynamics of oligopoly, authoritarianism, and a narrow-based mobilization, "both government and local community safety practitioners will need to foster the conditions in which partnerships can flourish and to nurture forms of co-operation, rooted in mutual acceptance of difference and inter-organisational trust" (Crawford, 1998: 244–5). As Anthony Giddens (1994) points out, the tricky question is how diverse groups can cohere or be integrated into the wider social order, while at the same time respecting cultural differences. What is needed are forms of social cohesion that foster social solidarities, yet preserve a cosmopolitan acceptance of cultural differences. This requires "social dynamics" that seek to increase public interaction between different groups (Crawford, 1997: 289–90). For Robert Putnam (2000), the path to cohesive and well-functioning communities and societies that are heterogeneous and complex is paved with what he calls "bridging social capital," which are the bonds of trust, reciprocity, and connectedness that can be formed across diverse social groups and which can reduce tensions through "the beneficial effects of interpersonal contact across previously delineated group boundaries, such as race and class" (Stukas and Dunlap, 2002: 414). The diversity and potential for conflict and disagreements in such neighbourhoods must be carefully harnessed to ensure that inter-group cleavages are not exacerbated, but instead contribute to greater interaction, understanding, trust, cooperation, collective empowerment, and joint problem solving.

Efforts to forge an inclusive, collective identity and local social cohesion within disadvantaged neighbourhoods must transcend demographic characteristics and other perceived differences, which build upon, but do not obliterate such differences or smother individual identities. One must also accept the importance of individuality and diversity within the larger shared identity and acknowledge that one's identification with a community or a movement "does not necessarily mean completely sharing a systematic and coherent vision of the world" (Della Porta and Diani, 1999: 100, 109). What is desirable is the nurturing of what I call an "inclusive pooled identity" – the development of a highly individualized mosaic for a local community that borrows from different existing identities of local residents, which is meant to help them share in the broader community identity while retaining their existing individual and/or group identity(ies). This idea borrows from the concept of multiculturalism advocated by Parekh (2000: 220), who views the hallmarks of a multicultural society as those in which each culture has incorporated some elements of the other(s). This new multicultural dimension imaginatively transforms "the elements borrowed from different traditions into something wholly different."

Preferably, efforts to foster social cohesion, social capital, and a collective identity, on the one hand, with action-oriented community development and local social problem-solving strategies, on the other, should be joined. Community building and development projects should be combined so that attention is "focused on producing unified activities that require the energy of diverse people to reach a shared goal. It is not enough to simply try to negotiate group differences. These common projects should address community conditions, such as housing, education, and recreation" (Vertovec, 1997). One technique that can be employed to foster social cohesion and collective identity, while incorporating a strategic, joint problem-solving ancillary, is a "search conference" (Sinclair, 1994). This structured form of an action-oriented, deliberative, and unifying dialogue is meant to bring together people from opposing camps concerning a particular issue. The goal of the search conference is to discover common interests and goals and to "search" for a shared, desirable future without trampling upon existing values or stifling opinions. As with other types of "deliberative dialogue" models, a search conference is often used as part of a process that helps groups develop strategic plans, and is especially suited for a diverse assemblage of stakeholders. In this strategic, action-oriented context, a search conference first promotes a dialogue among participating individuals and (opposing) groups that seeks to open new channels of communication and to promote the exploration and development of cooperative efforts. Once this common ground is established, participants can then develop a plan of action. For Jacksteit and Kaufmann (1997), dialogue is the key to opening the door to common ground. Dialogue is different from debate, which is about persuading others that your views are "right" and that the views of others are "wrong." Dialogue is concerned with increasing understanding and being understood, rather than persuading others or proving your position is the only correct one. While a search for common ground includes making compromises to arrive at "a middle position," it is really about identifying shared values and concerns. People are not asked to change their views on a particular issue or to force or simulate agreement where it does not exist. Instead, they are encouraged to be curious about different viewpoints and their reasoning; to look beyond labels, stereotypes, and prejudices; and, most importantly, to understand and establish empathy with one another (Jacksteit and Kaufmann, 1997).

Jacksteit and Kaufmann (1997) describe a basic search conference design for promoting dialogue, understanding, dialogue, and action. The workshop is designed as an all-day affair, which is necessary for the often time-consuming processes of building trust, finding common ground, and developing solutions while accommodating deliberative dialogue techniques. The workshop, which is guided by one or more trained facilitators, begins with a round of introductions by participants, including why they chose to attend the workshop and what role they will play. The purpose of the search conference and the ground rules that participants agree to at the time of their registration are then explained. Participants then complete a questionnaire specific to the issue(s) to be discussed. The questionnaire has two parts: (1) respondents answer as themselves, and (2) respondents answer as they think participants in the workshop who are on the opposite side of the issue would answer. The large group breaks into smaller groups of four or five, including a facilitator. In these small group settings, participants are asked to share their view on the issue and how and why they arrived at this view. The dialogue usually begins with the sharing of personal experience because these "experiences cannot be argued about nor agreed or disagreed with." Conveying experiences also "invites understanding responses from those who hear them" (Jacksteit and Kaufmann, 1997: 14). Participants are then invited to discuss what they might learn from the opinions of those on the other side of the issue. After everyone has had a chance to speak, the full conference then reconvenes for about 30 minutes to share their insights and discoveries and to discuss their experiences in small-group dialogue. After lunch, the results of the survey are presented and participants are asked to identify points of agreement and disagreement, including any misconceptions stemming from the survey findings. The small groups then reconvene in the afternoon. The question for dialogue in this session varies, but often the participants are asked to speak about their feelings and experiences in relation to how those on the other side of the issue view the former participants' ideas, beliefs, and opinions, and how it feels to be misunderstood and/or stereotyped. The group may also be asked to identify a mutually agreeable goal and how they can work together towards reaching it. At the end of the day, all conference participants reconvene for the final time to share what they learned, to present any resolutions reached in their small-group sessions, to explore the implications of the day's experience, and to bring some final closure to the conference (which may be a resolution, an action plan, an accord or common ground that was reached, or simply an agreement to meet again). These workshops often close by having participants describe their experience, what they have learned, and what empathy, if any, they have developed for those on the opposite side of the issue.

Social Inclusion/Stake in the Community

An overarching goal of a community development approach to crime prevention, especially when applied to disadvantaged and mixed-status neighbourhoods, is to stimulate a broad-based, inclusive, and representative mobilization of residents around crime and other local social problems. The implications of an inclusive mobilization of residents in heterogeneous neighbourhoods are twofold. First, appeals to community and a common identity must not exclude anyone based on demographic characteristics. Second, emphasis must be placed on creating opportunities and incentives for those who are often marginalized and excluded from the public sphere due to poverty, a lack of education, mental health issues, language or cultural barriers, and so on. These two implications for an inclusive mobilization strategy are interconnected, because those who are excluded from local collective action are disproportionately made up of individuals and groups who suffer from the greater problem of social exclusion. Shorthand terms such as social exclusion, social isolation, alienation, marginalization, or disenfranchisement are used to denote a by-product of "what can happen when people or areas suffer from a combination of linked problems such as unemployment, poor skills, low incomes, unfair discrimination, poor housing, high crime, bad health and family breakdown" (Office of the Deputy Prime Minister, 2004: 4). Social exclusion is characterized by a social and physical detachment and isolation, a lack of supportive and sustaining relationships with others, low self-esteem, and higher rates of depression (Bloom and Kilgore, 2003: 440). Social isolation, according to Duncan (1999: 9), refers to the segregation of poor people from middle- and upper-income citizens, resources, activities, and opportunities; in other words, "it keeps the haves out of contact with the have-nots."

Efforts to build a truly inclusive democratic civil society must involve the integration of marginalized groups and individuals into "mainstream" society. Strategies that nurture a socially cohesive neighbourhood and a local common identity must logically stress the integration of the neighbourhood's residents, which is measured by the nature and scope of an individual resident's local social network, local social interaction, and participation in local civic action, as well as his or her belonging and attachment to the local community. As Zenaida, Rajulton, and Turcotte (2003) put it, social integration is social cohesion measured at the individual level. Reaching out to and including the socially marginalized within the local community and society at large must occur along four dimensions: economic (inclusion), socio-economic (development), political (participation), and socio-cultural (sense of belonging).

A lack of integration in and attachment to a neighbourhood in which one lives is a principal reason why people do not become involved in local collective action; the willingness of people to act communally for the good of a neighbourhood is related to their sense of local attachment and belonging and the way they view their own role within the community (Flint, 2002: 261). Thus, the question is, how do you get people in poor communities, especially those who are socially isolated, to "buy a stake" in their community? At the very least, efforts to integrate those who are socially isolated and excluded need to be sincerely asked why they do not take part in local group activities or why they shy away from other forms of social interaction. They should also be asked, What would make you feel more welcome in the community? What would it take to get you more involved? and What do you hope and desire for your community, especially as it relates to your own life?

The extent to which residents are locally integrated is also dependent on their ability to identify with others who make up the local community or neighbourhood group. The more strongly one identifies with other members of a community, the greater the chance that local integration, a sense of belonging, and group participation will occur. As detailed in previous chapters, research into civic participation, collective action, and social movements, including community crime prevention, indicates that those who become involved tend to identify with the larger group (and not just the issues addressed by the group). According to Pratkanis and Turner (1996), one tactic to recruit and sustain participation in collective action is to provide individuals with a social identity. People "often strive to maintain self-esteem via a collective self-orientation," and do so by "becoming committed to a group, participating in its activities, identifying with its behaviours, adopting its symbols and attitudes and so on." Thus, efforts to include those who are locally and socially isolated should involve helping them identify what they have in common with others in the neighbourhood, especially those active in local groups and activities. This can be facilitated, in part, through vehicles already spelled out in this chapter, such as the block-level action groups, block parties, and search conferences.

Within mixed-status neighbourhoods, responsibility for identifying commonalities among residents, and the broader goal of integrating the poor and socially isolated into the local community, falls upon the shoulders of those more affluent, empowered, and civically minded residents, who should begin by providing (local) support networks for disadvantaged and marginalized residents. Bloom and Kilgore (2003) describe the U.S.-based Family Partners Program, which is run by the Beyond Welfare group (www.beyondwelfare.org). Through this program, middle-class families help socially integrate and better the lives of those less fortunate by pairing middle-class volunteers with families struggling to emerge from poverty. Middle-class volunteers are expected to meet with low-income participants regularly to provide a peer relationship and to build trust; to help them develop a plan to move out of poverty; to listen and help with their problems; to help them access community services; to provide support when dealing with government agencies, schools, and other institutions; and to simply be a supportive friend. In their research into this program, Bloom and Kilgore found that volunteers undertook many practical activities, such as babysitting, giving driving lessons, providing transportation, donating clothes, helping with home repairs, and accompanying participants when they attended school, legal appointments, or social service meetings. In addition to reducing the social isolation that people living in poverty often experience, this program also endeavours to spur middle-class volunteers to examine and move past any biases they may have towards people living in poverty and to increase their understanding of the challenges that poverty presents to individuals and the community at large. All of these ancillary goals are meant to help motivate and sustain the participation of the middle class in eradicating poverty (Bloom and Kilgore, 2003: 434–5).

Indeed, the most useful way that the more affluent members of society can promote greater social inclusion among the poor and marginalized is to help them climb the socio-economic ladder. For neighbourhood groups, this means working with other key partners (including the state) in tangible ways to directly address the immediate and long-term needs of their most vulnerable neighbours. By way of example, Fisher and Kling (1987: 37) cite the Unemployed Councils, a wing of the American Communist party in the 1920s and 1930s, which talked less about the coming revolution and more about practical ways of helping people survive and prosper in the present. "The practice of mobilizing people around locally based political demands – grievances – was supplemented by the practice of helping them out on the most immediate level of their problems." Granted, this assistance was also used as an organizing tactic and could be more manipulative than sincere. Yet, the lesson for a community development approach to crime prevention is clear: to be successful, inclusive community organizing in disadvantaged neighbourhoods must endeavour to address the immediate material needs of the most impoverished residents through both short-term problem solving and long-term personal socio-economic development.

The Social Integration, Empowerment, and Engagement of Youth

Local social inclusion and integration can also be promoted by the principles of decentralization detailed earlier in this chapter, whereby individual community members are given the power to make decisions and determine the allocation of resources that affect their lives in the community. Research shows that this is particularly important for including and nurturing the pro-social development of young people. If youth are to develop attachments to their community and society, and become more civically engaged, they must be provided with genuine and meaningful opportunities to participate in and serve their community, a voice in what happens to them, and a chance to be part of the solution and to have an impact on the problems that concern them. Young people must be made to feel that they are useful and of value, not in a paternalistic or patronizing way, but in a spirit that genuinely recognizes and respects the experiences and knowledge that they can bring to public problem solving (Smith, 1993; National Crime Prevention Centre, 1995; Pearson and Voke, 2003). As a means to achieve both developmental and social integration goals, particular attention should be paid to those youth who are most disadvantaged, those at risk of chronic offending, those who have been in trouble with the law, and youth who are from first-generation families, racial minority groups, and aboriginal groups. In his research into youth crime on English council estates, Purdue (2001: 2218) observed that while youth are widely perceived as the source of problems on the estates, they were largely absent from any decision-making structures. This contributed to difficulties in truly addressing their needs, and deprived decision-makers of personal perspectives on how these needs could be met to help avoid delinquency problems. Rob White (2000) writes that a "greater democratization of decision-making at the neighborhood level" should incorporate the input of young people, including young offenders, directly into the decision-making process, especially decisions that affect their lives. "This can be done both on an *ad hoc* basis, and through institutionalization of youth advocacy, youth policy and youth participation through local government bodies." Youth councils have been enacted in numerous jurisdictions as adjuncts to the governance of schools, community centres, youth drop-in facilities, and city councils. By creating opportunities for input from the perspective of young people, youth councils represent an ideal operational nexus for the combined principles of decentralization, development, empowerment, and integration.

Social developmental, empowerment, and integration strategies aimed at youth should also be accompanied by programs and practices that help them become civically engaged in the present and the future. All youth should be encouraged to volunteer and become involved in civic organizations and the political process. Parents and other role models can best encourage youth to become politically involved by setting an example. Schools should offer civics classes, provide "service learning" options where students get credit for volunteering, and "increase the quality and quantity of activities in schools that support engagement skills including reports, persuasive debate, discussion, and group service activities." (Pearson and Voke, 2003: 26). At the Cesar Chavez Public Charter High School for Public Policy in Washington, DC, a full-time public policy director is employed who "works with faculty and staff to weave public policy themes into the curriculum and to help students learn how policy is shaped and how citizens can have a profound influence on the policies that affect their communities" (16). Schools should also "walk the walk" by creating a democratic environment within which civic and democratic ideals can best be taught. This will help foster "democratic communities in schools in which students can live the idea of democracy." To this end, students should be given greater opportunities to provide input into school administration, policies, and curriculum (26). One innovative example is the Philadelphia Student Union, a student-run organization originally developed at one local high school "by a group of young people who were angry about the low quality of education in their schools and wanted to do something about it." The Union has since become a city-wide student advocacy group, and on 25 October 2000, 409 students from twenty-seven high schools from around Philadelphia came together to ratify a platform for school reform that called for greater funding for public schools; smaller schools and class sizes; a more interactive, multicultural, and engaging curriculum; greater student involvement in decision-making that affects their education; increased school safety; and assistance for underachieving schools (Philadelphia Student Union, Internet web site). Young people who have not finished school or do not go on to receive a post-secondary education should not be forgotten. One project that targets the latter group is "Youth VOICES" a university-based, youth civic engagement initiative, also in Philadelphia, that provides young adults who do not attend university with the opportunity to attend a six-week summer academy, where they "work to identify and define an issue of interest to their peers that concerns their community." As part of this academy, the group "develops a strategy for addressing the problem, determines timelines, and builds partnerships to address the problem with community-based organizations, businesses, and others." This program has the added benefit of exposing these young people to the university environment – students and professors who assist them with their projects – which may lead in turn to their future enrolment (Pearson and Voke, 2003: 5).

Mentorship programs that connect adults with youth, such as Big Brothers and Big Sisters, also help in the integration process, while providing them with positive role models. In the United States, the Office of Juvenile Justice and Delinquency Prevention (OJJDP) administers the Juvenile Mentoring Program (JUMP), which is designed to provide one-to-one mentoring for youth at risk of delinquency, gang involvement, educational failure, or dropping out of school. Through the JUMP program, the OJJDP awards three-year grants to community organizations to support the implementation and expansion of collaborative mentoring projects. What makes JUMP unique is that mentors are encouraged to work in partnership with other community agencies and institutions to help provide a "multi-dimensional intervention" that maximizes a "comprehensive continuum of care for the youth they are serving" (Office of Juvenile Justice and Delinquency Prevention, 1998: 14). Typically, such coordination involves schools, mental health centres, substance abuse treatment programs, recreation centres, or medical service providers, among others. Many JUMP projects also supplement their core mentoring activities with additional services for youth participants and their families, including parent support groups, self-help groups, and referrals to other community organizations (Office of Juvenile Justice and Delinquency Prevention, 1998). Rob White (2000) suggests that cultural activities such as dance, art, music, story-telling, computer games, and fashion embody skills and activities that can help engage and include at-risk young people in local communities. Because young people, and especially young offenders, know the streets, they are also in a good position to be knowledgeable about safety and security issues and can be employed in novel ways as agents of public safety (White, 2000). For Smith (1993) a national youth service program is an effective way of providing youth with constructive opportunities to make significant contributions to society and to be rewarded for their work. All youth should be eligible to volunteer for selected work in public service, and, in return, they would receive various benefits, including education scholarships, unemployment compensation, cash bonuses, or other desirable rewards for their public service. The value of the benefits received could be determined by length of service and national priorities. Youth could also be involved in both the design and implementation of the program to reinforce the basic principles of participation, learning, earning, and serving. In

France, young people undertaking national service have been recruited by schools as mentors and "recreational counsellors" and also help monitor schoolyards to protect students against bullies and other forms of victimization (Pitts and Hope, 1997: 47).

Integrating Members of Immigrant and Visible Minority Groups

Intensive efforts to draw new immigrants into local multicultural social networks are particularly important because of the difficulty they may experience in adjusting to a new society, culture, and language. The integration of refugees and other immigrants into existing multicultural social networks is also central to a broad-based mobilization of disadvantaged neighbourhoods, not only because many find themselves settling in such neighbourhoods, but also because exclusive ties to an ethnic community may lead people to withdraw from civic engagement in the larger multicultural community. According to Uslaner and Conley (2003: 333), "Our research, like other studies of Asian American and Latino political behavior, emphasizes how minorities' acculturation or socialization into American society plays a central role in civic participation." While this conclusion may be heavily influenced by America's melting pot orientation towards cultural assimilation, research in Mount Pleasant, Canada, indicates that new immigrants are often socially isolated from the larger community network, and the lack of social cohesion in the neighbourhood is due in part to a fractionalization along ethnic and racial lines. Neighbourhood groups can play a leading role in integrating and acculturating immigrants into their new society. In the introduction to a report on innovative practices in the local integration of new immigrants, Aristide Zolberg and Alison Clarkin (2003: 5) state that "research on the subject indicates very clearly that many of the most interesting and constructive experiences occur outside the sphere of 'government,' within that of 'civil society,' i.e., community organizations." Individuals, families, and community organizations can "adopt" and help educate and acculturate new immigrants while introducing them to political, social, and economic institutions, and the government, community, health care, and social services available to them.

Most major cities have non-governmental organizations that offer settlement and other social services to immigrants. In Vancouver, the mandate of SUCCESS is to "promote the well being" of immigrant Canadians, which includes encouraging "their involvement in the community" through "the provision of social, educational and health services, business and community development, and advocacy" (SUC-CESS, 2004). Neighbourhood groups that represent areas with a large immigrant population should work closely with, assist, and complement the work of these city-wide or regional immigrant organizations. In France, one area of focus for the Parisian Association of Women Mediators is advising and assisting immigrants in various domains such as health, schooling, housing, and employment. The mediators are immigrants themselves who were selected because of their first-hand understanding of the difficulties of being a newcomer in French society. An objective of the program is to overcome barriers associated with immigrants' potential distrust of public authorities and to provide a wide array of mediating services, such as overcoming language barriers (part of the mediators' mission is to act as interpreters), educating immigrants on how French institutions work, and what rights and duties they have (to promote their autonomy and to guide them towards available public services), fostering mutual understanding between immigrants and service providers they come in contact with (teachers, doctors, social workers, etc.), dealing with family problems (including the adaptation of cultural family issues to French norms and laws), as well as problems related to discrimination (Zolberg and Clarkin, 2003: 18–19).

Neighbourhood-based social gatherings are another effective way to integrate new immigrant families into the local communal fold, especially when such events revolve around children. Because children often integrate and acculturate faster than their parents, the social networks they establish with their peers from other races and ethnicities can serve as a springboard to integrate parents and older siblings. Social gatherings that revolve around the culture of new immigrant families, whereby they are asked to prepare indigenous foods and discuss and educate others on their cultural or religious beliefs can also be seen as a welcoming gesture. As with underprivileged children and youth in general, community-based team sports can be effective in integrating immigrant children and youth (and their parents), while promoting other benefits and pro-social behaviours such as physical exercise and teamwork. Creating local remedial educational resources and opportunities for immigrant children, young people,[2] and adults is also crucial to their integration. Specialized outreach efforts should also be developed to involve and empower first-generation women of colour. In describing her unsuccessful struggles to engage the participation of immigrant Chinese women in English classes at the YWCA in Vancouver, Marilyn Callahan (1997: 179–80) learned they in fact "did not wish to learn another language," as well as other valuable lessons: "Their children were bilingual, they themselves did not work outside the home, and they had a large, close circle of friends and family, none of whom spoke English. While there were likely other reasons for their disinterest, I learned a fundamental lesson: that successful community developers begin by listening to the needs of others and moving at their pace, in their directions, using their methods. I also learned that outsiders, particularly those from dominant cultures, often do not understand the realities of women of colour who cope daily with gender and race both within and outside their culture."

With this in mind, Lorraine Gutierrez and Edith Lewis (1998: 110–11) provide the following principles for organizing women of colour:

1 Organizers must have intricate knowledge of and willingness to participate in the woman's ethnic community.
2 Effective feminist organizing with women of colour requires that women of colour be in leadership roles.
3 The organizer must be willing to serve as a facilitator and to allow the problem to be studied through the "lens" or "vision" of women of colour.
4 The organizer must utilize the process of praxis to understand the historical, political, and social context of the organizing effort.
5 An effective strategy for organizing women of colour is the small group.
6 Women of colour who are involved in feminist organizing must anticipate the possible backlash from within their own community of origin, the wider society, and the feminist movement (due to the notion that organizing groups of women can be divisive, such as dealing directly with incidents of homophobia or sexism within communities of colour).
7 Feminist organizers must recognize ways in which women of colour have worked effectively within their own communities.

Communication and Dialogue: Personal, Deliberative, and Undistorted

An inherent characteristic of many of the prescriptions and strategies advocated throughout this chapter – including those that revolve around outreach, community building, and problem solving – is interpersonal communication, and, more specifically, face-to-face dialogue. Because dialogue has historically been the main form of communication at the local level (Young, 2001: 36), it should also be the communicative basis upon which neighbourhood residents are mobilized to build community and to address local problems. Interpersonal communication and face-to-face dialogue at the neighbourhood level represents an important means to achieve at least two essential prerequisites for local collective action and healthy communities: positive social interaction and local social cohesion. Face-to-face dialogue is especially important for mobilizing neighbourhoods because, as research has shown, personal contact is often the most effective way to solicit participation in local collective action, especially when carried out by trusted and motivational local leaders or members of the potential participant's social network. Dialogue may also be a more successful means to reach out to marginalized populations because of its affective-emotional basis, which tends to avoid the more impersonal, pedantic, cerebral, and technical traits of reports, mail-outs, the media, and so on. Indeed, dialogue stands in contrast to social guidance models of governance that stress the technical aspects of written communication, a legacy of the positivist tradition of "objectified, systematized knowledge that exists independently of any person who expresses these ideas" (Daly, 1978: 199). While research and technical reports will always be necessary communicative components of local organizing and problem solving, their moral and deliberative weight can only be realized when fully and thoughtfully discussed by community members. For Mathews (1994: 40), the most basic form of politics is conversation about what is really in the public's interest. Dialogue is the vehicle that best facilitates the collection and sharing of information, theories, opinions, perspectives, and analyses, and is the optimal means by which people can pool information, share personal experiences, spark ideas, test ideas, generate possible solutions, or modify existing propositions. In short, a fundamental aspect of the democratic and fully engaged community is a free and open discussion, especially one that takes place in a group context (Bridges, 1994: 69–70).

Despite the positive and empowering aspects of dialogue, uninformed, dogmatic, prejudiced, or careless opinions will contribute little to a cohesive group identity or lasting solutions to complex social problems such as crime. As such, public dialogue must be premised on a thoughtful deliberation of relevant issues and problems by key stakeholders. Recent advances in public dialogue models are based upon critiques of modern techniques of soliciting public input on social issues such as polling and public opinion surveys, which generally do not allow for thoughtful judgments by respondents. Newer techniques of "deliberative public dialogue" are characterized by an informed and pensive discussion and consideration of relevant issues. The Holy Grail of a deliberative public dialogue is no less than the achievement of an active and democratic civil society where people participate in public affairs equally, sincerely, and thoughtfully. David Mathews (1994: 136) uses the term "deliberative democracy" to refer to a process of public dialogue where people concentrate "on carefully defining and, if need be, redefining problems before moving onto solutions." He distinguishes this "citizen politics" from conventional politics, which "concentrates more on getting to solutions quickly." A deliberative democracy recognizes that the highest expression of human rationality is achieved, not through scientific models, but in forums where individuals and entire communities come together to speak and reason on issues of common concern (40). Deliberative public dialogue is premised on the belief that the ideal democracy is one where all key partners assemble for a full discussion of salient issues, which are explored and debated in depth and where action-oriented decisions are reached through a democratic process (Fishkin, 1995: 34). For Yankelovich (1991: xii), citizen dialogue means moving from public opinion to public judgment, which is "a genuine form of knowledge that on certain aspects of issues deserves to carry more weight than that of scientific experts." He uses the term "public judgment" to refer to a particular form of public opinion that involves a "genuine engagement with the issue" and the consideration and weighing of a wide variety of factors, perspectives, opinions, and options (5). The deliberation process includes such analytical elements as awareness-raising, information gathering and dissemination, education, understanding, brainstorming, choice-making, and judgment. It involves a statement of individual and community values and aspirations, a problem definition, a discussion of and deliberation on potential solutions to problems, the choice of the most appropriate option, the group's acceptance of the consequences of this action, and the resolve to act. Those people who are affected by the issue under deliberation or by the consequence of the action are the main participants in a public dialogue. For Mathews (1994: 41), public dialogue is ultimately action-oriented; something must come out of the discussion: "The public dialogue is not an end in itself; rather, it is a means to an end, to making a decision" (Dillon, 1994: 10).

Within the context of a community development approach to crime prevention, a deliberative public dialogue is well suited to the block-level action group, which facilitates personal, face-to-face communication. This small-group dialogue can then form the basis of a deliberative discussion at the wider community level. At both block and community levels a structured deliberative discussion can employ the techniques of the so-called "study circles," which are small groups of people who meet over a period of days, weeks, or even months to deliberate on important public issues. Study circles are structured to ensure all participants have an equal say and to help the group explore complex issues through an informed and thoughtful deliberation process. A typical study circle progresses from a session on personal experience (How does the issue affect me?) to sessions providing a broader perspective (What are others saying about the issue?) and concludes with a session on action (What can we do about the issue?). Study circles attempt to help citizens gain "ownership" of public issues, a recognition that there can be a connection between personal experiences and public issues, a deeper understanding of their own and others' perspectives and concerns, and a discovery of common ground among opposing viewpoints or groups. An important part of the study circle process is educating participants so they can engage in a more thoughtful discussion and make informed judgments. Prior to the study circle, participants are encouraged to read materials or watch educational videos about the issue under discussion. Throughout the process, participants are presented with information on the issues from different perspectives, giving them a range of realistic choices, with the pros and cons of each spelled out to help them arrive at a decision and formulate an action plan (Sinclair, 1994).

A study circle format was employed by the Vancouver Police Department and the Vancouver Police Board, which co-hosted a community "deliberative dialogue" session at the Morris J. Wosk Centre for Dialogue on 27 March 2004. According to the Vancouver Police Department web site, the deliberative dialogue session "allowed the VPD and the Police Board to hear what matters to the community" in order to "prioritize the top safety issues in Vancouver." When combined with input from police members, the results of the session was used "to develop a comprehensive plan to improve community safety" and was to contribute to the development of a new Vancouver Police Strategic

Plan for 2004 to 2008 (Vancouver Police Department and Vancouver Police Board, n.d.). Participants were invited from each of the twenty-three spatial communities that make up the city of Vancouver. Along with members of the Vancouver Police Board and senior management of the Vancouver Police Department, this session brought together 103 participants "with diverse backgrounds and perspectives from all over Vancouver" (Vancouver Police Department and Vancouver Police Board, n.d.: 4). Two weeks before the session, participants were sent reading material that included an overview of the policing situation in Vancouver, crime statistics, and a series of relevant media articles. The session took place from 9:00 A.M. to 4:30 P.M. The participants were randomly seated at nineteen (circular) tables of eight people each. Each table included a representative from either the Vancouver Police Board or the Vancouver Police Department, and a facilitator. The participants took part in nine conversations throughout the day, each of which had a different (although overlapping) theme, including different options for VPD enforcement. The session closed with participants reflecting on their experiences participating in the session. These nine themes are listed below, including some sample questions asked under each:

1 *Community Safety Issues in Vancouver:* How do the media stories reflect your daily reality? What are the top community safety issues from your perspective? Why?
2 *Root Causes of Crime:* What are the root causes behind the top community safety issues in Vancouver?
3 *Vancouver – The Safest Major City in Canada by 2008:* In 2008, what would the new headlines and images be?
4 *Service Delivery – Strategic Option A:* The Vancouver Police Department should deploy the majority of available police officers on the street to eliminate street disorder.
5 *Service Delivery – Strategic Option B:* The Vancouver Police Department should dedicate more of their resources to deal with perceived root social causes of crime such as inadequate parenting, poverty, addiction and youth at risk.
6 *Service Delivery – Strategic Option C:* The Vancouver Police Department should deploy more of their personnel conducting analysis of general and specific crimes thereby allowing for a more strategic approach to addressing crime issues.
7 *Service Delivery – Strategic Option D:* The Vancouver Police Department should allocate more of their resources to developing commu-

nity policing centres and working in partnership with the community to address safety and crime concerns.

8 *Service Delivery – Common Ground:* What ideas from any of the four Strategic Options (or any other) do we agree would best address the root causes and improve community safety in Vancouver?

9 *Deliberative Dialogue Closing Words:* Your experience today. One idea, feeling, commitment, or learning you are taking with you.

According to the document produced from this session, "over 3800 comments, thoughts and ideas were expressed by the participants and recorded by the police representatives during the deliberative dialogue session" (Vancouver Police Department and the Vancouver Police Board, n.d.: 6).

Communicative Policing

While dialogue remains a key communicative foundation for community action and development, when used inappropriately it may in fact serve as an obstacle to participation. As documented in the Mount Pleasant case study, inappropriate communications between local organizers and their constituents, and a lack of two-way communication between police and residents, were cited as factors that helped to obstruct a broad-based mobilization of residents. Previous sections of this chapter have mostly explored alternative ways to fashion dialogue and communication *horizontally* within heterogeneous neighbourhoods to help build cohesive and inclusive communities. This section explores communication that operates along the *vertical* dimensions of power connecting two key partners in crime prevention: neighbourhoods and the police. Of particular concern is how asymmetrical power relations between police and disadvantaged neighbourhoods can serve to obstruct empathetic and partnership-building dialogue. In order to overcome these communicative obstacles, this section relies on the critical theory of Jürgen Habermas as a conceptual framework within which the power relations between police and disadvantaged neighbourhoods (and other marginalized groups) can be examined and made more symmetrical. The ultimate goal of this theoretical approach is a new relationship that transcends community policing and enters a realm of what I call "communicative policing." A theory of communicative policing strives to instil in police a cognitive interest that moves them from that which is technical in its orientation to that which is emancipatory. This would be accomplished by emphasizing how police could identify and remove obstacles to undistorted communications, and promote mutual understanding between themselves and less powerful neighbourhoods or social groups. This may serve to lessen the asymmetrical power relations, thereby promoting not only more effective community policing, but greater participation in collective community development and safety efforts by (marginalized) members of disadvantaged neighbourhoods.

The construction of this communicative policing theory begins with the assumption that a fundamental aspect of community policing is communication. As Skolnick and Bayley (1988: 6) point out, the words "community" and "communicate" both share a common prefix. As such, "community-based policing suggests active communication with the public." Community policing initiatives such as neighbourhood offices, foot patrols, and bike patrols represent an attempt to overcome the real and psychological barriers to communication that the roving and reactive squad car presents (8). For Leighton (1991: 10), community policing relies on private citizens as a major source of information and intelligence: "Much of the success of policing depends on how well its personnel operate as information managers who engage in 'interactive policing' by routinely exchanging information on a reciprocal basis with community members through close formal contacts and numerous informal networks." According to Skogan (1990: 15), when community policing succeeds, it opens up channels of communication for the flow of information from citizens to police, including requests for action, which are then sincerely considered for action by police.

An analysis of the role of communication and dialogue as tools in exposing and deconstructing asymmetrical power structures is informed by Habermas's (1979, 1987) theory of "communicative action," which works towards ensuring a mutual understanding among social actors and institutions and the larger goal of overcoming asymmetrical power relationships that negatively impact on human and social development. Habermas critiques Marx by arguing that society in the course of its historical development is formed, not simply by its mode of production, but also by the way people interact through language and communication, which for Habermas are the keys to uncovering the undiscovered potential of modernity. For modernity is itself a dialectic: on the one hand, there is vast potential for human betterment, equality, and an inclusive democratic society; on the other, however, there continues to be exclusion and hierarchy. Habermas believes the unrequited task for modernity – the search for a universal knowledge and morality that is rooted in equality and emancipation – can best be found in language, communication, dialogue, and understanding. The ultimate emancipatory goal, and the role of language and communication in achieving such a goal, is best comprehended by examining Habermas's linkage between human knowledge and cognitive interests, and their orientation towards human and social development. In his earlier works, Habermas (1968, 1971) distinguishes between three types of knowledge: empirical-analytical, hermeneutic, and critical. Each has its own distinctive methodological approach, but all are necessary to human development. Each type of knowledge is based on a "cognitive interest," which is the purpose for which the knowledge is developed. In turn, each purpose provides us with an interest in the knowledge and its development. These interests are called "knowledge-constitutive" because they determine the objects and kinds of knowledge.

Habermas also identifies three primary cognitive interests: technical, practical, and emancipatory. Each of these cognitive interests is rooted in a respective dimension of human social existence: work, symbolic interaction, and power. Work or labour ("instrumental action") is grounded in a technical interest geared towards mastering and controlling natural processes and using them to society's advantage. This interest is manifested in positivism or purposive rationality, which Habermas calls the "empirico-analytical sciences." The second means by which human beings transform their environment is language, which incorporates a "practical interest" that gives rise to the "hermeneutic sciences."[3] The practical interest develops through a medium of symbolic interaction, which is guided by norms that make reciprocal expectations about human action possible. Habermas is particularly concerned with the way in which interaction is distorted and confused by social structures. People can be wrong in their understanding of each other, and they also can be systematically misled and manipulated, especially through language (Craib, 1992: 233–4). Thus, this practical interest must give rise to a third "emancipatory interest" that, while still based on language, is concerned with power relations and serves to rid interaction and communication of their distorted elements as they are manifested in relations of power. The social theory of Habermas examines politico-economic structures and power relations as operative communication structures. He believes that society must overcome the type of disabling and distorting communications that take place between different groups in society (especially between the powerful and the powerless) or that emanate from authoritarian or bureaucratic institutions. Instead, society must strive towards the collective enabling power of democratic political discourse and mutual understanding through a communicative action that involves discussion and choice and is aimed at reaching an understanding or consensus, ideally without attempting unduly to influence others. For Habermas, it is through communicative action that we can reach an inclusive, democratic society and an ideal form of life in which communication is free from distortion and where everybody participates equally in society.

The application of this analytical framework to policing in Mount Pleasant first reveals the existence of asymmetrical power relationships between police and the public they serve. This asymmetrical power relationship is especially pronounced in relation to marginalized groups, such as the poor, the mentally ill, and immigrants from developing countries. This power relationship is reflected in, and perpetuated by, communicative acts by Vancouver police members, including a lack of proactive dialogue with these groups, an absence of a two-way communication, the inability or unwillingness of police to speak in the native language of immigrant constituents, a tendency to monopolize crime control initiatives, and other non-dialogical acts, such as the police uniform and service revolver or perceptions of disrespect by police towards different cultural norms. As argued in chapter 5, this asymmetrical power relationship and distorted communications help erect obstacles to participation in community safety programs by marginalized individuals and groups within Mount Pleasant.

Distortion in communications between the police and poor neighbourhoods can be viewed in the context of how policing has increasingly been shaped by the positivist tradition and the scientific method. In its response to crime, police work has become more sophisticated and in doing so has embodied the positivist legacy of the Enlightenment: scientific control over its domain. Computerized databases, crime and policing statistics, geographical crime analysis, forensic sciences, profiling, and DNA testing have all contributed to a scientific cadre within law enforcement agencies that has rationalized many forms of police work. As policing has evolved, it has become a manifestation of positivism; it has become a science. Police science, while a relatively young discipline, has incorporated all the trappings of positivism, in particular a scientific approach to policing driven by a technical interest in human knowledge (substantiating Habermas's view of labour as constituting an empirical-analytical form of knowledge). In turn, the scientific paradigm has instilled in police work and communications a reliance on instrumental approaches to problem solving, a rigid adherence to established policy and procedure, a dependence on traditional institutions and methods, a technical language, a detached objectivity towards social problems, and, in some cases, an unempathetic and unsympathetic attitude towards some communities served by the police. Aggravating the detached nature of police work was the creation of the modern police force, which is characterized by a centralized command and control, the radio-directed roaming patrol car (which removed and isolated police physically and symbolically from the communities they serve), and an increased focus on law enforcement and crime control (as opposed to the broader community safety and "peacemaking" goals). In their relationship and communications with individual citizens, groups, and neighbourhoods, this instrumental and technical approach to policing can result in distorted communications and a lack of mutual understanding. The traditional policing model has served to distance the police from many communities and obstructs a democratic basis to crime prevention that is fundamental to community policing. By pursuing a technical approach to policing, especially in disadvantaged neighbourhoods, a police force may undermine an active and empowered community, the very foundation of community policing and crime prevention. It can also promote an unequal influence over crime control and prevention policies and practices through the professional (technical) power of the police. An analogy can be drawn with the relationship between government planners and community residents. Planning theorist John Friedmann (1973) suggests that the barriers to effective communication between planners and their "clients" are caused by the fact that the former rely primarily on abstract, technical, "processed knowledge" that is different from the public's personal, "experiential knowledge." These differences in knowledge also translate into differences in language; the planner's language is technical, conceptual, and abstract whereas the language of the public is less cerebral and more emotional and personalized.

Community policing attempts to transcend the limitations inherent in this instrumental and technical approach to policing. Using Habermas's linkage between human knowledge and cognitive interests and their orientation towards social problem solving, the concept of community policing represents a move from the technical, cognitive interest imbedded in traditional policing as an empirico-analytical science to a more communicative basis that incorporates a practical interest. This in turn propels policing into the realm of the hermeneutic sciences. It is here that the practical interest of community policing (i.e., clarifying the conditions and substance of communication with neighbourhood) can be pursued and replaces the technical interest of traditional policing that perpetuates a dominance and control over disadvantaged neighbourhoods. Yet, regardless of the positive communicative advances made in the hermeneutic community policing approach, and despite efforts by police to promote dialogue and understanding with neighbourhood residents, interaction and communications can remain distorted. This is because police are imbued with an enormous amount of power by virtue of the statutory authority to arrest, to detain, and even to kill. This power is visually symbolized by the police officer's service revolver and his uniform. The most vivid examples of how the uniformed police officer automatically creates personal asymmetrical power relations with marginalized groups in Mount Pleasant were the uneasiness displayed towards police by the mentally ill or new immigrants from developing countries. For members of these groups, the uniformed police officer, especially in crisis situations, communicates and symbolizes the asymmetrical power between the two groups. The police automatically enter into a discourse with private citizens from a position of power that is manifested and perpetuated by their dialogical and non-dialogical communicative acts. These ongoing power relations are confirmed by Gilling (1993), who, in analysing a multi-agency approach to crime prevention, concludes that despite attempts at forming interdependent relationships between police and other groups, police discourse, being much the more powerful, is likely to dominate any informal discussions and collaboration.

For community policing to maximize the participation of disadvantaged neighbourhoods in local crime prevention initiatives, it must transcend its historical-hermeneutic approach where the cognitive interest is practical and the objective is clarification of the conditions of communication. This practical interest of community policing must give way to an emancipatory interest that, while still based on communication, is concerned with power relations and serves to exorcize the distorted elements from the interaction and communication between the police and the communities they serve. The differences between traditional, community, and communicative policing, as seen through the lens of Habermas's critical theory, are summarized in table 7.1. The

Table 7.1 A typology of policing, viewed through the lens of Habermas's critical theory

	Type of knowledge		
	Empirical-analytical	Hermeneutic	Critical
Concern	Work	Language (symbolic interaction)	Power relations
Cognitive interest	Technical-instrumental	Practical (communicative)	Emancipatory
Policing	Traditional policing	Community policing	Communicative policing
Concern	Law and order	Relationship and communication with communities	Reducing power relations between police and disadvantaged neighbourhoods and marginalized groups
Cognitive interest	Order maintenance/ Formal social control	Community safety, prevention of crime, peacekeeping	Development, empowerment, and emancipation of disadvantaged neighbourhoods and marginalized groups

transition from community policing to communicative policing begins when police enter into a dialogue that embodies an emancipatory spirit – one that lifts the disadvantaged neighbourhoods from powerlessness to equality. As Habermas argues, communicative action promotes equal power relations through undistorted communications and mutual understanding, emphasizing a mutually conducive form of dialogue. This is the normative basis for a theory of communicative policing: to repair systematically distorted communication between police and less powerful groups as a means of making these two groups equal partners in crime prevention and community development. Constituting the more powerful partner in the relationship, much (but not all) of the onus for correcting distorted communications falls upon the police. The removal of distorted communication by the police would begin as a self-reflective process whereby they examine their own communication and ensure that in every communicative act a police officer speaks comprehensibly, sincerely, empathetically, appropriately, and accurately. Individual police officers would have to understand that they are symbols of powerful state institutions that reproduce existing asymmetrical and inequitable social relations. At the very least, police must ensure that there is always a two-way channel of communication with community members, that feedback to residents is timely, that people's concerns are taken seriously, and that opportunities are omnipresent for citizen's complaints and input into policing policies and priorities. Police officers would enter continually into reflective dialogue with community members and listen with sincerity, empathy, and sympathy. They would emphasize conversation and avoid lecturing and the use of technical jargon or "legalese." Distorted communications with first-generation immigrants could be lessened if police would serve these groups in their native language. Police must also internalize the capacity to understand their own potential for stereotyping certain populations as well as prejudices, biases, and abuses that may be perpetrated against some groups.

Distortions may take place not only in the content of what is said, but also in how the content is represented and the context in which it is expressed. Winkel (1991) found that the differing perceptions and conflict between police and visible minorities in the Netherlands is partially the result of non-verbal communication errors. As detailed in chapter 4, instances where non-verbal acts of communication between police and marginalized groups in Mount Pleasant impeded their relationship (e.g., the sight of a police uniform by new immigrants or those with a mental illness). Thus, communicative policing must also emphasize non-dialogical acts that attempt to reduce distortions and asymmetrical power relations between police and less powerful groups (especially those groups that have poor relations with police). Meeting on the community's turf and leaving the police uniform and gun at the office may help balance power relations and reduce anxiety among marginalized populations. Ongoing proactive contact and communication between police and members of marginalized, immigrant, or racial minority groups may foster increased participation of these groups in anti-crime activities. Again, this contact must take place outside of conflictual situations. Evidence from the Mount Pleasant case study suggests that when individual police officers are well known to and gain the trust of members of these groups, they become a conduit for crime reporting that may not exist otherwise. This observation is also reflected in a study of crime reporting by minority ethnic groups, which found that those "who had had involuntary contacts with the police were less likely to say that they would report a crime, whereas those who had had voluntary contacts were more willing to report" (Davis and Henderson, 2003: 577). Another study found that "voluntary contacts with the police involving citizens in various community policing programs tended to increase confidence in the police" (Ren et al., 2005: 62). When dealing with certain ethnic and immigrant groups, police must be cognizant that their cultural norms and physical gestures may offend. Ultimately, communicative policing is about establishing greater trust between police and those communities that are often distrustful of police. As Lynn (2002) points out, "positive, ongoing, personal action by law enforcement personnel is vital to gaining access and establishing trust in immigrant and refugee communities not only to reduce crime but to reduce the fear of crime."

As a means to overcome distorted communications and to promote joint problem solving, this theory of communicative policing also incorporates John Friedmann's (1987) concept of "mutual learning" in which the processed knowledge of police is combined with the experiential knowledge of neighbourhood residents. This concept of mutual learning demands a more intensive, formal, and ongoing partnership between the police and disadvantaged groups that promotes a better appreciation of the different perspectives on crime, crime prevention, and community safety held by each party. The goal of this enhanced relationship is mutual understanding, where the police learn from the community and the community gains a greater appreciation of the challenges and obstacles faced by police. One vehicle to facilitate such a mutual dialogue would be "citizen police academies," which traditionally have used to educate the community about the police function, but can also be adapted to educate the police about the community. Citizen volunteering that maximizes contact with police officers should also be encouraged, not only because this contact increases volunteers' confidence in police as a link between the public and the police, but also because volunteers can help police become "a part of and not apart from" the community they serve (Albrecht and Green, 1977).

In order to reduce asymmetrical power relations, communicative action would also be reflected in the sharing of control over crime prevention decision-making and resources. As emphasized earlier in the chapter, neighbourhoods would have much greater input and control over those public policies and programs that affect their lives. Ultimately, a theory of communicative policing requires an understanding of what Jones and colleagues (1994: 44) refer to as "a set of criteria for the purpose of testing how far the arrangements for making policing policy follow democratic principles." The criteria they set out are: equity, delivery of services, responsiveness, distribution of power, information, redress, and participation (Jones, Newburn, and Smith, 1994: 42–8; as cited in Crawford, 1997: 244).

Overcoming Organizational Obstacles to Collective Action

Much of this chapter has focused on theories, principles, and strategies concerned with overcoming some of the social, demographic, and structural impediments to local collective action. The Mount Pleasant case study, as well as other research into CCP and collective action, also illustrates quite clearly the central importance of community-based organizations and leadership in soliciting and sustaining participation. As detailed in chapter 4, successful crime prevention organizing in Mount Pleasant and other Vancouver communities was characterized by strong, motivational, and stable leaders who used intensive, varied, personal, and appropriate communications and programs that appealed to both crime concerns and a sense of community, often targeting a specific group and/or concentrating on a small spatial area. The crime prevention offices (CPOs) that were successful in attracting a large number of volunteers created an environment that recognized and valued this unpaid work. Tasks were assigned that were commensurate with the skill level of volunteers, but which would also contribute to their personal development. The CPOs that were most effective in both attracting volunteers and program delivery were also characterized by a productive relationship with other organizations both within and outside the community.

Recruiting and Retaining Volunteer Participants

One of the most challenging and time consuming tasks facing community groups is attracting, working with, and sustaining the participation of group members and volunteers. CCP organizations that communicate effectively ensure that the message appeals to both instrumental (crime concerns) and affective-emotional sentiments (social interaction and integration, social cohesion, etc.), while promoting the material, solidary, and purposive benefits of involvement. Generally speaking, to attract participation in community safety initiatives, local groups must be able to convince prospective members that benefits will accrue to them personally and/or to the community as a whole. Communication and the program itself must ensure that community members realize "net benefits" of participation, which means that the benefits of involvement (e.g., a greater sense of safety and security) outweigh the costs of participating (e.g., time commitment). Participants should also be shown that involvement comes with "relative benefits," in which they realize benefits not available to those who do not participate (such as home insurance discounts, a monthly newsletter with security tips, a free security audit of their home by police, etc.). In fact, to maximize the appeal of participation, organizations should offer participants a combination of incentives, which include *material incentives* (insurance discounts, free food and drinks, awards and prizes for volunteering, skills development, acculturation, gift certificates from local retailers, discounts for programs or classes at the local community school or college, etc.), *solidary incentives* (social interaction and integration, a sense of belonging, supportive social networks), and *purposive incentives* (a sense of accomplishment, altruism, personal feelings of efficacy and empowerment). These incentives should also be tailored to specific demographic groups. For example, middle-class homeowners would be more receptive to communications that stress solidary incentives, while emphasis should be placed on communicating tangible, needs-based, material incentives for poorer residents. When reaching out to the poor and socially excluded, community groups should stress the immediate benefits of participation and volunteering, such as the acquisition of new skills and local connections that can enhance employment opportunities.

Communication should be frequent, appropriate, and varied, with particular emphasis on personal contact. Technical language and jargon should be avoided, and all communications should be translated into the dominant languages spoken in the community, ensuring the messages are culturally sensitive to each group. In the same vein, messages should be tailored to make them appropriate and appealing to the different target audiences. Prior to developing communications strategies and messages, organizers should conduct research that assesses the needs and desires of the local population, determine those benefits and incentives that can best motivate community members to become involved, and then develop and test various messages through "market research" such as focus groups. The program contents, strategies, and volunteer responsibilities and tasks will also influence the level of participation in a local group or activity. Research with Vancouver crime prevention groups found that the activities that attracted the highest participation were those that combined community beautification projects (murals, garbage clean-up, public gardening, etc.) with a social element. For example, food and drinks should always be served at meetings and volunteer-based projects. This contributes to a more social atmosphere, sends a positive message to participants, can help keep physical energy levels up, and can help induce participation by those who live below the poverty line.

Of equal importance are the steps that local groups must undertake to retain volunteers and sustain an active group membership. This is especially important for CCP, given the high dropout rate that afflicts passive programs such as NW. Judith Feins (1983) notes that crime prevention activities are particularly ill-suited to sustain membership. People become bored with watching and patrolling, and, ironically, the more successful the program is at reducing crime, the more difficult it is to keep people involved (once the problems of crime lessen, there is a tendency for people to relax their efforts). Crime prevention and other local initiatives must factor in participation maintenance techniques to keep volunteers involved. In Seattle, a maintenance program for Neighbourhood Watch captains was devised and consisted of three elements: (1) a short questionnaire to help block captains identify problems that required particular attention or follow-up; (2) personal visits by police personnel to block captains to address such issues as resident turnover and training; and (3) the formation of a network and/or periodic meetings of block captains in a particular neighbourhood or jurisdiction, to acquaint them with each other and with police personnel in the area, to foster and support communication and organizing efforts, to facilitate the sharing of ideas about addressing common problems, and to develop inter-neighbourhood strategies, and so on (Feins, 1983: 40). Regardless of the crime prevention activity or vehicle, strong leadership will keep volunteers committed to and working on the cause. The roles and responsibilities for volunteer members should be clearly defined and fully understood by them. Initial and ongoing training should be provided. The work undertaken by participants should be personally meaningful. In assigning tasks, the skill level and time constraints of participants should be taken into consideration, while ensuring, when possible, that assigned tasks contribute to the personal development of volunteers (this is especially true of young people, the undereducated, unemployed, unskilled immigrants, etc.). Community organizers should communicate frequently with volunteers and local residents in general (even if it is just a monthly newsletter), and opportunities must be created to encourage volunteers to provide input. Given the challenging and long-term nature of crime prevention, organizers must ensure that the issue of crime and its prevention are not viewed as so overwhelming that residents will be too intimidated to volunteer or inclined to drop out if they do not perceive that tangible or immediate results will be realized. What must be constantly stressed and communicated to participants are the small, yet concrete and incremental steps that can be and are being achieved to address long-term goals. For Hinkle et al. (1996: 49), this translates into ensuring that potential and current participants realize some form of personal and collective accomplishment and efficacy, which underscores the importance of "structuring grassroots activities in terms of incremental, reasonably attainable goals," allowing participants the opportunity to achieve certain goals and milestones, no matter how small. Last, but not least, group members and volunteers must be made to feel that their efforts are appreciated. This includes periodically recognizing their contributions with special awards or prizes.

Leadership

Leadership, writes Charles Dobson in *The Citizen's Handbook* (2005), is a skill, and like any other skill it is learned, not inherited, and it takes practice. Good community organizers do not tell other people what to do, but help others take charge. They do not grab the limelight, but nudge others into it. "They are not interested in being The Leader, but in trying to create more leaders." They know how and when to delegate and then allow their colleagues to carry the tasks out in their own way. Good leaders show appreciation for work well done, welcome criticism, help people to believe in themselves, inspire trust, herald a higher purpose, and convince others they can lead (Dobson, 2005: n.p.). Strong leaders must be able to succinctly, yet profoundly, articulate and communicate the broader purpose of the group and foster a shared identity and meaning for those involved. Leaders inspire trust and confidence among group participants and do so by helping them understand the group's overall purpose and strategies, how each member of the group personally contributes to achieving key goals, and by constantly communicating with and providing information and feedback to all those involved. Organizers must be able to "actively manage a process that shifts meaningful expertise, capacity, and control, to groups without being overly directive and influential so as to dampen volunteer engagement" (Gittell and Vidal, 1998: 85). For Purdue (2001), community leaders require pragmatic organizational skills and expertise in the issues being addressed, but must also inspire others to follow and articulate a wider "moral vision" that includes a sense of justice and equality. Community leaders, especially within poor, marginalized neighbourhoods, must be agents of change. The entrepreneurial side of the community organizer includes "an ability to cope with risk and uncertainty; creativity in solving problems through divergent thinking," and a competitive streak that still prizes collaboration. Community leaders must be able to raise funds, while being efficient in the use of available resources. Leaders are "quick to spot an opportunity to turn contingencies to their advantage," and will learn from their mistakes without dwelling on them. They are willing to work within the available conditions (without being too conformist), which includes taking advantage of the existing political opportunity structure. They integrate new ideas into their thinking and then experiment with these ideas. Community leaders must create a network of partnerships and strategic alliances with other neighbourhood groups and external agencies and act as key points of contact between them. They must also be able to run democratic meetings, facilitate complex deliberative discussions, and help guide meetings towards tangible, action-oriented results (Purdue, 2001: 2215–17).

Crime Prevention and Multi-purpose Community Organizations

Two overlapping questions concerning crime prevention organizing and program implementation are (1) Should the focus be placed specifically on the prevention of crime and community safety or should the broader goals of social and community development be pursued? and (2) Should crime prevention activities be the main focus of a local group or part of a broader agenda of a multi-issue neighbourhood organization? Given this study's conclusion that many of the problems experienced by disadvantaged neighbourhoods are rooted in the same causal factors combined with the development-based approach detailed throughout this chapter, it is appropriate to advocate that neighbourhoods pursue crime prevention and community safety initiatives through an omnibus, multi-issue organization that addresses the problems of a neighbourhood in a holistic, integrated, and problem-oriented, development-based fashion.

Some researchers suggest that a comprehensive approach to local issues and problems, pursued through a multi-issue neighbourhood association can contribute to greater participation levels. Lewis and Salem (1981: 417) claim that participation in crime prevention "appears to be most closely associated with membership in community organizations with diverse purposes." Podolefsky and Dubow (1981) found that participation in crime prevention activities and programs was more likely when such programs were adopted by an organization with multiple purposes with which neighbourhood residents were already committed. Judith Feins (1983: 25–7) advises, "Anyone wishing to start a crime prevention program should first look to established neighbourhood organizations. Members of neighbourhood-based organizations can suggest that the issue of crime be added as one of their concerns." An organization with a history or track record of benefiting the neighbourhood in issue areas other than crime and safety is a more promising vehicle for anti-crime activity because its reputation for success can potentially help sustain crime prevention initiatives. Existing organizations may already have the resources, including staff and volunteers, which can be dedicated to crime prevention, and many have in place a system of communication that can serve as a vehicle for getting residents informed about local crime problems and strategies to address them. In their book on community organizing, Gittell and Vidal (1998: 177–8) state that one way to encourage the "breadth and continuity of participation" is to structure the intervention so that it offers both a range of opportunities for participation and reasons for commitment. Some researchers blame the difficulties in sustaining participation in Neighbourhood Watch partly on its single issue focus. In their article entitled, "Decaying interest in burglary prevention," Gillham and Barnett (1994: 43) suggest that crime prevention should be part of a larger effort to meet the inevitable variety of needs among neighbourhood residents. "This has the advantage of encouraging continuing contact with residents on other issues without having to talk only about crime. Residents, otherwise, eventually get bored with such a narrow, repetitive focus." Finally, Crawford (1997: 312) concludes that crime alone may not be the most appropriate focus around which to organize open, tolerant, and inclusive communities. Such a focus may lead to greater defensiveness, exclusivity, and parochialism. The nurturing of tolerant communities, their institutions and structures, must be shaped around discussions and foci that are integrating, rather than exclusive and bifurcating, as is the case with crime.

The Role of the State

Despite the primacy that communities must assume in crime prevention and local problem solving in general, there will always be a role for the state. The specific role to be played by the state varies with the level of government. Federal as well as state/provincial governments are much more resource-rich than municipal governments, and as such they are often better placed as a funding source. However, this should not be their only role. As succinctly stated by the United Nations Congress for the Prevention of Crime and the Treatment of Offenders (1993), "Leadership and support by national governments are needed for cities who have limited resources and jurisdictional competence. National governments must pass legislation, create prevention councils, encourage research evaluation and training and maintain adequate financing."

Because municipal governments control local policing, they can play a tremendous role in crime prevention. More than any other municipal government agency, a police department that is not committed to crime prevention and community policing can completely undermine any progressive community safety policies and programs established by a municipal government. Yet, the role to be played in crime prevention by municipal governments transcends policing. In fact, municipal governments may constitute the most important government player in crime prevention, in part because they are the government that is closest to communities. Municipal governments also set the tone for crime control at the local level, are responsible for a number of relevant policy areas (housing, schools, urban planning, sanitation, recreation), can identify and mobilize key partners, are essential to team-building, and can provide funding and other resources to build capacity at the local level.

What is fundamentally required of any level of government is the fulfilment of one its most basic roles in society: ensuring an equitable distribution of resources, with particular emphasis on helping those who are the most disadvantaged. With this as a goal, the four most important tasks that governments can play in crime prevention and community development are: (1) minimize the distorting and harmful effects of market forces on those who are most vulnerable, while ensuring that social resources are more equitably distributed for this purpose; (2) foster, fund, and help implement (social developmental) policies and programs that address the root causes of crime, targeting at-risk families, children, youth, and communities; (3) support and help build capacity within communities, while promoting an active citizenry to undertake local initiatives to prevent crime and to solve other local problems; and (4) complement citizen-based preventative approaches to crime through the criminal justice system.

The broader context of the role of the state is creating opportunities for an engaged civic society, direct democracy, and local social problem solving, while promoting and defending, diversity, equality, and inclusion (Crawford, 1997: 246). Governments must create an environment whereby everyone in society has a role to play in building strong, vibrant, and healthy communities. As advocated at the outset of this chapter, this includes a greater decentralization of public resources and decision-making power to the community level. In short, the state must be prepared to relinquish some power and give up some resources to non governmental organizations. At the same time, governments must be equal partners with local communities, working to empower and guide groups and individuals along a path of civic engagement and community building that distributes basic rights and resources responsibly and equitably.

The most ill-advised approach a government can take towards crime is to exclusively or overwhelmingly pursue a punitive, enforcement-based philosophy. To be sure, the criminal justice system is a complement to the proactive, development-based, preventative approaches undertaken at the community level. However, policies that place too much emphasis on enforcement, harsh sentences, and incarceration as a way to address crime can nonetheless send the message that the reactive, "get-tough," retributive, enforcement, and punishment-based system is the best or the only way to address crime. It can also usurp the contribution made by communities, as all of these aforementioned functions fall exclusively under the purview of the state. Governments must demonstrate, through policies, resource allocation, and actions that it does view proactive, preventative approaches as a priority.

Conclusion

A fundamental premise of community crime prevention is that the criminal justice system is unable to cope with the quantity of crime, fails to identify many criminal offenders and bring them to justice, falls short of rehabilitating offenders, and does not address the root causes of crime and criminality (Standing Committee on Justice and the Solicitor General, 1993: 1). Crime prevention is a philosophy that in many respects is antithetical to that of the criminal justice system: responsibility for crime control and public safety is in the hands of the public, not the state; the emphasis is on proactive interventions, as opposed to the reactive response that is the hallmark of the criminal justice system; concern is shifted from the offender to the potential offender and victim; and attention is paid to targeting not only crime, but also fear, disorder, and the root causes of criminality. The ascension of community crime prevention since the early 1970s can be seen as a significant historical development in how Western societies deal with crime and disorder. It can also serve as a microcosm for much larger debates, such as the most appropriate role of the state and the citizenry in social problem solving. The partial transfer of responsibility for crime control from the state to the public reflects the growing recognition of the dwindling role, capacity, and unwillingness of the state to unilaterally solve society's ills, and, concomitantly, the increased expectations for social problem solving that are being thrust upon civil society. Ironically, this development is occurring in a period of history for many Western countries in which there are strong doubts as to the willingness or capacity of large swaths of the public to become civically, politically, and locally active.

Despite this dilemma, and the ongoing challenges facing CCP programs in attracting and sustaining membership, community crime prevention remains a politically attractive medium and message that can be evoked by those on both the right and left of the political spectrum (Walklate, 2001). At the core of the messages on either side of the political divide is the venerable notion of community. For the Right, despite its support for the expansion of the criminal justice system that is implicit in its punitive approach to crime control, philosophically, the community, as an embodiment of the virtues of individual responsibility and self-reliance, represents the most appropriate and most capable instrument in local social problem solving, especially when compared to the reviled welfare state. The Left, by contrast, sees the community as the bridgehead for grass-roots activism, a buffer against the negative impact of private capital, and a self-empowering force for the marginalized and less powerful in society. The fact that the community can be readily called upon to serve the ideological agendas of both the Right and the Left in their crime control policies very much infers that crime and crime prevention are examples of how social problems and their solutions are socially constructed for ends that are as much political or ideological as they are practical (Gilling, 1997: 10). Regardless, the sociological concept of community will continue to represent a vital foundation, and indeed a major quest, for the theory and practice of crime prevention.

Anthropologist Anthony Cohen notes that "the concept of community has been one of the most compelling and attractive themes in modern social science" (Cohen 1985: 7). Like other essential elements of CCP – collective action social interaction and cohesion, informal social control, self-help, empowerment, partnerships, and so on – there is an almost unquestioned presumption that communities are a good thing (Walklate, 2001). The community is an "angel in marble" (Grine, 1994: 441) and a vast reservoir of untapped resources to be mined, while "voluntary collective action is the under-exploited 'rough diamond' of civil society, which can be polished and turned to the provision of essential local goods and services" (Crawford, 1997: 166–167). The concept of community is viewed as a social and moral good in itself, as well as a means of achieving certain policy goals: "The reinvigoration of 'moral authority'; citizen empowerment; the relegitimation of public institutions; the transfer of responsibilities from the state to individuals and groups for their own security; and as a source of resources to be tapped and exploited" (199). Community-based collective action represents one attempt to "reawaken dormant moral energies" in civil society (Flint, 2002: 250).

While the "community" can be harnessed to promote the ideals of civil society, within the context of crime prevention it can also be used as the basis for reactive, excessive, socially unjust, divisive, prejudicial, and exclusionary approaches. The task at hand for crime prevention theorists, policy makers, and practitioners is to guard against these human tendencies, while harnessing and promoting the great ideals and powers of community and civil society, such as inclusiveness, social justice, equality, cooperation, partnerships, empathy, and thoughtful deliberative dialogue. The pursuit of these virtues in the context of CCP is particularly important for disadvantaged neighbourhoods. Indeed, one of the greatest challenges facing advanced Western societies is the spatial concentration of poverty, despair, social exclusion, crime, and civic disengagement (which in turn is part of a larger trend: the fragmentation of civil society along ethnic, religious, ideological and socio-economic lines and the accompanying concentration of economic and political power among the few). One part of the solution to the spatial concentration of poverty, crime, and civic disengagement is to help turn impoverished neighbourhoods into cohesive, caring, healthy, non-alienating, civically engaged, democratic, and politically empowered collectives. And because the state appears to be incapable or unwilling to intercede effectively in the broader structural forces and processes that perpetuate the creation and growth of these inner-city islands of neglect, it has become clear that these neighbourhoods must become more self-reliant through organized collective action. Simply put, "organized community groups have emerged as our primary hope for reshaping the destiny of threatened urban neighbourhoods" (Skogan, 1990: 16). Accepting the inherent value of civil society, local self-governance, and participatory democracy, greater efforts must be sought in engaging, empowering, and mobilizing disadvantaged neighbourhoods to address their plight. This challenge is made all the more daunting by the need to craft solutions that transcend crime and other symptoms, and to deal with the root causes of these problems, all the while recognizing that the structural forces that are so highly influential in creating and spatially concentrating many of society's ills are beyond the scope of any single organization, neighbourhood, or government.

The critically oriented, community development approach to crime prevention presented in this chapter is one modest contribution to the broader efforts to address endemic social problems through a comprehensive strategy that ultimately is based on a reinvigoration of civil society, the centrality of the local community in social problem solving, and the empowerment and participation of those who are in the most need. This means that a greater share of public resources and power be allocated to the local level and to the poorest communities in particular. There are no doubt many who will view these aspirations as radical, utopian, and naive. Reversing the centralization of economic and political power that has been ongoing within most countries is a Herculean task, to say the least. Even within the realm of crime control, despite the emergence and acceptance of the role of the community in crime prevention, the criminal justice system will continue to constitute and be accepted as the most dominant institution in this regard. However, who among us would have predicted forty years ago that police agencies in some countries would be mandated by law to consult with the public in their crime control strategies (Stevens, 1998: 10), or that Michalowski's (1983) idea of citizen courts would find expression through the principles and practice of restorative justice? There are a multitude of forces at work that are popularizing the traditional criminal justice system to accommodate the input of the public, and to make it more responsive to their needs. The critically oriented approach to CCP spelled out in this chapter is an attempt to increase the breadth and depth of these reforms by advocating more fundamental changes which can accommodate the safety and developmental needs of society's most vulnerable individuals, groups, and neighbourhoods.

Notes

Introduction

1 For the purpose of this study, a disadvantaged neighbourhood is an inner-city urban area characterized by a low socio-economic status, a high crime rate, a high population turnover, demographic heterogeneity, a low level of social cohesion, and physical deterioration.

2. Mount Pleasant, Community Crime Prevention, and Participation in Local Collective Action

1 In addition to directly accessing 1996 and 2001 census data for the Mount Pleasant census tracts from Statistics Canada, collated census data were also taken from two other sources: (1) Community profiles calculated by the city of Vancouver (http://www.city.vancouver.bc.ca/commsvcs/Census2001/MountPleasant03.pdf), and (2) census tract profiles calculated by the Mount Pleasant Business Improvement Association. I would like to thank Martha Welsh, executive director of the BIA, as well as Jennifer Miles who collated and analysed the census tract data for Mount Pleasant.

2 The volatile nature of Mount Pleasant is compounded by its close proximity to the Downtown Eastside, officially Canada's poorest and most crime-ridden neighbourhood. Because it is also the epicentre of Vancouver's street-level drug trade, it has a highly concentrated population of intra-venous drug users, and, as a result, one of the highest rates of HIV and hepatitis C in Canada.

3 All income figures are in 2000 dollars.

4 While there were a number of social developmental programs implemented in Mount Pleasant that include the participation of local residents (e.g., the

Kivan Boys and Girls Club, the Mount Pleasant Family Centre, the Mount Pleasant Neighbourhood House, etc.), they were initiated and funded largely by government agencies, local schools, or city-wide charitable organizations Few, if any, social developmental activities were implemented by the CPO, the Safer Community Society, or any of the other anti-crime groups that emerged from the neighbourhood, nor was there much interaction between the social developmental organizations and the crime prevention groups that were the focus of this study.

3. Obstacles to Participation and Collective Action at the Individual and Neighbourhood Level

1 Notwithstanding the influential role of the police in mobilizing the occupants of the buildings, the impressive turnout of residents for the initial Neighbourhood Watch meetings in both buildings indicates that in some circumstances success can be achieved in mobilizing low-income, multiethnic rental buildings. This and other success stories of crime prevention organizing are described in chapter 4.
2 "Welfare Wednesday" refers to the third Wednesday of every month, when provincial welfare cheques are distributed.
3 The Tait houses are homes on Mount Pleasant's Carolina Street owned by the Tait family, who, during the research period, rented out several subdivided homes in the neighbourhood. These landlords were often accused of renting to undesirable and unruly tenants, including drug traffickers, pimps, and prostitutes. The houses to which this research participant referred became the focus of the Carolina Street Neighbourhood Group.
4 Vancouver and Victoria were the scenes of at least three riots targeting Asian immigrants in the late nineteenth and early twentieth centuries. As Anthony Chan (1983: 140) recounts, the most infamous example occurred on 7 September 1907, when white agitators violently attacked Vancouver's Chinese and Japanese communities. "Whipped into a frenzy of hatred by speeches from labor, church and Asiatic Exclusion League demagogues, a crowd of about 1,000 left their meeting and headed to the nearby streets of Chinatown. A rock crashed through a window of a Chinese tailor shop. The riot escalated quickly from there. The mob surged through the streets, smashing windows, looting and threatening to assault Chinese merchants. A few blocks away, Japanese shops and businesses were also attacked."
5 Because there are no streets in Mount Pleasant that are populated predominantly by Chinese or Vietnamese families, there is a lack of data to address

whether a street with a homogeneous Chinese or Vietnamese population would be prone to mobilize collectively around crime prevention.

4. Organizational Obstacles to Participation in Community Crime Prevention

1 Indeed, in the evolution of the CPO some of the weaknesses identified through this research have been recognized and to some extent addressed, although greater participation has not necessarily followed.

2 Notable exceptions were the promotion of the annual general meeting of the MPSCS in 1996, in which a concerted effort was made to reach out to the Asian population in the community, including the translation and distribution of flyers and personal promotion among recognized leaders of the Chinese, Vietnamese, and Cambodian communities. This effort was initiated and spearheaded by myself, in part as a quasi-experiment to determine if the participation of these groups could be solicited through intensive and appropriate communications. As documented in chapter 3, this outreach was unsuccessful.

3 Following the initial research period, the lack of two-way communication was raised by the Mount Pleasant CPO coordinator with police management. The police responded by developing a uniform reporting system for all CPOs. The report that is submitted by the CPO to police includes a section where the police indicate action taken on the referral. Following the implementation of this reporting system, Vancouver Police Department management began to more consistently inform the coordinator of their follow-up to referrals made to them by the CPO.

4 The "success" of the case studies documented in this chapter is measured exclusively in terms of the ability of a local group to promote an inclusive mobilization of local residents around crime prevention. It is beyond the scope of this study to determine whether this mobilization actually had an impact on crime.

5. Structural Obstacles to Collective Action Crime Prevention

1 In 1996, the Mount Pleasant CPO was approached about the potential of free office space in a proposed building by a real estate development firm. While the initial overtures of the president of this company were imbued with philanthropy, it was discovered in the course of negotiations that the CPO was being used by the developer to wring concessions out of the city government for one of its other real estate developments. When these concessions were

not forthcoming, the negotiations with the CPO were abruptly halted by the developer. In response to my appeal for donated space, a representative of the developer who was involved in the negotiations bluntly reminded me that the purpose of his company was to make a profit, not to provide "community services."

2 The proclivity of the middle class to monopolize public resources is not restricted to crime prevention. According to a study conducted by Pierre Lefebvre of the Université du Québec à Montréal, the bulk of Quebec's government-subsidized daycare spots have been filled by middle-class and more affluent families. Almost 60 per cent of children filling subsidized spots are from two-parent families earning more than $60,000 a year, even though less than half of families with daycare-age children fall into that income category in Quebec. Families earning less that $40,000 account for more than a quarter of Quebec's children, but used less than 20 per cent of the subsidized daycare spaces (as cited in Sokoloff, *Globe and Mail*, 4 June 2004).

3 Shaughnessy is one of Vancouver's most affluent communities. Located on the west side of the city, the average household income, according to 1996 census data was $131,148.

4 Elections Canada, 2004, Internet web site, accessed 22 January 2006. http://www.elections.ca/content.asp?section=pas&document=turnout& lang=e&textonly=false.

5 Target hardening refers to efforts to make sites more impenetrable to offenders, through, for example, the use of locks, gated entrances, alarms, reinforced doors or windows, etc.

6 This argument follows Crawford's (1994: 508) hypothesis that community crime prevention initiatives are in danger of becoming "part of the broader management and administration of the social crises induced by post-welfarism and the market economy." For Crawford, fundamental public issues are being marginalized except insofar as they are defined in terms of their crimogenic qualities: "The danger is that, as a consequence, we will come to view poor housing, unemployment, racism, failed educational facilities, the lack of youth leisure facilities, etc. no longer as important public issues in themselves. Rather their importance will be seen to derive from the belief that they lead to crime and disorder. The fact that they may do exactly that is no reason not to assert their importance in their own right. The concern is that social deficiencies are being redefined as 'crime problems' that need to be controlled and managed, rather than addressed in themselves."

7 Government attention to, and funding for, crime prevention and community policing were further eroded following the terrorist attacks of 11 September

2001, as the focus and resources of national, regional, and municipal government and law enforcement shifted to combating terrorism. In the United States, this has had a direct impact on federal funding for crime prevention. Under the provisions of the 2004 omnibus spending bill, which was given final approach by Congress on 22 January 2004, deep cuts were made in such Justice Department programs as the Office of Community Oriented Policing Services and the Local Law Enforcement Block Grant program (*Law Enforcement News*, 2004).

8 The income statement for the 1996/97 fiscal year of the Mount Pleasant Safer Community Society listed their funding sources as follows: Donations: $10,299.15; Provincial Government Grant: $20,000; Casino Night: $20,686.69; Projects: $901.94; and Interest: $290.11, for a total of $52,177.89. "Casino Night" is a provincial government program that uses for-profit casinos to raise money for charitable societies. Together, direct and indirect government funding constituted $40,686.69 or 78 per cent of the total income for the Mount Pleasant Safer Community Society. (Ironically, this information was taken from an income statement submitted as part of a government grant application for the 1997/98 fiscal year. The application was successful and the Society received $25,000.)

9 Interviews conducted among police and city officials in 1999 for this research exposed a common refrain that the number of CPOs had mushroomed beyond control, without any overall strategic direction, and that there were far too many to be sustained and supported by the local government and police. This was reflected in a memo to Vancouver City Council, which read, "the growth of the CPCs, from 4 in 1996 to 21 in 2000, happened in many cases without a set of requirements and guidelines, but was rather a reaction to immediate identified needs in each of the areas where these CPCs were created. As a result of this reactive approach, we now have 6 CPCs in District One, 6 in District Two, 5 in District Three and 4 in District Four" (Lee and Lemcke, 2000).

6. Community Crime Prevention as Collective Action

1 In contrast, Heckathorn (1993) identifies research into the impact of group heterogeneity on collective action. He argues that the presence of actors with diverse characteristics facilitates collective action because it increases the likelihood that a "critical mass" of highly motivated contributors will emerge to initiate action (Olson, 1965; Hardin, 1982; Oliver et al., 1985). However, these studies do not deal with the combined forces of socio-economic and racial heterogeneity at the neighbourhood level.

7. Crime Prevention through Community Development

1 These critical theorists share the assumption that the substantive and process-oriented objectives of CCP and community development can be achieved. This places the normative prescriptions of this chapter firmly in the camp of critical (idealist) criminologists (Michalowski, 1983; O'Reilly-Fleming, 1996), as opposed to "left realists" (Lea and Young, 1984; McLean, 1991). Presumably, a left realist would argue that participation in CCP will always be limited and that organizing strategies should focus on a small but committed segment of the population.

2 The rioting that took place in France in 2005, which was attributed to youth of North African descent who had been effectively excluded and marginalized from mainstream French society and denied adequate educational and employment opportunities, is one striking lesson in the importance of integrating immigrant and ethnic minority youth into "mainstream" society.

3 Hermeneutics is the science of interpretation, which attempts to make sense of what people say and think, and its connection with their actions. It is a label attached usually to an abstract form of philosophical argument concerned with different conceptualizations of "understanding" and how people understand (Craib, 1992: 233).

References

Adorno, T.W., E. Frenkel-Brunswick, D.J. Levinson, and R.N. Sanford. 1950. *The Authoritarian Personality*. New York: Harper.

Agnew, J. 1978. "Market relations and locational conflict in cross-national perspective." In K. R. Cox (ed.), *Urbanization and Conflict in Market Societies*, pp. 128–43. Chicago: Maaroufa Press.

Albrecht, J.G. 1985. *Planning as a Social Process: The Use of Critical Theory*. Princeton, NJ: Princeton University Press.

Albrecht, S.L., and M. Green. 1977. "Attitudes towards the policing and the larger attitude complex: Implications for police community relationships." *Criminology* 15: 67–86.

Alinsky, S. 1971. *Rules for Radicals*. New York: Vintage Books.

Allen, J., and G. Cars. 2001. "Multiculturalism and governing neighbourhoods." *Urban Studies* 38(12): 2195–209.

Allardt, E., P. Jartti, F. Jyrkila, and Y. Littunen. 1958. "On the cumulative nature of leisure activities." *Acta Sociologica* 3: 165–72.

Alsford, S. 2005. "Frankpledge." In *Medieval English Towns – Glossary*. Accessed 23 January 2006 from http://www.trytel.com/~tristan/towns/glossary.html#frankpledge.

Arnstein, S.R. 1969. "A ladder of citizen participation." *Journal of the American Institute of Planners* 35: 216–24.

Ashby, W.R. 1956. *An Introduction to Cybernetics*. London: Chapman and Hall.

Atkinson, R., and S. Cope. 1995. "Community participation and the evaluation of urban regeneration strategies." Paper presented at the Interdisciplinary Conference on "Ideas of Community." Centre for Social and Economic Research, University of the West of England. 13–15 September.

Bagguley, P. 1992. "Social change, the middle class and the emergence of 'new social movements': A critical analysis." *Sociological Review* 40(1): 26–48.

Barker, I., and R. Linden. 1985. *Community Crime Prevention*. Ottawa: Ministry of the Solicitor General Canada.

Barr, R., and J. Tagg. 1995. "From teaching to learning: A new paradigm for undergraduate education." *Change* 27(6): 13–25.

Bazemore, G. 2000. "Building community and nurturing justice: A review of the community justice ideal."*Contemporary Justice Review* 3(2): 225–34.

Beck, U. 1992. *Risk Society: Towards a New Modernity*. Trans. Mark Ritter. London and Newbury Park, CA: Sage.

Beckett, K. 2001. "Crime and control in the culture of late modernity." *Law and Society Review* 35(4): 899–929.

Bell, D. 1976. *The Cultural Contradictions of Capitalism*. New York: Basic Books.

Bellah, R., R. Madsen, W.M. Sullivan, A. Swidler, and S.M. Tipton. 1985. *Habits of the Heart: Individualism and Commitment in American Life*. Berkeley: University of California Press.

Bellah, R.N., R. Madsen, S.M. Tipton, W.M. Sullivan, and A. Swidler, 1991. *The Good Society*. New York: Knopf.

Bellair, P.E. 1997. "Social interaction and community crime prevention: Examining the importance of neighbour networks." *Criminology* 35(4): 677–703.

Bender, T. 1978. *Community and Social Change in America*. New Brunswick, NJ: Rutgers University Press.

Bennett, S. 1995. "Community organizations and crime." *Annals of the Academy of Political and Social Science* 539 (May): 72–84.

Bennett, S., B.S. Fisher, and P.J. Lavrakas. 1986. "Awareness and participation in the Eisenhower neighborhood program." Paper presented at the annual meeting of the American Society of Criminology. Atlanta, GA.

Bennett, S., and P.J. Lavrakas. 1989. "Community-based crime prevention: An assessment of the Eisenhower Foundation." *Crime and Delinquency* 35 (July): 345–64.

Bennett, T. 1989. "Factors related to participation in neighborhood watch schemes." *British Journal of Criminology* 29(3): 207–18.

Berelson, B.R., P.F. Lazarsfeld, and W.N. McPhee. 1954. *Voting: A Study of Opinion Formation in a Presidential Campaign*. Chicago: University of Chicago Press.

Berk, R.A. 1974. *Collective Behaviour*. Dubuque, IA: W.C. Brown.

Beyond Welfare Group. 2005. Accessed 22 November from www.beyondwelfare.org.

Bloom, L.R. and D. Kilgore. 2003. "The volunteer citizen after welfare reform in the United States: An ethnographic study of volunteerism in action." *Voluntas: International Journal of Voluntary and Nonprofit Organizations* 14(4): 431–54.

Blunkett, D. 2003. "Active citizens, strong communities: Progressing civil renewal." Home Secretary's Scarman Lecture, Citizens" Convention. London: Home Office.

Body-Gendrot, S. 2001. "The politics of urban crime." *Urban Studies* 38(5/6): 915–29.

Boland, B. 1998. "The Manhattan experiment: Community prosecution." In *Crime and Place: Plenary Papers of the 1997 Conference on Criminal Justice Research and Evaluation*, pp. 51–68. Washington, DC: National Institute of Justice. July.

Boostrom, R.L., and J.H. Henderson. 1983. "Community action and crime prevention: Some unresolved issues." *Crime and Social Justice* 19: 24–30.

Boostrom, R.L., and J.H. Henderson. 1988. "The ideology of community crime prevention." *Journal of Security Administration* 11(1): 53–66.

Booth, A. 1972. "Sex and social participation." *American Sociological Review* 37: 183–92.

Boothroyd, P. 1994. "Managing population-environment linkages: A general systems theory perspective." In P. Boothroyd (ed.), *Population-Environment Linkages: Toward a Conceptual Framework*, pp. 141–60. Halifax: School for Resource and Environmental Studies.

Botes, L., and D. van Rensburg. 2000. "Community participation in development: Nine plagues and twelve commandments." *Community Development Journal* 35(1): 41–58.

Bottoms, A.E. 1995. *Intensive Community Supervision for Young Offenders: Outcomes, Process and Cost*. Cambridge: Cambridge Institute of Criminology.

Brantingham, P. 1986. "Trends in Canadian crime prevention." In K. Heal and G. Laycock (eds.), *Situational Crime Prevention: From Theory into Practice*, pp. 102–12. London: Her Majesty's Stationary Office.

Brantingham, P.L., and P.J. Brantingham. 1981. *Patterns in Crime*. New York: Macmillan.

Bridges, D. 1994. "Deliberation and decision making." In J.T. Dillon (ed.), *Deliberation in Education and Society*, pp. 67–80. Norwood, NJ: Ablex.

British Broadcasting Corporation. 2004. "Call for crime message re-think," 30 August. Accessed 5 September 2004 from http://news.bbc.co.uk/2/hi/uk_news/england/tees/3610102.stm.

Brown, B.B. 1985. "Residential territories: Cues to burglary vulnerability." *Journal of Architectural and Planning Research* 2(4): 231–43.

Buerger, M.E. 1994. "A tale of two targets: limitations of community anti-crime actions." *Crime and Delinquency* 40 (July): 411–36.

Bula, F. 1994. "Residents vow to testify against johns in prostitution cases." *Vancouver Sun*. 19 October, A1.

Bula, F. 1995. "Community policing office faces cash crisis." *Vancouver Sun.* 2 November, B1.

Bula, F. 2003. "Boards refuse to turn assets over to police." *Vancouver Sun.* 29 April, B1.

Bula, F., and P. Fong. 2003. "City will pay for crackdown, mayor says. Do what you have to do in Downtown Eastside, Campbell tells police." *Vancouver Sun,* 10 July, A1.

Bursik, R.J., and H.G. Grasmick. 1993a. *Neighborhoods and Crime: The Dimensions of Effective Community Control.* New York: Lexington Books.

Bursik, R.J., and H.G. Grasmick. 1993b. "Economic deprivation and neighborhood crime rates, 1960–1980." *Law and Society Review* 27: 263–83.

Cable, S., and B. Degutis. 1991. "The transformation of community consciousness: The effects of citizens' organizations on host communities." *International Journal of Mass Emergencies and Disasters* 9(3): 383–99.

Callahan, M. 1997. "Feminist community organizing in Canada: Postcards from the edge." In B. Wharf and M. Clague (eds.), *Community Organizing: Canadian Experiences,* pp. 181–204. Toronto: Oxford University Press.

Campbell, A., P.E. Converse, D.E. Stokes, and W.E. Miller. 1960. *The American Voter.* New York: John Wiley and Sons.

Canadian Criminal Justice Association. 1989. "Safer communities: A social strategy for crime prevention in Canada." *Canadian Journal of Criminology* 31(4): 360–579.

Canadian Press. 2006. "Pickton to plead not guilty in trial Monday." 29 January.

Carr, T., M. Dixon, and R. Ogles. 1976. "Perceptions of community life which distinguish between participants and nonparticipants in a neighbourhood self-help organization." *American Journal of Community Psychology* 4: 357–66.

Castells, M. 1983. *The City and the Grass Roots: A Cross-Cultural Theory of Urban Movements.* London: Edward Arnold.

Central Office of Information. 1989. *Practical Ways to Crack Crime: The Handbook.* London: Central Office of Information.

Chan. A. 1983. *Gold Mountain: The Chinese in the New World.* Vancouver: New Star Books.

Chavis, D.M., and G. Wandersman. 1990. "Sense of community in the urban environment: A catalyst for participation and community development." *American Journal of Community Psychology* 18: 55–81.

Checkoway, B. 2003. "Citizen participation and training." In K. Christensen and D. Levinson, (eds.), *Encyclopedia of Community* (vol. 1), pp. 158–60. Boston: Sage.

Checkoway, B., and M.A. Zimmerman. 1992. "Correlates of participation in neighbourhood organizations." *Administration in Social Work* 16(3–4): 45–64.

Chicago Community Policing Consortium. 2000. *Public Involvement: Community Policing in Chicago.* Chicago: Northwestern University, Center for Urban Affairs and Policy Research.

Chicago Community Policing Consortium. 1999. *Community Policing in Chicago, Years Five-Six: An Interim Report.* Chicago: Institute for Policy Research, Northwestern University. Accessed 22 April 2004 from http://www.northwestern.edu/ipr/publications/policing_papers/caps99.pdf.

Chicago Community Policing Consortium. 1996. *Community Policing in Chicago: Year Three.* Chicago: Illinois Criminal Justice Information Authority.

Chief Constable. Vancouver Police Department. 1994. *Policy Report: Community Policing.* Presented to Vancouver City Council. September.

Chief Electoral Officer of Canada. 2004. *Report of the Chief Electoral Officer of Canada on the 38th General Election Held on June 28, 2004.* Ottawa: Elections Canada.

Chong, D. 1993. "Coordinating demands for social change." *Annals of the American Academy of Political and Social Science* 528 (July): 126–41.

Churchman, C.W. 1968. *The Systems Approach.* New York: Dell.

City of Vancouver. Director of the Housing Centre. 2001. *State of Social Housing in Vancouver.* Policy Report submitted to Vancouver City Council, 3 October. Accessed 28 January 2006 from http://vancouver.ca/ctyclerk/cclerk/011016/RR1.htm.

City of Vancouver. Planning Department. 1994. *Mount Pleasant: Community Profile.* Community Profile Series, no 13. Vancouver: City of Vancouver Planning Department.

City of Vancouver. Planning Department. 1995. *Vancouver Local Areas, 1981–1991.* Vancouver: City of Vancouver Planning Department. July.

City of Vancouver. Planning Department. 1997. *Vancouver Local Areas, 1995/1996. 100% and 20% Data from the Canada Census.* Vancouver: City of Vancouver Planning Department.

Clapper, V.A. 1995. "Citizen participation: Demotic or elitist." *Politeia* (Pretoria) 14(1): 102–5.

Clark, P.B., and J.Q. Wilson. 1961. "Incentive systems: A theory of organizations." *Administrative Science Quarterly* 6: 129–66.

Clarke, R.V. and D.B. Cornish. 1985. "Modeling offenders' decisions: A framework for policy and research." In M. Tonry and N. Morris (eds.), *Crime and Justice: An Annual Review of Research* (vol. 6.), pp. 147–86. Chicago: University of Chicago Press.

Clary, E.G. and M. Snyder. 2002. "Community involvement: Opportunities and challenges in socializing adults to participate in society." *Journal of Social Issues* 58(3): 581–91.

Classen, R. 1996. "Restorative justice: Fundamental principles." Paper presented at UN Alliance of NGOs Working Party on Restorative Justice. Accessed 13 May 2003 from www.fresno.edu/pacs/alternative youth justiceprinc.html.

Clear, T.R., and G.F. Cole. 1986. *American Corrections.* Belmont, CA: Brooks/Cole.

Clear, T.R., and D. Karp. 1999. *The Community Justice Ideal.* Boulder, CO: Westview Press.

Cler-Cunningham, L. 2001. "Sins of the city. Plight ignored: An innovative group working to save sex trade workers from violence and illness meets a bureaucratic brick wall." *Vancouver Sun.* 28 March, p. A23.

Clotfelter, C.T. 1980. "Explaining unselfish behavior: Crime and the helpful bystander." *Journal of Urban Economics* 8: 196–212.

Cloward, R.A. and L.E. Ohlin. 1960. *Delinquency and Opportunity.* Glencoe, IL.: Free Press.

Clutterbuck, P. 1983. *Neighbourhoods under Stress.* Toronto: Social Planning Council.

Coakes, S.J., and B.J. Bishop. 1998. "Where do I fit in? Factors influencing women's participation in rural communities." *Community, Work and Family* 1(3): 249–71.

Cohen, A. 1985. *The Symbolic Construction of Community.* London: Routledge.

Cohen, J.L., and A. Arato. 1992. *Civil Society and Political Theory.* Cambridge, MA: MIT Press.

Cohen, L.E., and M. Felson. 1979. "Social change and crime rate trends: A routine activity approach." *American Sociological Review* 44: 588–608.

Commission on Social Justice. 1994. *Social Justice Strategies for National Renewal.* London: Vintage.

Conge, P.J. 1988. "The concept of political participation: Toward a definition." *Comparative Politics* 20(2): 241–49.

Conklin, J.E. 1975. *The Impact of Crime.* New York: Macmillan.

Consultation Centre. 1987. *Coquitlam Block Watch Program: Review and Assessment.* Final Report prepared for the Solicitor General of Canada. (Unpublished.)

Craib, I. 1992. *Modern Social Theory: From Parsons to Habermas.* New York: Harvester Wheatsheaf.

Crank, J. 1994. "Watchman and community: Myth and institutionalization in policing." *Law and Society Review* 28(2): 325–51.

Crawford, A. 1994. "The partnership approach to community crime prevention: Corporatism at the local level?" *Social and Legal Studies* 3(4): 497–519.

Crawford, A. 1995. "Appeals to community and crime prevention." *Crime, Law and Social Change* 22: 97–126.

Crawford, A. 1997. *The Local Governance of Crime: Appeals to Community and Partnerships.* Oxford: Clarendon Press.

Crawford, A. 1998. "Community safety and the quest for security: Holding back the dynamics of social exclusion." *Policy Studies* 19(3/4): 237–53.

Crawford, A. 1999. "Questioning appeals to community within crime prevention and control." *European Journal on Criminal Policy and Research* 7: 509–30.

Crawford, A. 2002. "The growth of crime prevention in France as contrasted with the English experience." In G. Hughes, E. MacLaughlin, and J. Muncie (eds.), *Crime Prevention and Community Safety: New Directions*, pp. 214–39. Thousand Oaks, CA: Sage.

Crawley, M. 1996. "Three die in karaoke bar stabbings: Weekend deaths are the latest in a list of violent crimes that police suspect are gang-related. No arrests have been made. Weekend stabbings continue long list of gang-related violence." *Vancouver Sun.* 8 April, B1.

Critchley, T.A. 1972. *A History of Police in England and Wales.* Monclair, NJ: Paterson-Smith.

Curtis, R.L., and B.E. Aguirre (eds.). 1993. *Collective Behavior and Social Movements.* Boston: Allyn and Bacon.

Daly, K.W. 1978. "Planning theory in search of an audience." In H.A. Goldstein and S.A. Rosenberry (eds.), *The Structural Crisis of the 1970s and Beyond: The Need for a New Planning Theory*, pp. 192–201. Blacksburg: Virginia Polytechnic Institute and State University.

Davids, C. 1995. "Understanding the significance and persistence of Neighbourhood Watch in Victoria." *Law in Context* 13(1): 57–80.

Davis, R.C., and N.J. Henderson. 2003. "Willingness to report crimes: The role of ethnic group membership and community efficacy." *Crime and Delinquency* 49(4): 564–80.

DeKeseredy, W.S., S. Alvi, M.D. Schwartz, and E.A. Tomaszewski. 2003. *Under Siege: Poverty and Crime in a Public Housing Community.* Boulder, CO: Lexington Books.

Delgado, G. 1993. "Building multiracial alliances: The case of People United for a Better Oak." In R. Fisher and J. Kling (eds.), *Mobilizing the Community: Local Politics in the Era of the Global City*, pp. 103–27. Newbury Park, CA: Sage.

Della Porta, D., and M. Diani. 1999. *Social Movements: An Introduction.* Oxford and Malden, MA: Blackwell.

Dewey, J. 1958 [1929]. *Experience and Nature.* New York: Dover.

Diani, M. 1992. "The concept of social movement." *Sociological Review* 40(1): 1–25.

Diani, M. 1995. *Green Networks: A Structural Analysis of the Italian Environmental Movement.* Edinburgh: Edinburgh University Press.

Dillon, J.T. 1994. "The questions of deliberation." In J.T. Dillon (ed.), *Deliberation in Education and Society*, pp. 3–24. Norwood, NJ: Ablex.

Dobson, C. 2005. *The Citizen's Handbook.* Vancouver: Vancouver Citizens' Committee. Accessed 26 January 2006 from http://www.vcn.bc.ca/citizens-handbook/.

Donnelly, P.G., and T.J. Majka. 1998. "Residents' efforts at neighborhood stabilization: Facing the challenges of inner-city neighborhoods." *Sociological Forum* 13(2).

Dowds, L., and P. Mayhew. 1994. "Participation in Neighbourhood Watch: Findings from the 1992 British Crime Survey." *Home Office Research and Statistics Department: Research Findings* (11): 1–4.

Downtown Eastside Residents Association. 1997. "Demographic and crime rate data." (Unpublished.)

Dubow, F., and D. Emmons. 1981. "The community hypothesis." In D.A. Lewis (ed.), *Reactions to Crime.* Beverly Hills, CA: Sage.

Dubow, F., and A. Podolefsky. 1979. *Citizen Participation in Collective Responses to Crime.* Evanston, IL: Center for Urban Affairs, Northwestern University.

Dubow, F., M. McPherson, and G. Silloway. 1985. "Organizing for the state: Neighborhood Watch as a strategy of community crime prevention." Paper presented at the annual meeting of the American Society of Criminology. San Diego, CA.

Duncan, C.M. 1999. *Worlds Apart: Why Poverty Persists in Rural America.* New Haven, CT: Yale University Press.

Durkheim, E. 1933. *The Division of Labor in Society.* New York: Free Press.

East Ender. 1984. "Mount Pleasant residents organize to address crime, prostitution." 13 September.

Eder, K. 1995. "Does social class matter in the study of social movements?" In L. Maheu (ed.), *Social Movements and Social Classes*, pp. 21–54. Thousand Oaks, CA: Sage.

Egerton, M. 2002. "Higher education and civic engagement." *British Journal of Sociology* 53(4): 603–20.

Einstadter, W.J. 1984. "Citizen patrols: Prevention or control." *Crime and Social Justice* (no. 21/22): 200–13.

Enns, C., and J. Wilson. 1999. "Sense of community and neighbourliness in Vancouver suburban communities: The picket fence project." *Plan Canada* 39(4): 12–15.

Epstein, B. 1990. "Rethinking social movements." *Socialist Review* 20(1): 35–65.

Ersing, R. 2003. "Community empowerment." In K. Christensen and D. Levinson (eds.), *Encyclopedia of Community* (vol. 1), pp. 261–4. Boston: Sage.

Etzioni, A. 1968. *The Active Society: A Theory of Societal and Political Processes.* New York: Free Press.

Etzioni, A. 1993. *The Spirit of Community: The Reinvention of American Society.* New York: Simon and Schuster.

Etzioni, A. 1995. *The Spirit of Community.* London: Fontana.

Etzioni, A. 2003. "Communitarianism." In K. Christensen and D. Levinson (eds.), *Encyclopedia of Community* (vol. 1), pp. 224–8. Boston: Sage.

Fagan, J. 1987. "Neighborhood education, mobilization, and organization for juvenile crime prevention." *Annals of the American Academy of Political and Social Sciences* 494 (November): 54–70.

Fainstein, N., and S. Fainstein. 1974. *Urban Political Movements: The Search for Power by Minority Groups in American Cities.* Englewood Cliffs, NJ: Prentice Hall.

Fainstein, N., and S. Fainstein 1979. "New debates in urban planning." *International Journal of Urban and Regional Research* 3: 381–403.

Fainstein, N., and S. Fainstein 1993. "Participation in New York and London: Community and market urban capitalism." In R. Fisher and J. Kling (eds.), *Mobilizing the Community: Local Politics in the Era of the Global City,* pp. 52–71. Newbury Park, CA: Sage.

Farrington, D.P. 1994. *Psychological Explanations of Crime.* Aldershot, UK: Dartmouth.

Feenstra, G. 2003. "Community becomes dustpan for police sweep in Downtown Eastside." Letter to the editor. *Vancouver Sun.* 11 July, p. A11.

Feins, J. 1983. *Partnerships for Neighbourhood Crime Prevention.* Washington, DC: National Institute of Justice.

Felson, M. 1987. "Routine activities and crime prevention in the developing metropolis." *Criminology* 25(4): 911–31.

Felson, M. 1994. *Crime and Everyday Life.* Thousand Oaks, CA: Pine Forge Press.

Feuer, L. 1969. *The Conflict of Generations: The Character and Significance of Student Movements.* New York: Basic Books.

Fielding, N. 2001. "Community policing: Fighting crime or fighting colleagues?" *International Journal of Police Science and Management* 3(4): 289–302.

Findlay, M., and U. Zvekic. 1988. *Analysing Informal Mechanisms of Crime Control: A Cross-cultural Perspective.* Rome: UN Social Defence Research Institute.

Fisher, B. 1993. "What works: Block Watch meetings or crime prevention seminars?" *Journal of Crime and Justice* 16(1): 1–28.

Fisher, C.S., R.M. Jackson, C.A. Stueve, K. Gerson, L.M. Jones, and M. Baldassare. 1977. *Network and Places: Social Relations in the Urban Setting.* New York: Free Press.

Fisher R., and J. Kling. 1987. "Leading the people: Two approaches to the role of ideology in community organizing." *Radical America* 21(1): 31–45.

Fisher, R., and J. Kling. 1993. "Introduction: The continued vitality of community mobilization." In R. Fisher and J. Kling (eds.), *Mobilizing the Community: Local Politics in the Era of the Global City*, pp. xi–xxiii. Newbury Park, CA: Sage.

Fishkin, J. 1995. *The Voice of the People: Public Opinion and Democracy*. New Haven, CT: Yale University Press.

Fitzgerald, R., M. Wisener, and J. Savoie. 2001. *Neighbourhood Characteristics and the Distribution of Crime in Winnipeg*. Ottawa: Statistics Canada. Accessed 13 June 2004 from http://www.statcan.ca/english/research/85-561-MIE/85-561-MIE2004004.htm.

Flint, J. 2002. "Return of the governors: Citizenship and the new governance of neighbourhood disorder in the UK." *Citizenship Studies* 6(3): 245–64.

Forester, J. 1982. "Planning in the face of power." *Journal of the American Planning Association* 48: 67–80.

Forester, J. 1985. *Critical Theory and Public Life*. Cambridge, MA: MIT Press.

Forester, J. 1989. *Planning in the Face of Power*. Berkeley: University of California Press.

Forester, J. 1993. *Critical Theory, Public Policy, and Planning Practice: Toward a Critical Pragmatism*. Albany: State University of New York Press.

Forrest, R., and A. Kearns. 2001. "Social cohesion, social capital and the neighbourhood. *Urban Studies* 38(12): 2125–43.

Forst, M.L., and G. Bazemore. 1986. "Community responses to crime." *Journal of California Law Enforcement* 20(3): 100–5.

Foster, J., and T. Hope. 1990. *Housing, Community and Crime: The Impact of the Priority Estates Project: Phase Two*. Crime Prevention Unit Paper No. 23. London: Home Office.

Foster, J., T. Hope, L. Dowds, and M. Sutton. 1993. *Housing, Community and Crime: The Impact of the Priority Estates Project*. London: Her Majesty's Stationary Office.

Fowler, F.J., and T.W. Mangione. 1982. *Neighborhood Crime, Fear and Social Control: A Second Look at the Hartford Program*. Washington, DC: U.S. Department of Justice.

Fowler, F.J., and T.W. Mangione. 1986. "A three-pronged effort to reduce crime and fear of crime: The Hartford Experiment." In D.P. Rosenbaum and M. Cahn (eds.), *Community Crime Prevention: Does It Work?*, pp. 87–108. Beverly Hills, CA: Sage.

Fowler, F.J., M.E. McCalla, and T.W. Mangione. 1979. *Reducing Residential Crime and Fear: The Hartford Neighborhood Crime Prevention Program*. Washington, DC: U.S. Department of Justice.

Freidman, W. 1998. "Volunteerism and the decline of violent crime." *Journal of Criminal Law and Criminology* 88(4): 1453–74.

Friedmann, J. 1973. *Retracking America: A Theory of Transactive Planning.* Garden City, NY: Anchor Press/Doubleday.

Friedmann, J. 1979. *The Good Society.* Cambridge, MA: MIT Press.

Friedmann, J. 1982. "Urban communes, self-management, and the reconstruction of the local state." *Journal of Planning Education and Research* 2(1): 37–53.

Friedmann, J. 1987. *Planning in the Public Domain: From Knowledge to Action.* Princeton, NJ: Princeton University Press.

Friedmann, J., and M. Douglas. 1975. *"Agropolitan Development: Towards a New Strategy for Regional Planning in Asia.* New York: United Nations Centre for Regional Development.

Friedmann, R.R. 1992. *Community Policing: Comparative Perspectives and Prospects.* New York: St. Martin's Press.

Galaway, B., and J. Hudson (eds.). 1990. *Criminal Justice, Restitution, and Reconciliation.* Monsey, NY: Criminal Justice Press.

Galloway, G. 2004. "The rich got richer ... The little economic growth there was in the '90s was concentrated among high-income earners, Statscan finds." *Globe and Mail.* 8 April, p. A10.

Gamson, J. 1995. "Must identity movements self destruct? A queer dilemma." *Social Problems* 42(3): 390–407.

Gamson, W.A. 1968. *Power and Discontent.* Homewood, IL: Dorsey.

Gans, H.J. 1962. *The Urban Villagers.* New York: Free Press.

Garland, D. 1990. *Punishment and Modern Society.* Oxford: Clarendon Press.

Garland, D. 1996. "The limits of the sovereign state: Strategies of crime control in contemporary society." *British Journal of Criminology* 36(4): 445–71.

Garland, D. 2001. *The Culture of Control: Crime and Social Order in Contemporary Society.* Chicago: University of Chicago Press.

Garland, D. 2002. "Governmentality and the problem of crime." In S. Russell (ed.), *Governable Places: Readings on Governmentality and Crime Control,* pp. 15–44. Brookfield, VT: Ashgate.

Garnson, W. 1975. *The Strategy of Social Protest.* Homewood, IL: Dorsey.

Garofalo, J., and M. McLeod. 1988. *Improving the Use and Effectiveness of Neighborhood Watch Programs.* Washington, DC: National Institute of Justice, U.S. Department of Justice.

Garofalo, J., and M. McLeod. 1989. "The structure and operations of Neighborhood Watch programs in the United States." *Crime and Delinquency* 35(3): 327–44.

Gatti, U., and E. Tremblay. 2000. "Civic community as a factor of containment of violent crime: A criminological study of Italian regions and provinces." *Polis* 14(2): 279–99.

Geason, S., and P.R. Wilson. 1998. *Crime prevention: Theory and Practice.* Canberra: Australian Institute of Criminology.

Geller, W. 1999. "Suppose we were really serious about police departments becoming 'learning organizations.'" *National Institute of Justice Journal* 234 (December): 2–7.

Giddens, A. 1994. "Brave new world: The new context of politics." In D. Miliband (ed.), *Reinventing the Left,* pp. 21–38. Cambridge: Polity Press.

Giddens, A. 1998. *The Third Way: The Renewal of Social Democracy.* Cambridge, UK, and Malden, MA: Polity Press.

Gillham, J.R., and G.A. Barnett. 1994. "Decaying interest in burglary prevention: Residence on a block with an active block club and community linkage." *Journal of Crime and Justice* 17(2): 23–48.

Gilling, D. 1993. "Crime prevention discourses and the multi-agency approach." *International Journal of the Sociology of Law* 21(2): 145–57.

Gilling, D. 1997. *Crime Prevention: Theory, Policy and Politics.* London: UCL Press.

Gillis, A.R., and J. Hagen. 1983. "Bystander apathy and the territorial imperative." *Sociological Inquiry* 53(4): 449–60.

Girling, E., I. Loader, and R. Sparks. 2000. *Crime and Social Change in Middle England: Questions of Order in an English Town.* New York: Routledge.

Gittell, M. 1980. *Limits to Citizen Participation: The Decline of Community Organizations.* Beverly Hills, CA: Sage.

Gittell, R., and A. Vidal. 1998. *Community Organizing: Building Social Capital as a Development Strategy.* Thousand Oaks, CA: Sage.

Goldstein, H. 1990. *Problem-Oriented Policing.* Philadelphia: Temple University Press.

Goris, P. 2001. "Community crime prevention and the 'partnership approach': A safe community for everyone?" *European Journal of Criminal Policy and Research* 9: 447–57.

Gottfredson, D. 1990. "Changing school structures to benefit high-risk youths." In P.E. Leone (Ed.), *Understanding Troubled and Troubling Youth: Multidisciplinary Perspectives,* pp. 246–71. Newbury Park, CA: Sage.

Government of British Columbia. Ministry of Management Services. 1996. *1996 Census Profile Vancouver-Mount Pleasant Provincial Electoral District.* Victoria: Government of British Columbia. Ministry of Management Services. Accessed 12 November 2004 from http://www.bcstats.gov.bc.ca/data/cen96/ped96new/ped00_71.pdf.

Grabow, S., and A. Heskin. 1973. "Foundations for a radical concept of planning." *Journal of the American Institute of Planners* 39(2): 106–14.

Graham, J. 1995. *Crime Prevention Strategies in Europe and North America.* Helsinki, Finland: Helsinki Institute for Crime Prevention and Control.

Gram, K. 1994. "Harcourt reply on prostitution angers residents." *Vancouver Sun.* 15 August, p. A3.

Gram, K. 2001. "Neighbourhood poverty holds kids back – study: A research map links readiness for school with the wealth of a child's neighbourhood." *Vancouver Sun.* 2 January, p. B1.

Grasmick, H.G., P. Jacobs, and C.B. McCallam. 1983. "Social class and social control: An application of deterrence theory." *Social Forces* 62 (December): 359–74.

Greenberg, M.R. 2001. "Elements and test of a theory of neighborhood civic participation." *Human Ecology Review* 8(2): 40–51.

Greenberg, S.W., W.M. Rohe, and J.R. Williams. 1982. *Safe and Secure Neighborhoods: Physical Characteristics and Informal Territorial Control in High and Low Crime Neighborhoods.* Washington, DC: U.S. Department of Justice, National Institute of Justice.

Greenberg, S.W., W.M. Rohe and J.R. Williams. 1983. "Neighborhood conditions and community crime control." *Journal of Community Action.* 19(5): 39–42.

Greenberg, S.W., W.M. Rohe, and J.R. Williams. 1984. "Neighborhood design and crime: A test of two perspectives." *Journal of the American Planning Association* 50 (Winter): 48–61.

Greenberg, S.W., W.M. Rohe, and J.R. Williams. 1985. *Informal Citizen Action and Crime Prevention at the Neighborhood Level: Synthesis and Assessment of the Research.* Washington, DC: U.S. Department of Justice, National Institute of Justice.

Grine, R.M. 1994. "'Angels in marble': Problems in stimulating community involvement in community policing." *Crime and Delinquency* 40(3): pp. 437–68.

Guest, A., and S. Wierzbicki. 1999. "Social ties at the neighbourhood level: Two decades of GSS evidence." *Urban Affairs Review* 35(1): 92–111.

Gurr, T.R. 1970. *Why Men Rebel.* Princeton, NJ: Princeton University Press.

Gutierrez, L.M., and E.A. Lewis. 1998. "A feminist perspective on organizing with women of color." In F.G. Rivera and J. Erlich (eds.), *Community Organizing in a Diverse Society,* pp. 97–116. Boston: Allyn and Bacon.

Habermas, J. 1968. *Towards a Rational Society.* Boston: Beacon Press.

Habermas, J. 1971. *Knowledge and Human Interests.* Boston: Beacon Press.

Habermas, J. 1973. *Legitimation Crisis.* Boston: Beacon Press.

Habermas, J. 1979. *Communication and the Evolution of Society*. Boston: Beacon Press.

Habermas, J. 1987. *The Theory of Communicative Action*. Vol. 2. *A Critique of Functionalist Reason*. Oxford: Polity Press.

Haeberle, S.H. 1987. "Neighborhood identity and citizen participation." *Administration and Security* 19: 178–96.

Hall, B.L. 1981. "Participatory research, popular knowledge and power: A personal reflection." *Convergence* 14(3): 6–17.

Hall, M., T. Knighton, P. Reed, P. Bussière, D. McRae, and P. Bowen. 1997. *Caring Canadians, Involved Canadians: Highlights from the 1997 National Survey of Giving, Volunteering and Participating*. Ottawa: Industry Canada.

Hall, M., L. McKeown, and K. Roberts. 2001. *Caring Canadians, Involved Canadians: Highlights from the 2000 National Survey of Giving, Volunteering and Participating*. Ottawa: Industry Canada.

Hall, P. 1999. "Social capital in Britain." *British Journal of Political Science* 29(3): 417–61.

Hancock, L. 2001. *Community, Crime, and Disorder: Safety and Regeneration in Urban Neighbourhoods*. New York: Palgrave.

Hancock, L., and R. Matthews. 2001. "Crime, community safety and toleration." In R. Matthews and J. Pitts (eds.), *Crime, Disorder, and Community Safety: A New Agenda?*, pp. 98–119. London: Routledge.

Hardin, G. 1982. *Rational Choice*. Baltimore, MA: Johns Hopkins University Press.

Harvey, D. 1981. "The urban process under capitalism: A framework for analysis." In M. Dear and A. Scott (eds.), *Urbanization and Urban Planning in Capitalist Society*, pp. 91–121. New York: Methuen.

Harvey, D. 1985. *The Urbanization of Capital: Studies in the History and Theory of Capitalist Urbanization*. Baltimore, MD: John Hopkins University Press.

Hauser, S.M. 2000. "Education, ability, and civic engagement in the contemporary United States." *Social Science Research* 29: 556–82.

Heckathorn, D.D. 1993. "Collective action and group heterogeneity: Voluntary provision verses selective incentives." *American Sociological Review* 15(3): 329–50.

Heller, K., R. Price, S. Reinharz, S. Riger, and A. Wandersman. 1984. *Psychology and Community Change: Challenges for the Future*. Homewood, IL: Dorsey.

Henig, J.R. 1982. *Neighborhood Mobilization: Redevelopment and Response*. New Brunswick, NJ: Rutgers University Press.

Herbst, L., and S. Walker. 2001. "Language barriers in the delivery of police services: A study of police and Hispanic interactions in a midwestern city." *Journal of Criminal Justice* 29(4): 329–40.

Hertzman, C., S. McLean, D. Kohen, J. Dunn, and T. Evans. 2002. *Early Development in Vancouver: Report of the Community Asset Mapping Project (CAMP)*. Vancouver: Human Early Learning Partnership, University of British Columbia.

Hicks, H.M. 1962. *Citizen Participation in Neighbourhood Rehabilitation: A Pilot Study of a Sample Area (Lower Mount Pleasant)*. Master's thesis. University of British Columbia, Vancouver.

Hills, J. 1998. *Income Gap Remains Wide Despite Mid-1990s Fall in Inequality*. London: Joseph Rowntree Foundation. Accessed 25 August 2004 from http://www.jrf.org.uk/knowledge/findings/socialpolicy/spr368.asp.

Hinkle, S., L. Fox-Cardamone, J.A. Haseleu, R. Brown, and L.M. Irwin. 1996. "Grassroots Political Action as an Intergroup Phenomenon." *Journal of Social Issues* 52(1): 39–51.

Hirschman, A. 1982. *Shifting Involvement*. Princeton, NJ: Princeton University Press.

Hoch, C.J. 1984. "Pragmatism, planning and power." *Journal of Planning Education and Research* 4(2): 86–96.

Hope, T. 1984. "Building design and burglary." In R. Clarke and T. Hope (eds.), *Coping with Burglary*, pp. 45–60. Boston: Kluwer-Nijhoff.

Hope, T. 1988. "Support for Neighborhood Watch: A British crime survey analysis." In T. Hope and M. Shaw (eds.), *Communities and Crime Reduction*, pp. 146–63. London: Her Majesty's Stationary Office.

Hope, T. 1995. "Community crime prevention." In M. Tonry and D. Farrington (eds.), *Building a Safer Society: Strategic Approaches to Crime Prevention*, pp. 21–89. Chicago: University of Chicago Press.

Hope, T., 1997. "Inequality and the future of community crime prevention." In S.P. Lab (ed.), *Crime Prevention at a Crossroads*, pp. 143–58. Cincinnati: Anderson.

Hope, T., and J. Foster. 1992. "Conflicting forces: Changing the dynamics of crime and community on a 'problem' estate." *British Journal of Criminology* 32(4): 488–504.

Hope, T., and S. Lab. 2001. "Variation in crime prevention participation: Evidence from the British Crime Survey." *Crime Prevention and Community Safety: An International Journal* 3(1): 7–22.

Horvath, P. 1998. "Agency and social adaptation." *Applied Behavioral Science Review* 6(2): 137–52.

Hourihan, K. 1987. "Local community involvement and participation in Neighbourhood Watch: A case-study in Cork, Ireland." *Urban Studies* 24(2): 129–36.

Howell, M. 2002a. "Mt. Pleasant police centre needs more volunteer help: City grant could be cancelled." *Vancouver Courier*. 29 September, p. 26.

Howell, M. 2002b. "Crime prevention lacking in Mt. Pleasant. Community policing centre in Kingsgate Mall to close at end of year." *Vancouver Courier.* 2 December, p. 7.

Huckfeldt, R. 1979. "Political participation and the neighbourhood social context." *American Journal of Political Science* 23(3): 579–92.

Hughes, Gordon. 2002. "The shifting sands of crime prevention and community safety." In G. Hughes, E. MacLaughlin, and J. Muncie (eds.), *Crime Prevention and Community Safety: New Directions*, pp. 1–10. Thousand Oaks, CA: Sage.

Hunter, A., and T.L. Baumer. 1982. "Street traffic, social integration and fear of crime." *Sociological Inquiry* 52: 122–31.

Hyman, H., and C. Wright. 1971. "Trends in voluntary association memberships of American adults: Replication based on secondary analysis of national sample surveys." *American Sociological Review* 36: 191–206.

Inglehart, R. 1988. "New participation in post-industrial society." *Rivista Italiana di Scienza Politica* 18(3): 403–45.

Jacksteit, M., and A. Kaufmann. 1997. *Finding Common Ground in the Abortion Conflict: A Manual.* Washington, DC: Common Ground Network for Life and Choice.

Jacobs, J. 1961. *Death and Life of Great American Cities.* New York: Random House.

Johnston, L. 2001. "Crime, fear and civil policing." *Urban Studies* 38(5/6): 959–66.

Jones, T., T. Newburn, and D. Smith. 1994. *Democracy and Policing.* London: Policy Studies Institute.

Jones-Finer, C. and M. Nellis (eds.). 1998. *Crime and Social Exclusion.* Oxford: Blackwell.

Kearns, A., and R. Forrest. 2000. "Social cohesion and multilevel urban governance." *Urban Studies* 37(5/6): 995–1017.

Kelling, G.L. 1987. "Acquiring a taste for order: The community and police." *Crime and Delinquency* 33(1): 90–102.

Kelling, G.L., and C. Coles. 1996. *Broken Windows: Restoring Order and Reducing Crime in Our Communities.* New York: Free Press.

Kenny, C.B. 1992. "Political participation and effects from the social environment." *American Journal of Political Science* 36(1): 259–67.

Khan, N.A. 1993. "Towards an understanding of participation: The conceptual labyrinth revisited." *Administrative Change* 20(1–2): 106–20.

Kines. L. 1992. "Neighbors band together to save their community." *Vancouver Sun.* 6 February, p. A1.

King, M. 1988. *How to Make Social Crime Prevention Work: The French Experience.* London: National Association for the Care and Resettlement of Offenders.

Klandermans, B. 1993. "A theoretical framework for comparisons of social movement participation." *Sociological Forum* 8(3): 383–402.

Klandermans B., and D. Oegema. 1987. "Potentials, networks, motivations, and barriers: Steps towards participation in social movements." *American Sociological Review* 52(4): 519–31.

Kling, J. 1993. "Complex society/complex cities: New social movements and the restructuring of urban space." In R. Fisher and J. Kling (eds.), *Mobilizing the Community: Local Politics in the Era of the Global City,* pp. 28–51. Urban Affairs Annual Review. Beverly Hills, CA: Sage.

Kornhauser, W. 1959. *The Politics of Mass Society.* Glencoe, IL: Free Press.

Kumar, S. 2002. *Models for Community Participation. A Complete Guide for Practitioners.* London: ITDG Publishing.

Kuttschreuter, M., and O. Wiegman. 1997. "Crime communication at information meetings." *British Journal of Criminology* 37(1): 46–62.

Lab, S. 1990. "Citizen crime prevention: Domains and participation." *Justice Quarterly* 7(3): 467–91.

Lab, S. 1997. "Crime prevention: Where have we been and which way should we go?" In Steven Lab (ed.), *Crime Prevention at a Crossroads,* pp. 1–13. Cincinnati: Anderson.

Lab, S., and D.K. Das. (eds.). 2001. *International Perspectives on Community Policing and Crime Prevention.* Upper Saddle River, NJ: Prentice Hall.

Lab, S., and T. Stanich. 1994. "Crime prevention participation: An exploratory analysis." *American Journal of Criminal Justice* 18(1): 1–23.

Lasch, C. 1979. *The Culture of Narcissism.* New York: W.W. Norton.

Lau, S., and Kuan, H. 1995. "The attentive spectators: Political participation of the Hong Kong Chinese." *Journal of Northeast Asian Studies* 14(1): 3–24.

Lavrakas, P.J. 1981. "On households." In D.A. Lewis (ed.), *Reactions to crime,* pp. 67–85. Beverly Hills, CA: Sage.

Lavrakas, P.J. 1982. "Fear of crime and behavioral restrictions in urban and suburban neighborhoods." *Population and Environment* 52: 42–64.

Lavrakas, P.J. 1985. "Citizen self-help and neighborhood crime prevention policy." In L.A. Curtis (ed.), *American Violence and Public Policy,* pp. 87–115. New Haven: Yale University Press.

Lavrakas, P.J., and L. Herz. 1982. "Citizen participation in neighborhood crime prevention." *Criminology* 20: 479–98.

Lavrakas, P.J., and D.A. Lewis 1980. "The conceptualization and measurement of citizens' crime prevention behaviors." *Journal of Research in Crime and Delinquency* 17: 254–72.

Lavrakas, P.J., J. Normoyle, W.K. Skogan, E. Herz, G. Salem, and D.A. Lewis. 1980. *Factors Related to Citizen Involvement in Personal, Household, and Neighborhood Anti-crime Measures.* Final Report of the National Institute of Justice. Evanston, IL: Northwestern University, Center for Urban Affairs.

Law Enforcement News. 2004. "The federal well is running dry: Spending bill, Bush budget deliver bad news for aid to locals." 30(615): 1, 12.

Laycock, G., and N Tilley. 1995. *Policing and Neighbourhood Watch: Strategic Issues.* London: Great Britain Home Office Police Research Group.

Lea, J., and J. Young. 1984. *What Is to Be Done about Law and Order?* London: Penguin.

Lee, T. 1968. "Urban neighbourhood as a socio-spatial scheme." *Human Relations* 21: 241–68.

Lee, M., and W. Lemcke. 2000. Administrative report submitted to Vancouver City Council from the chief constable and the director of social planning. *Community Policing Program Review.* 6 September. Accessed 13 June 2004 from http://www.city.vancouver.bc.ca/ctyclerk/cclerk/000926/rr1.htm.

Lee, M. 2002. Administrative report submitted to the Standing Committee on City Services and Budgets from the director of social planning and the chief constable of the Vancouver Police Department. *Community Safety Grant – Mount Pleasant.* 11 September. Accessed 13 June 2004 from http://www.city.vancouver.bc.ca/ctyclerk/cclerk/021003/csb2.htm.

Lee, M., and B. Goddard. 2003. Administrative report submitted to the Standing Committee on City Services and Budgets from the chief constable and the director of social planning. *New Community Policing Centres Model."* 18 June. Accessed 13 June 2004 from http://www.city.vancouver.bc.ca/ctyclerk/cclerk/20030626/csb3.htm.

Lee, M. 2000. Administrative report submitted to Vancouver City Council from the chief constable and the director of social planning. *Grant Allocations of Year 2000 – Community Safety Funding Program.* 11 September. Accessed 13 June 2004 from http://www.city.vancouver.bc.ca/ctyclerk/cclerk/000222/a7.htm.

Leighton, B. 1988. "The community concept in criminology: Toward a social network approach." *Journal of Research in Crime and Delinquency* 25(4): 351–74.

Leighton, B. 1991. "Visions of community policing: Rhetoric and reality in Canada." *Canadian Journal of Criminology* 33(3–4): 485–522.

Lenski, G.E. 1966. *Power and Privilege: A Theory of Social Stratification.* New York: McGraw-Hill.

Léonard, L., G. Rosario, C. Scott, and J. Bressan. 2005. "Building safer communities: Lessons learned from Canada's national strategy." *Canadian Journal of Criminology and Criminal Justice* 47 (2 April): 233–50.

Lewis, D.A. 1979. "Design problems in public policy development: The case of the community anti-crime program." *Criminology* 17(August): 172–83.

Lewis, D.A., and G. Salem. 1981. "Community crime prevention: An analysis of a developing perspective." *Crime and Delinquency* 27: 405–21.

Lewis, D.A., J.A. Grant, and D.P. Rosenbaum. 1988. *The Social Construction of Reform: Community Organizations and Crime Prevention.* New Brunswick, NJ: Transaction Books.

Lichterman, P. 1995. "Beyond the seesaw model: Public commitment in a culture of self-fulfilment." *Sociological Theory* 13(3): 275–300.

Linden, R. 1996. *Building a Safer Community: A Community-based Crime Prevention Manual.* Ottawa: Department of Justice.

Lindsay, B., and D. McGillis. 1986. "Citywide community crime prevention: An assessment of the Seattle Program." In D.P. Rosenbaum (ed.), *Community Crime Prevention: Does It Work?*, pp. 46–7. Beverly Hills, CA: Sage.

Lipsky, M. 1969. *Protest in City Politics, Rent Strikes, Housing and the Power of the Poor.* Chicago: Rand McNally.

Little, B. 2004. "Canada scores poorly on poverty test." *Globe and Mail.* 30 August, p. B4.

Lockwood, D. 1999. "Civic integration and social cohesion." In I. Gough and G. Olofsson (eds.), *Capitalism and Social Cohesion: Essays on Exclusion and Integration*, pp. 63–83. London: Macmillan.

Lofland, L.H. 1983. "Understanding urban life: The Chicago legacy." *Urban Life* 11(4): 491–511.

Lotz, J. 1997. "The beginning of community development in English-speaking Canada." In B. Wharf and M. Clague (eds.), *Community Organizing: Canadian Experiences*, pp. 15–29. Toronto: Oxford University Press.

Low, N.P. 1990. "Class, politics: From reductionism to pluralism in Marxist class analysis." *Environment and Planning – A.* 22(8): 1091–14.

Lowman, J. 1992. "Street prostitution control: Some Canadian reflections on the Finsbury Experience." *British Journal of Criminology* 32(1): 1–17.

Lowman, J. 2000. "Violence and the outlaw status of (street) prostitution in Canada." *Violence against Women* 6(9): 987–1011.

Lowman, J., and L. Fraser. 1995a. *Technical Report – Violence against Persons Who Prostitute: The Experience in British Columbia.* Report submitted to the Department of Justice Canada, Research, Statistics and Evaluation Directorate. Accessed 24 July 2004 from http://users.uniserve.com/~lowman/violence/2.htm.

Lowman, J., and L. Fraser. 1995b. *Technical Report – Violence against Persons Who Prostitute: The Experience in British Columbia.* Report submitted to the Department of Justice Canada, Research, Statistics and Evaluation Directorate.

Accessed 24 July 2004 from http://users.uniserve.com/~lowman/violence/8.htm.

Lowman, J., and L. Fraser. 1995c. *Technical Report – Violence against Persons Who Prostitute: The Experience in British Columbia.* Report submitted to the Department of Justice Canada, Research, Statistics and Evaluation Directorate. Accessed 24 July 2004 from http://users.uniserve.com/~lowman/violence/7.htm.

Lurigio, A.J., and D.P. Rosenbaum. 1986. "Evaluation research in community crime prevention: A critical look at the field." In D.P. Rosenbaum (ed.), *Community Crime Prevention: Does it Work?*, pp. 19–44. Beverly Hills, CA: Sage. Sage Criminal Justice System Annuals. Vol. 22.

Lyet, P. 1998. "L'Organisation du benevolat, un defi pour les acteurs du champ social." *La Revue du Mauss* 11: 280–94.

Lynn, D.B. 2002. "Forging creative partnerships: The alliance of public health and public safety among immigrant populations." *Policy Studies Journal* 30 (1): 132–47.

Lyons, M., C. Smuts, and A. Stephens. 2001. "Participation, empowerment and sustainability: (How) do the links work?" *Urban Studies* 38(8): 1233–51.

Lyons, W., and J. Scheb. 1998. "Reflections on the survey." *Knoxville News-Sentinel.* 19 July.

Maccoby, E.E., J.P. Church, and R.M. Church. 1958. "Community integration and the social control of juvenile delinquency." *Journal of Social Issues* 14: 38–51.

Mackie, J. 1999a. "It's a neighbourhood of distinct areas." *Vancouver Sun.* 3 April, p. B8.

Mackie, J. 1999b. "East side, west side are different stories." *Vancouver Sun.* 3 April, p. B8.

Mackie, J. 1999c "Mount Pleasant: The restoration of heritage houses was the start, and now a proud old neighbourhood is basking in a new glory." *Vancouver Sun.* 3 April, p. B7.

Mackie, J. 2003. "Mount Pleasant to be more so." *Vancouver Sun.* 26 May, p. B7.

MacLaughlin, E. 2002. "The crisis of the social and the political materialization of community safety." In G. Hughes, E. MacLaughlin, and J. Muncie (eds.), *Crime Prevention and Community Safety: New Directions*, pp. 77–100. Thousand Oaks, CA: Sage.

Marans, R.W. 1976. "Perceived quality of residential environments: Some methodological issues." In L. Craik and E. Zube (eds.), *Perceiving Environmental Quality: Research and Applications*, pp. 123–47. New York: Plenum Press.

Marris, P. 1982a. "Social change and reintegration." *Journal of Planning Education and Research* 2: 54–61.

Marris, P. 1982b. *Community Planning and Conceptions of Change.* London and Boston: Routledge and Kegan Paul.

Marsh, G. 1999. "The community of circumstance: A tale of three cities: Community participation in St. Kilda, Knox, and Lewisham." *Research in Community Sociology* 9: 65–86.

Marston, S.A., and G. Towers. 1993. "Private spaces and the politics of places: Spatioeconomic restructuring and community organizing in Tuscon and El Paso." In R. Fisher and J. Kling (eds.), *Mobilizing the Community: Local Politics in the Era of the Global City,* pp. 75–102. Newbury Park, CA: Sage.

Martin, E. 1920. *The Behaviour of Crowds.* London and New York: Harper and Brothers.

Marwell, G., P.E. Oliver, and R. Prahl. 1988. "Social networks and collective action: A theory of the critical mass." *American Journal of Sociology* 94(3): 502–34.

Marx, G.T. 1989. "Commentary: Some trends and issues in citizen involvement in the law enforcement process." *Crime and Delinquency* 35(3): 500–19.

Marx, G.T., and D. Archer. 1971. "Citizen involvement in the law enforcement process: The case of community police patrols." *American Behavioral Scientist* 15: 52–72.

Marx, G.T., and D. McAdam. 1994. *Collective Behavior and Social Movements.* Englewood Cliffs, NJ: Prentice Hall.

Masterson-Allen, S., and P. Brown. 1990. "Public reaction to toxic waste contamination: Analysis of a social movement." *International Journal of Health Services* 20(3): 485–500.

Mastrofski, S.D. 1991. "Community policing as reform: A cautionary tale." In C.B. Klockers and S.D. Mastrofski (eds.), *Thinking about Policing.* pp. 47–67. New York: McGraw Hill.

Mathews, D. 1994. *Politics for People: Finding a Responsible Public Voice.* Chicago: University of Illinois Press.

Matthews, Hugh. 2001. "Citizenship, youth councils and young people's participation." *Journal of Youth Studies* 4(3): 299–318.

Matthews, R., and J. Pitts. 2001. "Introduction: Beyond criminology." In R. Matthews and J. Pitts (eds.), *Crime, Disorder, and Community Safety: A New Agenda?*, pp. 1–25. London: Routledge.

McAdam, D. 1994. "Culture and social movements." In E. Lavana, H. Johnston, and J.R. Gusfield (eds.), *New Social Movements: From Ideology to Identity,* pp. 36–57. Philadelphia: Temple University Press.

McCarthy, J.D., and M.N. Zald 1977. "Resource mobilization and social movements: A partial theory." *American Journal of Sociology* 82(6): 1212–41.

McConville, M. and D. Shepherd. 1992. *Watching Police Watching Communities.* London and New York: Routledge.

McCourt, K. 1977. *Working-Class Women and Grass-Roots Politics.* Bloomington: Indiana University Press.

McEvoy, K., B. Gormally, and H. Mika. 2002. "Conflict, crime control and the re-construction of state-community relations in Northern Ireland." In G. Hughes, E. MacLaughlin, and J. Muncie (eds.), *Crime Prevention and Community Safety: New Directions,* pp. 182–212. Thousand Oaks, CA: Sage.

McLean, B. 1991. "Introduction: The origins of left realism: Some theoretical and methodological concerns of the local crime survey." *Crime, Law and Social Change* 15(3): 213–54.

McLean, M. 2000. *Vancouver Drug Epidemiology and Drug Crime Statistics 2000.* Vancouver: Canadian Community Epidemiology Network on Drug Use.

McPherson, M., and G. Silloway. 1981. "Planning to prevent crime." In D.A. Lewis (ed.) *Reactions to Crime,* pp. 149–66. Beverly Hills, CA: Sage.

Meeker, J.W., and J. Dombrink. 1988. "The undocumented and their legal needs." *Humboldt Journal of Social Relations* 15(2): 105–32.

Melucci, A. 1980. "The new social movements: A theoretical approach." *Social Science Information* 19: 199–226.

Melucci, A. 1985. "The symbolic challenge of contemporary movements." *Social Research* 52: 789–816.

Melucci, A. 1989. *Nomads of the Present: Social Movements and Individual Needs in Contemporary Society.* Philadelphia: Temple University Press.

Melucci, A. 1992. "Liberation of meaning? Social movements, culture and democracy." *Development and Change* 23(3): 43–77.

Merkl, P. 1987. "How new the brave new world: New social movements in West Germany." *German Studies Review* 10: 125–47.

Merry, S.E. 1981. "Defensible space undefended: Social factors in crime control through environmental design." *Urban Affairs Quarterly* 16(4): 397–422.

Merton, R. 1938. "Social structure and anomie." *American Sociological Review* 3(October): 672–82.

Messner, S.F., and R.M. Golden. 1992. "Racial inequality and racially disaggregated homicide rates: An assessment of alternative theoretical explanations." *Criminology* 30: 421–45.

Metro Action Committee on Public Violence against Women and Children (METRAC). 1989. *Moving Forward: Making Transit Safer for Women.* Toronto: METRAC.

Michalowski, R.J. 1983. "Crime control in the 1980s: A progressive agenda." *Crime and Social Justice* 20: 13–23.

Michalowski, R.J. 1992. "Crime and justice in socialist Cuba: What can left realists learn?" In J. Lowman and B. McLean (eds.), *Realist Criminology: Crime Control and Policing in the 1990s,* pp. 115–38. Toronto: University of Toronto Press.

Michelson, W. 1970. *Man and His Urban Environment: A Sociological Approach.*
Reading, MA: Addison-Wesley.

Milbrath, L. 1965. *Political Participation: How and Why People Get Involved with
Politics.* Skokie, IL: Rand McNally.

Miller, B. 2000. *Geography and Social Movements.* Minneapolis: University of
Minnesota Press.

Miller, L.L. 2001. *The Politics of Community Crime Prevention: Implementing
Operation Weed and Seed in Seattle.* Aldershot, UK; Burlington, VT: Ashgate-
Dartmouth.

Miller, S. 2004. "Beyond welfare reform: An overview of our approach."
Accessed 22 July 2004 from http://www.beyondwelfare.org.

Miller, W.E., and J.M. Shanks. 1996. *The New American Voter.* Cambridge, MA:
Harvard University Press.

Morenoff, J.D., R.J. Sampson, and S.W. Raudenbush. 2001. "Neighborhood
inequality, collective efficacy, and the spatial dynamics of urban violence."
Criminology 39: 517–59.

Mount Pleasant Citizens' Planning Committee. 1989. *Community Development
Plan for Mount Pleasant.* Vancouver: City of Vancouver.

Mount Pleasant Triangle. Citizens N.I.P Committee. Vancouver City Planning
Department. 1976. *Mount Pleasant Triangle Concept Plan.* Vancouver: Vancouver City Planning Department.

Mukherjee, S., and P. Wilson. 1987. "Neighborhood Watch: Issues and policy
implications." *Trends and Issues in Crime and Criminal Justice* (no. 8). Canberra:
Australian Institute of Criminology.

Mulberg, A. 1976. *Bellevue Citizen Involvement in Burglary Prevention.* King
County, WA: Law and Justice Planning Office.

Muller, J. 1990. "Management of urban neighbourhoods through Alinksy-style
organizing: Redevelopment and local area planning." In R. Ng, G. Walker,
and J. Muller (eds.), *Community Organization and the Canadian State,* pp. 203–
12. Toronto: Garamond Press.

Munk, A. 2002. "Social partnerships in distressed neighbourhoods: The Danish
case." *European Journal of Housing Policy* 2(3): 223–45.

Murphy, C. 1988. "Community problems, problem communities and community policing in Toronto." *Journal of Research in Crime and Delinquency* 25: 392–
410.

Murphy, C., and G. Muir. 1985. *Community-Based Policing: A Review of the Critical Issues.* Ottawa: Solicitor General of Canada.

Murray, C.A. 1983. "The physical environment and community control of
crime." In J.Q. Wilson (ed.), *Crime and Public Policy,* pp. 107–22. San Francisco: Institute for Contemporary Studies.

National Crime Prevention Centre (Canada). 1995. *Clear Limits and Real Opportunities: The Keys to Preventing Youth Crimes.* Ottawa: NCPC.

National Federation of Settlements and Neighborhood Centers. 1968. *Making Democracy Work: A Study of Neighborhood Organizations.* New York: National Federation of Settlements and Neighborhood Centers.

Nelson, R.F. 1976. *The Illusions of Urban Man.* Ottawa: Ministry of State for Urban Affairs Canada.

Newman, O. 1972. *Defensible Space: People and Design in the Violent City.* New York: Macmillan.

Newman, O., and K.A. Franck. 1982. "The effects of building size on personal crime and fear of crime." *Population and Environment* 5(4): 203–20.

Nicholas, S., D. Povey, A. Walker, and C. Kershaw. 2005. *Crime in England and Wales, 2004/2005.* London: Home Office.

Nie, N.H., J. Junn, and K. Stehlik-Barry. 1996. *Education and Democratic Citizenship in America.* Chicago: University of Chicago Press.

Nihei, N. 2003. "Who is a 'volunteer'? A reconsideration of assumptions about participation in theories of civil society." *Soshioroji* 48(1): 93–109.

Normandeau, A., and B. Leighton. 1990. *A Vision of the Future of Policing in Canada.* Ottawa: Solicitor General of Canada.

Norris, F.H., and K. Kaniasty. 1992. "A longitudinal study of the effects of various crime prevention strategies on criminal victimization, fear of crime, and psychological distress." *American Journal of Community Psychology* 20(5): 625–48.

Oberschall, A. 1973. *Social Conflict and Social Movements.* Englewood Cliffs, NJ: Prentice Hall.

O'Connor, T. 2006. "A brief guide to police history." *MegaLinks in Criminal Justice.* Accessed 23 January 2006 from http://faculty.ncwc.edu/toconnor/205/2051ect04.htm.

Offe, C. 1985. "New social movements: Changing boundaries of the political." *Social Research* 52: 817–68.

Office of the Deputy Prime Minister. Social Exclusion Unit. 1998. *Bringing Britain Together: A National Strategy for Neighbourhood Renewal.* London: Home Office.

Office of the Deputy Prime Minister. Social Exclusion Unit. 2004. *Tackling Social Exclusion: Taking Stock and Looking to the Future: Emerging Findings.* London: ODPM Publications.

Office of Juvenile Justice and Delinquency Prevention. 1996. *Juvenile Offenders and Victims: A National Report.* Washington, DC: OJJDP.

Office of Juvenile Justice and Delinquency Prevention. 1998. *Juvenile Mentoring Program: 1998 Report to Congress.* Washington, DC: OJJDP.

Oliver, P. 2003. "Collective action." In K. Christensen and D. Levinson (eds.), *Encyclopedia of Community* (vol. 1), pp. 198–203. Boston: Sage.

Oliver, P.E., G. Marwell, and R. Teixeira. 1985. "A theory of the critical mass: Interdependence, group heterogeneity, and the production of collective action." *American Journal of Sociology* 91: 522–56.

Olofsson, G. 1988. "After the working-class movement? An essay on what's 'new' and what's 'social' in the new social movements." *Acta sociologica* 31(1): 15–34.

Olsen, M.E. 1970. "Social and political participation of blacks." *American Sociological Review* 35(4): 682–97.

Olson, M. 1965. *The Logic of Collective Action: Public Goods and the Theory of Groups.* Cambridge, MA: Harvard University Press.

O'Malley, P. 1992. "Risk, power and crime prevention." *Economy and Society* 21(3): 252–75.

O'Malley, P. 1996. "Risk and responsibility." In A. Barry, T. Osborne, and N. Rose (eds.), *Foucault and Political Reason: Liberalism, Neo-liberalism and Rationalities of Government*, pp. 189–208. Chicago: University of Chicago Press.

Oppal, Mr Justice W. 1994. *Closing the Gap: Policing and the Community: The Report.* Victoria, BC: Queen's Printer.

O'Reilly-Fleming, T. (ed.). 1996. *Post-Critical Criminology.* Scarborough, ON: Prentice Hall.

Pantoja, A., and W. Perry. 1998. "Community development and restoration: A perspective and case study." In F.G. Rivera and J.L. Erlich (eds.), *Community Organizing in a Diverse Society*, pp. 220–42. Boston: Allyn and Bacon.

Parekh, B. 2000. *Rethinking Multiculturalism: Cultural Diversity and Political Theory.* London: Macmillan.

Passy, F. 2003. "Social networks matter, but how?" In M. Diani and D. McAdam (eds.), *Social Movements and Networks: Relational Approaches to Collective Action*, pp. 21–48. Oxford and New York: Oxford University Press.

Pavlich, G. 2002. "Preventing crime: 'Social' versus 'community' governance in Aotearoa/New Zealand." In R. Smandych (ed.), *Governable Places: Readings on Governmentality and Crime Control*, pp. 103–31. Brookfield, VT: Ashgate.

Pearce, S.C., and J. Olderman. 1995. *Community Corrections in the United States: A Summary of Research Findings.* North Carolina Sentencing and Policy Advisory Commission. Washington, DC: National Institute of Justice

Pearson, S.S., and H.M. Voke. 2003. *Building an Effective Citizenry: Lessons Learned from Initiatives in Youth Engagement.* Washington, DC: American Youth Policy Forum. http://www.aypf.org/publications/building-an-effective-citizenry.pdf.

Pemberton, K. 1989a. "Drug dealers pushing into Pleasant district." *Vancouver Sun.* 26 April, p. E8.

Pemberton, K. 1989b. "Police probe Mount Pleasant in hooker deaths." *Vancouver Sun.* 8 June, p. B7.

Pemberton, K. 1993. "Old-fashioned community policing under review." *Vancouver Sun.* 10 February, p. B1.

Pemberton, K., and D. Ward. 2003. "Closing of 'crack houses' cheered." *Vancouver Sun.* 12 April, p. B1.

Pennell S., C. Curtis, J. Henderson, and J. Tayman. 1989. "Guardian Angels: A unique approach to crime prevention." *Crime and Delinquency* 35: 378–400.

Penner, L.A. 2002. "Dispositional and organizational influences on sustained volunteerism: An interactionist perspective." *Journal of Social Issues* 58(3): pp. 447–67.

Pepinsky, H.E. 1989. "Issues of citizen involvement in policing." *Crime and Delinquency* 35(3): 458–70.

Pepinsky, H.E. 1991. *Geometry of Violence and Democracy.* Bloomington: Indiana University Press.

Perkins, D.D., B.B. Brown, and R.B Taylor. 1996. "The ecology of empowerment: Predicting participation in community organizations." *Journal of Social Issues* 52(1): 85–110.

Perkins, D.D., P. Florin, R.C. Rich, D.M. Chavis, and A. Wandersman. 1990. "Participation and the social and physical environment of residential blocks: Crime and community context." *American Journal of Community Psychology* 18(1): 83–115.

Perlman, J. 1979. "Grassroots Empowerment and Government Response." *Social Policy* 10(2): 16–21.

Perry, J.B. 1989. "Public support of the Guardian Angels: Vigilante protection against crime." *Sociology and Social Research* 73(3): 129–31.

Perry, S.E., M. Lewis, and J-M Fontan. 1992. *Revitalizing Canada's Neighbourhoods: A Research Report on Urban Community Economic Development.* Vernon, BC: Centre for Community Enterprise.

Philadelphia Student Union. Internet web site. Accessed 30 January 2006 from http://www.phillystudentunion.org/main.html.

Pilisuk, M., J. McAllister, and J. Rothman. 1996. "Coming together for action: The challenge of contemporary grassroots community organizing." *Journal of Social Issues* 52(1): 15–37.

Pitts, J., and T. Hope. 1997. "The local politics of inclusion: The state and community safety." *Social Policy and Administration* 31(5): 37–58.

Piven, F.F. 1966. "Participation of residents in neighbourhood community action programs." *Social Work* 1 (January): 73–80.

Piven, F.F., and R.A. Cloward. 1977. *Poor People's Movements: Why They Succeed, How They Fail.* New York: Vintage Books.

Piven, F.F., and R.A. Cloward. 1982. *The New Class War.* New York: Pantheon.

Plaster, S. 2002. "Community CPTED." *CPTED Journal* 1(1): 15–18.

Plaster, S., and S. Carter. 1993. *Planning for Prevention: Sarasota, Florida's Approach to Crime Prevention through Environmental Design.* Tallahassee: Florida Criminal Justice Executive Institute, Florida Department of Law Enforcement.

Pleasant Times. 2003a. "Business Block Watch arriving soon in UpTown!" 13(1): 1.

Pleasant Times. 2003b. "Business Block Watch." 13(2): 2.

Podolefsky, A.M. 1985. "Rejecting crime prevention programs: The dynamics of program implementation in high need communities." *Human Organization* 44: 30–40.

Podolefsky, A.M., and F. Dubow. 1981. *Strategies for Community Crime Prevention: Collective responses to Crime in Urban America.* Springfield, IL: Thomas.

Pratkanis, A.R., and M.E. Turner. 1996. "Persuasion and democracy: Strategies for increasing deliberative participation and enacting social change." *Journal of Social Issues* 52(1): 187–205.

Prokopy, J.J. 1998. "Obstacles to participation in community-based development: A case study from northern Thailand." *Society for the Study of Social Problems.* (Unpublished.)

Purdue, Derrick. 2001. "Neighbourhood governance: Leadership, trust and social capital." *Urban Studies* 38(12): 2211–24.

Putnam, R.D. 1995. "Bowling alone: America's declining social capital. *Journal of Democracy* 6(1): 65–78.

Putnam, R.D. 1996. "The strange disappearance of civic America. *The American Prospect.* Accessed 26 January from http://www.prospect.org/print/V7/24/putnam-r.html.

Putnam, R.D. 2000. *Bowling Alone: The Collapse and Revival of American Community.* New York: Simon and Schuster.

Putnam, R.D., with R. Leonardi and R.Y. Nanetti. 1993. *Making Democracy Work: Civic Traditions in Modern Italy.* Princeton, NJ: Princeton University Press.

Rand, A. 1943. *The Fountainhead.* Indianapolis, IN: Bobbs-Merrill.

Rand, A. 1957. *Atlas Shrugged.* New York: Random House.

Randall, J.E. 1983. *Metro Vancouver: Industrial Decentralization and Port Activity on the Lower Fraser River.* Toronto: University of Toronto/York University.

Ravanera, Z.R., F. Rajulton, and P. Turcotte. 2003. "Youth integration and social capital: An analysis of the Canadian General Social Surveys on time use." *Youth and Society* 35(2): 158–82.

Reed, P.B., and L.K. Selbee. 2001. "The civic core in Canada: Disproportionality in charitable giving, volunteering, and civic participation." *Nonprofit and Voluntary Sector Quarterly* 30(4): 761–80.

Rena, L., C. Liqun, N. Lovrich, and M. Gaffney. 2005. "Linking confidence in the police with the performance of the police: Community policing can make a difference." *Journal of Criminal Justice* 33: 55–66.

Rex, J.A. 1971. "The concept of housing class and the sociology of race relations." *Race* 12 (January): 293–301.

Rex, J.A., and R. Moore. 1967. *Race, Community and Conflict*. New York: Oxford University Press.

Rich, R.C. 1980. "The dynamics of leadership in neighborhood organizations." *Social Science Quarterly* 60: 570–87.

Rivera, F.G., and J. Elrich. *Community Organizing in a Diverse Society*. Boston: Allyn and Bacon.

Rochon, T.R. 1993. "Social movements and the policy process." *Annals of the American Academy of Political and Social Science* 528 (July): 75–87.

Roehl, J. 1984. *Evaluation of the Urban Crime Prevention Program*. Washington, DC: U.S. National Institute of Justice, Institute for Social Analysis.

Rohe, W.M. 1985. "Crime prevention through informal social control." *Social Science Newsletter* 70(3): 162–5.

Rose, N. 2000. "Government and control." *British Journal of Criminology* 40(2): 321–99.

Rosenbaum, D.P. 1987. "The theory and research behind Neighborhood Watch: Is it a sound fear and crime reduction strategy?" *Crime and Delinquency* 33: 103–34.

Rosenbaum, D.P. 1988a. "Community crime prevention: A review and synthesis of the literature." *Justice Quarterly* 5: 323–95.

Rosenbaum, D.P. 1988b. "A critical eye on Neighbourhood Watch: Does it reduce crime and fear?" In T. Hope and M. Shaw (eds.), *Communities and Crime Reduction*, pp. 126–45. London: H.M. Stationery Office.

Rosenbaum, D.P. (ed.). 1986. *Community Crime Prevention: Does It Work?* Beverly Hills, CA: Sage.

Rosenbaum, D.P., D.A. Lewis, and J.A. Grant. 1985. *The Impact of Community Crime Prevention Programs in Chicago: Can Neighborhood Organizations Make a Difference?* Evanston, IL: Northwestern University, Center for Urban Affairs and Policy Research.

Rosenstone, S.J., and J.M. Hansen. 1993. *Mobilization, Participation, and Democracy in America*. New York: Macmillan.

Royal Canadian Mounted Police. 2004. *Drug Situation in Canada – 2003*. Ottawa: RCMP, Criminal Intelligence Directorate.

Rubin, H.J., and I.S. Rubin. 1992. *Community Organizing and Development*. New York: Macmillan.

Rule, J.B. 1989. "Rationality and non-rationality in militant collective actions." *Sociological Theory* 7: 145–60.

Rutherford, A. 1993. *Criminal Justice and the Pursuit of Decency*. Oxford: Oxford University Press.

Safe in Tees Valley and the Home Office. 2003. *Informing the Effective Use of Publicity and Media Campaigns to Reduce Crime and the Fear of Crime*. Stockton on Tees: Safe in Tees Valley. Accessed 20 September 2004 from http://www.safeinteesvalley.org/CrimePreventionAndTheMediaReportIssue4.pdf.

Salisbury, R. 1969. "An exchange theory of interest groups." *Midwest Journal of Political Science* 8: 1–32.

Sampson, A. 1988. "Crime, localities and the multi-agency approach." *British Journal of Criminology* 28(4): 478–93.

Sampson, R. 1985. "Neighborhood and crime: The structural determinants of personal victimisation." *Journal of Crime and Delinquency* 22: 7–40.

Sampson, R. 1987. "Communities and crime." In M.R. Gottfredson and T. Hirchi (eds.), *Positive Criminology*. Newbury Park, CA: Sage.

Sampson, R.J., S.W. Raudenbush, and F. Earls. 1997. "Neighborhoods and violent crime: A multilevel study of collective efficacy." *Science* 277: 918–23.

Sasson, T., and M. Nelson. 1996. "Danger, community, and the meaning of Crime Watch: An analysis of the discourses of African American and white participants." *Journal of Contemporary Ethnography* 25(2): 171–200.

Saunders, P. 1978. "Domestic property and social class." *International Journal of Urban and Regional Research* 2 (June): 233–51.

Saunders, P., and J. Thompson. 2004. "Indepth, Pickton: The missing women of Vancouver." *CBC News Online*, 27 January. Accessed 28 January 2004 from http://www.cbc.ca/news/background/pickton/.

Savolainen, J. 2005. "Think nationally, act locally: The municipal-level effects of the National Crime Prevention Program in Finland." *European Journal on Criminal Policy and Research* 11(2): 175–91.

Schneider, A.L. 1987. "Co-production of public and private safety: An analysis of bystander intervention, private neighboring and personal protection." *Western Political Science Quarterly* 40: 611–30.

Schneider, A.L., and P.R. Schneider. 1978. *Private and Public-Minded Citizen Responses to a Neighborhood-based Crime Prevention Strategy*. Eugene, OR: Institute for Policy Analysis.

Schwartz, A.I., and S. Clarren. 1978. *The Cincinnati Team Policing Experiment*. Washington, DC: Police Foundation.

Scott, A.J., and S.T. Roweis. 1977. "Urban planning in theory and practice: A reappraisal." *Environment and Planning – A.* 9: 1097–119.

Segatti, P. 1990. "New social movements, new forms of public commitment: A new step towards a larger political equality?" *Rassegna Italiana di Sociologica* 31(4): 447–92.

Selener, D. 1992. *Participatory Action Research and Social Change: Approaches and Critiques.* PhD diss. Department of Anthropology. Cornell University, Ithaca, NY.

Shaw, C., and H. McKay. 1942. *Juvenile Delinquency and Urban Areas.* Chicago: University of Chicago Press.

Shaw, M.E. 1981. *Group Dynamics.* New York: McGraw-Hill.

Sherman, L.W. 1997a. "Thinking about crime prevention." In L.W. Sherman, D. Gottfredson, D. MacKenzie, J. Eck, P. Reuter, and S. Bushway, *Preventing Crime: What Works, What Doesn't, What's Promising. A report to the United States Congress,* pp. 27–57. Washington, DC: National Institute of Justice.

Sherman, L.W. 1997b. "Communities and crime prevention." In L.W. Sherman, D. Gottfredson, D. MacKenzie, J. Eck, P. Reuter, and S. Bushway, *Preventing Crime: What Works, What Doesn't, What's Promising. A Report to the United States Congress,* pp. 58–109 Washington, DC: National Institute of Justice.

Sherman, L.W., C.H. Milton, and T. Kelly. 1973. *Team Policing: Seven Case Studies.* Washington, DC: Police Foundation.

Sherman, L.W., D. Farrington, B. Welsh, and D. MacKenzie. 2002. *Evidence Based Crime Prevention.* New York: Routledge.

Sherman, L.W., J.W. Shaw, and D.P. Rogan. 1995. *The Kansas City Gun Experiment: Research in Brief.* Washington, DC: National Institute of Justice.

Shonholtz, R. 1987. "The citizens' role in justice: Building a primary justice and prevention system at the neighbourhood level." *Annals of the American Academy of Political and Social Science* 494 (November): 43–53.

Shorter, E., and C. Tilly. 1974. *Strikes in France, 1830–1968.* London and New York: Cambridge University Press.

Sietrov, M.I. 1989. "Myths and fetishes of the General Systems Movement." *Cybernetics and Systems: An International Journal* 20: 215–18.

Sinclair, A. 1994. "Participation programs and techniques." In W. Sarkissian and D. Perlgut (eds.), pp. 17–35. *The Community Participation Handbook,* Perth, Western Australia: Institute for Science and Technology, Murdoch University.

Skelton, C. 1999. "Immigrants often silent when crime strikes home: Many newcomers, especially the Asians, are reluctant to inform police about crime, believing the police can't protect them." *Vancouver Sun.* 10 April, p. B6.

Skogan, W.G. 1988. "Community organizations and crime." In M. Tonry and

N. Morris (eds.), *Crime and Justice: A Review of Research* (vol. 10), pp. 39–78. Chicago: University of Chicago Press.

Skogan, W.G. 1989. "Communities, crime and neighborhood organization." *Crime and Delinquency* 35(3): 437–57.

Skogan, W.G. 1990. *Disorder and Decline: Crime and the Spiral of Decay in American Neighborhoods.* New York: Free Press.

Skogan, W.G. 1996. Paper presented to the Conference on Problem-Oriented Policing as Crime Prevention. Swedish National Police College, Stockholm.

Skogan, W.G. 2004. "Representing the community in community policing. In W.G. Skogan (ed.), *Community Policing: Can It Work?*, pp. 57–75. Washington: National Institute of Justice.

Skogan, W.G., and N.G. Maxfield. 1981. *Coping with Crime: Individual and Neighborhood Reactions.* Beverly Hills, CA: Sage.

Skogan, W.G., and M.A. Wycoff. 1986. "Storefront police offices: The Houston field test." In D. Rosenbaum (ed.), *Community Crime Prevention: Does It Work?*, pp. 179–99. Sage Criminal Justice Systems Annuals, vol. 22. Beverly Hills, CA: Sage.

Skolnick, J.H., and D.H. Bayley. 1988. *Community Policing: Issues and Practices around the World.* Washington, DC: U.S. Government Printing Office.

Smelser, N.J. 1963. *Theory of Collective Behavior.* New York: Macmillan.

Smelser, N.J. 1993. "The nature of collective behaviour." In R.L. Curtis and B.E. Aguirre (eds.), *Collective Behavior and Social Movements*, pp. 21–28. Boston: Allyn and Bacon.

Smith, A. 1976. "Mount Pleasant." In Chuck Davis (ed.), *The Vancouver Book*, pp. 91–3. North Vancouver: J.J. Douglas.

Smith, D.H. 1975. "Voluntary action and voluntary groups." In A. Inkeles, J. Coleman, and N. Smelser (eds.), *Annual Review of Sociology* (vol. 1), pp. 247–70. Palo Alto, CA: Annual Reviews.

Smith, M.P. 1989. "Urbanism: Medium or outcome of human agency." *Urban Affairs Quarterly* 24(3): pp. 353–58.

Smith, R.L. 1993. "In the service of youth: A common denominator." *Juvenile Justice* 1(2): 9–15.

Sokoloff, H. 2004. "Day care: Ballooning Quebec plan model for Grits." *Globe and Mail.* 4 June, p. A6.

Sommer, R. 1969. *Personal Space: The Behavioral Basis of Design.* Englewood Cliffs, NJ: Prentice Hall.

Spicker, P. 1992. "Equality versus solidarity." *Government and Opposition* 27: 66–77.

Spitzer, S. 1977. "The rationalization of crime control in capitalist society." *Contemporary Crises* 3 (2): 187–206.

Standing Committee on Justice and the Solicitor General. 1993. *Crime Prevention in Canada: Toward a National Strategy.* Twelfth Report of the Standing Committee on Justice and the Solicitor General, Parliament of Canada. Ottawa: Queen's Printer for Canada.

Stansfield, R.T. 1996. *Issues in Policing: A Canadian Perspective.* Toronto: Thompson Educational.

Staples, L. 1984. *Roots to Power: A Manual for Grassroots Organizing.* New York: Praeger.

Statistics Canada. 1997. *Census of Canada, 1996.* Study Area data. PA 925 Areas (City of Vancouver). [Computer file]. Ottawa: Statistics Canada.

Statistics Canada. 2004a. "Low income in census metropolitan areas. 1980 to 2000." *The Daily.* Ottawa: Statistics Canada. April. Accessed 30 April 2004 from http://www.statcan.ca/Daily/English/040407/d040407a.htm.

Statistics Canada. 2004b. "Literacy scores, human capital and growth 1960 to 1995." *The Daily.* Ottawa: Statistics Canada. Accessed 4 October 2004 from http://www.statcan.ca/Daily/English/040622/d040622d.htm.

Statistics Canada. 2004c. "Study: Neighbourhood characteristics and the distribution of crime in Winnipeg. *Daily.* 16 September. Accessed 3 May 2006 from http://www.statcan.ca/Daily/English/040916/d040916c.htm.

Stevens, John. 1998. "Reducing crime and disorder: A British perspective." In *The Role of the Police in Crime Prevention. Synthesis Report. Montreal Seminar: Program of Exchange Expertise on the Role of the Police in Crime Prevention,* 10–13 November 1998. Montreal: International Centre for the Prevention of Crime.

Stoecker, R. 1990. "Taming the beast: Maintaining democracy in community-controlled redevelopment." *Berkeley Journal of Sociology* 35: 106–26.

Stukas, A.A., and M.R. Dunlap. 2002. "Community involvement: Theoretical approaches and educational initiatives. *Journal of Social Issues* 58(3): 411–27.

SUCCESS. 2004. Internet Web Site. Accessed 23 January 2006 from http://www.success.bc.ca/eng/.

Suttles, G.D. 1972. *The Social Construction of Communities.* Chicago: University of Chicago Press.

Talen, E. 1999. "Sense of community and neighbourhood form: An assessment of the social doctrine." *Urban Studies* 36(8): 1361–79.

Tarrow, S. 1996. "Social Movements." In A. Kuper and J. Kuper (eds.), *The Social Science Encyclopedia,* pp. 792–95. London: Routledge.

Taub, R.P., D.G. Taylor, and J. Dunham. 1984. *Patterns of Neighborhood Change: Race and Crime in Urban America.* Chicago: University of Chicago Press.

Taylor, C. 1991. *The Malaise of Modernity.* Concord, ON: Anansi.

Taylor, I. 1981. *Law and Order: Arguments for Socialism.* London: Macmillan.

Taylor, I. 1996. "Fear of crime, urban fortunes and suburban social movements: Some reflections from Manchester." *Sociology* 30(2): 317–37.

Taylor, I. 1999. *Crime in Context: A Critical Criminology of Market Societies.* Boulder, CO: Westview Press.

Taylor, R. 1996. "Neighborhood responses to disorder and local attachments: The systemic model of attachment, social disorganization, and neighborhood use value." *Sociological Forum* 11: 41–74.

Taylor, R.B., and S. Gottfredson. 1986. "Environmental design, crime and prevention: An examination of community dynamics." In A. Reiss and M. Tonry (eds.), *Communities and Crime*, pp. 387–416. Chicago: University of Chicago Press.

Taylor, R.B., S.D. Gotfredson, and S. Bower. 1984. "Block crime and fear: Defensible space, local social ties and territorial functioning." *Journal of Research in Crime and Delinquency* 21(4): 303–31.

Teixeira, V. 2003. *HNCPC Volunteer Survey, 2003: How Are We Doing as a Volunteer Organization?* Vancouver: Hastings North Community Policing Centre.

Thacher, D. 2001. "Conflicting values in community policing." *Law and Society Review* (35)4: 765–98.

Todhunter, C. 2001. "Undertaking action research: Negotiating the road ahead." UNIS *Social Research Update* (issue 34), University of Surrey. Accessed 23 January 2006 from http://www.soc.surrey.ac.uk/sru/SRU34.html.

Toner, R., and D.D. Kirkpatrick. 2004. "Social conservatives wield influence on platform." *New York Times.* 31 August, p. A1.

Toumbourou, J.W. 1999. "Implementing communities that care in Australia: A community mobilisation approach to crime prevention." *Trends and Issues in Crime and Criminal Justice* 122 (July). Canberra: Australian Institute of Criminology.

Touraine, A. 1985. "An introduction to the study of social movements." *Social Research* 52: 749–87.

Touraine, A. 1988. *The Return of the Actor.* Minneapolis: University of Minnesota Press.

Trickett, A., D. Ellingworth, and K. Pease. 1992. *Changes in Area Inequality in Crime Victimisation, 1982–88: Findings from the British Crime Surveys.* Manchester: University of Manchester Press.

Trojanowicz, R.C. 1986. "Evaluating a neighborhood foot patrol program: The Flint, Michigan Project." In D.P. Rosenbaum (ed.), *Community Crime Prevention: Does It Work?* pp. 157–78. Beverly Hills, CA: Sage.

Trojanowicz, R.C. and B. Bucqueroux. 1991. *Community Policing and the Challenge of Diversity.* East Lansing, MI: National Center for Community Policing.

Troyer, R.J., and R.D. Wright. 1985. "Community response to crime: Two middle class anti-crime patrols." *Journal of Criminal Justice* 13: 227–41.

Turner, R.H., and L.M. Killian. 1987 [1957]. *Collective Behavior.* Englewood Cliffs, NJ: Prentice Hall.

Turner, R.H., and L.M. Killian. 1993. "The field of collective behaviour." In R.L. Curtis and B.E. Aguirre (eds.), *Collective Behavior and Social Movements,* pp. 5–20. Boston: Allyn and Bacon.

Umbreit, M.S. 1994. *Victim Meets Offender: The Impact of Restorative Justice and Mediation.* Monsey, NY: Willow Tree Press.

United Nations Congress for the Prevention of Crime and the Treatment of Offenders. 1993. *Urban Policies and Crime Prevention.* Vienna: UN.

United Nations Development Programme. 2004. *Human Development Report 2004: Cultural Liberty in Today's Diverse World.* New York: United Nations Development Program.

United States. Department of Justice. 1978. *Guidelines Manual: Guide to Discretionary Grant Programs.* Washington, DC: U.S. Government Printing Office.

United States. National Advisory Council on Criminal Justice Standards and Goals. 1973. *A National Strategy to Reduce Crime.* Washington, DC: U.S. Government Printing Office.

University of British Columbia, School of Community and Regional Planning. 1994. *Mount Pleasant Community Development Plan Review.* Vancouver: School of Community and Regional Planning.

Uslaner, E., and R. Conley. 2003. "Civic engagement and particularized trust: The ties that bind people to their ethnic communities." *American Politics Research* 31(4): 331–60.

Vadhansinhdhu, P. 1995. *Local Knowledge in Physical Design and Planning: A Case Study of Chiangmai, Thailand.* PhD diss., Department of Community and Regional Planning, University of British Columbia, Vancouver.

Vancouver Echo. 1992. "Mount Pleasant residents protest prostitution." 12 March, p. 1.

Vancouver Police Department. Vice Intelligence Unit. 1990. *Engaging in Prostitution Enforcement, Section 213, Criminal Code.* Unpublished statistical report, 30 May.

Vancouver Police Department. 1997. "Criminal Code and Statute offences, January 1st to June 24th, 1997." Vancouver: Vancouver Police Department, Crime Analysis Unit. (Unpublished.)

Vancouver Police Department. 2004a. *Statistical Reports.* Vancouver: Vancouver Police Department Planning and Research Section. Accessed 23 August 2004 from http://www.city.vancouver.bc.ca/police/Planning/reports.htm.

Vancouver Police Department. 2004b. *Community Deliberative Dialogue Session.* Vancouver Police Department. Internet web site. Accessed 23 August 2004 from www.city.vancouver.bc.ca/police/What%27sNew/ DeliberativeDialogue.htm.

Vancouver Police Department and Vancouver Police Board. n.d. *Improving Community Safety: Community Deliberative Dialogue Session. (Saturday, 27 March 2004)* Morris J. Wosk Centre for Dialogue. Session Summary Report. Accessed 23 August 2004 from www.city.vancouver.bc.ca/police/ What%27sNew/DeliberativeDialogue.pdf.

Vancouver School Board. 1995. *First Languages Table: Mount Pleasant, 1994/95.* Vancouver: Vancouver School Board. (Unpublished.)

Vancouver Sun. 1985. "Apathy affects Mount Pleasant development: City report." 29 May, p. B3.

Vancouver Sun. 1999a. "Centre bridges gap between police, citizens: Patrick Kwok teaches new immigrants what to do when they need police help." 10 April, p. B6.

Vancouver Sun. 1999b. "Block Watch set for review." 29 November, p. B1.

van den Hemel, M. 1999. "Crime prevention efforts need boost." *Richmond Review.* 1 December.

Vasoo, S. 1991. "Grass-root mobilisation and citizen participation: Issues and challenges." *Community Development Journal* 26(1): 1–7.

Verba, S., and N.H. Nie. 1972. *Participation in America: Political Democracy and Social Equality.* New York: Harper and Row.

Verba, S., K.L Schlozman, and H.E. Brady. 1995. *Voice and Equality: Civic Voluntarism in American Politics.* Cambridge, MA.: Harvard University Press.

Vertovec, S. 1997. *Social Cohesion and Tolerance.* Metropolis International web site. Accessed 15 December 2005 from http://international.metropolis.net/ research-policy/social/index_e.html.

Walker, C.R., and S.G. Walker. 1993. *The Role of Citizen Volunteers.* Ottawa: Solicitor General Canada. User Report Community Policing Series 1993–06.

Walker, S. 1977. *A Critical History of Police Reform: The Emergence of Professionalism.* Lexington, MA: Lexington Books.

Walklate, S.L. 2001. "Fearful communities?" *Urban Studies* 38(5/6): 929–39.

Waller, I., and D. Sansfaçon. 2000. *Investing Wisely in Crime Prevention.* Washington, DC: U.S. Department of Justice, Office of Justice Programs, Bureau of Justice Assistance.

Walsh, M.L. 1997. *Building Citizen Involvement: Strategies for Local Government.* Washington, DC: National League of Cities, International City/County Management Association.

Wandersman, A. 1981. "A framework of participation in community organizations." *Journal of Applied Behavioral Science* 17(1): 27–58.

Ward, C.S. 1998. *Community Education and Crime Prevention: Confronting Foreground and Background Causes of Criminal Behavior.* Westport, CT: Bergin and Garvey.

Warwick, L. 2001. "Slur against mall out of date." *Vancouver Sun.* 24 October, p. A19.

Washnis, G.J. 1976. *Citizen Involvement in Crime Prevention.* Lexington, MA: Heath.

Welton, M.R., and J. Lecky. 1997. "Volunteerism as the seedbed of democracy: The educational thought and practice of Guy Henson of Nova Scotia." *Studies in the Education of Adults.* 29(1): 25–38.

Weinberg, D.H. 1996. *A Brief Look at Postwar U.S. Income Inequality.* Washington: United States Census Bureau. Accessed 24 February 2004 from http://www.census.gov/hhes/www/img/p60–191.pdf.

Weinstein, S.P. 1998. "Community Prosecution." *FBI Law Enforcement Bulletin* 67(4): 19–24.

Weimer, M. 2002. *Learner-Centered Teaching: Five Key Changes to Practice.* San Francisco: Jossey-Bass.

Wharf-Higgens, J. 1997. "Who participates? Citizen participation in health reform in B.C." In B. Wharf and M. Clague (eds.), *Community Organizing: Canadian Experiences*, pp. 273–301. Toronto: Oxford University Press.

Whitaker, C.J. 1986. *Crime Prevention Measures. Bureau of Justice Statistics.* Special Report. Washington, DC: U.S. Department of Justice.

White, R. 2000. "Social justice, community building, and restorative strategies." *Contemporary Justice Review* 3(1): 55–72.

Whiteley, P.F. 1995. "Rational choice and political participation: Evaluating the debate." *Political Research Quarterly* 48(1): 211–33.

Williams, K. 1995. "Community mobilization against urban crime: Guiding orientations and strategic choices in grassroots politics." *Urban Affairs Review* 30(3): 407–31.

Wilson, J. 1983. "Crime and American culture." *Public Interest* 70: 22–48.

Wilson, J. 1973. *Introduction to Social Movements.* New York: Basic Books.

Wilson, J. 1975. *Thinking about Crime.* New York: Academic.

Wilson, J., and G. Kelling. 1982. "Broken windows." *Atlantic Monthly.* 31 March.

Wilson, P. 1976. *Public Housing for Australia.* St Lucia: University of Queensland Press.

Winkel, F.W. 1991. "Interaction between police and minority group members: Victimization through the incorrect interpretation of nonverbal behavior." *International Review of Victimology* 2(1): 15–27.

Wirth, L. 1938. "Urbanism, migration and tolerance: A reassessment." *American Sociological Review* 56: 117–23.

Wolff, L., and D. Geissel. 1994. "Street prostitution in Canada." *Canadian Social Trends* (Summer): 18–22.

Women's Action Centre against Violence (Ottawa-Carleton). 1995. *Safety Audit Tools and Housing: The State of the Art and Implications for CMHC*. Ottawa: Canada Mortgage and Housing Corporation.

Wong, K.C. 2001. "Crime prevention in China: A community policing approach." In S.P. Lab and D.K. Das (eds.), *International Perspectives on Community Policing and Crime Prevention*, pp. 207–23. Upper Saddle River, NJ: Prentice-Hall.

Wood, J.L., and M. Jackson. 1982. *Social Movements*. Belmont, CA: Wadsworth.

XTRAWest. 2003. "CPCs remain independent." 7 August, p. 7.

Yanay, U. 1994. "The big brother function of Block Watch." *International Journal of Sociology and Social Policy* 14(9): 44–58.

Yankelovich, D. 1991. *Coming to Public Judgement: Making Democracy Work in a Complex World*. Syracuse, NY: Syracuse University Press.

Yarwood, R., and B. Edwards. 1995. "Voluntary action in rural areas: The case of Neighbourhood Watch." *Journal of Rural Studies* 11(4): 447–59.

Yeich, S. 1996. "Grassroots organizing with homeless people: A participatory research approach." *Journal of Social Issues* 52(1): 111–21.

Young, J. 1999. *The Exclusive Society: Social Exclusion, Crime and Difference in Late Modernity*. London: Sage.

Young, J. 2001. "Identity, community and social exclusion." In M. Roger and J. Pitts (eds.), *Crime, Disorder, and Community Safety: A New Agenda?*, pp. 26–53. London: Routledge.

Youth Service Canada. Safer Neighbourhood Initiative. 1996. *A Security Audit of Mount Pleasant Businesses*. (Unpublished.) Vancouver: Youth Service Canada.

Zacharias, Y. 2000. "Neighbours sick of sex trade: Pushed out of Mount Pleasant, hookers and dealers moved on to Kingsway. Now that neighbourhood aims to see them on their way." *Vancouver Sun*. 27 October, p. B4.

Zedner, L., and N. Lacey. 2000. "Community and governance: A cultural comparison." In S. Karstedt and K.T. Bussman (eds.), *Social Dynamics of Crime and Control*, pp. 157–70. Portland, OR: Hart Publishing.

Zenaida R.R., F. Rajulton, and P. Turcotte. 2003. "Youth integration and social capital: An analysis of the Canadian General Social Surveys on time use." *Youth and Society*. 35(2): 158–82.

Zevitz, R. 2002. "Breaking the routine: Assessing the effectiveness of a multi-neighborhood anticrime initiative through qualitative interviewing." *Justice Professional* 15(2): 127–47.

Zhang, L., S.F. Messner, A.E. Liska, M.D. Krohn, J. Liu, and Z. Lu. 1996. "Crime prevention in a communitarian society: 'Bang-jiao' and 'tiao-jie' in the People's Republic of China." *Justice Quarterly* 13(2): 199–222.

Zolberg, A.R., and A.J. Clarkin (eds). 2003. *Sharing Integration Experiences: Innovative Community Practices on Two Continents*. New York: New School University.

Index

apartment buildings and crime prevention, 39, 75–6, 91–2, 95–7, 117–19, 134–5. *See also* Crime Free Multi-Housing Program

Block Watch. *See* Neighbourhood Watch
British Crime Survey: crime rate statistics, 160–1; participation in community crime prevention programs, 34, 36–7; security measures, in private households, 173
broken windows metaphor, 24–5, 62
Business Watch, 75, 81

Carolina Street Neighbourhood Group (Vancouver), 66–7, 69, 75, 99, 145
Chicago, 21–4, 39, 41, 42
Chicago School of Sociology: and informal social control, 24; and social disorganization theory, 21–2, 84–5, 160
Chinatown (Vancouver), 105, 127–8, 150
Chinese Community Policing Centre (Vancouver), 103, 127–8

citizen patrols: anti-prostitution efforts, 66–9, 76, 90, 99, 105, 131; and Hastings Community Policing Centre, 139; and informal social control, 24; and opportunity reduction, 29; participation in, 36
civic engagement. *See* participation
collective action (*see also* social movements): and community crime prevention, 3–11, 27–31; definition of, 206–7; and disadvantaged neighbourhoods, 34–6, 41–6; and education, 210–11, 250–3; factors related to, 11, 207–43; and homogeneity of a neighbourhood, 39–41, 219–20, 236, 238–43, 266; and identity (group), 4, 9, 96, 128, 169, 178, 201, 206–7, 229–38, 269–73, 275; and leadership, 95, 99, 131–52, 223–4, 246–7, 299–300; obstacles to participation in, 207–43; participation in, 207–43; and purposive rationality, 178–81, 225; and social capital, 208, 269–74; and social cohesion, 170–8, 220, 224–6, 238–43, 269–74; social environmental factors influencing, 219–21; social movements,